Daylighting

The focus of daylighting design is the comfort and happiness of users. People respond in many ways to light, and experience it in terms of what is recognised and felt, not as photometric values. So good design is subtle and many-faceted. It is a concern for the human body's dependence on daylight, for what gives joy and interest, for the creation of 'place', for a building's effect on its surroundings. A focus on people is essential to the creation of buildings which are sustainable within the natural world.

This authoritative and multi-disciplinary book provides architects, lighting specialists, and anyone else working daylight into design, with all the tools needed to incorporate this most fundamental element of architecture.

The book is centred on practical daylighting design. It describes how new thinking about peoples' needs and about the requirements of sustainability is leading to a radical shift in daylighting design practice. It includes:

- An overview of current practice of daylighting in architecture and urban planning
- A review of recent research on daylighting and what this means to the practitioner
- A global vision of architectural lighting which is linked to the climates of the world and which integrates view, sunlight, diffuse skylight and electric lighting
- Up-to-date tools for design in practice
- Delivery of information in a variety of ways for interdisciplinary readers: graphics, mathematics, text, photographs and in-depth illustrations
- A clear structure: eleven chapters covering different aspects of lighting, a set of worksheets giving step-by-step examples of calculations and design procedures for use in practice, and a collection of algorithms and equations for reference by specialists and software designers

Daylighting: Architecture and Lighting Design is a book which should trigger creative thought. It recognizes that good lighting design needs both knowledge and imagination.

Peter Tregenza is Emeritus Professor in the School of Architecture at the University of Sheffield. As an architect and engineer he has been fascinated by the beauty and complexity of daylight for more than forty years, teaching and studying the subject internationally. He has been Visiting Professor at the National University of Singapore and at the Chinese University of Hong Kong, and has worked in schools of architecture in the UK, North and South America, Australia and New Zealand, and China. He has been involved in the research activities of the Commission International de l'Eclairage, especially the CIE/WMO International Daylight Measurement Project and European Union programmes. His publications include many research papers on daylighting and he is the co-author with David Loe of *The Design of Lighting* (Routledge, 1998).

Michael Wilson is Principal Research Fellow in the School of Architecture and Built Environment at the University of Westminster, UK. He was Director of the Low Energy Architecture Research Unit from 1987 until 2010. He has undertaken more than 25 research, dissemination and demonstration projects in daylighting, acoustics and energy for the European Commission. In particular he coordinated a research project on sun tracking systems and projects producing interactive teaching packages on daylight. He has lectured in the UK, throughout Europe, in South America and South Africa.

Daylighting

Architecture and lighting design

Peter Tregenza and Michael Wilson

Routledge
Taylor & Francis Group

LONDON AND NEW YORK

First published 2011
by Routledge
2 Park Square, Milton Park, Abingdon, Oxon, OX14 4RN

Simultaneously published in the USA and Canada
by Routledge
270 Madison Avenue, New York, NY 10016

Routledge is an imprint of the Taylor & Francis Group, an informa business

Typeset in Univers by Glyph International
Printed and bound in Great Britain by
Bell & Bain Ltd, Glasgow

British Library Cataloguing in Publication Data
A catalogue record for this book is available from the British Library

Library of Congress Cataloging-in-Publication Data
Tregenza, Peter.
Daylighting : architecture and lighting design / Peter Tregenza and Michael Wilson.
p. cm.
Includes bibliographical references and index.
1. Daylighting. 2. Architectural design. 3. Light in architecture.
I. Wilson, Michael (Michael Peter), 1949- II. Title.
NA2794.T74 2011
729'.28–dc22   2010028616

ISBN 978-0-419-25700-4

Contents

Acknowledgements

We are grateful to many for their help in producing this book. Firstly, there are academic colleagues from whom over many years we have learnt much about lighting; we would especially like to thank Professor John Page and Professor Steve Sharples at the University of Sheffield, Professor Edward Ng at the Chinese University of Hong Kong, former colleagues in LEARN at London Metropolitan University, Axel Jacobs, John Solomon, Livio Venturi, Dr Marc Zanchetta, Dr Luisa Brotas and Professor Fergus Nicol, Dr Aris Tsangrassoulis from the University of Thessaly, Professor Mick Hutchins from Sonnergy, Wilfried Pohl from Bartenbach Lichtlabor, and Tony Corlett for help with the graphics. Next, our thanks go to friends in the Society of Light and Lighting, in the CIBSE Daylight Group, in CIE committees and in other international research groups; their enthusiasm and scholarship has continually renewed our fascination with daylight. We acknowledge, too, the debt we owe to those who have worked with us as research students: the stimulus of sharing knowledge with challenging and lively minds has been invaluable.

We would like to thank the editorial and production staff at Taylor & Francis: they have been encouraging, supportive and tolerant – the qualities that authors most need in a publisher.

We are grateful to those who read and commented on various parts of this book during its writing, bringing errors and omissions to our notice. The mistakes that remain are entirely our fault. We know they must exist: we just don't know where they are. Please let us know of any that you find.

How to use this book

This book is about natural light and its use in buildings. It covers sunlight and diffuse skylight; it also discusses the design of electric lighting, because often the most sustainable scheme employs natural and electric lighting together through the day. It relates daylight to climate, and thus to buildings that are sustainable because their design is linked to the natural world of their site.

The book has two aims. The first is to give an overall view that includes some of the innovative ideas in daylighting that have arisen during the last few years. The second aim is to provide both the practitioner and the researcher with some up-to-date tools.

Daylighting is a subject that crosses professional boundaries and academic disciplines. It features in books on architecture, urban design, environmental physics and psychology. You might have a professional interest in the topic if you are involved in property law or in health care. If you are a researcher, your background might lie in atmospheric physics, social science, engineering or any of several other disciplines.

Unfortunately, a common interest does not imply a common approach. What you need to know about daylighting depends on your background and your purpose. So does the form in which you can most comfortably assimilate it: are you happiest working graphically? Or with reasoned writing? Or with mathematics?

We have tried to organise the book in a way that makes it accessible to readers from different disciplines, and to be useful at different technical levels. We have also attempted to balance a readable introduction to the subject with a structure that provides a convenient source of reference.

There are three elements of the book:

1 *The central text*. Ten chapters introduce the main ideas. They are in a sequence that runs broadly from design to research – starting with the aims and criteria of lighting design; then looking at the behaviour of light, and concepts of climate and sustainability; then at physical aspects of windows; and finally at theoretical models of daylighting. The topics within each chapter are written so that you can read into them as far as you need and skip the unnecessary. Chapter 11, *Notes and references*, comments on the main text, gives the sources of material in the book and shows where additional information can be found.

2 *Worksheets*. These are stand-alone documents aimed at the everyday needs of the designer. They summarise key ideas from the main text and describe, step by step, how to analyse the daylight at a site, how to predict how a building or a lighting scheme will perform, and how to assess the quality of lighting in existing buildings. They include data sheets giving information needed in calculations, and graphic tools.

3 *Algorithms and equations*. Intended for the researcher or the software developer, this is a list of formulae needed to construct numerical models of daylighting. It treats natural light as a series of transformations of the solar beam, from molecular scattering in the upper atmosphere to the compound interreflection within a room. This section begins with a list of symbols and ends with a list of sources.

You will find two themes running through the book. The first is the *essential variability* of daylight. Every place on earth has its own visual climate. Daylight varies with season, with global position, and with landmass and ocean. In the tropics, night and day are almost equal and vary little between June and December, while in arctic regions, a 24-hour summer day balances a 24-hour winter night. In cloudless arid regions, the pattern of sky brightness changes only gradually with time and place, while in cloudy regions, the variation can be rapid and chaotic.

But this spatial and temporal changeability is not a disadvantage. Quite the contrary: it is fundamental to life. It governs the seasonal growth of plants and animals and their diurnal behaviour. It affects the forms they adopt, their materials and colouring. It affects us humans: physiologically – often without our awareness – and in our cognitive and emotional behaviour. We can infer, from the changing daylight around us in a room, whether we are in a city or the country, in a tropical climate or a temperate one, what the weather is now, what time of day it is, what human activity there is outside. The variability of daylight is not random, and the information that it carries is as important for us as its energy.

The second theme of the book is the *centrality* of people to lighting design. Daylighting is an essential part of sustainable architecture, and design for good daylight can generate architecture that is unique to place and function. But sustainability depends not only on the building being appropriate to the climate: it is also essential that the people who use the building are satisfied with it.

The focus of daylighting design is the comfort and happiness of users, and this implies the creation of buildings that are part of the natural world. People respond in many ways to light, and experience it in terms of what is recognised and felt, not as photometric values. So good design is subtle and many-faceted. It is a concern for the human body's dependence on daylight, for what gives joy and interest, for the creation of 'place', for a building's effect on its surroundings.

This is essentially a technical book, but we hope that it might trigger your creative imagination as well as providing knowledge, because both are needed in design and in research.

## one

Criteria of good daylighting

The human body evolved in the diurnal cycle of light and dark, and is tuned to the spectrum of the sun's radiation. We respond to daylight in many ways: our luminous environment affects our health; it triggers responses in us that can be traced to require-ments for safety and survival; it affects our interaction with other people; it determines the ease with which we carry out visual tasks. Crucial to all of these is that daylight is not a constant flow of light but something dynamic, varying with time and place.

The essentials

This chapter, and everything about daylighting design in the rest of the book, could be reduced to three rules:

* Make the building appropriate to the climate.
* Preserve the natural variation of daylght.
* Give users control of their own environment.

1.1
Light carries meaning. A child's perception of the world of brightness and colour is linked with the growth of language and conceptualisation.

These are central to the aim of satisfying the users of the building and to the aim of sustainable architecture. The reasoning for them is developed gradually through the book.

Physical measures and what we see

These are complaints recorded during surveys of buildings in use:

- 'The room is gloomy.'
- 'The whole character of the place is wrong.'
- 'There's a shiny reflection in my computer screen.'
- 'The sunlight is dazzling.'
- 'I can't control the blinds and I can't open a window.'
- 'It's OK if you sit by the windows but too dark at the back of the room.'
- 'The electric lights are on all day even though there is plenty of daylight.'
- 'I can't see out of the window.'
- 'It's too exposed, not enough privacy.'
- 'There is so much light that my curtains are fading.'
- 'The new building opposite is reducing my daylight.'

There are as many criteria of good lighting as there are ways in which a design can fail. These complaints are typical, and each points to some factor that the designer has to consider. Their implications extend across the whole scale of building design, from the orientation and block planning of the site to interior detail. The first conclusion to be drawn is that the aim of lighting design goes far beyond the mere provision of some given quantity of illumination.

The essential variability of daylight

Natural light is always changing. It varies in time, sometimes smoothly and slowly, sometimes rapidly and chaotically. It varies spatially at many scales from the differing daylight climates across the globe to the complex and subtle distribution of brightness at the scale of an individual room.

If you are in a daylit room now, look around you. Can you tell where light has been reflected by the ground

1.2

Design for a cloudy climate: an eighteenth-century window giving the interior of the room the view of a large angle of sky.
The Library, Stevenstone, Devon, UK.

outside? Where it has come directly from the sky? Where a patch of brightness is due to reflected sunlight? Look at Figure 1.2. What can you deduce about other windows in the room?[1]

Any daylit room at any moment is unique. Its pattern of brightness depends on where it is in the world, and on the time of year and time of day. Variability in space and time is the dominating characteristic of natural light. For much of

---

1 It's a subtle effect, but if you look at the white panel below the window, you realise that there must be another source of light in the room. There are, in fact, windows in the opposite wall.

the twentieth century, this variability, especially its apparent randomness in cloudy regions, was seen as a serious drawback. In offices, classrooms and most other types of interior, uniformity of illumination was taken to be an essential characteristic of good lighting.

But people like daylight. Most prefer to live and work in daylit rooms. If some activity requires a windowless space, there is an urge to take a regular break, to 'get some daylight and fresh air'. There has not been enough research to be certain why we have this desire for daylight. Strong but circumstantial evidence implies that changeability is crucial: the continual variation of brightness in a daylight room is, literally, stimulating because our senses respond to change, not to unvarying conditions.

It is not changeability in itself that matters: natural light, by its spatial and temporal variability, carries information, and this information is at least as important to us as the energy of the radiation. For people in a building, the light that flows in through windows is worth much more than its value simply as radiant energy. It tells about the world outside, and it is natural to us because our bodies evolved in the swing of night and day, summer and winter.

There is a fundamental difference between an objective description of light and what we perceive. The daylight flowing into a room can be described physically in several ways: as luminous flux; as a luminance distribution; as radiant energy that varies in spectrum, time and direction. Subjectively, we could visualise it as a mere pattern of brightness, but this is not normal perception: looking outside, we see a view; and inside we see walls, ceiling and floor, and all the things and people they enclose.

But exactly what we perceive, and what it means to us, depends on our individual experiences and expectations: no two people 'see' the same room. Moreover, the perceived environment is not dependent on visual stimuli alone: it is influenced by other physical factors, such as noise and heat, and it is affected by the social environment. Our awareness is of a place as a whole, and our reactions to it are influenced by our frame of mind, our motivation and our interest in whatever we are doing. Lighting affects mood: but the mood it creates depends on us. The sunlight of an early spring morning can lift the spirits and give a new enthusiasm for the tasks of the day; or have an opposite effect if we fear what the day may bring.

Standards and reality

Daylight varies in a complex and not wholly predictable way; so does human response to daylight. But design criteria, the standards and guidance required in practice, must be objective and simple, consistent and replicable. It must be possible to test whether or not a lighting situation reaches stated criteria or to calculate whether a design, when built, would do so; and both measurements and calculations should be easy and robust.

This is discussed more fully in Chapter 6, and the conclusion reached is this: meeting the requirements of published standards, no matter how assiduously they are followed or how extensive the criteria, does not necessarily produce good lighting. Well-conceived standards give points of support in the process of designing but they are no substitute for the designer's understanding of the needs and wishes of the people who will live or work or play in the building being created.

Health 1: the need for regular exposure to daylight

Electromagnetic radiation affects the body, both harmfully and beneficially. We evolved in the environment of light from the sun, and we require it for the maintenance of health. But exposure must be controlled: excessive short-wavelength radiation – x-rays and beyond – causes deep-tissue damage; radiation at wavelengths near the visual range can damage the skin and the eyes. The harmful effects can be both rapid (such as burning) and long-term (such as stimulation of cancer growth). Direct sunlight on the body can be valuable, but there must be a balance between the risks of over-exposure to sunlight and under-exposure.

The design of a building cannot by itself ensure the optimum exposure to daylight for maintenance of mental and physical health: the way a person lives and, in the case of residential buildings, the management regime of the institution are crucial factors, but a poor building can have a seriously detrimental effect. The fundamental needs are:

1　A 24-hour cycle of illumination that includes periods of darkness and of bright light
2　Exposure to bright daylight during winter months

3   The need of building users for a sense of contact with the outside world

4   Avoidance of glare that causes discomfort or reduces visibility of hazards

The importance of each of these depends on the building type and the circumstances of the users. The influence of the built environment on health is greatest for those who are confined – the old and the sick, those in prison, those whose work keeps them indoors through the hours of daylight.

Circadian rhythms, SAD and the need for light

The natural 24-hour cycle of light and dark is used by the body to regulate the daily sequence of physiological changes – of sleep, hunger, body temperature, alertness, and of almost all hormone production. Circadian rhythms are 'clocks' in the bodies of mammals and many other organisms that control these changes. Disrupting them gives the symptoms of jet-lag and shift-work, and of sleep disorders. There may be long-term consequences: for instance, confinement in windowless cells may contribute to mental health disorders in prisons.

Our various circadian rhythms are interlinked and together have an inherent cycle time of slightly more than 24 hours; but, crucially, they are modified by external stimuli, and exposure to light is probably the most important of these. In the retina, there are photoreceptors other than those used for vision, and these trigger hormonal changes associated with the day–night cycle.

The effect of light on the hormonal changes increases with illuminance but values as low as 100 lx on the eye have a measurable effect. The spectral sensitivity to radiation of the non-visual retinal receptors differs slightly from that of the rods and cones (which define 'light'), the peak sensitivity occurring at the wavelengths where we see blue–green. Periods of darkness are as necessary as exposure to bright light, and in a healthy state the light–dark cycle is synchronised with the person's diurnal activity–sleep cycle. With older people, especial care must be taken to ensure sufficient illumination, because the transparent parts of the eye become yellowed with age and thus reduce the blue–green disproportionally.

There are categories of people with a higher than average probability of suffering from deprivation of light or from conditions associated with disturbed circadian cycles. They include shift workers; people who are disabled by advanced age or other chronic conditions and are unable to go outside; people confined within an institutional building where there is continuous lighting for care or for security; and people who frequently make long-haul flights. There is substantial research evidence that, with people of all ages, good sleep and associated improvements in behaviour are associated with therapeutic exposure to bright daylight within a 24-hour light–dark cycle.

Seasonal affective disorder (SAD) is a depressive illness that varies with the time of year. It can occur during winter, with symptoms common to other types of mental depression such as oversleeping, mood changes, lack of energy and over-eating; there is also a summer form in which the symptoms tend to be the opposite – lack of sleep, loss of appetite, weight loss. The winter form is the more usual and is found mainly in young adults, but it also affects older people, and women more than men.

The mechanism of the winter disease is clearly related to exposure to light: the symptoms are relieved when the sufferer receives daily exposure to a bright source of light, they disappear with the onset of summer and recur in autumn, and they are found predominantly in people living at latitudes distant from the equator. The summer form of SAD is much rarer and is not necessarily a response to high levels of light; it may be due to other factors such as overheating or behavioural changes during hot summer months.

Although the type of daylight climate in which SAD tends to occur is known, further research is required about the regime of illuminances that triggers the disease. The evidence available suggests that the risk of SAD becomes significant where people live in an environment in which illuminance on the eye is below 1 klx for much of the day. Therapeutic doses are better understood: when daily exposure to bright light is used clinically as an antidepressive, typically the patient spends 30 minutes every morning facing a 'light box' – fluorescent lamps mounted behind a diffusing screen – which produces 10 klx at the patient's eyes. A lower level of light, 2.5 klx, may be used for a period of 1–2 hours. The total dosage required, the product of illuminance and time, tends thus to be about 5 klx h. Radiation towards and beyond the blue end of the visible spectrum is more effective than longer wavelengths. It is found also that the light treatment for SAD patients is more effective during the morning than the afternoon, and the normal recommendation is for exposure to light immediately after waking.

Figure 1.3 shows how typical winter values of illuminance outdoors vary with latitude; they give mean daylight levels not for the shortest day of the year but a month later, 21 January, which is more representative of the winter period as a whole. The horizontal axes of the graphs extend from 20°, just within the tropics, to 60°, close to the Arctic Circle. Figure 1.3(a) shows illuminance on a vertical surface and is approximately the illuminance on the eyes. The two upper curves give values at 9 am and mid-day when the sun is shining and the receiving surface is orientated to face the sun; the two lower curves show the average illuminance on the surface when the sun is obscured. Figure 1.3(b) gives the time of sunrise on 21 January.

It can be seen that at latitudes of 50° and above, not only are the hours of daylight short but, outdoors in cloudy weather, the mean diffuse illuminance on the eye barely exceeds the levels needed for SAD therapy. Indoors on an overcast day, an exposure to light equivalent to a therapeutic dose could be received only by a person remaining close to a window for several hours. When the sun shines in through a window, however, there is ample light. It is probably not just for its warmth that sunlight is welcomed in cold weather: its high brightness may stimulate a real uplifting of mood in those affected by winter depression.

The conclusion to be drawn is that in cool climates the conditions that engender SAD are likely to be experienced by anyone who is confined indoors. This applies to a significant proportion of the population and to several building types, but is a particular important consideration for people in care buildings. It has been found, for instance, that dementia patients, and older people in residential homes generally, tend to have significantly less exposure to environmental daylight than other people living in the district.

Sunlight, synthesis of vitamin D and other health factors

A deficiency of vitamin D is associated with rickets and poor bone growth generally; among older people, it may hasten skeletal frailty and thus an increased risk of fractures. Exposure to sunlight is the natural means by which the body produces vitamin D.

Overexposure to sunlight causes skin damage that leads ultimately to cancer. Different groups of the population, by their styles of living, have opposite risks to health: the young and the rich from excessive exposure to the sun, the old and the poor from inadequate exposure.

Conclusions for design

1 Buildings in which the occupants are confined during the hours of daylight, such as residential care homes, prisons, hospitals and factories with shift working, should have freely accessible internal areas with strong daylight. In cool climates, these areas should receive direct sunlight, but there should be blinds or other means of control. The daylit areas should be useable for normal daytime activities. Intermediate indoor–outdoor spaces such as conservatories satisfy these requirements.

2 Bedrooms and dormitories generally, and places such as hospital wards where residents regularly sleep, should have very low levels of light during the normal sleeping

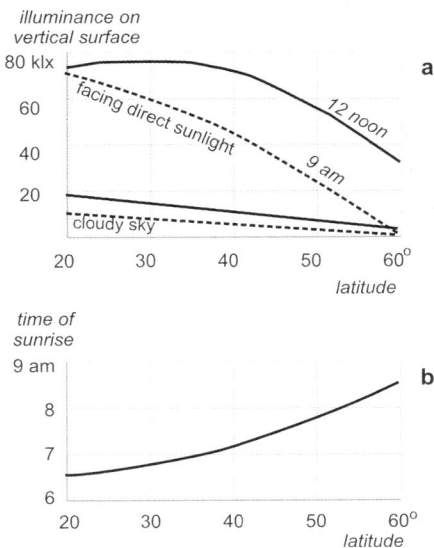

1.3
Winter daylight: January 21 in the Northern Hemisphere. (**a**) Average illuminance on a vertical surface outdoors at 9am and noon, facing the sun and on a cloudy day. (**b**) Time of sunrise (in solar time).

1.4
What we like to look at. A general view containing elements that are preferred: natural things – trees, grass, water; some activity; a range from nearby ground to distant objects and sky.
King's Park, Perth, Western Australia

1.5
The type of view that is not preferred: built, not natural, objects; a short distance range, no sky. But usually a room looking onto this would be preferred to a windowless interior, and if the viewer had a personal interest in the place, or if there were security needs, such a view might be considered essential.

periods of residents or patients. Curtains or blinds should exclude unwanted light from outdoors; this includes stray beams from exterior night-time lighting, and daylight of the early morning and late evening in high-latitude places. Where needs of safety or security require illumination for supervision, this should be screened from the view of those sleeping; controls such as movement detectors should be used to allow near-darkness wherever possible. Many people, particularly the elderly, wake from time to time at night; local lighting should always be provided, controllable from the bedside.

Health 2: the need for a view

This is a topic where recent research has greatly altered thinking. Until recently, standards and daylighting codes have tended to treat a window has having two visual functions: 'view', what you see looking outwards, and 'daylight', the illumination that is coming in. But this distinction is misleading: it is the daylight that carries the view. Or, putting this more precisely, the perception of a view is one of the ways in which the body responds to daylight. When we look outwards through a window, daylight reaches the eyes from many angles.

Some of the incident light is direct from the sky, maybe the sun itself, some is reflected by exterior surfaces such as the ground and other buildings. This field of light varies in intensity and colour with direction. The miracle of vision is that we can use this complexity to construct an image of the world before us.

Some rooms must be windowless: auditoria, film and television studios, art galleries displaying light-sensitive materials – in general, places where illumination must be controlled at low levels. But a windowless room is strongly disliked if there is no obvious reason why daylight should be excluded. Any view is better than none: if the only window in a basement flat looks out onto a brick wall, most people would far prefer that to a windowless interior. Even if the user keeps blinds or curtains always closed, the existence of a link with the outside is valued.

An attractive or interesting view can have a therapeutic effect. In particular, windows with views onto nature can enhance working and well-being. It was found, for example, that patients recovering from surgery in a ward with windows overlooking trees required less powerful analgesic drugs and had shorter recovery times than matched groups of patients in a ward with a view only of a brick wall. Similarly, the glare discomfort caused by a bright sky or by sunlight reflected from light-coloured surfaces is lower when there is an

1.6
This window controls sunlight penetration in a warm dry climate, while allowing air movement; it prevents an inward view (because the interior is dark compared with the surface of the lattice screen) but enables people inside to see outwards. *Iran*

interesting natural view than when the view is of an urban scene of the same brightness.

A substantial amount of research has been done on people's preferences for the content of views. In a typical experiment, subjects sit in a simulated room; images are projected onto screens seen through window-like openings and the subjects are asked to rank these. The following results have been found by several investigators:

1 Views that encompass a wide scale of distance are preferred to those of limited extent; the scenes ranked highest encompass some sky, distant landscape, a middle distance with movement or activities, and objects and the ground nearby.
2 Views of natural scenes are preferred to those of urban environment; scenes containing water are especially popular.
3 When a person is confined indoors, in buildings such as a care home, windows that overlook everyday activities in the community can provide some compensation for restricted social contact.

There are, however, two factors that override these preferences: security and privacy. The need for security normally implies a need to maintain awareness of specific external spaces: examples are supervision of children playing, awareness of people approaching the entrance, a general observation of the site to deter intruders. These activities constitute visual tasks and should be treated as such. The views they give do not necessarily meet the need for contact with the outside world.

The converse of a view out is privacy, the ability to prevent other people seeing in. This requirement is highly dependent on culture and it can take precedence over a view out. In most cultures, people in their home will close curtains or blinds if passers-by could invade privacy, even if this sacrifices a valued view. They would be dissatisfied, however, if the room were windowless.

The provision of an outward view and control over any inward view depend both on a building's site layout and block form, and on the fine detail of window design. Traditional architecture exhibits many solutions to the apparent conflict between criteria of inward and outward view; some are of great ingenuity and beauty, particularly in countries of the Middle East.

It is not just the direct view outwards that is valued. Daylight brings information even if a direct view is blocked.

The continuously varying illumination from a window gives awareness of the outside world even when there is no direct view. From the changing pattern of brightness within the room, we know whether it is sunny outdoors or overcast and raining, whether it is windy with a rapidly changing sky or is settled and calm; we sense also the time of day; and often in an urban building we are aware of reflections or moving shadows of road traffic.

Conclusions for design

1 Unless the function of the room is incompatible with daylighting, or it is used only for short periods, every workplace and every habitable room in a dwelling should have a view through a window to the outside. If a workplace must necessarily be a windowless room, workers should have free access to a nearby space with a good exterior view. A view into another internal space is less liked than an external view; and, if there can be only an internal view, this should be into a large daylit space, such as an atrium.
2 In hospitals, residential care buildings and other buildings where people are unable to move around freely, interesting views, particularly of natural scenes, should be visible to users from their normal daytime positions.
3 The variation of daylight on the walls and ceiling of a room should not be masked by electric lighting. If this is necessary to enhance task illumination or to brighten surfaces that receive little daylight, users should still be aware of the natural changeability of daylight.

The creation of place

A 'place' is somewhere with meaning, somewhere that arouses associations, that can trigger memories of earlier occasions, that can stimulate emotions.

In the greatest buildings and urban spaces, we find an inexhaustible richness of associations. Indeed, the possession of such richness could be the defining characteristic of great work in any art. But every building, anywhere in any town, can arouse thoughts and feelings, and this is an inevitable outcome of the processes by which we perceive the world. The experience of a place can be profound and it can be fleeting, but it is rarely neutral.

Architectural design is the creation of place. So, therefore, is the choosing of brightness and colour, because these are elements of architecture. The lighting and materials of a room, the distribution of light and dark, of chroma and texture, not only determine the physical visibility of things, but they establish the nature of the place, its character, its meaning. Whether or not the designer intends it, the room (or the building or the urban space) that is created will be associated in the mind of every user with places that he or she has previously experienced.

To see why this is so, and to understand the implications for people's expectations and satisfaction, we must make a brief review of perceptual theory.

Images and words

Look at the photograph in Figure 1.7. Suppose you were instructed to study this for one minute and then, half an hour later, sketch it from memory: could you do it? Almost certainly. The appearance of the sketch would depend on your drawing skill, but it is very likely that you could reproduce the picture in a recognisable way. And if you could draw the place, you could also describe it in words: 'It is a bedroom with two single beds with white bedspreads. It is daytime and there is a large square window …', and so on.

Consider an alternative. Suppose you were instructed to subdivide the picture into a grid of 1000 small squares and then, starting at the top left-hand corner, remember the brightness and colour in each square. This would be impossible – unless you had some method of reducing all these values to some pattern or formula.

The result of our perceptual process is not like a bit-mapped digital image from camera or scanner. We do not see an array of millions of luminous points: we recognise a 'room', a 'window', a 'chair'. Patterns of light and colour have meaning, and the 'meaning' is an outcome of the method used by the eye and brain to organise and remember a colossal quantity of information.

Perception is, in essence, the process of linking immediate sensory information with remembered experience. The distribution of brightness and colour that constitutes our visual environment is never treated as an abstract, meaningless pattern. For safety, for survival, we have always needed to identify things that might benefit or harm us. The result is that our awareness of a place goes beyond mere

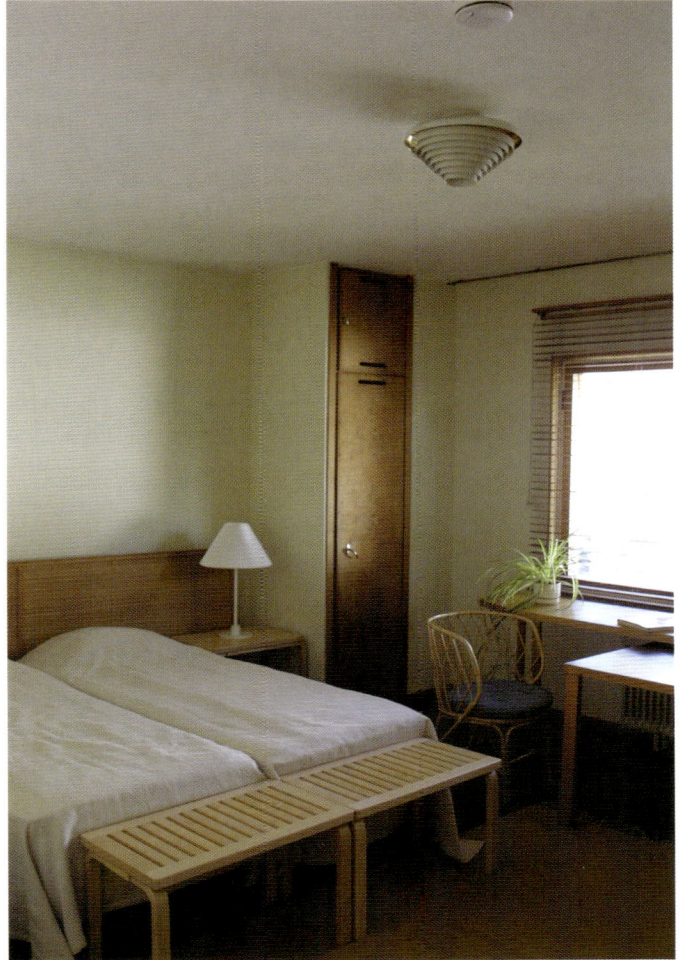

1.7
Could you look at this photograph for a minute then draw it from memory?
Aalto House, Munkkiniemi, Helsinki

recognition: what we see governs our expectations and our satisfaction, it affects our mood, our confidence, our approach to our activities there, and how we react with other people.

It is no accident that we can describe in words what we can draw. In developmental theory, a *schema* (plural *schemata*) is an organised set of memories that builds up though repeated experience. As we pass through different stages of childhood, schemata develop as we gain language: we learn that a 'chair' differs from a 'table' when we understand what 'sit' means. By experience, we begin to recognise the typical shape and dimensions of a chair; and when surprised by exceptions, we construct more complex schemata with the ability to recognise differing categories, such as 'armchair', 'car seat', 'throne'. Schemata link sensory memories with words and concepts.

Culture and climate

A 'culture' could be defined as a commonality of experience, a sharing of memories. Because perception is the process of relating what is immediately sensed to concepts derived from earlier experience, people with similar cultural backgrounds make similar associations between words, images and emotions. That is why a story-teller can trigger common emotions in a group of listeners, or why it is possible to use lighting to change a stage set of meaningless blocks into a scene that consistently conveys the nature of a play.

The converse is that people from dissimilar cultures 'see' quite different places. How would you describe the scene shown in Figure 1.8? Is it 'homely'? Or a place you recognise as a traditional English cottage but quite different from your own home? Or somewhere so foreign that you feel slightly threatened?

There are cultural differences due to different climatic experiences, and these affect expectations about comfort and discomfort. If, for example, a group of students of various nationalities is asked to write down their reaction to a picture of a dark room with small windows, those who come from a hot dry climate tend to say that the room looks pleasantly cool; those from a northern temperate climate tend to describe the room as gloomy.

Cognitive awareness of our personal environment can range from entirely subconscious to intolerably distracting: what determines this is, firstly, the extent to which the place is consistent with our schema, and, secondly, the extent to which we concentrate on some other topic. These interact: if what we are doing or thinking is important and the environment is unsettling, our performance or pleasure is diminished.

In a familiar situation, where all that we subconsciously sense is what we expect, we are likely not to notice the surroundings. If something is incongruous, or if we realise what sort of place it is but it is not our normal setting, we are

1.8
How would you describe this scene? What feelings does it arouse in you?

aware of this. If every clue to recognition implies something different, we are confused.

What we consciously remember from a scene, or what we include when asked later to describe it, varies between us as individuals, not only in 'subjective' judgements of mood or preference but also in 'objective' tasks such as estimating the size of one element in relation to another or discriminating between objects that differ only slightly. Both preference and task performance can be shown to vary systematically with characteristics of the individual and also with common characteristics that define a particular culture. There are also many results that imply that satisfaction with any particular circumstances depends on expectation. We are happy if we get more than we anticipated and dissatisfied if we get less, but the level of our expectation depends both on the immediate context and on all our earlier experience.

Assumptions and constancy

When we have insufficient evidence to recognise unambiguously a place or an element in a scene, we make assumptions – consciously and subconsciously – about both the social context and the physical. We do this continually in our perception of the three-dimensional environment. For instance, a daylit wall varies greatly in luminance, but we perceive this as a change of illumination rather than a variation in surface reflectance, because that is what experience tells us is probable. Look at Figure 1.9: what our eyes focus on is just a pattern of coloured inks on paper. But the distribution of brightness and colour of this pattern is like many we have experienced before; so we 'see', that is construct in our mind, the image of a three-dimensional object. What is more, we recognise it as a carved figure in a museum, a representation of a middle-aged man dressed in historical clothing. We would even be willing to attribute a mood and character to him.

The phenomenon of 'constancy' is the result in perception of assuming that one physical characteristic rather than another is varying. We take the most familiar explanation when there is ambiguity: coloured lighting falling on a person's face is recognised as that rather than as sudden colour changes in the skin. The ability to separate the effect of illumination from surface characteristics and deduce that it is the light that changes is 'lightness constancy'. It depends

1.9
You are looking at a two-dimensional printed pattern, but not only do you interpret it as a carved figure, you probably attribute to it emotion and character.
Medieval pilgrim, Museo das Peregrinacions, Santiago de Compostela

on our experience of similar physical situations and on the availability of clues to resolution of ambiguity.

But constancy can break down. If false clues invoke the wrong assumptions, we see 'illusions'. This can occur with familiar visual tricks like Figure 1.10, where an implication of a converging perspective makes the horizontal bars seem unequal. Constancy often breaks down when a source of light is hidden: a picture illuminated by a masked spotlight to a much higher brightness than its surroundings can look like a transparency lit from behind. And, in Figure 1.11, the church seems to be brightly painted, but the façade is grey stone and the illusion of a painted surface is the result of projected light.

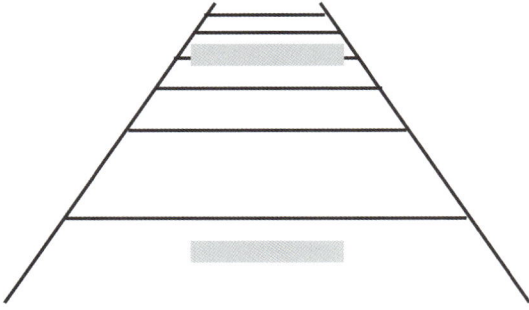

1.10

The Ponzo illusion. The converging lines carry an association with increasing distance, so the grey bars, which are identical, appear to be different sizes.

1.11

Projection of coloured lights gives an illusion of a painted façade.
Saint Nizier, Lyon

The church was photographed from several viewpoints; the images were coloured, detail-by-detail, then projected back on the façade from the original viewpoints.

Consistency

Perception is a process that integrates all the physical senses, not just the visual; and, crucially, it depends on the social environment. Our response to a place includes expectations both of specific physical characteristics and of the ways in which people would behave in that environment. Words like 'church', 'pub', 'school' invoke visual images and recognition of specific sensory environments: they also invoke behavioural memories. We know what a classroom is like and we expect it to differ from the interior of a church or a pub. We behave differently in different types of room and we expect others to do so. We form integrated concepts through repeated experiences: language, sensory awareness and social actions become interlinked.

Sound, smell, touch, air movement, air temperature, radiant heat – and the way these alter with time and with our own movements – all of these can affect what we 'see'. If there is inconsistency – for instance, if a restaurant looks luxurious and expensive but sounds like a fast-food place – we are puzzled or confused. We are more disturbed still if the behaviour of other people is inconsistent with our expectations of the place.

The process of place recognition is usually below the level of conscious awareness. It is a search through the schemata formed though previous experience for the one that best fits the present sensory stimuli. A place is identified when we have linked it with a specific schema. It then becomes associated with all the experiences that have accumulated in memory around the selected schemata. These associations then generate expectations about the physical and social nature of the place we see.

It is enough to imagine a room, or simply use its name, to invoke expectations. A type name, such as 'bedroom', implies that the room will have those features that define the type, the clues to recognition: in a bedroom there will be one or more beds; there will be conditions of heat, light and sound that make sleeping possible, and the room will have various other characteristics that distinguish it from, say, a bedroom furniture showroom in a department store. We know also that bedrooms vary greatly, but, because the majority lie within a fairly narrow range of size, shape, layout and materials, we could easily describe a typical example. We have an idea of what is typical for many types of space.

The 'normal' room

Let the term 'normal' mean a set of expectations about the physical environment, expectations that are evoked by the name of the place – either a generic name, such as 'bedroom', or the name of somewhere specific. The test of whether a 'normal' place exists in a person's mind is whether qualifying words can suggest something unusual. The phrase 'a very big bedroom' implies one much larger than most of those in our previous experience, and it is meaningless to say 'a very big bedroom' unless the hearer not only has a concept of a 'normal' bedroom, but has one that is similar to the speaker's. The fact that we use such expressions prolifically in everyday speech is evidence that, firstly, words such as 'bedroom' can conjure a clear image of a place and, secondly, there exist typical images, or sets of expectations, that are common between people.

This gives us a huge advantage in communication. It is not necessary to give detailed descriptions of things of shared experience. By triggering recall of memory in the hearer, a few words can, in effect, convey complex information about places, or people, or pictures. We have a highly developed ability to deduce the culture of other people from the particular words they use, and this influences our social behaviour.

The concept of 'normal' can be extended beyond particular types of room to the construction and shape of building elements – the slope of tiled roofs, for example, or the proportions of structural columns. If most of the buildings we have seen have similar shapes and dimensions when constructed of particular materials, these become 'normal'. We comment on exceptions: 'The roof of that house is very steep'; 'That column doesn't look safe!'

The rectilinear daylit room

There is a shape that occurs, with subtle climatic modifications, almost everywhere in the world. It is found in vernacular architecture wherever local building materials naturally lead to

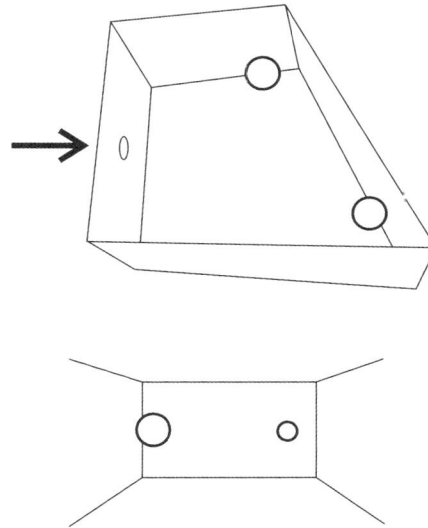

1.12
The Ames room, seen from above and (lower drawing) from the viewpoint indicated by the arrow.

planar forms (the timber frame, the masonry wall) and internationally with steel and glass, and the boxed shuttering of reinforced concrete. It is found where space needs to be subdivided regularly. The rectilinear room is the most common interior space: it is the living room, the classroom, the office – the kind of room in which most people spend many of their daytime hours and where many of the significant events of life take place.

There is convincing evidence that rectilinear room geometry is 'normal'. An example is the demonstration room invented by the American ophthalmologist and psychologist Adelbert Ames, Jr (1880–1955). It is shown in Figure 1.12, and may be built either as a scale model or full size. In plan and section, it is far from rectangular – the ceiling slopes downwards and opposite walls differ in length – but, when viewed from one position, a peephole in one of the walls, it appears in the perspective of a rectilinear room. The only peculiarity is that, seen from the peephole, people inside the room appear to change size as they walk around. So strong is the association between a rectilinear room and a visual pattern of converging lines that, faced with ambiguity, the brain causes us to perceive a familiar room form occupied by weirdly changing people rather than an unexpected room shape enclosing ordinary men and women. The illusion does not always work: if the viewer has previously seen the room from another position, the distortion is recognised from the viewpoint, or if a person inside the room is well known to the viewer.

In each case, additional knowledge causes the viewer to adopt an alternative schema.

The windows in a 'normal' rectilinear room are usually in one wall or two adjacent walls in buildings of domestic scale, for practical reasons of layout planning; larger spaces such as classrooms may have windows in opposite walls. Roof openings are less common than side windows, again for obvious practical reasons. Associated with 'normal' room dimensions are, therefore, 'normal' patterns of light, the characteristic patterns of daylight distribution. When windows are in one wall only, or in adjacent walls, the pattern of illumination is strongly asymmetrical. There are steep gradients of brightness across the room surfaces, and the relative amounts of light falling on vertical and horizontal surfaces changes with distance from a window. Most importantly, the pattern of surface brightness and the absolute quantity of light in the room are not constant but change with time in a way that is related to the world outside.

There is experimental evidence that supports the existence of 'normal' brightness distributions. The experiments used test rooms where illuminance on the walls, ceiling and desktop surfaces could be adjusted separately. Subjects were asked to adjust the lighting to their preferences or to select from preset luminance patterns. Those chosen had the characteristics of daylit spaces, even though the rooms were windowless. Subjects tended to prefer working-plane illuminances significantly greater than the minimum needed for office-type visual tasks; mean wall luminances were moderately high, but exhibited a large difference between maximum and minimum. 'Visually interesting' or non-uniform wall luminance patterns were preferred, together with acceptance of temporal variation. An important result from such experiments is that subjects are able to make consistent judgements about the lighting of a room and that they are consistent in the use of words and metaphors to describe particular lighting situations.

Daylight quantity

Surveys of daylighting preferences among different groups of users have produced widely varying results. Occupants of very high-density residential blocks in Hong Kong were found to be satisfied with much lower levels of daylight than expected in social housing in Western Europe; occupants of expensive modern apartments tend to expect more daylight (and more extensive views out) than those living in low-cost areas. The nature of the architecture is also significant: less light is expected in the cottages of a rural village than in a high-ceilinged Renaissance villa or a modern dwelling.

The question 'How much daylight should be provided for a particular room type?' implies two further questions: 'How much do people expect?' and thus 'What is "normal" for them?'

There is no universal criterion of daylight quantity. What is found to be satisfactory depends on the function of the building, its architectural nature and the culture of the users. Expectations probably also vary with time: as a population becomes used to a higher standard of housing, for example, or as fashions change, or as matters such as sustainability become widely accepted.

An indication of what was 'normal' in buildings can be inferred from published guidelines, rules of thumb and mandatory requirements. These go back as far as Vitruvius; they are found in key books on architectural principles by Palladio and other authors in the Italian Renaissance; there are eighteenth and nineteenth century European examples, and there are regulations, standards and byelaws published in many countries during the last 150 years.

These do, of course, describe what each author considered to be either minimum requirements or good practice rather than the conditions found in existing buildings of the time. We will take them as indications of what users might have expected in a good building. Most give required window sizes either in terms of the ratio of window area to floor area or in terms of the ratio of window area to inside window wall area. Some recommend specific proportions of windows and maximum room depths in relation to window height.

What is remarkable is the consistency of the recommendations over many centuries. For the window area : floor area ratio, typical ranges of values are

housing	8–13%
schools	17–25%

At the beginning of the twentieth century, the requirements of the London Building Act were 10% and 20% for the two building types, and these values were echoed in byelaws from other parts of Britain, continental European cities and cities in the USA. In some places, equivalent regulations exist now.

Figures from the first half of the last century must be seen in the context of rudimentary electric lighting and substantial atmospheric pollution from coal burning. Especially, it must be noted that daylighting was the principle method of illumination, and this was why relatively large glazing areas were required in schools and workplaces.

Expectations

'Normal' characteristics extend beyond particular place types. For example, some assumptions we make from common experience are:

- Floor and ground surfaces are usually dark-coloured, but not black; ceilings tend to be much lighter; walls tend to vary greatly because they are broken up by doors, windows, pictures and many other items.
- The flow of light is usually downwards, from the sky and from overhead electric lighting.
- Distant objects outdoors tend to appear weaker in colour saturation than nearby objects, owing to scattering by the atmosphere.

A place that differs from such norms can take a special character. A strongly lit white floor can trigger associations with snow or the sensation of walking on a cloud; an upward flow of light from a window and a bright ceiling suggests sunlight on the ground outside; a dark ceiling can make a room seem cave-like, especially if all the enclosing surfaces are dark-coloured and matt. Stage design uses these common assumptions to create illusion: a face lit from below looks threatening, even diabolical; a gradation from strong colour at the front of the stage towards a uniform pale blue at the horizon makes an illusion of great distance. The two images in Figure 1.13 illustrate the visual significance of the floor reflectance.

Expectations and the needs of the user

Should a bedroom 'look like a bedroom'? Should a building, or a room, or a source of light, draw attention to itself, or is it better that it remain part of an unnoticed background?

1.13
If the floor or ground surface is darkened, the perceived character of the place is changed. The interreflected light is reduced, thus reducing the brightness of other surfaces. *British Museum, London, original (upper) and modified image (lower)*

There is an important decision that the designer must make: it is whether a place should be 'normal'; whether, that is, a setting should be accepted subconsciously or should attract attention. A workplace must maintain stimulation but not be distracting; a display must not go unnoticed; a building where people are already overwhelmed with information must not add more. Awareness of our personal environment ranges from the entirely subconscious to the full focus of our attention. We can be so concentrated on a thought or an activity that we entirely miss what is happening around us; or the opposite – we can be so overwhelmed by a place of natural beauty or magnificent architecture that all else is forgotten. Sometimes there is conflict – we try to concentrate on a task but are continually distracted by something we can see.

The more 'normal' a place, the more likely that it will remain below the level of conscious experience. This is helpful where users are anxious or handicapped, such as unconfident travellers in a large airport terminal or patients in a hospital. A building that by self-display increases the amount of information that users have to assimilate can increase their distress.

But complexity and contradiction are elements of architectural composition, and these imply that a place should be noticed for its own sake. A building may provoke thought, and hold the viewer's attention by saying more than can be revealed at a quick glance. It can contain references to recent events, to cultural memories and to the other arts; but any resulting ambiguity may be worse than confusing to a distressed person.

For every place, there is an optimum level of consistency between the different senses, between the physical and the social environments, and between expectations and actuality – the balance between the 'normal' and the strange. When tasks demand concentration, the purpose of the building is to provide a comfortable helpful enclosure. Where users have sensory or cognitive disability, or are anxious or distressed, every aspect of the place should aid and guide. Not only must the place be 'normal', there must be consistency in every aspect.

But where display of the building itself is an objective – where the architecture can be stimulating, exciting, innovative – it is not enough to offer only the 'normal'. The aim is twofold: to provide sufficient clues to establish recognition of the type, and to present the unexpected. Both are necessary; if a place is so bizarre that it is not recognisable, the degree of innovation is not measurable.

Designers and the rest of the world

Successful design depends on anticipating users' expectations about the physical characteristics of the room. This depends on many physical and social factors. Expectations are shared between people of similar background, but vary with climate and culture. They may be different between the people who commission a building and those who will live and work there, because in most cases clients and users are different people.

A professional designer does not have the same perception of the visual environment as people untrained in the discipline. A five-year course in architecture, for instance, not only gives the student a technical competence: it creates new attitudes, new visual standards, and a changed meaning to many common words. Above all, we become sensitised to our specialism: a highway lighting engineer is much more aware than other people of glare from street lights; an architect looks more at buildings, and at different features of them. It is essential for the designer to be aware of this and to use language – both the language of speech and the language of the visual world – that carries meaning for the layman.

Conclusions for design

1 People have clear expectations about the appearance of a place. These depend on culture and personal experience; they govern how people behave in the place, their motivation to work and their attitude to change. There exist assumptions about the appearance and contents of particular types of building; these can be triggered by the name ('bedroom', 'department store', 'church') and by characteristics that lead to recognition of a particular type of place.
2 A designer's perception is likely to be different from that of a building's users. It is important to recognise this, especially when designing for users with disabilities such as dementia or from a different cultural background.

Places may be recognised differently, and behavioural clues misinterpreted.

3 The extent to which a place is consistent with people's expectations determines whether it is recognised as a particular type of place and whether it is noticed. Where task performance is crucial or where people may be stressed, it is important that the enclosure is not unsettling or distracting.

Work and comfort

Reading and writing are visual tasks; so are using tools, assembling components and many other activities in a workplace. But there are visual tasks of everyday life, for example:

- finding your way in an unfamiliar place;
- recognising peoples' faces;
- playing ball games;
- looking at the architectural features of a building;
- monitoring the ground while walking.

'Visual tasks' are activities that require the brain to collect information from some specific part of the visual surroundings. The term is used commonly in the context of the office, classroom or factory, but the principles of task lighting are more general: we carry out visual tasks all the time, mainly subconsciously.

The normal process of perception is abstracting what we need to know from what we see, and this is also the essence of task performance. Task design is therefore not a special part of lighting activity; it is something applicable across the whole scope of design. In practice, this means that techniques that are usually discussed in the context of workplace performance can be used advantageously whenever it is important for something to be visible.

Size, brightness and contrast

Task illuminance – the amount of light falling on the task – affects the speed and accuracy of working. But only up to a point: if you a reading by the light of a single candle then adding a second candle will help greatly; if you are already in a bright room, doubling the illuminance on the page may give no perceptible improvement.

There is a point beyond which additional light makes little improvement to the speed and accuracy of task performance. Where this point occurs depends on the size and contrast of the task detail: with small grey print on grey paper, a much greater illuminance is required before you reach your optimum performance than when reading large black type on white paper; nor will your performance be as good however much light you add. Try reading the small writing in Figure 1.14 under different levels of light, or looking at it with half-closed eyes.

Figure 1.15 shows the relationship between performance and task illuminance. The most important conclusion to be drawn from it is that, no matter how much task illuminance is increased, the speed and accuracy of carrying out a visually difficult task is less than that of one with greater contrast and bigger detail. This means that designing the task and its surroundings to increase these factors – with, for example, the use of directional lighting to enhance solid forms, the systematic use of colour, and the use of optical aids such as magnification – is more effective than increased illuminance alone. Notice in the lowest two items in Figure 1.14 how colour contrast can enhance visibility.

Illuminance/performance curves such as those in Figure 1.15 are average values: they are the lines that best fit a broad scatter of measurements. In experimental data, there is much variation between individual subjects, even when factors such as ageing, motivation, adaptation and visual handicaps are taken into account. Any attempt to make recommendations for task illuminance also depends on judgements of value: do you set the level at 90% or at 99% of optimum performance – one might imply an illuminance ten times the other? And how do the tightly controlled simplified tasks used in the laboratory relate to the varying and complex visual fields of the normal workplace?

For purposes of standardisation, such judgements have to be made, and schedules of recommended illuminance such as the list at the end of this chapter are the bases of lighting design throughout the world. They ensure that minimum standards are achieved and they serve as a benchmark for contractual purposes and for analysing factors such as energy consumption. But the sensitivity of task illuminance values must be interpreted in the context described: a doubling of illuminance from 500 lx to 1000 lx may have some effect on

Size, brightness and contrast

Size, brightness and contrast

Size, brightness and contrast

Size, brightness and contrast

Size, brightness and contrast

Size, brightness and contrast

Size, brightness and contrast

1.14

Size, brightness and contrast are the three primary characteristics of visual tasks that affect visibility.

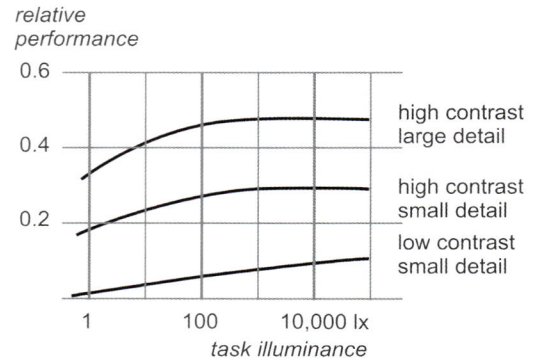

1.15

The relationship between illuminance and task performance. The curves are trend lines drawn through very scattered data.
Based on work by Weston [50].

the performance of a visually demanding task, but an increase from 500 lx to 550 lx is likely to remain imperceptible.

There is some evidence that a lower illuminance is required from daylight than from electric lighting, to maintain a given level of performance. The reasons for this are not certain: it is possible that both physiological and psychological processes are involved. It is known, for instance, that performance is better when the colour rendering quality of the source is improved; the flow of light from a side window is soft but directional, giving good three-dimensional modelling; it is also true that people prefer daylit rooms, so improved motivation might be a factor.

The principal aim of lighting design is often taken to be the provision of plenty of light. Possibly, this is because the development of lighting technology has, throughout history, been a search for increasingly efficient sources. It is also a view reinforced by the fact that most standards use illuminance, a measure of light quantity, as the principal criterion of lighting merit. But to think in this way is to miss the point completely: the purpose of lighting is to convey information. The light that reaches our eyes varies in time and direction, the result of interactions with surrounding surfaces. From this variability, we are each able to construct a mental model of our own immediate world.

It is helpful to think of our senses not as instruments that measure energy, like photometers, but as receivers of signals. It is then clear that the essential requirement with respect to light intensity is that the illumination reaching the eye has sufficient energy to carry the signal. This gives a theoretical basis for performance/illuminance curves such as those in

Figure 1.15. The more information to be carried, the greater the signal bandwidth needed. Where the spatial resolution must be high (that is, where fine detail must be seen) or if sensitive discrimination is required between different levels of brightness or colour (where contrast in a visual task is small), or when the visual field is changing rapidly, a carrier of more energy is needed than when a simple clear pattern is the information conveyed: this is illustrated by the differences in the graph between lines representing different size/contrast combinations. It follows also that if a signal is already suffi-ciently strong to embody all the information required, no advantage will be gained by increasing its energy: this is shown by flattening of the curves as illuminance increases.

Geometry

Good task lighting design does not begin with numbers. When the aim is to achieve comfort coupled with the best possible visibility of a task object, the design strategy is to answer four groups of questions. The first two define the problem:

1 What characteristics of the task need to be visible? Is it a surface pattern, such as a printed page? The three-dimensional shape of an object? The surface texture?
2 Who is doing the task? Is the person for whom we are designing very young or old? Does he or she have normal eyesight? Any physical handicaps? Is the task repetitive over a long period, or short in duration? Is it done in a fixed position – sitting or standing – or does the person move around?

The two questions draw out the solution:

1 What form of lighting best enhances the critical character-istics of the task? Should there be a beam of light just skimming the surface to exaggerate texture, or diffuse light to mask it? Is the surface pattern more important than the shape of the object? Is the surface shiny or matt? Is colour important? Is there movement?
2 Where should the light sources be, in relation to the task and the viewer? What is the background? Is any screening needed?

With daylight, this last group of questions is crucial. The geometry of the layout – the positions of windows in relation to the tasks and positions of users – predominantly determines the quality of workplace lighting.

Where the lighting is faulty – with users feeling discomfort or being unable to work with the speed and accuracy that they should achieve – the fault is usually due to the geometry of the layout. Worksheet 12 gives a diagnostic procedure for finding the causes of discomfort or weak performance due to poor workplace lighting. Faults fall into five categories:

1 *Glare from a direct view of the source.* The sky or other bright objects are visible close to the task in a user's line of sight. If the contrast is sufficiently great, this can be uncomfortable; but performance can be lessened by bright views close to the task even when there is no discomfort.
2 *Glare from reflections.* Sources of light reflected in shiny surfaces cause discomfort or impair performance by being bright patches in the field of view.
3 *Task contrast reduced by reflections.* Bright objects reflected in the task area itself act as a veil of brightness over the detail of the task. This is often a serious problem with VDUs in offices and with whiteboards or traditional chalkboards in classrooms, as in Figure 1.16. The person in Figure 1.17 is handicapped by several lighting faults that would impair his visual ability by reducing the effective contrast in the visual task: he is facing a bright sky; sunlight falls on his desk; there are shiny reflections in the book he is reading and in the surrounding desktop.
4 *Dazzle.* The brightness of the task surface is so great that the eye cannot adapt to it comfortably. Bright sunlight on white paper is a common cause of this in schools and offices. In industry, processes such as welding require protective screens. Excessive brightness can be dangerous in the short term owing to accidents from temporary blindness. Frequent or prolonged exposure causes permanent eye damage.
5 *Low illuminance.* Insufficient light falls on the task. If the original lighting installation was adequate, low illuminance on task areas can be the result of shadows – from rearranged furniture, for instance, or where a user sits with his back to a window, blocking daylight that should fall on the work surface. A frequent cause of inadequate illuminance is poor building maintenance – failure to replace lamps, to clean luminaires or to repair blinds. The practice of keeping blinds permanently closed to exclude

1.16
Veiling reflections on a book and a VDU screen. The bright fuzzy pattern in the screen is the reflection of a view though a window.

1.17
The person sitting here suffers from major faults in the lighting. He faces the bright sky, he has sunlight falling on his task area, and his vision of the task will be reduced by shiny reflections.

sunlight or reduce sky glare is also a common cause of low illuminance.

The geometry of source–task–user is a factor in all these categories of fault. Its importance cannot be overestimated: an apparently minor change in a user's working position can transform good task lighting to bad, and vice versa. There is a simple rule which applies to most situations: windows should be to the side of users; the lines of sight of users should be parallel with the window wall. When a person is using a VDU, or working with papers at a desk, or using machine tools, there is a high risk of diminished task visibility when a window is either directly behind or directly in front of the user.

The corollary of this is that if windows occupy a large fraction of two adjacent walls, good task lighting is very difficult to achieve. In such cases, a practical solution is to lower the blinds of all windows in one orientation. This again emphasises the rule that good daylighting depends on decisions made in the early design stages of a building. It is the block form of a building and its orientation that determine the availability of sunlight, the view and the amount of skylight falling on windows; and it is the shape and layout of rooms and the location of windows that determine the extent to which the incident daylight can be used as workplace lighting.

People vary very much in the daylight illuminance they choose to work in. If they can freely adjust window blinds and electric lighting in their workplace, they usually change the settings little after they set them up initially when moving into the space. Those who work primarily on computers tend to set up a lower illuminance on the desktop than those who use computers occasionally. This may occur for several reasons, particularly (a) to reduce distracting brightness from a direct view or reflection of windows or luminaires, and (b) to achieve a lower overall background brightness to the screen.

People with impaired vision

Older people and those with impaired vision from other causes need special consideration. Visual impairment has several symptoms, varying with the cause of the disorder. These are common problems:

1   Reduction in the fraction of the light entering the eye that reaches the retina. Owing to yellowing of the lens, the shorter wavelengths of the spectrum are especially attenuated, so the sensitivity to blue light is seriously reduced.
2   Slower responses. Brightness adaptation is slow, and so is focusing on objects.
3   Reduced colour saturation and reduced contrast.
4   Increased sensation of glare.

In most cases, but not all, higher illuminances are required on visual tasks; the optimum level is typically double or more the amount needed for the same task by young people with good vision. More important still are two requirements: high contrast between object and background, and within visual tasks; and a minimising of bright sources that could be glaring.

As in task design generally, enhancing contrast by changes of surface colour and clarifying the task detail can have a greater effect than increases of illuminance.

'Too much daylight'

It is comfortable reading a book outside provided that it is not in direct sunlight. If the sun is 60° above the horizon (approximate solar elevation at noon in summer in the UK), the illuminance on the ground from sun and sky can exceed 100 klx (100,000 lx). That illuminance on the white pages of a book is dazzling. With the sun hidden by cloud, the average horizontal illuminance is typically 40 klx at that solar elevation. For most people, this is no longer dazzling.

Compared with these external values, illuminances inside a building are small: 500 lx is the typical recommended value

in a general office. Nevertheless, desktop Illuminances of only three or four times the recommended amount have been judged as 'too bright' in some field studies. Clearly this is not due to the illuminance itself, a value maybe one-twentieth of an acceptable external illuminance. What it shows is that to achieve a high value of daylight in a working position, there is a risk of discomfort or visual disability from direct glare or glossy reflections. The problems are likely to be more severe if there is a large brightness difference between surfaces at the back of the room and those close to windows.

Peripheral and central vision

We depend on our peripheral vision to warn us about any change in the space around us. When we look at something, we move our eyes so that the centre of interest is focused on the fovea, a small area in the centre of the retina. Peripheral vision is the rest of our visual field, everything that is focused on the retina outside the fovea. Much of the time we are not conscious of it. The peripheral field remains below the level of awareness until something within it changes. Then we notice something and direct our interest, and our foveal vision, towards it.

The periphery of the visual field is especially sensitive to movement. We continuously monitor our surroundings; we become aware of anything moving into our visual field. If the ground surface changes as we walk, we glance downwards; a large unexpected movement overhead makes us shield our head. Because of the nature of our peripheral vision, flashing warnings are more noticeable at the edge of vision than in the direct gaze.

Having the central field of vision only is like using a bright narrow-beamed torch in a large dark unfamiliar room: you can see detail clearly but it is hard to gain a sense of the place as a whole. A dim diffuse light in the room might be inadequate for reading small detail but you can see the form of the room and sense its character. This is an analogy of the part that the outer area of the visual field plays in the perceptual process. Complete vision requires both parts.

So task lighting design does not stop at the edge of the visual task. Firstly, as we discussed above, the brightness and colour of the immediate surround to the task affect the visibility of the task itself. Secondly, the nature of the peripheral field can enhance or distract from concentration on the task. Rapid movements and flickering lamps interfere with performance. Conversely, a task environment that conforms to expectations, that is 'normal', is supportive. Daylight, with its variability and the information that this gives, is part of what is 'normal' in many room types.

Brightness adaptation

The human body is able to change physiologically as the immediate environment changes. When conditions cool, the blood vessels near the skin rapidly become constricted to minimise heat loss; in hot conditions, they dilate, and the skin perspires, to maximise cooling. There are also long-term physiological changes that occur when a person goes to live in a warmer or cooler climate.

The eye adapts to motion and to particular shapes, to colour and to brightness. These latter two are particularly relevant to daylight. Over a period of an hour or so during a calm sunny afternoon, the light entering a window may fall to a quarter of its initial amount and its colour may vary from a cool blue to a warm white; but, even if you are sitting working in daylight at a desk near the window, you are very likely not to notice these changes. In signal processing terms, the adaptation of the eye is like a filter that blocks slow changes of brightness and colour.

Three mechanisms of the eye are used in brightness adaptation. The first is the opening and closing of the iris; this is a fine adjustment comparable to the way a photographer reduces the camera aperture to obtain greater depth of field when there is ample light. The second is a neural process, transformation of sensory data in the eye–brain system; this is responsible for the almost immediate adaptation that occurs in situations where the luminance range is not large. The third mechanism is the bleaching out and regeneration of pigment in the photosensitive cells of the retina; with this, adaptation from dark to light is rapid; the regeneration of pigment needed for light-to-dark adaptation can take up to an hour. Combined, the mechanisms give a range of sensitivity that enables us to see in conditions from starlight to bright sunlight. Figure 1.18 illustrates this.

The reduced visibility of a task when light from bright objects in the background falls on the eye is the result of inappropriate adaptation: in photographic terms, the task

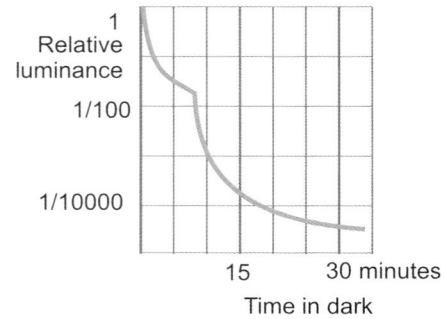

1.18
Adaptation to low levels of brightness. Subjects sit in a dark room after being adapted to strong light. At intervals, they are shown short flashes of light of different luminance. The graph shows the lowest luminance they detect plotted against the time they have spent in darkness. The angle in the curve indicates transition between the photoreceptors active at daytime levels of light (cones) to the more sensitive cells of the retina active at low levels (rods). Based on work by Arden [51].

area is underexposed because the background illumination has reduced the eye's sensitivity.

There are situations where the brightness adaptation of users must be controlled. The lighting of roadway tunnels must provide zones of intermediate brightness as drivers enter and leave. In a cinema, where users may enter from a daylit street, the sequence of spaces from the entrance, through the ticketing area, the foyer and the approach to the auditorium should be a progression of reducing brightness. The same strategy may be necessary in an art gallery, where the illuminance on the pictures displayed has to be low to minimise radiation damage. The visitor is taken through a sequence of spaces where the brightness of the displays gradually diminishes and users' vision becomes increasingly sensitive.

There are two requirements of spaces entered by people adapted to a higher illuminance. The first is to ensure that the light falling on their eyes is minimised, so their visual sensitivity is enhanced; the second is that essential objects are sufficiently bright to be well visible. These requirements do not necessarily conflict: the illuminance on the eye from a source depends on its luminance and its angular size. So the aim is to provide small areas of relatively high luminance that enable users to find their way, gain information and appreciate the displays. The same applies to emergency lighting that enables escape when the normal lighting fails. At very low lighting levels, colour can be used selectively.

The eye's photoreceptors that operate at daytime brightness are relatively much more sensitive to light at the red end of the spectrum than are the receptors that provide night vision. Red lights can be used as beacons or warning indicators without significantly affecting dark adaptation.

Most of the ways of dealing with brightness adaptation depend on the basic planning of the building – the sequence of display spaces in an art gallery, the location of the entrance and the layout of foyers in a cinema, the views from inside to outside. Again we reach the conclusion that successful lighting in architecture depends on decisions made at early stages of design.

Discomfort glare

Glare can be thought of as optical noise, masking the information sought. If intense, it causes physical discomfort.

In large rooms, such as open plan offices, a desk worker may be able to see row upon row of ceiling-mounted luminaires; if these are bright in the direction of the viewer, the result can be strong discomfort. The glare can be eliminated by choosing luminaires that emit light predominantly downwards; the luminance of the side of the fittings is then low. But a strongly directional flow of light is often unsatisfactory in a workplace: it gives bright reflections in horizontal desktops; it casts hard shadows that can impair task visibility; it can give unattractive modelling, especially of people's faces; and more luminaires are necessary because they must be spaced more closely to achieve uniformity of illumination. A better luminaire output distribution is found when the peak intensity of the light output is not vertical but diagonally downwards and coupled with a sharp cut-off of light towards the horizontal. It is also an advantage to spill some light onto the ceiling.

Research on glare has focused on quantifying the level of discomfort. This led to the concept of a 'glare index', a formula that allows alternative designs for the lighting of a space to be compared numerically.

Using laboratory studies of peoples' reactions, it was found that the degree of discomfort experienced when a subject was exposed to a small bright light depended on four factors:

* the luminance of the light source
* the size of the source

* the luminance of the background
* the angle of the source from the subject's line of vision.

The first two have a positive association with discomfort: as source luminance and size increase, discomfort becomes greater. The latter two reduce discomfort as they increase. This implies that discomfort glare is, in effect, the result of excessive contrast within the visual field, a function of source luminance against the luminance of the background. The glare from a source can be reduced by making the background brighter.

The same four parameters are found to be important factors in glare from large sources, such as windows, although the glare index equation changes as sources get bigger. Daylight glare calculations have not been widely adopted in practice.

Existing formulae are not good predictors of peoples' reactions to window glare. If a large number of subjects are asked to describe the discomfort they experience in various situations, and if glare indices are calculated from size and luminance measurements taken in each situation, a graph plotted from the results shows a wide scatter.

There must be other factors than the four given above that affect the sensation of discomfort from a glaring window. These include the age of the viewer, as we noted earlier. The brightness pattern of the glare source is a factor: it is not enough to measure only the mean luminance of a window. A large uniformly bright screen is judged to be less glaring than a non-uniform screen that gives the same illuminance at the viewer's eye; and some patterns, such as black-and-white striations, can be very much more uncomfortable.

It is not purely photometric characteristics that affect the sensation of discomfort: the viewer's interest in the glare source influences the degree of discomfort. Very bright television screens carrying an interesting picture are judged less glaring than blank white screens of the same mean luminance. Windows looking out on to an extensive view are less glaring than those looking onto the blank wall of an adjacent building. Views of natural scenes – hills, trees, water – are found to be less glaring than those of buildings, roads and the hard urban landscape. Such results from laboratory studies, in which subjects assess glare from scenes matched in brightness and luminance pattern, show that the sensation of discomfort is moderated by our interest in the cause of it, and whether we have a prior liking or disliking of the situation.

These research findings are further evidence that human response to light is influenced by the information that the light carries.

There are many analogies in other situations. We tend to be more disturbed by a neighbour's noise – a barking dog, for example – than by our own, and sensitivity is increased further if that sound has already been the subject of complaints.

Calculations of glare can be helpful, but they must not override common sense. A late-afternoon sky is beautiful and the beam from the setting sun that falls on the window gives pleasure, even though the glare index would predict it to be intolerably uncomfortable.

Conclusions for design

1   The essence of good task lighting is the geometrical relationship of task : light source : viewer. Firstly, light must fall on the task at an angle that enhances visibility of the object, but it must not fall strongly on the eyes of the viewer. Secondly, bright sources of light should not be visible to the viewer from reflections in and around the task. This imposes constraints on the layout of a daylight room, especially with side windows. Generally, viewers' lines of sight should be parallel with the window wall.

2   Users need to control their workplaces, to adapt to changing conditions. They must be able to control the entry of direct sunlight and to switch supplementary light sources on and off.

3   The quantity of light falling on the task area must be adequate for the task. In rooms of at least medium size, supplementary electric lighting is usually required.

4   If users are visually frail or handicapped, special lighting may be used to enhance their performance, and the task itself may be altered to enhance the size of detail and to increase contrasts. Most older people prefer higher levels of illuminance than young people.

Display

Good lighting in a shop or an exhibition does three things: it establishes the nature and character of the place; it draws the attention of viewers to the items on display; and it enables the users to see clearly the detail within these items. So far in this chapter, we have covered the first and last of these things; this final section looks at display lighting, especially the use of daylight.

Display lighting is the use of light and colour to draw and hold the user's attention. It is a primary requirement in museums, galleries and shops, but it is a consideration in almost every situation. It is found at all scales, from the floodlighting of a historic city to the layout of controls in a car.

As a source of light for display, daylight has qualities quite different from those of any artificial source: the high intensity of the sun's beam; the large angular size of the diffuse sky; variation in brightness associated with natural events; and variation in colour coupled with excellent colour rendering. But daylight is difficult to control. Throughout the world of optics, the larger the source, the larger the optical devices required to focus its output. The most common technique of display lighting is to make the object on display brighter than its surroundings, and this is usually achieved with the precise narrow beams of spotlights. Skylight cannot be focused in this way and, in addition, it is cumbersome to control in intensity.

Shopping malls and other large spaces

Many shopping malls have large windows, usually in the form of rooflights. These give the space a daylit appearance, which is popular. Displays of merchandise, though, are almost invariably lit with electric sources, and so are posters, banners, signs and other features in the public areas. The crucial part in the design of such a space is the treatment of intermediate conditions: in time, as the daylight fades, and spatially, in those areas for which the daylight is inadequate.

There is a phenomenon of perception that can be employed here: if a strong source of light is visible, there is a tendency to assume that all the ambient light is due to this source. If an atrium has high windows and in addition there is high-level electric lighting providing a downward flow of light of similar colour to the daylight, the floor and walls of the atrium can seem daylit even if the illuminance from the lamps is as great as that from the windows. It ceases to work when the external daylight falls to a level inconsistent with the indoor illuminance, or when the electric lighting masks the spatial variation of light from windows. The guideline remains: preserve the natural variation of daylighting.

So a strategy for daylight design of buildings such as shopping malls and for large atrium spaces in general is as follows:

1 Establish the daytime appearance as being a daylit space. Supplement the daylight in intermediate zones with luminaires that broadly mimic the distribution of light from the window.
2 Create distinctly different daytime and night-time modes. The junction between them could be slow and gradual or it could be an event with orchestrated changes as lights switch on and off. Several lighting modes could be set up: winter daylight, summer daylight, dusk, early evening, late night.
3 Use visible electric sources to create a hierarchy of display brightness, the highest levels being on the most important items displayed. Do not aim for a uniform illuminance. The amount of electric lighting may have to be greater in daylit areas than in those that receive little natural light, but it is normally necessary to ensure that deep spaces opening onto a daylit atrium are sufficiently well lit to avoid a dark cave-like appearance.

This strategy of using daylight to establish the fundamental character of a space and to use electric light in two ways, to supplement daylight subtly and to provide display and task illumination overtly, is powerful and widely applicable.

Galleries and museums

How a work of art is perceived, what it means to the viewer, is hugely influenced by the situation in which it is viewed: an altarpiece by Tintoretto seen in a Venetian church is an experience quite different from that given by a similar painting hung in a gallery; so is the sculpture on the pediment of a Doric temple seen on a Mediterranean island, compared with a reproduction of it on the façade of a nineteenth-century commercial building in a northern

European city. It is a strong argument that a work of art is best viewed in the place for which it was originally created. If this is not possible or desirable, we could suggest the following principle:

A work of art is best viewed in a luminous environment similar to that for which it was created.

We shall adopt this as a working rule and examine its implications.

The first conclusion is that paintings and other objects produced before the mid-nineteenth century were most likely to have been produced, used and exhibited in natural light; and probably this would not have been the controlled daylight of the Victorian art gallery but the inconstant unpredictable light of the church or the walls of the patron's villa, or the civic building.

The second conclusion is that this lighting might not be very good by modern standards of task and display design. The type of place where a painting was first shown was often something quite different from an exhibition of pictures, and a painting that we now consider to be of major importance might have been just one of many items. Furthermore, we have sources and luminaires that were not available when the painting was made. We can focus light onto a picture, enhancing the initial impression of a piece and making the detail of the painting far easier to see. This in turn has affected our expectations of how works of art should be displayed.

There is, however, a factor that can override all considerations of display: this is the need for conservation. Light, as radiant energy, causes organic materials to deteriorate. Those affected include leather, fabrics and paper; they also include some of the pigments used in paint. Pigments change differentially: some fade rapidly, while others, particularly mineral colours, are unaffected. The result is that the balance of colour in a painting changes gradually and irreversibly with exposure to light. Especially sensitive are works such as old watercolour paintings and Japanese woodblock prints.

Most national art galleries and many conservation organisations have a legal duty to preserve their collections for the next generation. They also have a duty to make the works available for the present generation to enjoy and to study. The curator thus has to reconcile four conflicting aims in the display of a work of art:

1   To illuminate the work and its surroundings in a historically accurate way; that is, in a way that would match the expectations of the artist.
2   To display it so that the impact of the work is maximised.
3   To display it so that the detail of the work is most clearly visible.
4   To cause no damage or change to the work.

The solution depends on the nature of the object, its value and importance, its robustness to damage, the purpose of the exhibition, and for whom the display is presented. We can begin the process of finding this solution by asking three broad questions:

1   What constraints are imposed by requirements of conservation: what is the maximum acceptable illuminance on the object and the period for which it is to be displayed?
2   What is the purpose of the exhibition: for example, are the objects displayed for sale, or is it a theatrical display, a

reconstruction of a historical scene, or a scholarly presentation? And who are the viewers: children, tourists, the general public, academic students?
3   What is the ideal form of lighting for display: for example, direct sunlight for stone sculpture, or natural room lighting for pictures, or small-scale individual lamps for miniature objects?

The answers to these questions should point towards the degree to which daylight is used in the display space. Table 1.1 summarises the possibilities.

A conclusion that can be drawn from the table is that daylighting should not be considered separately from the layout and form of the building as a whole, or from the design of electric lighting. Here is an example. People entering an exhibition have to make a transition between daylight outside and much lower levels of light in display spaces. On a bright day, the ratio of the mean external illuminance to the mean illuminance in a gallery displaying light-sensitive materials can be 2000:1. Significant brightness adaptation is needed; therefore the route of visitors should be gradual through a sequence of spaces of decreasing brightness. The extent to

Table 1.1: Daylight in galleries and exhibition spaces

	Advantages for display	Disadvantages
Windowless interior.	Permits the creation of a complete environment, and use of the full range of display and theatrical techniques.	In most cases, unrealistic in relation to the original environment of art works. Disadvantages of windowless rooms generally.
Windows providing general room lighting and views out; supplementary lighting on pictures.	Appearance of a daylit room. May simulate the original ambience of an art work.	Depends on the basic plan form and orientation of the building. Difficult to achieve very low illuminances on light-sensitive materials.
Side windows providing illumination on art works.	May simulate the original ambience. Good colour rendering. Good modelling of three-dimensional form.	Difficult to avoid glare and bright reflections in art works. Difficult to control illuminance.
Specially designed roof lights illuminating art works.	Basic form of nineteenth- and twentieth-century picture galleries. Was the setting for which many works were produced. Good colour rendering. Direction of light reduces shiny reflections. Daylight can be controlled with louvres and blinds. Can be supplemented with electric lighting.	Institutional appearance may not be appropriate. General appearance of room can be dull. Incoming daylight can be controlled to the extent that all the natural variation is lost.
Semi-outdoor space, highly glazed.	Can be used to simulate the external environment of art works. Direct sunlight available.	Thermal attributes of highly glazed spaces. Unsuitable for light-sensitive materials.

which this is possible depends on the basic form of the building; and it is a constraint on the layout of any exhibition in the building and on the electric lighting.

The prime reason for the use of daylight in buildings such as art galleries is the quality that we have argued is important in all buildings: its variation and the meaning it has to the viewer. Moreover, natural lighting provides a powerful means of connecting our present experience of a work with that of its artist.

Objects and background

Good display lighting design begins with the objects to be displayed. Like the design of task lighting, there are questions to be posed:

1 What is to be enhanced? For instance, is it silhouette? Colour? Texture? Surface pattern? 3D form?
2 Who is looking at it, and from where? What is the background? Does the object have to grab attention in a complex visual environment? Is the object or the viewer in motion? What are the relative locations of viewer, object and light sources?
3 What is the balance between the need to attract attention to an exhibit and the need to see it in detail?

The answer to the third of these questions depends on the purpose of the display. It differs between a shop window and a museum. In art gallery design, it is necessary to compromise between the differing visual requirements of display and assimilation. For example, pictures displayed on a white, evenly lit wall attract immediate attention, especially if they widely spaced. There is an economical approach to the renovation of an old building as a gallery: paint the walls, ceiling and beams – all the upper surfaces – white; strip the floor surface to its original wood or stone; provide plenty of daylight and many small spotlights; and let pictures alone provide strong colour. It is a strategy used by many small shops and restaurants. It is found in the traditional streets of the Greek islands, as in Figure 1.19.

But when a picture is seen against a bright white background, the apparent range of colours in the picture itself is contracted. This is especially noticeable in greyscale images. The photographer Ansel Adams, known for his technical skill

1.19

White surrounding surfaces make coloured patches prominent and enhance the silhouette of superimposed objects. There is much interreflected light, increasing the sense of brightness, a characteristic of traditional Greek villages.

Rhodes, Greece

in creating prints with a consistent tonal scale over the whole black–white range, preferred to display his work on a background with a reflectance of 0.18, a mid-grey close to the average reflectance of the images.

It is a decision that the exhibition designer or the gallery curator must make: setting pictures on a strongly contrasting background emphasises their outline shape and enhances their visibility as objects in the room, but at the cost of a smaller tonal range or reduced apparent contrast within the pictures themselves. With a background consistent with the tonal range of the pictures, the opposite is true. What choice

is made depends on the nature of the display: in a shop, the need is for the objects to catch the glance of a potential buyer; in a national museum, the aim is to display the true quality of the work.

Conclusions for design

The designer's approach can be summarised by the checklist in Table 1.2.

Table 1.2: Checklist for the beginning of display design

1	What is the purpose of the display? To sell? To entertain? To educate? To shock?
2	What is the overall character of the display? Cool and understated? A complete enclosing environment? Noisy and multicoloured? Set within an existing architecture?
3	Take the objects on display. Decide what characteristics should be enhanced, what limitations there are on lighting (maximum illuminance, security, etc.). Decide what background they should be seen against.
4	Consider the people viewing the display. How will they look at the objects? How far away? For how long? Are they static or moving? Are they families? Children? . . .

1.20

The lightness of the surround affects the degree to which an image stands out and it also affects the apparent contrast within the image.

two

What light does

This chapter introduces the physics of lighting. It can be read as a whole, you can dip into it to read about topics that are unfamiliar, or you can skip it altogether and use it as a reference later. It is structured in a way that allows you to look up a particular point, and go into the detail only as far as you need. If you read the first part of each section, you should gain a working knowledge of the main ideas and the words used to describe them; if you work through the chapter as a whole, you will cover much of the theoretical basis of illumination engineering.

A few simple principles underlie the subtle and complex patterns of brightness and colour within the translucent foliage of a plant – or in a cloudy sky or a daylit room. If you know the rules, you can explain why a particular lighting effect occurs or predict the appearance of a finished scheme when the design is no more than a sketch. You can also look at a rendered computer image and tell whether or not it is realistic.

2.1
The complex variation of luminance and colour in the foliage can be explained by simple processes of reflection and transmission of light.

2.2
We sense the radiation emitted by a candle in two ways: as warmth and as light. Originally, a candle was used as a reference for quantifying light. In present-day units, the flow of light from a candle is about 13 lumens.

Luminous energy

The principles described in this chapter apply to a physical world measured in millimetres, metres or kilometres – several orders of magnitude greater than the wavelength of light, the scale of people, buildings and towns. It is necessary to state this because the rules that predict the behaviour of light depend on the scale at which it is observed. We are fortunate: at the dimensions of the human world, light can be treated as just a flow of energy, a simplification not possible at the scale of quantum mechanics or at the scale of cosmology.

What we describe as light has no fundamental physical meaning, but is defined by human vision: it is simply radiation to which the eye is sensitive. Radio waves are electromagnetic radiation; so are ultraviolet light, x-rays and gamma radiation. They vary only in their wavelength, (which is usually measured in nanometres: 1 nm $=10^{-9}$ or 1/1,000,000,000 of a metre). We have various names for parts of the electromagnetic spectrum: the part we call 'light' is the band of wavelengths that are strongest in the solar radiation that reaches the earth. We have evolved in the rays of the sun and our bodies have grown to use solar radiation in the most efficient way.

There is an inherent problem in defining light in terms of the human eye: none of the normal physical units of energy can be used to quantify it. Light has, therefore, its own set of units. They are not used in other contexts and are not everyday measures – like kilograms, watts or metres – so we do not have a familiar sense of their meanings or their magnitudes. They need to be learnt. In all, there are four units of light and they will be introduced during the course of the chapter when they are needed. They are summarised in Worksheet 13.

The first lighting unit is the lumen (lm), which describes the rate at which luminous energy is flowing out of a lamp or through a window. Its physical equivalent is the watt (W), which can quantify the rate at which electrical energy is consumed: an incandescent lamp might use 100 W and emit about 1200 lm. A candle emits about 13 lm; a window in sunlight might admit 65,000 lm per square metre of glazing, but this depends on the height of the sun and the angle at which it strikes the window.

The ratio of the light output from a source to the total radiation emitted is known as luminous efficacy, measured in lumens per watt (lm/W). The luminous efficacy of an incandescent lamp is low, only about 13 lm/W, because most of the electric energy consumed by the lamp is emitted as heat; fluorescent lamps have a higher efficacy, typically about 80 lm/W.

Light is measured by photometers, instruments that respond to radiation in the same way as the human eye: at daytime levels of ambient light, the eye is insensitive to wavelengths shorter than about 380 nm, has a maximum response around 555 nm, then gradually reduces in sensitivity as wavelengths increase to 780 nm, above which it is again insensitive.

If, mathematically, a lamp output in watts needs to be converted to its light output in lumens, the spectrum is divided into narrow bands, the energy in each is multiplied by the eye sensitivity there, and the results are added up.

Light in the atmosphere

A projector beam can be seen in a smoky cinema but not when the air is clear: where there is pollution, particles suspended in the air divert a fraction of the beam and some stray light reaches the eye.

It is not just pollution that causes scattering. The sky is luminous because the solar beam is scattered by the molecules of gases as well as by small particles in the atmosphere. These atmospheric components vary with weather, time and place, so the sky changes in brightness and colour. The sunbeams in Figure 2.3 appear because water droplets in the air divert some of the sunlight that flows between gaps in the cloud layer.

The sky is the atmosphere made visible. It is not something above us, separate from us: we are within it, moving through it, changing it, breathing it. 'Sky' lies between us and everything we see. The distant peaks in Figure 2.4 are lighter and bluer than the nearer rocks because light reflected from their surfaces is scattered while other light passing through the intervening volume of atmosphere is diverted towards us.

2.3

Beams of sunlight made visible by dust in the atmosphere.
Desert, Iran

2.4

The blueness of distant mountains is the result of light scattering along the line of sight.

Hua Shan, Shaanxi province, China

2.5

The characteristic brightness pattern of a clear sky is caused by molecular scattering in the upper atmosphere.

The greater the density of particles or droplets in the air, the more the light is dispersed. In a very foggy atmosphere, a bright halo surrounds every source of light. This scattering attenuates the beam, making it weaker with distance. The density of particles also affects what we can see: in a thick fog, we can see only a few metres ahead because nearby droplets hide everything further away.

The combination of diffusion of light and reduction of the distance of vision is the cause of the characteristic patterns of sky brightness that occur with particular weather conditions. The cloudless blue sky is the result of light scattered out of the solar beam by the molecules of the atmospheric gases. If the sun is directly overhead in a clear sky, we see the

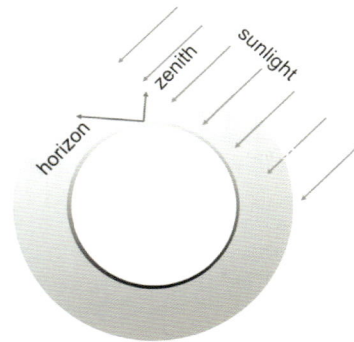

intense brightness of the solar disc surrounded by a flare that declines into deep blueness as the angle of vision from the sun increases: most of the scattered light is diverted out of the beam by only a few degrees. But the brightness of a clear sky increases again just above the horizon, because, although only a small fraction of the light is scattered to the viewer at this angle, there is a very long view through the atmosphere.

Molecular scattering varies greatly with wavelength; the blue end of the spectrum is affected more than the yellow–red. This creates the blueness of the upper sky; the deeper the colour, the clearer the atmosphere. The term 'turbidity' describes the scattering due to processes other than molecular – for example the effect of water droplets or solid airborne pollutants. These particles are larger than gas molecules, usually larger than the wavelength of light, and they re-mix the spectral colours. During the day, a cloudless sky of high turbidity looks much whiter than an unpolluted dry atmosphere.

2.6
A heavily overcast sky often has several layers of broken cloud. The sky tends to be brighter at the zenith than at lower angles of view, though there is often, as in the photograph, a skirt of brightness just above the horizon. *New South Wales, Australia*

A heavily overcast sky usually contains several layers of cloud, each reflecting and diffusing the downward light, and each darker within than the layer above. A directly upward view from the ground tends to penetrate to brighter clouds

than an oblique sightline; so, seen from a point on the ground, there is an increasing brightness from horizon to zenith. This brightness distribution that occurs on dull rainy days, the weather conditions when daylight tends to be at its minimum, has long been used as a reference sky for daylight calculations in a standardised form. There is more on this in Chapter 3.

The longer the atmospheric path of the sun's beam, the more the attenuation and the broader the directional separation of colour. A beam along a path almost parallel with the surface of the earth is seen as the setting sun. The rays have a long path through the atmosphere, so there is much scattering. Orange–red can dominate the view towards the sun, as in Figure 2.7; the sky in the opposite direction would be deep blue.

In most cases, there is little absorption of light in the atmosphere, only reflection and scattering, so most of the solar energy is preserved. However, in a highly polluted atmosphere, such as in Figure 2.8, particles and droplets suspended in the air absorb light, reducing the brightness of the scene, especially of distant objects.

Light on a surface and Lambert's law

Illuminance

In Figure 2.9, beams of sunlight make bright patches on the wall. To quantify this, we would take the amount of light (luminous flux, measured in lumens) and divide it by the area on which it falls (measured in square metres). The result is called illuminance, measured in lux (lx):

$$1 \text{ lux} = 1 \text{ lumen per square metre}$$

This is the second of the four units of light and is the one most frequently used to specify lighting requirements.

The beam of sunlight in Figure 2.9 falls at a glancing angle on the wall. If the wall could be turned to make a right angle with the beam, the sunlit patch would be smaller but brighter. The angle between a beam of light onto a surface and a line perpendicular to the surface is called the angle of incidence. When the surface directly faces the source of light, the angle

2.7
When the sun is low in the sky, its brightness is attenuated by a long path through the atmosphere. Light at the longer wavelengths, the part of the spectrum towards red, is scattered less than the shorter-wavelength blue.
Cornwall, UK

2.8
In a highly polluted atmosphere, solid particles and oil droplets absorb light and reduce contrast.
Xian, China

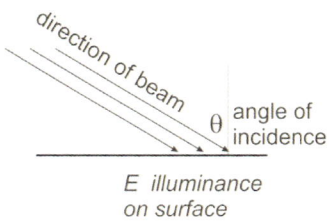

2.9
Illuminance from a beam of sunlight.
The Green Palace, Iran

of incidence is zero and the illuminance is highest. When the beam falls obliquely, the patch of light becomes larger, and so the illuminance, the amount of light falling on a given area of surface, is smaller. This effect is called Lambert's law, after the eighteenth-century mathematician Johann Heinrich Lambert, and it is written formally as follows:

Illuminance is proportional to the cosine of the angle between the direction of the incident light and a line at 90° to the surface.

It can be expressed much more concisely in symbols:

$$E \propto \cos\theta \qquad\qquad (2.1)$$

Large sources, small sources and ideal sources

We know from everyday experience that different types of light source produce characteristic patterns of light. We can recognise not only the presence of a window or luminaire that is hidden from view, but also its location, and its size and type. In Figure 2.10, for example, we know at once that the bright patches on the walls and ceiling are not caused by light from the windows, so we deduce that those protruding brackets are wall-mounted luminaires, shining upwards. Looking at Figure 2.11, we guess that there must be

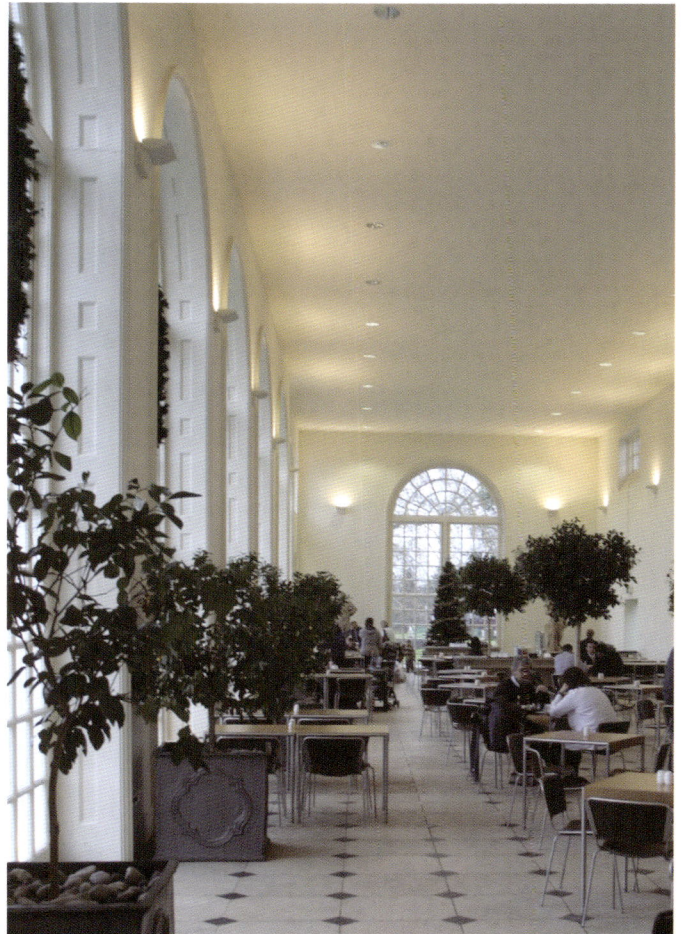

2.10
Large and small sources: daylight plus recessed spotlights in the ceiling and wall-mounted uplighters.
The Orangery, Kew Gardens, London

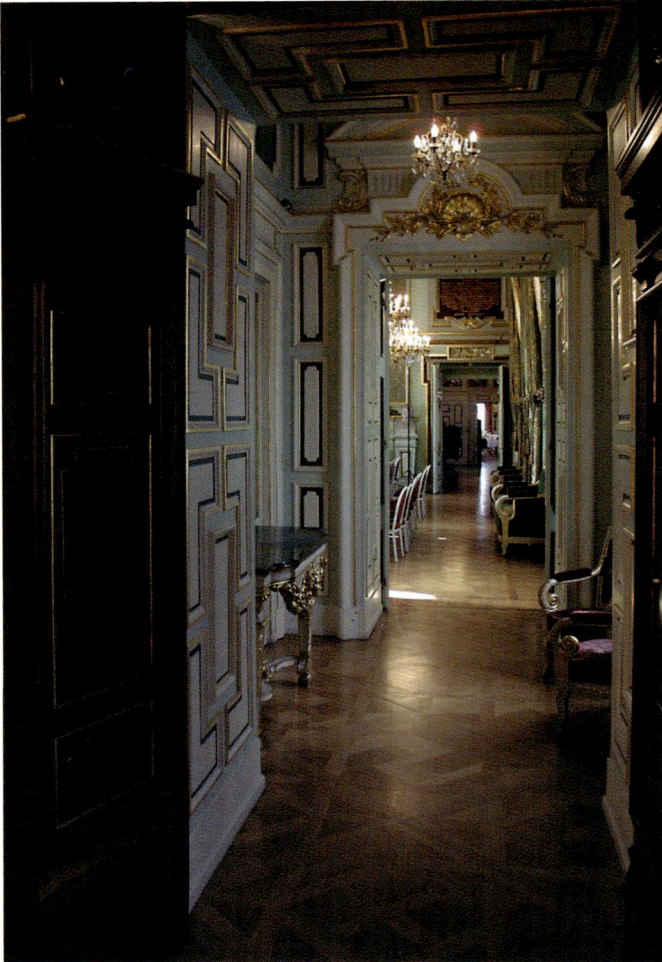

2.11

Some of the sources of light are hidden from the camera. Can you deduce where they are from the patterns of brightness on the room surfaces?

L' Hôtel de Ville, Lyon

windows just out of sight in the wall on the right because we know that the even illumination on the left-hand wall could not be produced by the small candle-like lamps in the chandeliers.

In architectural lighting, the size of a light source is crucial. A small lamp and one that is larger in area but less bright can produce the same illuminance at some chosen point, but, photometrically and visually, they differ. The small source looks very bright because all the light is emitted within a tiny area; this gives crisp shadows, but the illumination decreases rapidly with distance. A large source of light producing the same number of lumens looks far less bright; it casts soft-edged shadows, and the distance between source and receiver has less effect.

Much of the theory of lighting is based on hypothetical extremes. It asks what would happen if something were taken to the limit – if the source were infinitely small, infinitely large or infinitely far away. We begin by looking at what happens when a light source is very small.

Point sources, intensity and the inverse square law

Nothing real can be infinitely bright and of infinitesimal size, but many actual sources can, with negligible error, be treated as dimensionless. And if a source is point-like, the beautifully simple inverse square law applies. In symbols,

$$E \propto \frac{1}{r^2} \qquad (2.2)$$

In words,

Illuminance is inversely proportional to the square of the distance from source to surface.

If a spreading beam of light gives a patch of light 1 metre square on a wall, it produces a patch 2 metres square on a wall twice as far away. The patch area increases from 1 m² to 4 m², so the illuminance (flux divided by area) is reduced to one-quarter of the original value.

The inverse square law lies at the heart of lighting calculations. Here is an example:

- A projector 3 m away gives 100 lx on a screen. What is the effect of moving it back to 4 m away?
- The area illuminated increases by a factor of (4/3)2, so the illuminance on the screen falls to 100 ×(3/4)2, about 56 lx.

Luminous intensity

To fully describe the output from the projector, another unit of light is needed: the total in lumens would not be enough.

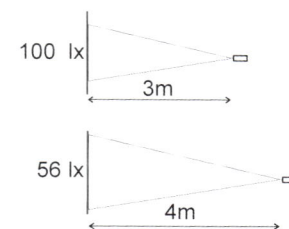

2.12

Light from a projector.

To specify the performance of lighting equipment, especially items such as projectors and spotlights, it is necessary to state how much light goes in a particular direction. This is the purpose of the third of the four units of light, the candela (cd).

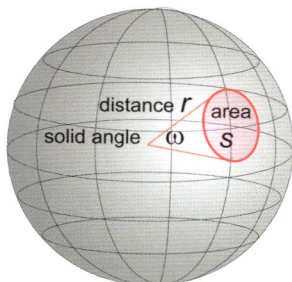

2.13

Solid angle.

Luminous intensity can be understood as follows. Picture a tiny lamp hanging at the centre of a transparent sphere one metre in radius. Imagine a circle drawn on the sphere. The intensity of the lamp in the direction of the circle is the number of lumens divided by the area of the circle. If the circle is linked back to the centre, it makes a cone. This cone could be made narrower, to be more precise about direction, but then it would be necessary to take into account the width of the cone. The normal way of doing this is to give the ratio of the surface area to the radius squared. This is called a solid angle, an angle in three-dimensional space, and is measured in steradians (sr). In symbols,

$$\omega = \frac{s}{r^2} \tag{2.3}$$

where ω is the angle in steradians, r is the radius of the sphere, and s the area of the surface patch (which can be any shape – it does not have to be circular).

So luminous intensity is defined as

$$I = \frac{F}{\omega} \tag{2.4}$$

The total angle surrounding a point in space, like the lamp in the centre of the sphere, is 4π steradians, so if a lamp emitting F lumens has an output that is the same in all directions, its intensity is $F/4\pi$ candelas.

The reason for the slightly difficult definition of intensity is that there is a simple outcome: the concepts of illuminance, intensity, Lambert's law and the inverse square law are interlinked. Together, they give the most important equation in lighting:

$$E = \frac{I\cos\theta}{r^2} \tag{2.5}$$

I is the intensity of the source in the direction of the surface, θ the angle of incidence on the surface and r the distance between source and surface.

The formula can be used with negligible error when the maximum dimension (for instance the diagonal size of a rectilinear luminaire) is less than one-fifth of the distance, $r/5$.

An infinite plane of light and the concept of luminance

Imagine a grey cloudy sky spreading uniformly bright towards the horizon in every direction. The illuminance on the ground might, if you measured it, seem higher than expected: everything looks dull in these conditions. If you walk to the top of a high hill, halfway toward the cloud base, the meter

2.14

A uniform sky. This photograph has been modified to remove sky luminance variation but it remains a realistic image.

reading may change little – getting closer to the source does not seem to affect the amount of light.

The key characteristic of a large source is its luminance. This value is the last of the four units of light. Luminance means objective brightness – what a meter reads – rather than the brightness perceived by the eye, which is affected by adaptation and by contrast in the visual field, and is referred to as apparent brightness.

The definition of luminance is again linked with the idea of an infinitesimal source. Imagine a bright surface, such as a translucent screen with a lamp behind it. Draw a circle on the surface and imagine another floating in the air just above the surface. The area within the surface patch is s square metres.

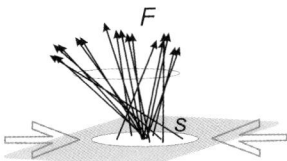

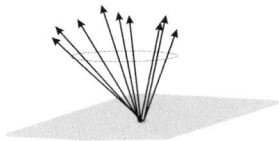

2.15
Defining luminance

Assume that F lumens emitted from the surface patch flow through the floating circle.

Now imagine the surface patch shrinking until it is almost a dimensionless point. The ratio F/s remains nearly the same, because both numbers are reduced, and the shape of the beam approaches a cone. So, if we take the value to which F/s is converging and then divide this by the angle of the cone, the result is a new concept: intensity divided by area. This is the meaning of luminance, and hence it is measured in candelas per square metre (cd/m²). Writing mathematically the limiting process we have just described, luminance is defined as

$$L = \lim \frac{I}{s}, s \to 0 \qquad (2.6)$$

There is a problem, though: how do you measure the area of the sky? The definition of luminance using a surface source makes no sense when the source is volumetric and infinite.

To deal quantitatively with sky brightness, we need to look at the situation the other way round.

Imagine a surface facing a bright screen and parallel to it. Draw a circle on the screen, as before, and one exactly opposite on the receiving surface. The area of each circle is s and the angle each circle makes from the centre of the opposite circle is ω. Now if ω is quite small, the circle on the screen can be treated as a point source, and the illuminance in the receiving circle by light received from the source circle is

$$E = \frac{I}{r^2} \qquad (2.7)$$

By the inverse square law, Equation (2.5) I is the source intensity and r the distance between the surfaces. (The angle of incidence, θ, is zero because the beam is perpendicular to the surface, so cos θ = 1 and we can ignore it.)

The intensity of the source is, by definition,

$$I = Ls$$

the luminance of the source in the direction of view multiplied by its area, but since

$$\omega = \frac{s}{r^2}$$

we can write

$$E = \frac{Ls}{r^2} = L\omega \qquad (2.8)$$

$$\text{so,} \quad L = \frac{E}{\omega}$$

The luminance of a patch of sky is the illuminance on a surface directly facing the patch divided by the angular size of the patch. The argument becomes rigorous if, as before, we define the equation as the limit when s approaches zero. What it means is that luminance does have a physical meaning when a source is not a surface.

Luminance meters work on this principle. In essence, they consist of a photocell, which gives an electrical signal when light falls on its surface; an electrical meter; and lenses or baffles that accept light from only a small angle of view.

The argument leading to Equation (2.8) is easy because the definitions of the four units of lighting – luminous flux (lumen), illuminance (lux), luminous intensity (candela) and luminance (candela per square metre) – ensure that they tie together in a clever way. In practice, we need to calculate the light flowing from one surface to another and the reflection from the second surface to a third, and so on. To do this, one more equation is needed.

If a surface scatters the light evenly, it is a perfect or 'Lambertian' diffuser. Its appearance is the same whatever the direction of the beam falling on it. Real surfaces are not perfect diffusers, but many of the materials of buildings can, with minor error, be treated as such. This assumption is made in much of the current software for lighting calculations.

If E is the illuminance on a Lambertian surface, its luminance is

$$L = \frac{E\rho}{\pi} \tag{2.9}$$

The symbol ρ stands for the reflectance of the surface, the proportion of the light landing on it that is reflected back: if $\rho = 0$, the surface is perfectly black; if $\rho = 1$, it is a perfect white.

The sky can be visualised as a diffuse plane stretching to infinity in every direction of view, or as a hemispherical dome over some point on the ground, or as a luminous gas surrounding us: these are equivalent in a definition of luminance. If the sky is taken to be equally bright in every direction, a useful first approximation, then there is a very simple rule linking sky luminance with illuminance on the ground:

$$E = \frac{L}{\pi} \tag{2.10}$$

The sky illumination on a vertical surface is exactly half that on the horizontal surface because it 'sees' only half a hemisphere of sky.

Finally, we can use Equations (2.9) and (2.10) to find the light reflected on the façade of a building. Assume that the ground surface is diffusing (which is a good approximation unless it is wet) and that the façade looks towards open ground. Then, if the illuminance on the ground is E_h and

the ground reflectance is ρ_g, the illuminance on a vertical surface is

$$E_v = \frac{E_h\,\rho_g}{2} \tag{2.11}$$

The illuminance on the façade from both direct skylight and the light reflected from the ground, under a uniform sky of luminance L_s, would be

$$
\begin{aligned}
E_v\text{(sky \& ground)} &= \frac{L_s}{2\pi} + \frac{L_s}{\pi}\frac{\rho_g}{2} \\
&= \frac{L_s(1+\rho_g)}{2\pi}
\end{aligned}
\tag{2.12}
$$

Parallel beams

The third of the ideal sources of light is one that gives a beam that does not diverge or converge – in technical language, a 'collimated beam'. As a source of finite area moves away towards infinity, its apparent size decreases and its beam appears more nearly parallel. The ultimate model is a bundle of straight parallel rays such as if there were a point source at the focus of a parabolic mirror. Because the beam does not diverge, there is no change of illuminance with distance; shadows cast from the beam are crisp and non-diverging.

For most lighting purposes, we can treat the sun as a source of parallel beams. It is only a small part of the sky, only one-half of a degree across in angular size, and this suggests that it should be treated as a point source. But its beam does not appear to diverge and solar illuminance seems to be unrelated to distance. The reason is, of course, that the sun is huge but a very long distance away. Distances of a few kilometres between places on the earth's surface are negligible in comparison with the distance between earth and sun.

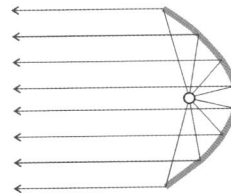

2.16
Parabolic mirror.

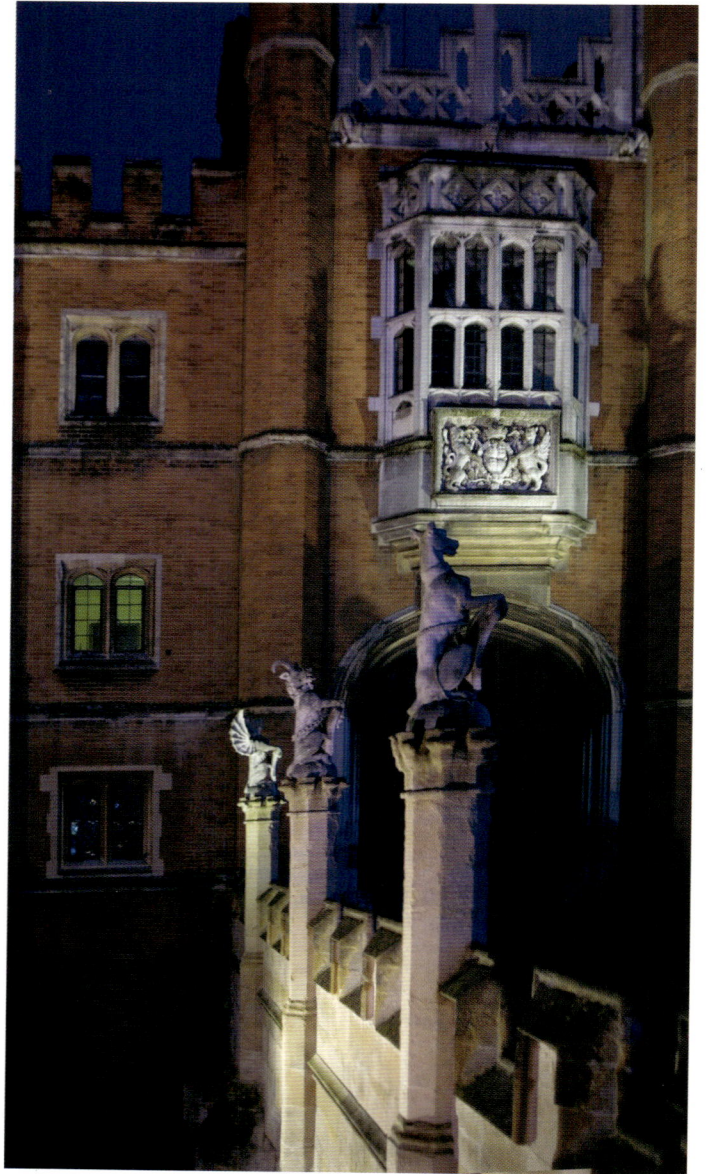

2.17

Left: Hampton Court Palace, on a winter afternoon. The diffuse light reduces contrast and three-dimensional appearance.
Right: Later on the same day. The directionality of the floodlighting selectively illuminates key areas; crisp shadows enhance form.
London UK

Using the ideal sources

These three 'ideal' sources of light – the point, the infinite plane and the parallel beam – can be a great help when trying to visualise a scheme at the design stage. The important results are summarised in Table 2.1.

Table 2.1: Ideal sources

Ideal source	Approximation to	Relationship between illuminance and distance	Shadow
Point	A small lamp	Illuminance decreases with square of distance	Hard-edged, diverging
Infinite plane	The diffuse sky; the ground	Constant	Indistinct edge
Parallel beam	The sun	Constant	Hard-edged, non-diverging

For urban spaces and the exterior of buildings, the visual difference between day and night can be represented as a change from illumination by an infinite plane source, the sky, plus sometimes a parallel beam, the sun, to illumination from many point-like sources. The difference is emphasised by differing directionality: the direct light from sky and sun is a downward flow, unaffected by distance; the light cast on buildings at night is primarily upwards and critically dependent on the distance between source and surface.

Figure 2.17 shows Hampton Court Palace in London on a winter afternoon and later, at dusk, with floodlighting. No sun falls on the façade that afternoon, and, under uniform illumination from the pale sky, the three-dimensional form is flattened and the overall appearance subdued. The floodlighting, by contrast, selectively enhances key areas;

pillars emphasise the three-dimensional shape of the elements. The place gets a theatrical character.

Look again at Figures 2.10 and 2.11 earlier in this chapter: they show the essential difference between large and small sources in the lighting of rooms. Daylight is illumination from a very large source, the sky, which is partially masked by the enclosing building. (Note that, photometrically and visually, this is not the same as a finite-area source, a diffusing screen perhaps, set in place of the window.) Skylight gives a gradually changing soft-edged brightness to room surfaces. If the sun shines into a room, there are hard-edged patches of very high but uniform illuminance. By comparison, small bright luminaires give points of high brightness; where their light falls on nearby surfaces, there is a pronounced brightness gradient; shadows are hard-edged.

2.18
Wrought-iron gateway.
Hampton Court Palace, London

Surfaces and the nature of reflection

There are two surface finishes on the gorgeous gates in Figure 2.18: an almost matt blue paint and a gold finish that is much glossier. Note how the two finishes differ in the way they reflect the late afternoon sunlight falling on them. The blue patches appear evenly lit; there are clear hard-edged shadows, and the brightness of areas in sunshine depends on the angle between the surface and the solar beam. No shadows, however, can be seen in the gold areas: the brightness and colour here depend primarily on what is reflected – the sun itself, the blue sky, the ground, other parts of the gate.

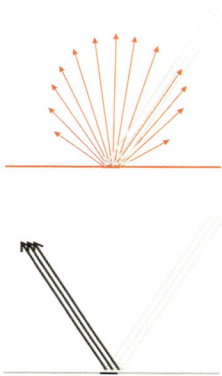

2.19
Diffuse (or Lambertian) and
specular reflection.

There are clearly two different types of reflection occurring here: the diffusing surface scatters the light; the specular (mirror-like) surface merely changes the direction of a beam, reducing its intensity by the amount that the material absorbs. Usually, this changes with the angle of incidence, the reflectance increasing as the beam becomes more nearly parallel to the surface.

If a transparent layer lies above a coloured light-scattering base, a bright glossy reflection can mask the base colour. In Figure 2.20, blue sky is reflected along the ripples where the line of sight makes a glancing angle with the water. Elsewhere on the ripples, the wave surface is almost perpendicular to the sightline, and the underlying objects are visible. In Figure 2.21, a layer of water on the leaf reflects the silhouettes of higher leaves.

Many building materials behave in this way. In Figure 2.23, the natural colour of the stone can be seen between the patches of shininess, the specular images of bright lamps. This composite behaviour of real materials explains why colours appear stronger, more saturated, in sunshine than under a cloudy sky. With a diffuse field of light falling on a surface, there is in every direction some shiny reflection; under a beam, the colour is undiluted in every direction except the line of sight towards the mirrored source.

2.20
Compound reflection. The
apparent colour of the water is
a varying combination of the
colours of the reflected sky, the
sea bed and the water itself.

A smooth finish appears increasingly glossy as the angle of incidence becomes large and the beam becomes more nearly parallel with the surface plan. With a matt surface, the opposite occurs: light falling at a glancing angle enhances the textured appearance of the material, and this effect becomes greater as the angle between light beam and view line increases. Shadows and highlights emphasise every miniature hill and valley of the surface in Figure 2.24; but these low-relief carved letters would be almost invisible under a general diffuse light or if illuminated by a beam parallel with the line of sight.

Just as with sources of light, it is useful to define 'ideal' surfaces that are extreme cases and simple to describe mathematically. Table 2.2 lists three ideal surfaces that are used extensively in lighting theory.

Table 2.2: Ideal surfaces

Ideal surface	Approximates to	Luminance and colour depend on	Effect of increasing angle of incidence of light
Specular	Polished metal; surface-silvered mirror	The luminance and colour of what is seen in reflection; this varies with direction of view	Increased reflectance
Lambertian	Blotting paper; woollen cloth; earth	The illuminance and colour of the surface; equally bright in every direction of view	Decreased illuminance; enhanced visibility of texture as angle between light beam and view angle increases
Compound: transparent layer over pigmented surface	Picture under glass; gloss paint; water	A combination of the two above, dependent on angle of view	Increased shininess, dilution of pigment colour

2.21

Compound reflection. The shapes of other leaves are reflected in the layer of water.

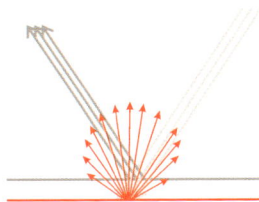

2.22

Compound reflection.

2.23

Glossy surfaces in buildings reflect in a similar way to shallow water. Note here how a step down is potentially hazardous because it is almost unnoticeable.

2.24

The texture of this incised granite slab is emphasised by the glancing angle of the incident light.

2.25

The Parthenon, Athens, in 1964.

An infinity of reflections

Forty years ago, before mass tourism and conservation became obviously incompatible, visitors could walk around the peristyle of the Parthenon. Now it is a forbidden pleasure, and looking from a protective distance is not the same experience. Within that colonnade, sunlight falling on the bare Pentellic marble is transformed by an infinity of interreflections into a diffuse field of light, an enclosing luminosity.

There is interreflected light in every daylit room (because no real surface is perfectly black, totally absorbing), and this interreflection makes room surfaces both brighter and more uniform. In a narrow street, the brightness of the walls depends crucially on the amount of interreflection: most of the light falling on the yellow wall in Figure 2.26 and on the left-hand wall has been reflected from the surface opposite.

2.26

Street brightness increased by interreflection between light-coloured walls. *Tallinn, Estonia.*

The amount of interreflected light in any enclosure – a room or a street – depends on three factors: the amount of light entering the enclosure, the surface area of the enclosing surfaces, and their reflectances.

The integrating sphere

To show what happens, there is another ideal. It is a large hollow sphere, matt-white inside. Called an integrating sphere because it adds up all the light received on its inner surface, it can be used to represent any enclosure that is fairly regular in shape and reasonably uniform in interior reflectance.

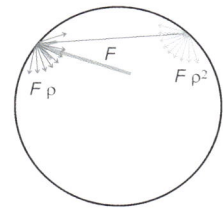

2.27

The integrating sphere.

Imagine that the sphere contains a lamp that emits F lumens. The average initial illuminance on the entire interior surface is F/s, where s m^2 is the area. Now if the surface reflectance is ρ, the flux bouncing back after the first reflection is $F\rho$ lumens. This falls again on the enclosing surface, and now $F\rho^2$ is the amount reflected back. With an infinite series of reflections, the average illuminance on the inside surface of the sphere is the total of all of these:

$$E = \frac{F}{s}(1 + \rho + \rho^2 + \rho^3 + \rho^4 + ...)$$
$$= \frac{F}{s(1-\rho)} \qquad (2.13)$$

This is variously called the integrating sphere equation and Sumpner's formula, after W E Sumpner, who described it in a 1894 paper. It is the basis of many daylight calculation methods, particularly those that predict the average illumination in a room.

When there is interreflection between surfaces, the final illuminance depends very heavily on reflectance: the graph in Figure 2.28, based on Equation (2.13), shows that the final illuminance is twice the initial illuminance if $\rho = 0.5$ and five times higher at $\rho = 0.8$. As the reflectance of an enclosure increases, the total amount of light becomes greater and its

relative
illuminance,
E

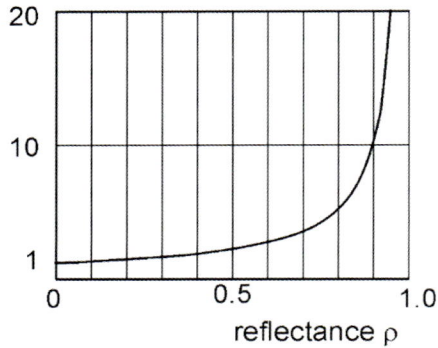

2.28

Sumpner's equation. When the reflectance of enclosing surfaces is high, the interreflected light increases surface illuminance greatly.

distribution more even. This occurs when the enclosure is only partial, such as a street or a niche in a wall.

Interreflection is the reason for the Parthenon's glowing luminance, and it can occur at any scale: in Figure 2.29, there is interreflection of a patch of sunlight in the reveal; and in Figure 2.31, the white glow inside the Merlion's mouth is interreflection of a small beam of sunlight entering between the jaws.

As a piece of laboratory equipment, the integrating sphere is used to measure the total light output (in lumens) of lamps and luminaires. The source is suspended in the centre; interreflection distributes its light uniformly over the white interior surface, and the total reflected illuminance is recorded by a photocell screened from the source to cut out the initial direct light.

When the source of light is hidden, an illuminated cavity has an unexpected brightness, as in Figure 2.29. If, however, the cavity is seen as a hole in a plane surface, it is darker than surrounding flat surface of the same colour.

2.29

A patch of sunlight, hidden from view, is revealed by diffuse reflection.

Cavity reflectance

Every time some of the light inside a cavity strikes a surface, some energy is reflected and some absorbed. Any light returning out of the cavity opening has, on average, had more than one bounce on the interior surfaces; if the cavity is deep and the opening small, the emerging light has been attenuated by many interreflections. A cavity therefore has a lower reflectance than a plane surface of the same material.

A simple equation that relates the effective reflectance of a cavity to the reflectance of a flat surface under the same lighting is given by a modification of Sumpner's formula:

$$\rho_c = \frac{k\rho}{1 - \rho(1-k)}$$

$$\text{where } k = \frac{\text{area of opening}}{\text{area of surfaces within cavity}} \qquad (2.14)$$

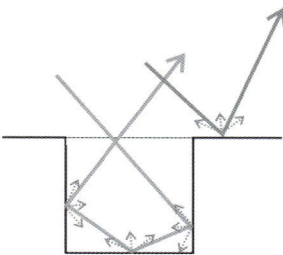

2.30

Cavity reflectance.

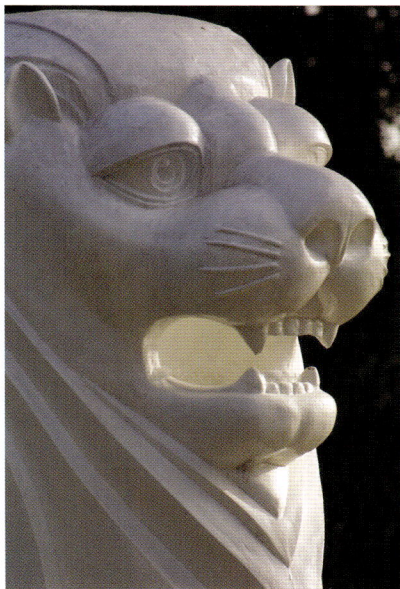

2.31

The Merlion, Singapore.

where ρ_c is the cavity reflectance and ρ the reflectance of the material on a plane surface.

The idea of cavity reflectance explains why a heavily textured material looks darker than one of the same colour with a smoother surface, and why a strongly moulded facade can have a relatively low overall reflectance.

When cavities are relatively shallow, such as the compound niches in Figure 2.32, and the incident light is strongly directional, like sunlight, reflectance varies with the angle of the beam and the direction of view. This is due to shadows within the cavities. A building façade with deep recesses may therefore vary less in appearance during the day than one with shallower moulding.

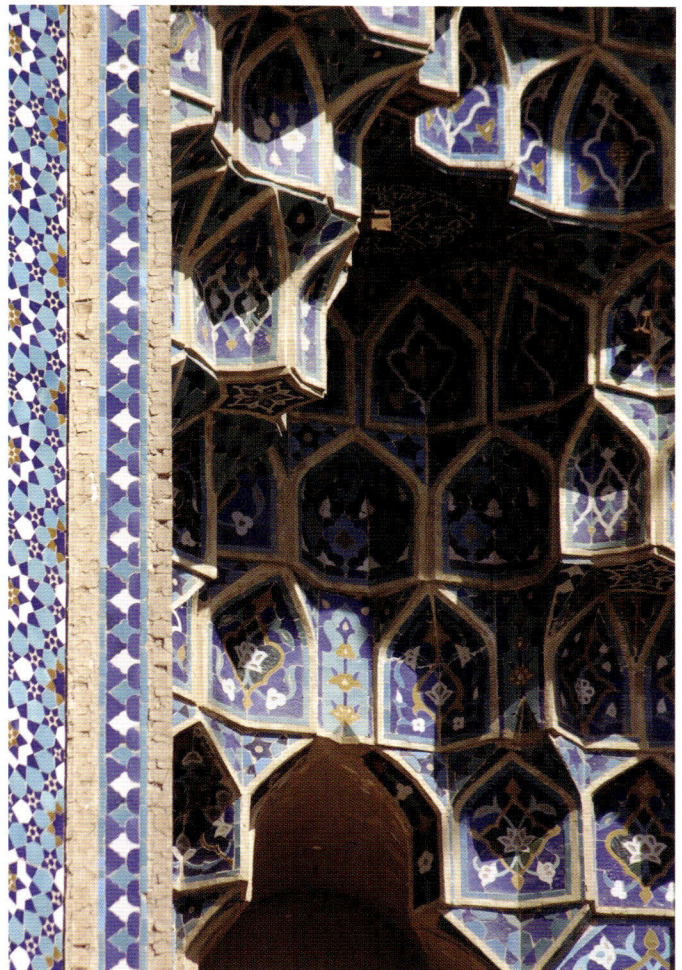

2.32

The deeper the recess, the darker it appears, but the overall pattern changes as the sun moves.

Isfahan, Iran

2.33
The Tudor kitchen.
Hampton Court Palace, London

The daylit room

Look at Figure 2.33. There are deep-set windows in thick walls, the surfaces are rough and the shape is irregular; it is not a normal kitchen. It shows very clearly, however, the characteristics of daylight from side windows. The photograph illustrates three main effects: Lambert's law, which relates illuminance to the angle at which light falls on a surface; the effect of a large source shining through small apertures; and diffuse reflection from matt surfaces.

When the photograph was taken, the sky was covered with thin cloud, so the light outside was diffuse and three-dimensional objects were illuminated evenly. But the deep window reveals of this room limit the view of the sky within the room, so the windows act as a hybrid of large area and parallel beam sources. Broad, diagonally downward, soft-edged beams illuminate nearby surfaces strongly (such as at 'a'), but wall brightness decreases noticeably with distance from a window. There are two reasons for this:

firstly, the angle of incidence changes, so Lambert's law applies; secondly, because the window is not a true parallel source, the beam of light diverges and therefore illuminance decreases with distance (though not as strongly as the inverse-square relationship of a point source).

Vertical surfaces facing a window (as on the reveal of an opening at 'b' and the opposite wall at 'c') receive more illumination than surfaces perpendicular to the window plane at the same distance, such as the cross-wall itself. Note that the beam from the left-hand window has a more defined edge than the beam from the right-hand window; the sky was brighter here, with the sun just visible through the cloud.

There is interreflection within the room. The magnitude of this can be estimated from wall areas that do not receive direct skylight. It is not insignificant because of the white-painted walls, but it would be much greater if the floor and other major surfaces were light-coloured.

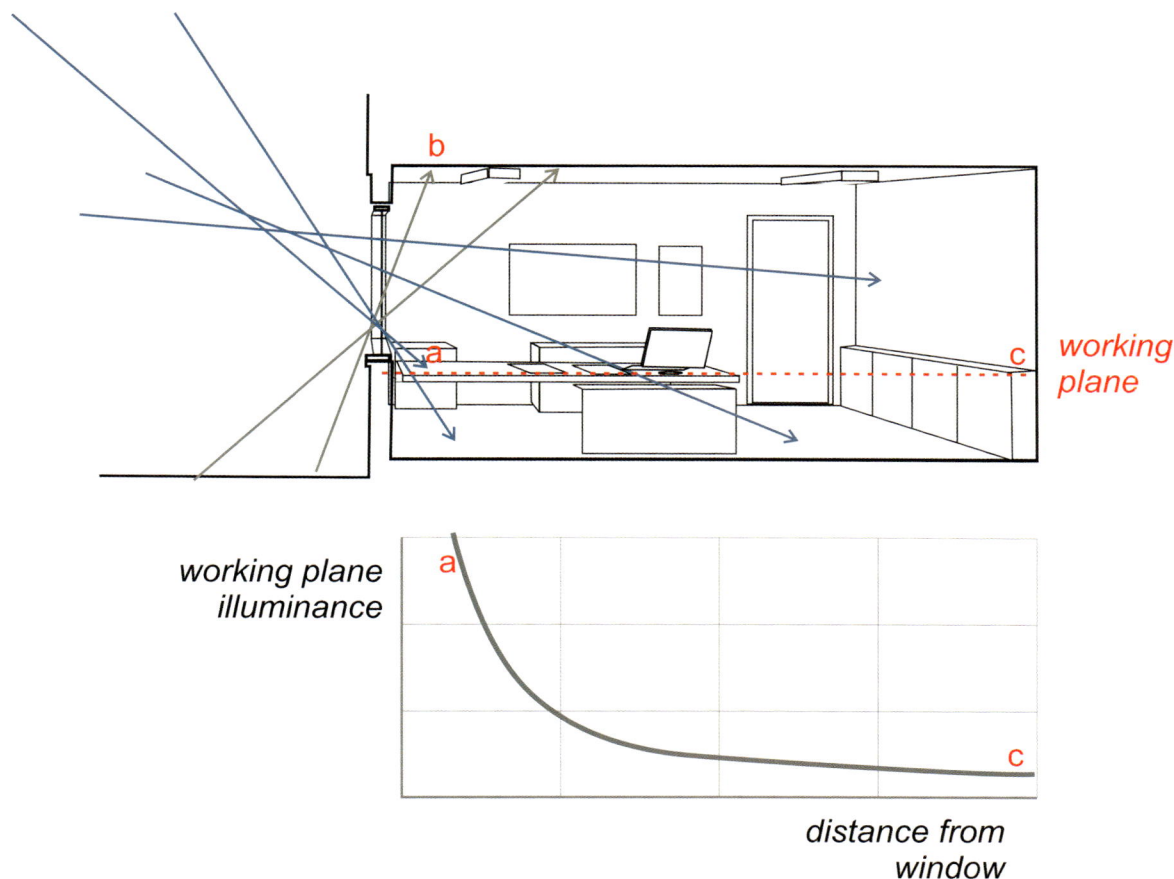

2.34

Distribution of working plane illuminance from a side window.

Figure 2.34 illustrates a small office in a temperate cloudy climate. With thinner window walls, the flow of light is not at all beam-like: in this example, incoming light diverges over a very wide angle. It includes light direct from the sky and reflected light from the ground and other external surfaces. The reduction in illuminance with distance from a window still occurs, though, and is especially noticeable on surfaces perpendicular to the window plane. Again, Lambert's law is the main principle involved.

The term 'working plane' usually refers to a horizontal plane across the room at desktop level, although it may describe any plane surface in which the task is situated. The graph shows how horizontal working plane illuminance decreases sharply with increasing distance from the window wall. Close to the window, a broad patch of sky can be seen from the working plane; further back, not only is the angular size of the visible sky patch much less but the light falls at only a glancing angle. The light falling on a vertical surface facing the window decreases more gradually, so at 'c' the desk illuminance can be far less than that on the adjacent wall.

Point 'a' sees a large patch of sky, and the illuminance there is broadly proportional to the average luminance of this sky patch. Far less of the sky is visible from point 'c', so not only is the illuminance there smaller but it fluctuates more in changing sky conditions. The initial illuminance at 'c', above the window, is due to light reflected from the ground, and so depends on ground reflectance and illuminance.

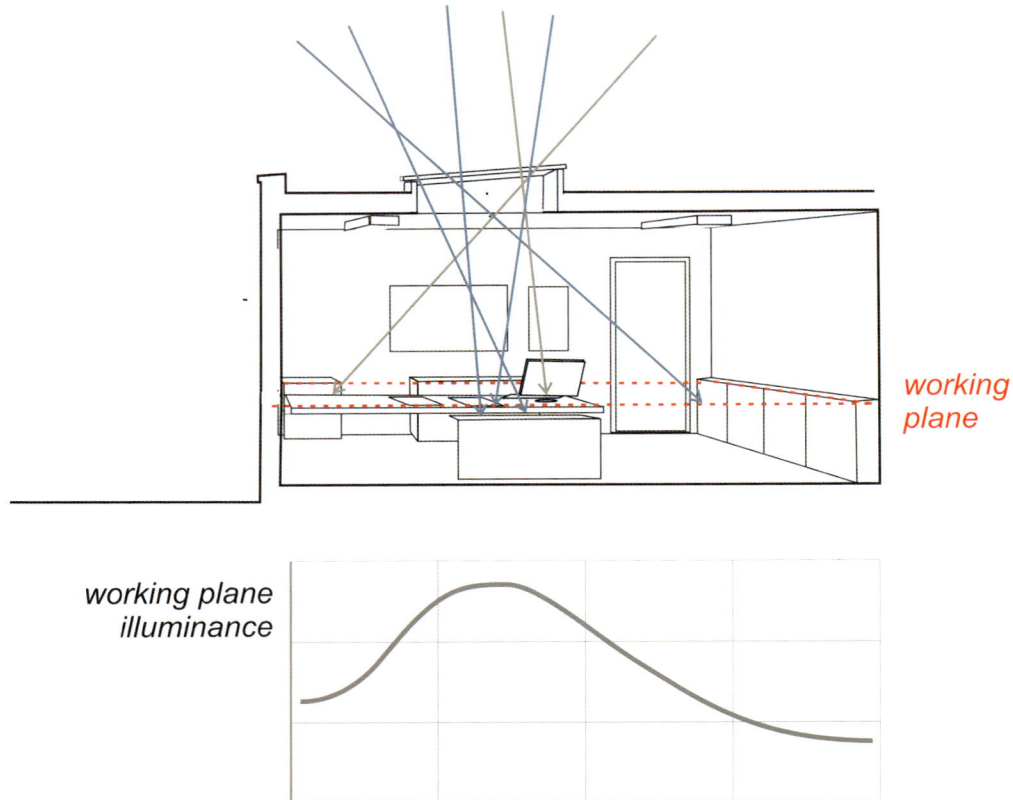

2.35

Distribution of working plane illuminance under a rooflight.

Daylight factors

The quantity of daylight in a room depends on the brightness outside. However, the appearance of a daylit room can remain broadly unchanged over a wide range of external illuminance, especially if the sky is changing slowly. This is because our eyes adapt to the ambient brightness and because we compare the interior lighting with the view to the outside.

The daylight factor is the ratio of daylight illuminance in a room to the simultaneous illuminance from the sky on an unobstructed horizontal surface. It assumes a heavily overcast sky and no sunlight, and is expressed as a percentage. It comes in two forms: the average daylight factor, which describes the mean daylight in a room, or over a given surface; and the daylight factor at a specific point.

A daylight factor can be a good indicator of the appearance of a room; it can be used to estimate the illuminance in a room and its potential electric lighting use. Chapter 7 and Worksheets 4 and 5 give much more detail.

Roof lights

Windows in a flat roof ('roof lights' or 'skylights') produce a higher illuminance on the floor or on a horizontal working plane than side windows of the same area for three reasons: there is a nearly perpendicular angle of incidence; the openings receive light from a large area of sky, and an overcast sky tends to be brightest at the zenith.

However, for several reasons, the use of roof lights alone to provide illumination to rooms such as offices or classrooms can be unsatisfactory: vertical surfaces of the room tend to be poorly illuminated unless openings are planned to cast light onto them; the ceiling is illuminated only by reflected light, so the brightness contrast between the visible sky and the surrounding ceiling area can be excessive; there are usually unwanted specular reflections of the sky in horizontal work surfaces; and three-dimensional modelling can be poor.

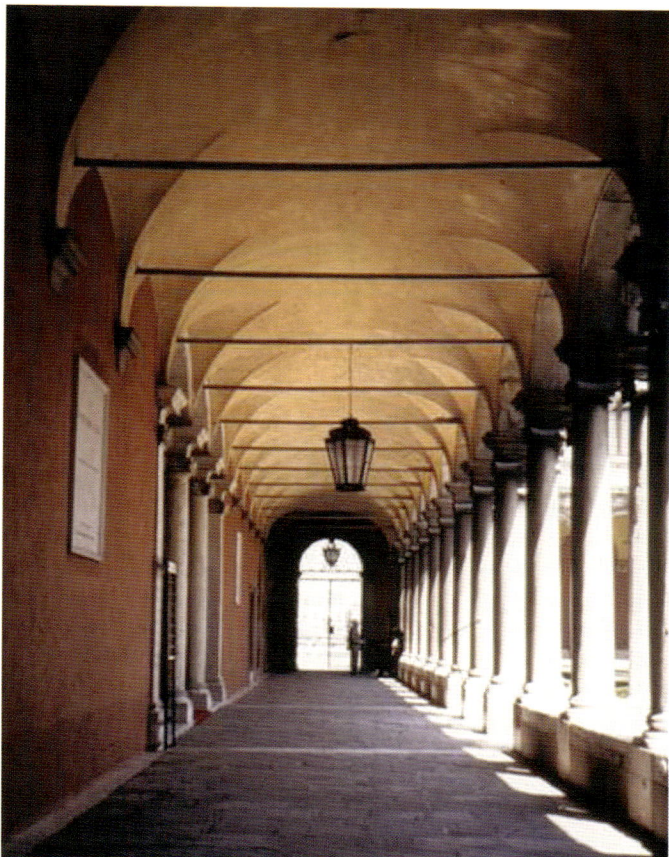

2.36

Reflected sunlight illuminating the ceiling.

San Giorgio Maggiore, Venice, Italy

2.37

Tall windows, high ceiling, low average surface reflectance.

Casa Guidi, Florence, Italy

Reflected sunlight

When there is strong sunlight outside, the luminance of light-coloured ground can be greater than that of the sky, except at angles near the sun. The ground behaves like an area source, so the upward light through the colonnade in Figure 2.36 is stronger than the downward component; in these conditions, the ceiling can have a higher illuminance than the floor.

A matt ceiling reflects the light diffusely, giving a much more even illuminance on the working plane than it would

receive from direct sunlight. A strategy for achieving high interior daylight illuminances in buildings in sunny climates is to seek a building form that excludes direct sunlight but exposes windows to sunlit exterior surfaces, ensuring that these are light-coloured. Under cloudy skies, the effect of other buildings is usually negative: obstructions reduce the light falling on a window. In sunny climates, the buildings immediately outside can be positively useful in two ways: by reflecting diffused sunlight into a room and by screening out direct sunshine.

Interreflection and brightness contrast

The room shown in Figure 2.37 is on the first floor of a house in Florence. The south-facing windows look onto the side elevation of a church across a narrow street; this obstructs most of the sky from view. During cloudy days in winter, the tall windows and high ceilings provide a level of daylight that is adequate for visual tasks such as reading and writing (the poets Robert and Elizabeth Barratt Browning lived and worked here). This zone extends about 3 m from each window.

Low-level sun is blocked by other buildings, but during the summer months it penetrates the windows at a high angle. The brightness of the room as a whole is not raised much by this direct sunlight, because it falls mainly on materials of low and medium reflectance, so about 80% of the light is absorbed at the first reflection, and is attenuated rapidly in subsequent interreflection because the average reflectance of all the room's surfaces is also low. A consequence of this is high contrast between the dark window wall and the bright patches of sunlight and visible sky.

Looking back at Figure 2.28, which relates illuminance to room surface reflectance, it can be seen that an increase of average reflection from, say, 0.2 to 0.3 has only a small effect. To obtain a very bright room where, for example, final illuminance is five times greater than the initial direct illuminance, the mean room surface reflectance must be about 0.8: as much surface area as possible has to be white.

Daylight and electric lighting

The daytime use of electric lighting is usually discussed in the context of interiors such as offices and classrooms. It is no less important in the lighting of historic buildings. In Brunelleschi's church of San Lorenzo in Florence (Figure 2.38), the regular windows and limited palette of surface colours produce a distribution of daylight that by its evenness gives the interior a character fundamentally different from that of the great mediaeval churches such as the cathedral at Chartres (Figure 2.39). San Lorenzo provided an image of a rational, ordered and re-born classical world, clearly distinguishable from an architecture of mediaeval theology.

In San Lorenzo now, daylight and the electric lighting are complementary. The general uniformity of light is the result of a layout of windows that gives comparable quantities of direct light to all the main spaces of the interior. There is a moderately high level of interreflection, to which the floor contributes substantially. The electric lighting raises

2.38
Windows give a continually changing illumination; electric lighting enhances the brightness range and increases the visibility of key areas.
San Lorenzo, Florence, Italy

the brightness range; it increases illumination of pictures in the aisles and side chapels, and, as the photograph shows, enhances the visibility of the ceiling paintings under the dome.

Daylight was always just part of the lighting in churches such as these. From the beginning, lamps and candles emphasised areas of special importance, they had liturgical significance and they gave extra illumination where visual tasks required it. The present lighting takes into account the knowledge that the majority of visitors come on cultural, not religious, pilgrimages. The importance of display, of theatricality, is increased: the need to emphasise important works of art and the architecture. The challenge is to do this and yet preserve the fundamental character of the church as a place of worship.

Throughout the world, most urban buildings use electric lighting to supplement light from windows during daytime. A design process that considers natural and artificial light to be different is technical nonsense and creatively incomplete. The designer has a palette of many sources of light – lamps and luminaires, the sky and windows. Each has different characteristics of light and colour, environmental gains and losses, costs, sizes, and subjective associations.

The quality of light in San Lorenzo is the result of different types of source used appropriately. It is an example of restrained sympathetic lighting design and can be seen not only as a model for lighting in other great churches or fine galleries, but as representing a holistic approach to the lighting design of any building.

2.39
The stained glass gives low illuminance inside the cathedral. As a result, the bright colours of the windows stand out in high contrast.
Chartres Cathedral, France

A summary

This chapter is a short introduction to lighting theory. These are the main points:

Luminous energy

1 'Light' is defined by the human eye's response to radiant energy.
2 Luminous flux – the flow of light – is measured in lumens. A 100 W incandescent lamp emits about 1300 lumens.
3 Luminous efficacy is the ratio of the visible radiation emitted by a source to the total radiation emitted. It is measured in lumens per watt.

Light in the atmosphere

1 A beam of light is invisible unless some of the energy falls on the eye.
2 The changing brightness and colour of the sky is the result of the different ways in which the solar beam is scattered in the atmosphere. The lower the sun is in the sky, the longer is the path of the solar beam and so the greater the scattering.
3 The blue sky is the result of scattering by air molecules in the upper atmosphere.
4 Clouds may lie in several layers in the atmosphere. They mix the scattered blue light back with the solar beam, and so look white. They reflect light back into space but absorb very little.
5 Low-level pollution absorbs light.

Light on a surface and Lambert's law

1 The rate at which light falls on a surface is called illuminance. It is measured in lux; 1 lux means 1 lumen per square metre.
2 When a beam of light falls on a surface, the illuminance depends on the angle between beam and surface. Lambert's law says that illuminance is proportional to the cosine of the angle of incidence.

Large sources, small sources and ideal sources

1 The effect of a light source depends on its size. A large source, such as a window under an overcast sky, gives soft shadows and an even illuminance on a surface, which decreases only gradually with distance. A small source, such as the bare filament of a clear incandescent lamp, gives hard-edged shadows, and the illuminance on a surface decreases sharply with distance.
2 As the size of the source becomes smaller and smaller, and approaches a point, the relationship between illuminance and distance becomes the inverse square law.
3 The candela describes the intensity of light from a source, the number of lumens in unit solid angle of the beam in a particular direction.

An infinite plane of light and the concept of luminance

1 Luminance is the objective brightness of a surface, as measured with a photometer. Apparent brightness is what we see, and is influenced by the eye's brightness adaptation and by the brightness of other parts of the field of view.
2 The luminance of a sky patch can be defined in terms of the illuminance on a surface directly facing the patch.
3 The four units of light, measuring luminous flux, illuminance, luminous intensity and luminance, are interlinked and can be used to calculate sequences of interreflection between different surfaces.

Parallel beams

1 Parallel or 'collimated' beams of light give hard-edged non-diverging shadows.
2 The three ideals – the point source, the large-area source and the collimated beam – are simple models of a small lamp, the diffuse sky and sunlight.

Surfaces and the nature of reflection

1 The brightness of a matt surface depends on the amount of light falling on it.
2 A glossy surface acts like a mirror, and its brightness depends on what it reflects.
3 When light falls on a rough material at a shallow angle, the surface texture is enhanced.
4 Most real materials are partly matt, partly glossy.

An infinity of reflections

1 Interreflected light in a room or a street increases the illuminance on surfaces and makes it more uniform. The amount of interreflection increases strongly with the reflectance of the individual surfaces.
2 A cavity has a lower reflectance than a plane surface of the same material.

The daylit room

1 In a side-lit room, the distribution of daylight is strongly asymmetric. The illuminance at a point on an interior surface depends on the following factors: the solid angle of the light source visible from the point in question (the sky, sunlit external surfaces); the luminance of the source; the angle of incidence on the interior surface; and the overall reflectance of the interior, and hence the interreflection in the room.
2 The daylight factor is the ratio of daylight illuminance in a room to the simultaneous illuminance outside on an overcast day, expressed as a percentage. It is widely used as an indicator of daylight adequacy. With side windows, the daylight factor at desktop level is typically 10% of the exterior illuminance beside the window, 2% two metres back into the room, 1% in the centre of the room and 0.5% at the back, furthest from the window.
3 Horizontal rooflights give a high working plane illuminance, but often at the cost of a relatively low wall illumination and poor modelling.
4 Electric lighting and daylight are complementary in their attributes, and their use jointly during daytime is normal for most sorts of building.

A homily

A designer's knowledge of the way light behaves is the equivalent of a writer's knowledge of vocabulary or a composer's experience of musical instruments and their sounds. Learning to design lighting is, to a large extent, the acquisition of experience of the fields of brightness and colour associated with particular forms, particular types of place and particular climates.

Observe, analyse, sketch, photograph, measure whenever there is something about the light and colour of a place that is interesting or moving, good or bad. Look at the sky and observe how the architecture of a region is a response to the daylight climate. Look at lamps and how they are used in luminaires, how they illuminate surfaces and how bright they are as objects. Watch how people use light in everyday activities, how they respond to unusual places; and, especially, note how you think and feel in response to your own luminous and chromatic world.

## three

The daylight climate

The intense solar radiation of interplanetary space is transformed by the earth's atmosphere into a source of energy that makes life possible.

This chapter describes the natural luminous environment that exists at the surface of the earth, and gives the data needed to calculate daylight within buildings.

3.1

Chaotic clouds. In unsettled weather, the brightness of a patch of sky and the illuminance at a point on the ground can fluctuate rapidly.

Derbyshire, UK

3.2
High cloud, a dust of ice crystals.

The luminous atmosphere

Outside the earth's atmosphere, the sun appears as a glaring disc, radiating energy; the stars are pinpricks; the moon is monochromatic and modelled, the earth colourful: but all are set in an unimaginable intense black.

The sky is the earth's atmosphere made luminous by the flow of energy from the sun. The sunlight is first scattered by molecules of the air, giving a halo of brightness around the sun; then, deeper into the atmosphere as the blackness of space softens to a deep blue, it becomes the sky pattern we see on a cloudless day: intensely bright around the solar disc, darkest blue opposite the sun, brighter again around the rim of the earth.

The highest clouds are just wisps of ice crystals, bright and white against the upper sky, as in Figure 3.2. Lower clouds are thicker and consist of water droplets. From above, they look bright: sunlight reveals complex shapes – visible bubbles of warm rising air, chains of rounded mountains drifting downwind. Inside, they are a thick mist; underneath, they look flat.

In a humid tropical climate (Figure 3.3), clouds can be mountainous – kilometres in extent from a base high above the ground to a towering top, with swirling air currents inside. In a temperate region, clouds may continue almost to ground level, alternating layers of white mist and open view. If they are dense, they reflect much light back upwards; beneath them, the sky looks grey and uniform, the sun is hidden, not revealed by even a trace of its brightness.

The lowest layers of the atmosphere change the sky again: particles and gases from industry and transport combine with natural condensation to absorb and scatter radiation. The ground surface has an effect, too, by reflecting light back onto the clouds, so the sky above a snowfield looks different from the sky over the ocean or over a large area of flowering crops.

In a city, Figure 3.5, much of the hemisphere of sky is hidden from view, masked by street facades, trees and any other surfaces that project above the horizon. These become, in effect, an artificial sky, lit by the real sky, enhanced by interreflection – a complex, changing visual world.

3.3
Towering clouds above a warm tropical sea. Sunlight is diffused and reflected back into space.

3.4
The atmosphere just above the ground and the earth's surface itself affect the brightness and colour of the sky.
Sussex, UK

3.5
In a city, much of the sky is masked by buildings and other objects. These become, in effect, an 'artificial sky'.
London, UK

Just under one-third of the solar radiation that comes into the atmosphere is diffused and reflected back into space. The rest is absorbed, warming the air, the oceans and the surfaces of the land. The energy is transformed into the winds, the ocean waves and the growth of living things. When these die, the energy they embody is absorbed in the material of the earth and stored. When coal and oil are burned, or electricity is derived from the motion of water and air, some of the energy again becomes light. Electric lighting is then the re-creation of daylight.

Seen from the surface of the earth, the flow of solar radiation is transformed by the atmosphere into two distinct sources of illumination: *sunlight*, the direct solar beam; and *skylight*, the diffuse light from the rest of the sky.

The distinction between these is fundamental to daylighting design:

- Sunlight is a very bright beam of nearly parallel rays; it casts sharp shadows. The position of the sun in the sky, and hence the direction of the beam, can be calculated accurately for any place and time; but, in many climates, whether cloud will hide the sun from view is purely a matter of probabilities.

- Skylight is the opposite: it is not a beam, it is diffuse, coming from all directions; shadows are soft-edged and often so weak that they are invisible. If the sky is clear of cloud, the upper blue sky has a stable, characteristic pattern of brightness; in cloudy climates, the constitution of the sky is again predictable only statistically.

The balance between sunlight and skylight is the most important characteristic of a daylight climate, because it determines which of two basic approaches to daylighting should be adopted: in a cloudy climate, the diffuse sky has to be the main source of light; where clear skies predominate, reflected sunlight can be the more effective. How this affects the basic form of the building, and the relationship with sustainable design, is described in Chapter 4.

The geometry of sunlight

Seen from the earth's surface, the daily solar path looks like a circular arc across the sky. Twice a year, on about 21 March and 23 September, day and night are equal (hence 'equinox'). The sun is above the horizon for 12 hours, rising due east and setting due west. Figure 3.6 shows this for a site at about 50°N latitude.

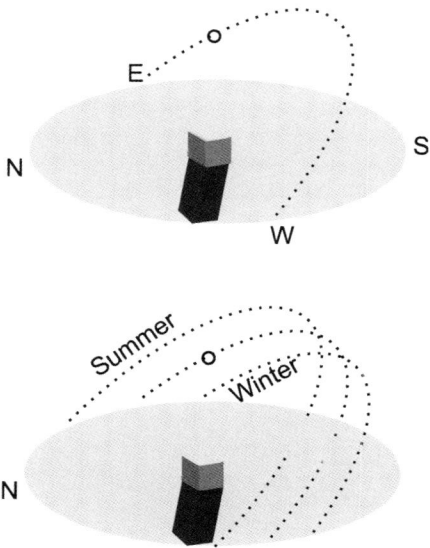

3.6
From a point on the earth's surface, the sun seems to follow a circular arc across the sky. This diagram shows the solar route at about 50°N latitude.

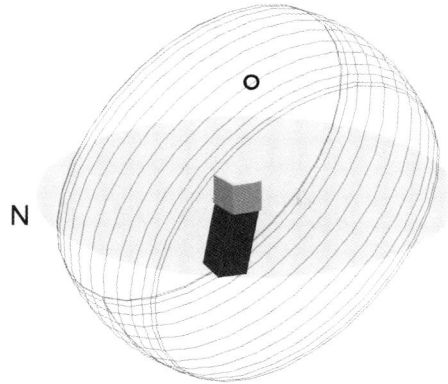

3.7
The complete annual sunpath is a spiral, tilted by the angle of latitude.

Except in the tropics, all through the summer, the sun is higher in the sky than at the equinox; sunrise is somewhere between east and north, sunset between west and north, and the sun is above the horizon for more than 12 hours. During winter months, the sunpath is lower in the sky; sunrise and sunset are towards south; the day is shorter than 12 hours. Between the tropics of Capricorn and Cancer, the sun is overhead twice during the year; on the equator, this is at the equinoxes, spring and autumn.

The daily sunpath is not exactly a circular loop across the sky. It is very slightly skewed, because the annual path is a spiral (think of 'helix', a spiral, and 'helios', the Greek word for the sun). Figure 3.7 illustrates this. The day-to-day change in the sun's path is greatest at the equinox and smallest in mid-winter and mid-summer (the 'solstice', which occurs on 22 December and 21 June, comes from a Latin phrase meaning 'stationary sun').

The sun's apparent position in the sky is normally defined by two angles: *solar azimuth* and *solar elevation* (or *solar altitude*). They are shown in Figure 3.8. Calculations of the solar angles are based on spherical trigonometry, which yields two equations for solar azimuth and elevation. But the earth's orbit is not exactly circular and it lasts slightly more than 365 days, so there are correcting factors. The result is a set of formulae that are not difficult but are cumbersome and best worked out by computer; they are listed in Section 2 of Algorithms and Equations.

The earth spins on its axis, which goes through the North and South Poles. This axis is tilted in relation to the plane of its orbit around the sun. The result is that for 6 months the sun is directly overhead somewhere in the Northern Hemisphere and for the other 6 months it is somewhere in the Southern Hemisphere. This accounts for summer and winter. The tilt of the earth's axis is 23.5°, which is why the tropics extend 23.5° north and south of the Equator.

The latitude at which the sun is directly overhead is the 'solar declination'. It changes day by day through the year; these are the key values:

(Northern) summer solstice, 21 June	+23.5°
Equinox, 22 March, 23 September	0°
(Northern) winter solstice, 22 December	−23.5°

The long equations for solar elevation and azimuth reduce to a very simple formula when the time is mid-day:

$$\text{maximum solar elevation} = 90° - \text{latitude} + \text{solar declination}$$

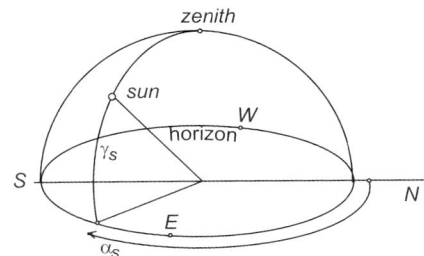

3.8
Solar angles: azimuth α_s, and elevation, γ_s.

For example, the latitude of London is approximately 51.5°, and the elevation of the sun at mid-day in mid-winter, the spring equinox and mid-summer's day is, respectively,

$$\gamma_{smax}(22\ \mathrm{Dec}) = 90° - 51.5 - 23.5 = 15°$$
$$\gamma_{smax}(21\ \mathrm{Mar}) = 90° - 51.5 + 0 = 38.5°$$
$$\gamma_{smax}(21\ \mathrm{Jun}) = 90° - 51.5 + 23.5 = 62°$$

'Mid-day' here means the moment in the day when the sun is highest, not when the clock indicates 12.00. Clock time and solar time differ. There are several reasons for this:

1   Clock time is set to the average solar time at standard meridians, lines of longitude 15° apart. If a site is east or west of the meridian to which local time is set, the time indicated by the sun will appear to be earlier or later than the clock. For example, in the UK, clock time is based on the Greenwich meridian, longitude zero, which passes through London. Penzance in south-west England has a longitude of 5.5° W. Since the rotation of the earth is 360° in 24 hours, 15° per hour, solar time in Penzance is 5.5/15 = 0.37 hours, or 22 minutes, behind clock time or solar time in London.

2   'Daylight saving' or 'summer time'. Clocks are deliberately set earlier or later than mean solar time. If clocks are advanced an hour in spring, and put back an hour in autumn, the sun will appear to rise an hour late on summer mornings and set correspondingly late in the evenings.

3   Eccentricity in the earth's orbit. Since the earth's path around the sun is not exactly circular, the day length differs slightly during the year, causing discrepancy with regular clock time. The effect is embodied in the 'equation of time', given in Algorithms and Equations. The discrepancy swings during the year between approximately +15 and −15 minutes.

Unless explicitly stated, tables and diagrams giving solar angles are based on solar time.

Sunpath diagrams are graphs of solar elevation and azimuth. The most common form is shown in Figure 3.9. It is plotted on a stereographic projection – this can be imagined as a perspective of the sky looking upwards with a very wide angle of view. It is similar to the image from a camera with a fish-eye lens.

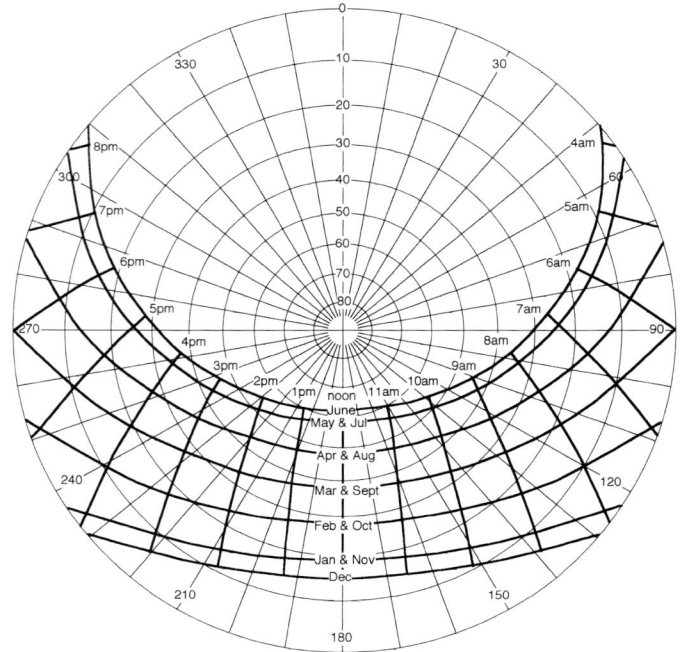

3.9

A stereographic diagram of the sky. The perimeter represents the horizon, and the concentric circles give the elevation of a sky point, with the zenith in the centre. The radial lines represent compass direction or azimuth, with north at the top, east at 90°. Superimposed are sunpaths for London, latitude 51° N. It can be seen that in mid-summer the sun rises in the north-east just before 4am, and sets in the north-west after 8pm. At noon, the solar elevation is at its maximum of about 62°. Equations for solar elevation and azimuth are in Section 2 of Algorithms and Equations.

For site investigations on the daylight climate of a site it is very convenient to superimpose sunpaths onto photographs, as in Figure 3.10.

Worksheets 8 and 9 describe the use of sunlight diagrams and fish-eye images. Worksheet 18 consists of sunpath and other types of sky diagram.

The lines across the patch of sky visible in Figure 3.10 give *possible sunlight hours* – the periods of sunshine that would occur with a clear sky. For cloudy climates, there is another measure: *probable sunlight hours*. This is found by combining solar geometry with meteorological records of sunshine duration. The probability of the sun being obscured at a particular time can be estimated. A useful way of presenting this information is a dot diagram, where the probable sunlight hours are proportional to the density of dots on the diagram, as in Figure 3.11.

3.10

A sunpath diagram superimposed on a fish-eye photograph taken at ground level close to a building. It shows when direct sunshine might fall on the ground here. This technique is very useful when assessing daylight availability at a site. The sunpath diagram is rotated to match the orientation of the photograph.

In Figure 3.12, the diagram is used to examine the extent to which sunlight might fall on a point in a room. The photograph taken at the point and the diagram are superimposed, and rotated to the orientation of the building (the window faces an azimuth of 185°, 5° west of south). It can be seen that during summer months, no sunlight would fall at the camera point; but during a winter day, the point could be in sunlight for about 4 hours. There are 27 crosses on the sky visible through the glazing; each represents 0.5% of probable sunlight hours; therefore, on average, the point on the desk receives sunshine for 13.5% of the time that there is sunlight outside.

Daylight availability

Wherever you are in the world, the amount of light falling on the ground depends on the solar elevation: the higher the sun, the greater the illuminance on the ground. This applies not only to sunny days, but to all weather conditions, even overcast days when the sun is entirely hidden. It occurs because, as the solar elevation increases, two things happen: the path of the rays through the atmosphere becomes shorter, and the angle at which sunlight falls on the ground and on the tops of clouds becomes more nearly perpendicular. This is illustrated in Figure 3.13.

Illuminance from sunlight

Figure 3.14 shows how the solar beam is attenuated by the atmosphere. The upper curve gives the illuminance from sunlight on a surface directly facing the solar disc. The lower curve, showing the illuminance of sunlight falling on level ground, illustrates the additional effect of a changing angle of incidence.

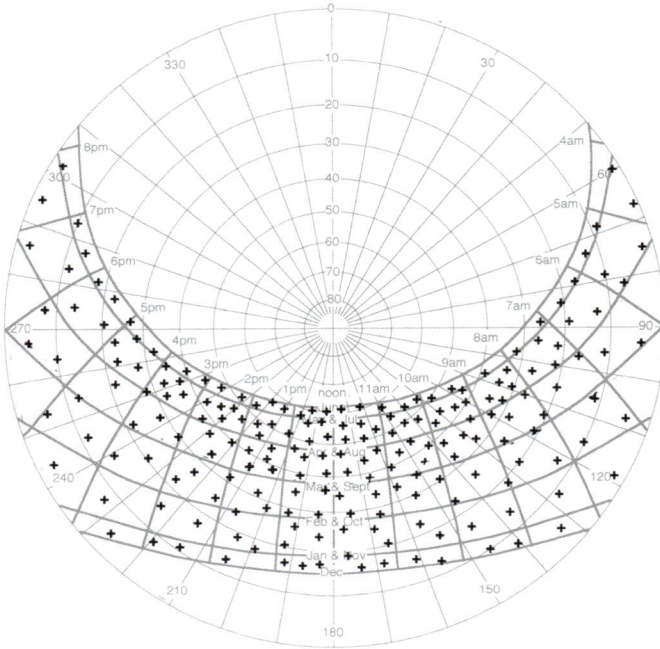

3.11

A stereographic diagram of the sky with a dot diagram of probable sunlight hours. Each cross represents 0.5% of the time that sunlight would fall on unobstructed ground.

London

3.12

The dot diagram is overlaid onto a fish-eye image taken from the centre of an office desk. The average number of hours that sunlight would fall at the camera point is proportional to the number of dots lying on the sky seen through the window.

The clear sky

The molecules that constitute the air of the upper atmosphere are sufficiently similar in size to the wavelength of the solar beam in the visible spectrum that their effect, called Rayleigh scattering, is wavelength-dependent: blue light is dispersed more than red light. The result is that

The intensity of sunlight is influenced by pollution and water vapour in the atmosphere: as the amounts of these increase, scattering and absorption become greater and the solar beam more attenuated. This effect is quantified by the *illuminance turbidity* of the atmosphere, T_{il}. If $T_{il} = 3$, the reduction in solar illuminance during its path through the atmosphere is equivalent to that from a path three times as long through clean dry air. Figure 3.15 shows the solar normal illuminance at different degrees of illuminance turbidity, from the clean atmosphere in mountainous regions to the heavily polluted conditions above an industrial city.

The solar elevation at a given time of day depends on the latitude of the site. Moving from the tropics towards the Arctic or Antarctic Circles, the difference between summer and winter becomes greater as latitude increase. Figure 3.16 shows the sunlight illuminance on the ground at three sites, 25°, 40° and 55°, on mid-summer's day and 6 months later in mid-winter.

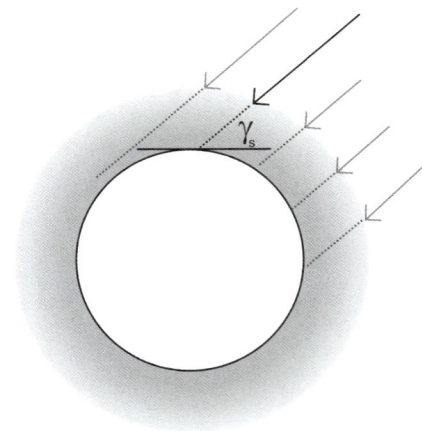

3.13

Both the length of the sunlight's path through the atmosphere and the angle of incidence at a point on the ground are related to the solar elevation γ_s.

solar illuminance, kilolux

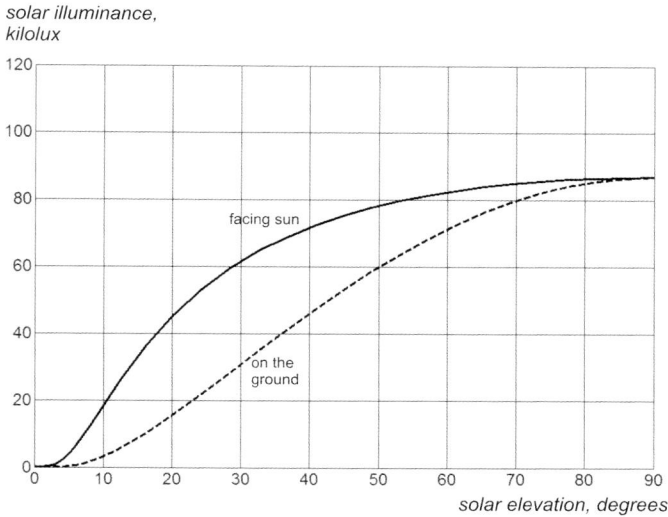

3.14

Illuminance from direct sunlight: solar normal illuminance (the amount of light falling on a surface perpendicular to the beam) and solar horizontal illuminance (the light falling on level ground). Outside the atmosphere, the solar normal illuminance is about 134 klx. (Illuminance turbidity = 3.5.) Equations for daylight illuminance are in Section 3 of Algorithms and Equations.

solar normal illuminance, kilolux

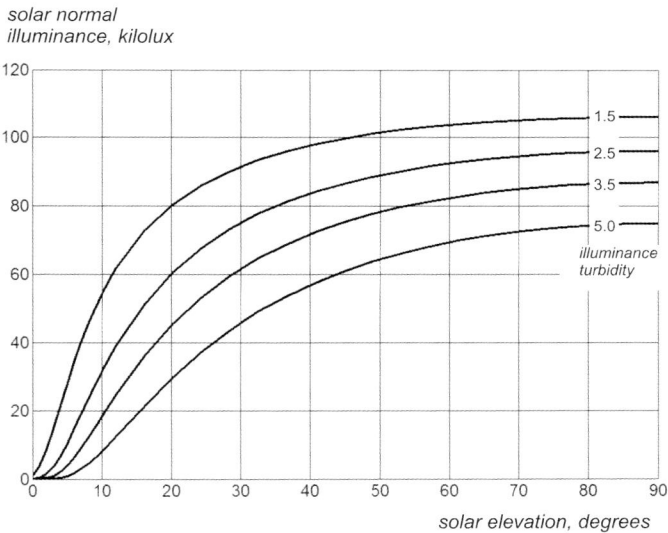

3.15

Solar normal illuminance at different values of illuminance turbidity T_{il}. Typically, they apply to:

$T_{il} = 1.5$: dry conditions in the high mountains

$T_{il} = 2.5$: rural

$T_{il} = 3.5$: urban

$T_{il} = 5.0$: industrial.

solar illuminance, kilolux

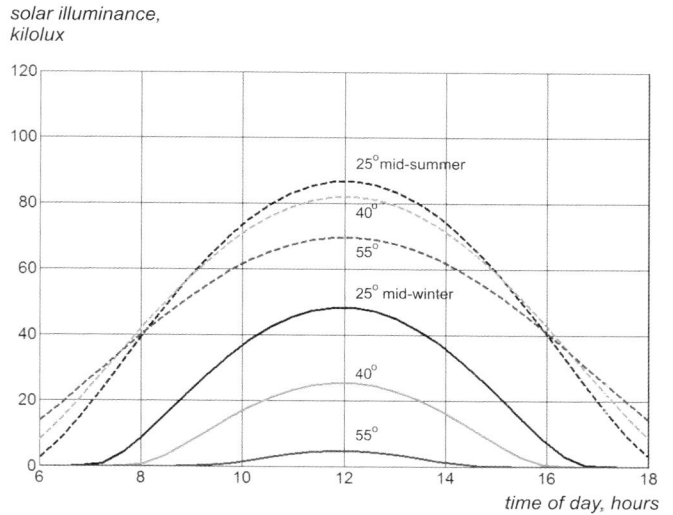

3.16

Sunlight on the ground: solar horizontal illuminance on 23 June and 23 December at three different latitudes. (Illuminance turbidity 3.5.) Note the very low level in winter at 55°.

sunlight falling through the atmosphere is transformed into an attenuated orange–red beam set in a diffuse field of blue. The longer the path through the atmosphere, the more the beam is scattered. In the high mountains on a dry day, the sky is a deep blue because only a small fraction of the beam has been scattered: the direct sunlight is intense.

In the visible range, very little of the sun's radiation is absorbed by the atmosphere, but there is highly significant absorption of the ultraviolet, mainly by oxygen and ozone; this is critical to life on the earth's surface. Other components of the atmosphere, particularly water and carbon dioxide, create a semi-opaque barrier to radiation of infrared wavelengths. The effect of the atmosphere is to change the ratio of visible to total radiation, a value called *luminous efficacy*. This varies with solar elevation and weather. Irradiance (the complete spectral quantity) from sun and sky is widely measured at meteorological stations, but illuminance is recorded at very few. Luminous efficacy can be used to derive daylight values from radiation data, but the efficacy figures must be carefully matched to the conditions.

There is more scattering of the solar beam as the atmosphere becomes moist or polluted, as turbidity increases. A turbid cloudless sky is brighter than one in a clean dry atmosphere, and areas that are deep blue with low

horizontal
illuminance, kilolux

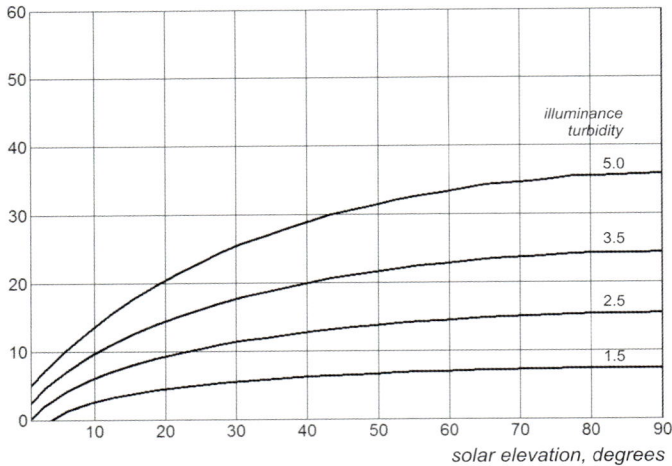

3.17
Horizontal illuminance from the clear sky alone (not sunlight). The illuminance is dependent on solar elevation. It increases with turbidity because more of the solar beam is scattered.

turbidity are much whiter. The circumsolar flare, the patch of very bright sky around the sun, becomes broader. The presence of heavy industrial or vehicular air pollution brings a yellow tinge; indeed, from an aircraft approaching one of those cities where in summer a bubble of warm polluted air is trapped by surrounding hills, the lower air is visible as a grey–brown fog.

If the illuminance turbidity can be estimated, the illuminance from a clear sky is quite predictable. Figure 3.17 shows this. But compare the curves with those in Figure 3.15: direct sunlight gives far higher illuminances than the clear sky. That is the argument for using reflected sunlight, wherever possible, as a source of interior lighting in sunny climates.

Cloud

The presence of clouds introduces apparent randomness. In many climates, predictability vanishes.

Figure 3.18 shows diffuse horizontal illuminance recorded at Nottingham, UK, between 1984 and 1985, and at Hong Kong between 2003 and 2005. Each dot is a single reading. It is evident that, although there is still some relationship between horizontal illuminance and solar elevation, the

diffuse horizontal
illuminance, kilolux

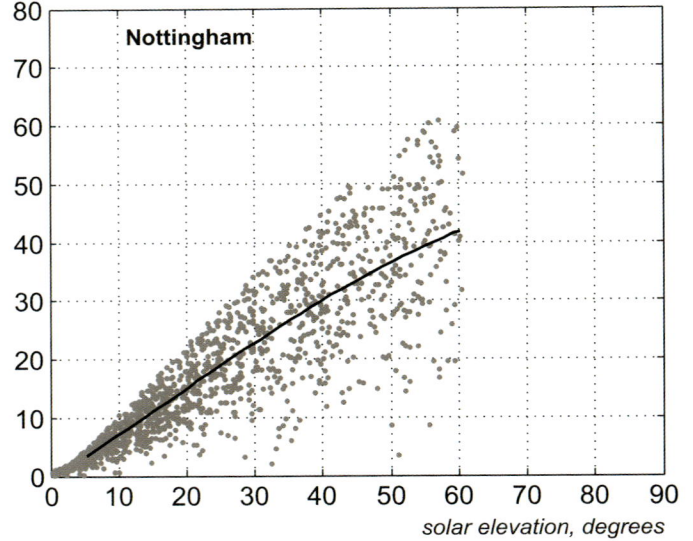

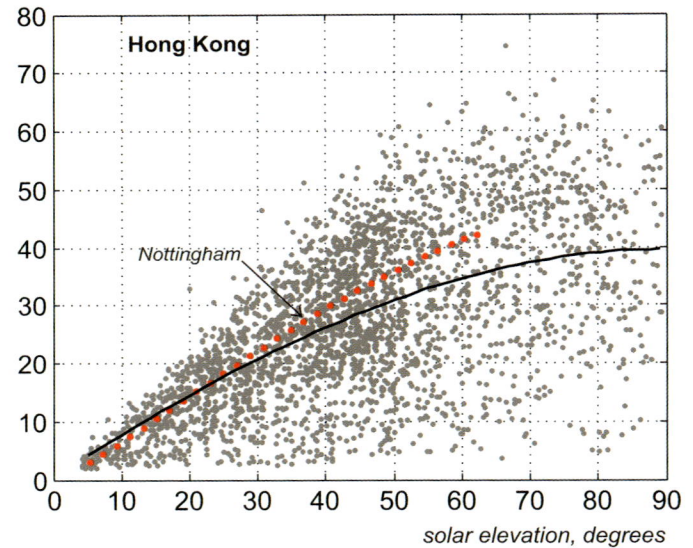

3.18
Diffuse horizontal illuminance. Measured values, excluding direct sunlight. The continuous line shows the mean value.
Based on measurements made in Nottingham, UK, and Hong Kong

scatter is so great that to base practical calculations on just the average values could be misleading.

Figure 3.19 shows the distributions more precisely. The histograms show how the actual illuminance varied in relation to the mean illuminance at any given solar elevation. Equations and statistics are given in Algorithms and Equations, Section 3.6. With these results, it is possible to

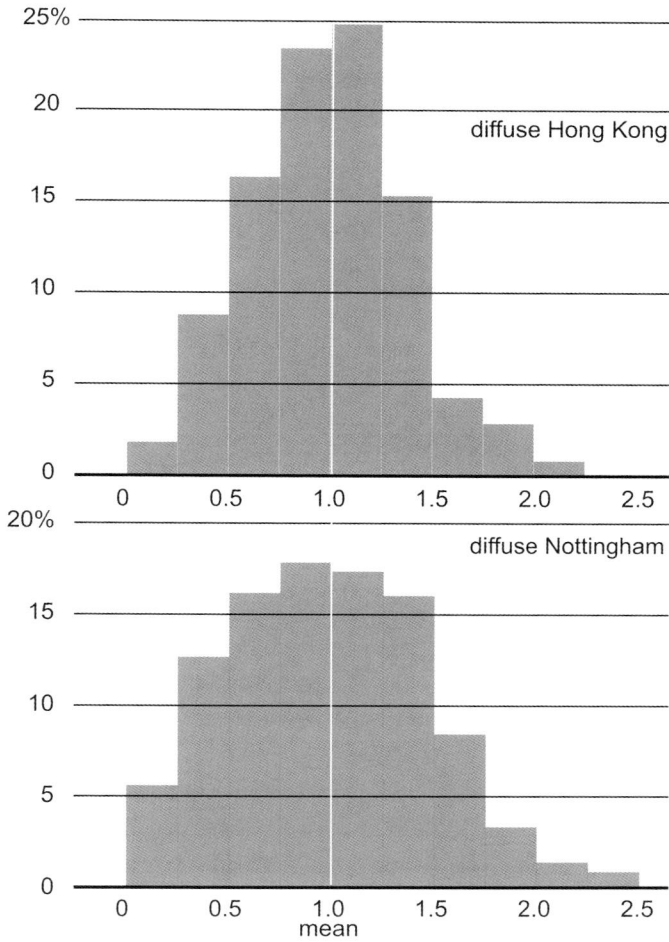

3.19

Diffuse horizontal illuminance. Frequency distributions of diffuse illuminance. Mean over solar elevations 5–60°.

Based on measurements made in Nottingham, UK and Hong Kong

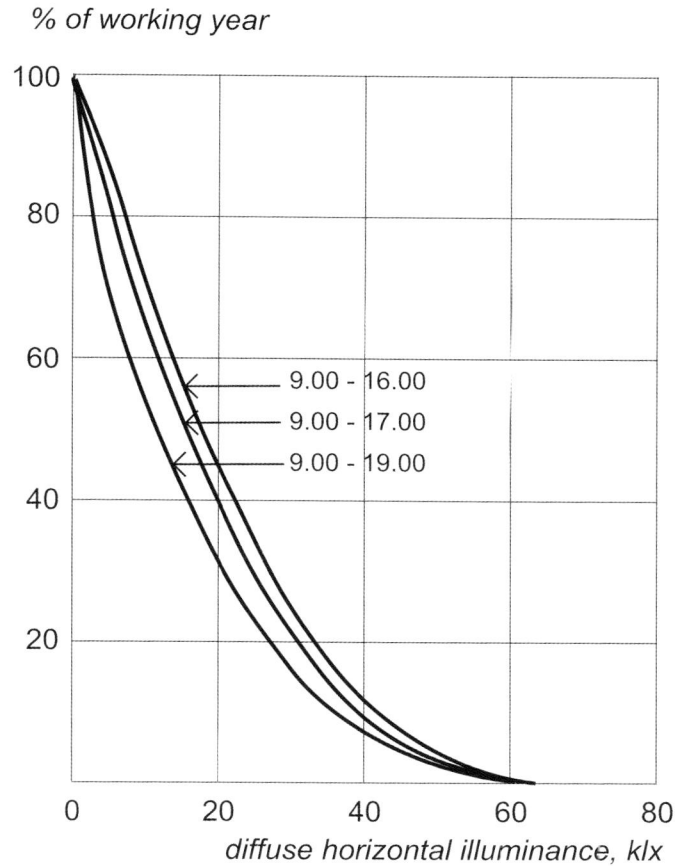

3.20

Diffuse horizontal illuminance during the working year. The curves show the frequency at which a given illuminance is exceeded for three different working-day periods.

Nottingham, UK

construct cumulative graphs such as Figure 3.20. This takes a working day between 09.00 and 17.00 and shows for a year the fraction of the total time that the illuminance (shown on the horizontal axis) is exceeded. Also plotted are curves for 09.00 to 16.00 and 09.00 to 19.00.

Cumulative graphs of this type are best plotted directly from the measured data. They can be constructed, however, with a computer program that takes the period required, calculates the solar elevation at, typically, 5-minute intervals, then uses the distribution values plotted in Figure 3.19 to find the distribution of illuminances at each occasion. From these, the range of illuminances over the total period is found. The advantage of this method is that arbitrary times

can be incorporated – such as the school day over a year, excluding holiday periods.

The two graphs in Figure 3.18 are remarkably similar despite the climatic differences. The Nottingham mean value curve is superimposed on the Hong Kong graph: it is slightly higher than the Hong Kong curve. This is to be expected: in warmer climates, clouds have a much greater vertical extent, which results in more reflection back into space. The result is that, at a given solar elevation, the diffuse horizontal illuminance tends to be less in cloudy tropical climates than at temperate latitudes. This is more than compensated by the higher solar elevations that occur in low-latitude climates, so, in warm moist climates, the diffuse illuminance can be very high. It is found that diffuse illuminance varies relatively little

*global horizontal
illuminance, klx*

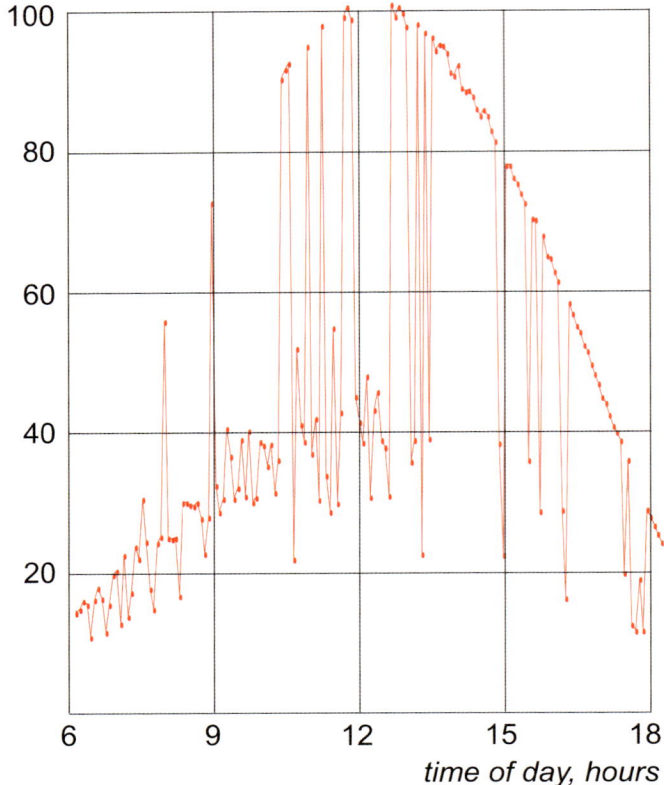

time of day, hours

3.21
Global horizontal illuminance on a summer day. There is broken cloud
during the morning but the sky becomes clearer in the early afternoon.
Nottingham, UK

over a region: the Nottingham data could be applied to similar
sites across north-west Europe and the Hong Kong results
are probably applicable to other maritime sub-tropical
locations.

Figure 3.21 illustrates the variation in global illuminance
(sun and sky together) during a typical day. It shows that in
the morning, the sky was about half covered with cumulus
cloud moving in a moderate breeze. The sun shone on the
ground for periods of a few minutes, then was obscured.
The illuminance fluctuated widely, dropping sometimes to
one-quarter of its value in strong sunshine. The cloud cover
gradually diminished, looking like Figure 3.22 just before noon
and a predominantly clear sky prevailed during the afternoon.

Cloud types differ in their effect. High-altitude clouds
consist of ice crystals. The wispy cirrus clouds shown earlier

in Figure 3.2 transmit most of the light incident on them; seen
in front of the sun, they create a bright halo around the solar
disk. Deep clouds of water droplets, which, from an aircraft
flying through them, appear to be a thick fog, reflect about
80% of incident light. There are often several distinct layers
of cloud.

The total amount of cloud in the sky, the fraction of the sky
that is covered, correlates very poorly with illuminance. The
graph in Figure 3.23 plots global illuminance measured over
many days when the solar elevation was 5°. The scatter of
values is very great, particularly with cloud covering more
than three-quarters of the sky: on some of these days, the
illuminance was higher than on totally cloudless mornings.

In humid tropical regions, the cloud base tends to be
higher above the ground, and the clouds themselves tend to
be much taller – a consequence of higher temperatures. This
gives the unexpected result that, at a given solar elevation,
the diffuse horizontal illuminance tends to be less in cloudy
tropical climates than at temperate latitudes, because more
light is reflected back into space and turbidity tends to be
higher. But higher solar elevations occur in low-latitude
climates, so in warm moist climates the diffuse illuminance
can be very high.

A continental zone has a different daylight climate from a
maritime region at the same latitude. Continental skies tend
to be more homogeneous and have cloud structures over
broad regions that change less rapidly than skies affected
by winds from the oceans. The presence of cloud is also
affected by large-scale landforms: mountains cause local
cloudiness and unstable weather.

Extreme values occur in storms. Under the vast cumulo-
nimbus clouds generated in thunderstorms, illuminances
can drop to one-thousandth of their usual value and, within
a minute or two, swing to exceptionally high levels.

Illuminance at low solar elevations

Much outdoor lighting is controlled by photocells that trigger
a switching off at dawn and switching on at dusk. It is often
necessary to estimate the electricity used by exterior lighting,
especially street lighting. In low-latitude regions, the daylight
illuminance changes rapidly as the sun rises and sets, and the
period of darkness varies little through the year. The further a

3.22
Clouds carried by wind give irregular periods of sunshine on the ground.
Manchester, UK

Global horizontal illuminance, kilolux

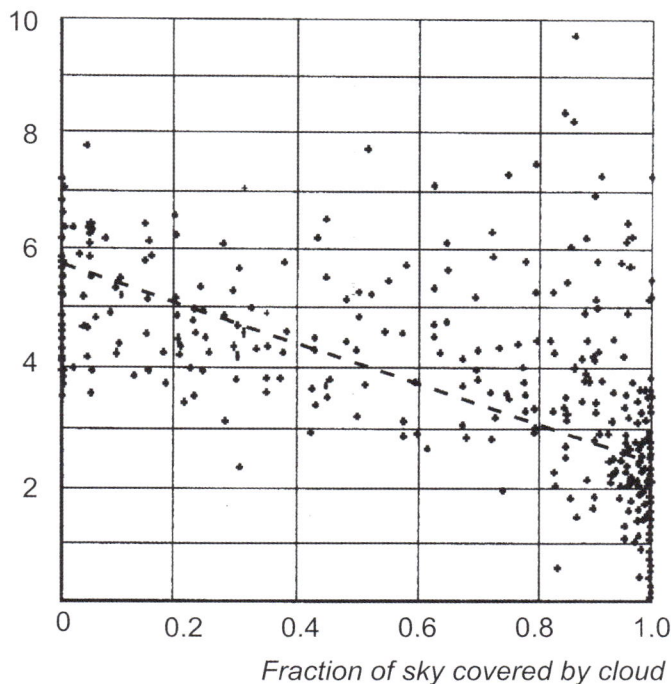

Fraction of sky covered by cloud

3.23
The relationship between cloud amount and illuminance at 5° solar elevation. The regression line is a very poor fit to the data.
Nottingham, UK

place is from the Equator, the longer the period of twilight and the greater the difference in night-time hours between summer and winter. This makes any calculation of the operating period of electric light increasingly more sensitive to the assumptions made.

As sunset approaches, global and diffuse horizontal illuminances converge. Figure 3.24 illustrates the relationship between solar elevation and the mean daylight illuminance on a horizontal surface. Figure 3.25 shows the proportion of readings below a given fraction of the mean. From these, it is possible to calculate the amount of time that ground illuminance is less than a given value.

It is found, though, that the total number of hours for which the global illuminance is less than a given value is relatively insensitive to change in this value and to variation of latitude. This is shown in Figure 3.26.

Luminance distribution of the sky

The amount of daylight in a room does not depend solely on the total amount of daylight outside: it is also affected by the pattern of brightness of the sky. A clear sky is brightest around the sun, has a bright ring just above the horizon, and is

$\overline{E}_{hg}$, *lux*

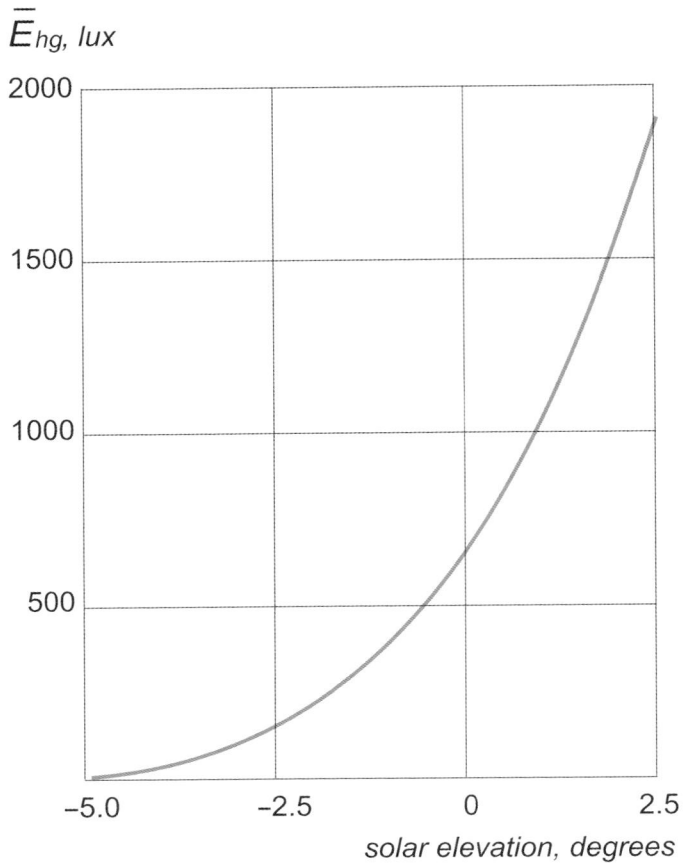

3.24

Mean illuminance on the ground at low solar elevation.

Nottingham, UK

proportion of occurrences

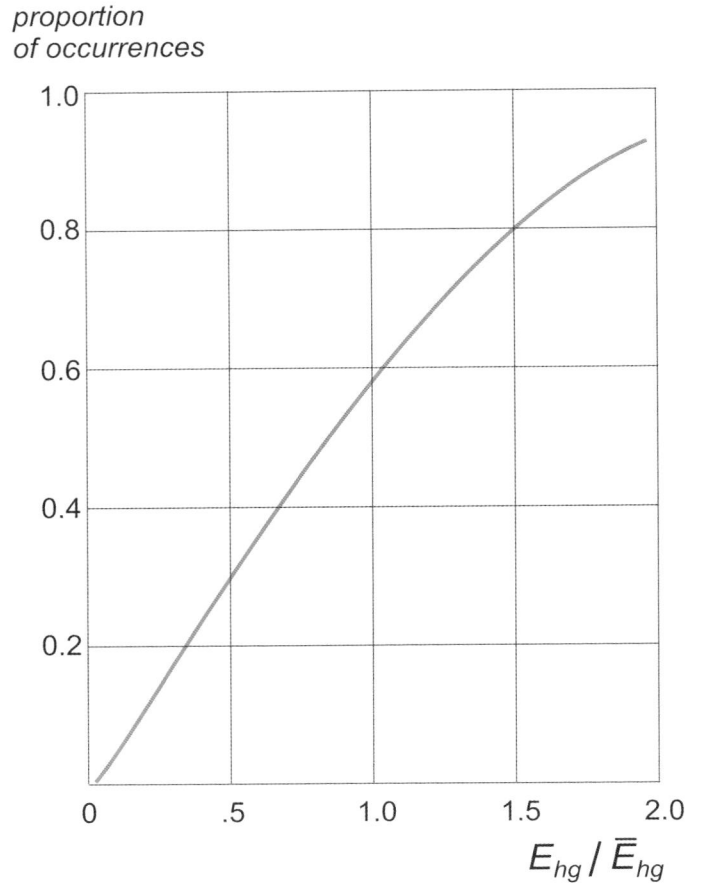

3.25

Proportion of recorded illuminances less than a given fraction of the mean value at the same solar elevation. Solar elevation –2.5° to 0°.

Nottingham, UK

total annual hours $E_{ref} < E_{hg}$

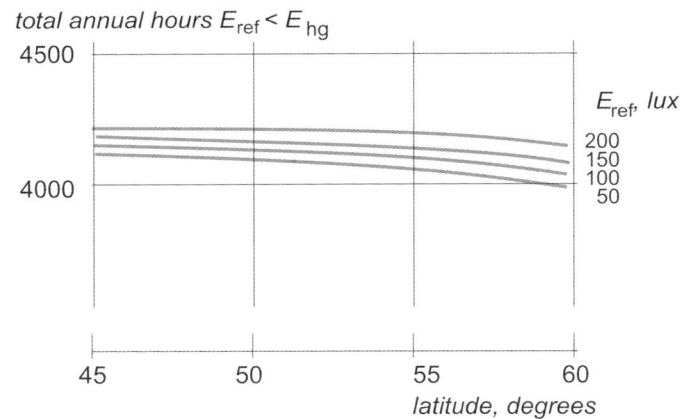

3.26

The total annual hours that daylight illuminance is less than a given value E_{ref}. The total hours are relatively insensitive to latitude and E_{ref}.

Nottingham, UK

darkest opposite to the azimuth of the sun. A thickly overcast sky tends to be brightest at the zenith (directly overhead) and darkest near the horizon. Tall clouds can be very bright when sunlight falls on them but dark when shaded.

Only a fraction of the whole sky is directly visible from a point in a room, and it is the luminance of this patch that mainly determines the daylight there in the room. From unobstructed ground outside, all the sky is visible. The brightness of a small patch varies more rapidly than the mean brightness of the whole sky so the ratio of room illuminance to horizontal illuminance – the daylight factor – tends to fluctuate. The daylight factor is therefore not precise as a predictor of instantaneous room illuminance. Chapter 8 describes this in more detail and shows how daylight factors can be linked with cumulate illuminance graphs, such as Figure 3.20, to obtain meaningful estimates of interior illuminance.

To calculate daylight illuminances accurately, the luminance distribution of the sky must be known. Until the 1990s, there were few measurements of this. Those that were available had mostly been measured with hand-held instruments and covered the sky with only a few points. There were no continuous measurements of sky brightness over periods of months and years.

In the late 1980s, the International Commission on Illumination (CIE) proposed a Daylight Measurement Year in which skylight and sunlight, together with other meteorological values, would be measured at research stations throughout the world. This became the International Daylight Measurement Project (IDMP), which began in 1991. Measurement sites were placed in two categories: General and Research. General class stations recorded illuminance and irradiance from the whole sky and from the sky without the solar zone. Research class stations, in addition, measured sky luminance at intervals of (typically) 5 minutes with scanning luminance probes – sensors that viewed patches of sky about 11° across. They covered the sky in a standard pattern of 145 zones.

The outcome of the IDMP was twofold: the ability to make accurate calculation of instantaneous internal illuminance with real data. This is done with the use of daylight coefficients, a method described in Chapter 10. The IDMP results gave also the scope for classifying the world's daylight climates in a new way – the CIE General Sky.

Standard skies

Daylight calculations, especially those done to show compliance with standards or regulations, need to be based on an agreed sky brightness pattern. 'Standard skies' are mathematical formulae that describe how the luminance of the sky varies with the elevation and azimuth of the direction in which it is viewed. The earliest to be fully adopted internationally was the CIE Standard Overcast sky. This describes the conditions under which the lowest steady levels of daylight tend to occur in temperate climates: the sky is grey and overcast; maybe there is rain. There may be several layers of cloud, some broken, some of them continuous sheets. The sun is entirely obscured and there is no hint of its position: looking up towards any point in the sky, then circling the sky at that elevation, the luminance remains the same. There is an increase in brightness as the eye moves upwards, so it is brightest around the zenith, but no change with azimuth. The distribution was originally called a Moon and Spencer sky after the authors of the paper in which it was formulated.

The luminance distribution varies only with the elevation of view. It gets brighter with increasing height above the horizon, but, at a given elevation, the luminance is the same in all horizontal directions. The relationship between luminance and the elevation of view is

$$L_\gamma = \frac{1+2\sin\gamma}{3} L_z \qquad (3.1)$$

The luminance L_γ of the sky at elevation γ is given as a fraction of the zenith luminance L_z; it is lowest at the horizon, where $L_0 = (1/3)L_z$. Figure 3.27 illustrates this.

Skies of this brightness distribution actually occur rarely even in predominantly cloudy climates, but the use of the standard overcast sky can be justified by taking it to represent stable worst-case conditions. The lowest levels of daylight that occur during storms usually last only minutes and are often part of a rapid fluctuation of illuminance from an unstable sky.

The Standard Overcast Sky was initially adopted by the CIE for lowland regions, and it is a good representation of a relatively rare but important sky condition. Measured ground illuminances under skies that are good approximations to the standard distribution do not vary as much as diffuse illuminances generally (Figure 3.32), but can range, still, from half to twice the mean value at a particular solar elevation.

The luminance of a cloudy sky, especially when there is a low-level sheet of stratus cloud, is affected by the reflectance of the ground, which is usually less than 0.2, and this is assumed in the formula for the Standard Overcast Sky. The effect of ground reflectance can be seen in agricultural areas where large-scale planting of a brightly coloured crop

zenith luminance
3 x horizon luminance

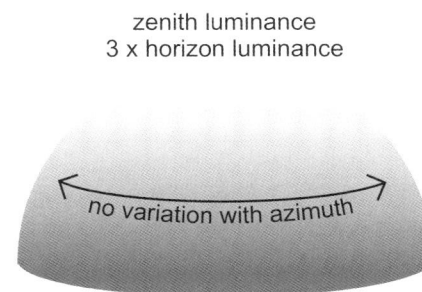

no variation with azimuth

3.27
The CIE Standard Overcast Sky.

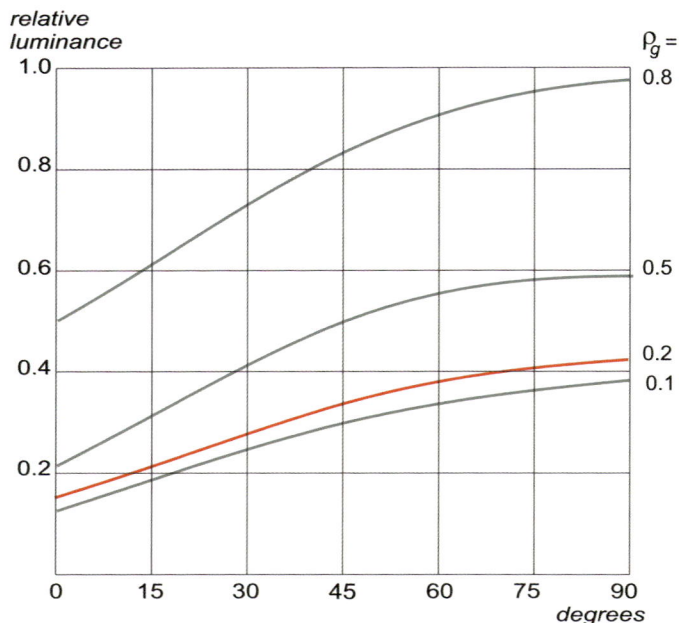

3.28

How the luminance of an overcast sky varies with ground reflectance. The horizontal axis gives the elevation above the horizon of the line of sight. Calculated for solar elevation 30°.

such as yellow oilseed rape gives a coloured tint to the base of clouds. When the ground is snow-covered, much more light is reflected upwards, making cloud bases brighter and superimposing onto them a uniform illumination that reduces the difference between zenith and horizon luminance.

Figure 3.28 illustrates this. Based on an empirical equation by Kittler (see Algorithms and Equations, Section 3.7), the four curves give the sky luminance at a given elevation: they correspond to four values of ground reflectance. Table 3.1 summarises the ratios of zenith luminance to luminance immediately above the horizon and the relative ground

Table 3.1: The effect of ground reflectance on the luminance and illuminance of an overcast sky

Ground reflectance	Ratio zenith luminance: horizon luminance	Relative ground illuminance
0	3.00	1.00
0.1	3.00	1.11
0.2	2.98	1.23
0.5	2.75	1.77
0.8	1.98	2.90

illuminances. Snow-covered ground can be brighter than the sky at low elevation, as in Figure 3.29.

The CIE Standard Clear Sky provided a similar basis for computing daylight in cloudless conditions. The formula has two parts that together mimic the two brightness gradients visible in the clear sky: a decrease in luminance with distance from the sun, and a decrease with elevation above the horizon (Figure 3.30). There were two versions: for low illuminance turbidity and for a polluted atmosphere.

The Overcast and Clear Sky standards were replaced in 2003 by the CIE Standard General Sky. The formula for this is in Section 4 of Algorithms and Equations and is a generalisation of the Clear Sky equation. By putting different parameters into the equation, a range of different sky brightness patterns can be produced. These include the earlier Overcast and Clear Sky distributions, and the Standard document lists 13 other sky types, ranging from an entirely uniform distribution to turbid skies with a pronounced solar corona.

The CIE standard skies have two important characteristics. First, they give only the relative luminance distribution – not absolute luminance values but sky brightness at any point as a fraction of the zenith luminance. And, secondly, they are models of homogeneous skies: they vary smoothly, not with the discontinuous brightness pattern given by a sky with individual clouds.

Most daylight factor calculation formulae are based on the Overcast Sky equation. The greatest potential use of the General Sky is as a means of categorising measured data. The daylight climate of a place can be summarised succinctly by the frequency with which General Sky types occur, and the illuminances and frequency of sunlight that occur with each sky type. It is also found that the use of the homogeneous distributions to represent skies with discrete clouds leads to insignificant error in subsequent calculations of daylight in rooms.

The whole climate

The natural luminous environment is not fully described by a set of graphs or a table of illuminances. The daylight climate is more than the light from sun and sky: and it is

3.29
Snow illuminated by the whole
sky can have a higher luminance
than cloud near the horizon.

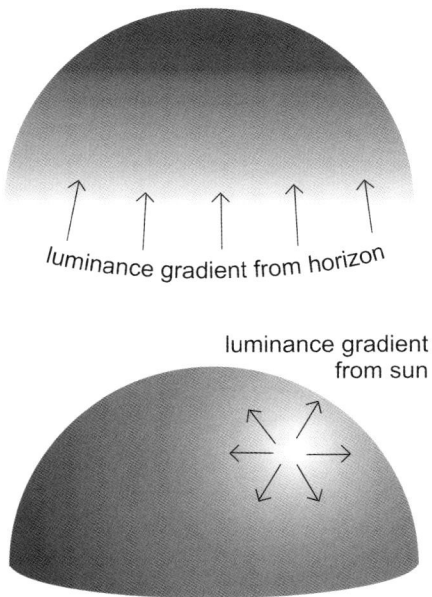

luminance gradient from horizon

luminance gradient
from sun

3.30
The CIE Clear Sky and the CIE General Sky define sky luminance as
a combination of two brightness gradients, one centred on the sun,
the other from horizon to zenith.

interlinked with all the other characteristics that determine
the climate of a place. The light falling on the face of a
building is affected by the nature of the ground, its colour
and reflectance; it depends on the vegetation, on whether
obstructing tree canopies are dense or open, and whether
leaves fall in winter; it depends on the forms of other
buildings, and the materials used in their construction.

The daylight climate that we perceive, the image we
construct of the visual nature of a place, is the meeting of
our expectations and our sensory experience. How warm
we are, what we hear and smell, the air movement we
feel – all the other responses we make to a climate – are
blended with what we visually perceive to form an
integrated awareness of the place we are in.

four

Daylight and the form of buildings

Decisions about the basic shape of a building, its orientation, and whether it is heavy or lightweight are crucial to the lifetime performance of the building. They determine its energy use, its effect on the microclimate of the surrounding site, the penetration of daylight into the interior, the available views and its exposure to sunlight. If a building's overall form is wrong, little can be done to compensate in the detailed design stages. This applies not only to skylight and sunlight but to other measures of building performance, such as noise control, thermal efficiency and structural efficiency.

Climate, environment and structure

The analogy of the natural

The climate of a place can be deduced from its ecology – the plants and animals that exist there, how they are distributed and how they interact. The traditional architecture of a place, often the outcome of many generations of trial and error, can also reflect its climatic environment.

A frequently used metaphor is that vernacular buildings 'evolve', which implies that the long-term development of building types is analogous to the sequence of variation and selection by which a natural species optimises its adaptation. This may or may not be valid; but when seeking the optimum

form for a building, comparison with nature is helpful because the same physical laws apply. The buildings in Figure 4.1 seem to be huddling together, facing inward, just as a group of people might do, caught outside in a blizzard. Heat loss is minimised by reducing the exposed surface area. Seaside hotels have facades spread out so that as many windows as possible face sun and sea, in the way the tree canopy in Figure 4.2 presents the leaves with the maximum exposure to sun and sky for photosynthesis; or as a sunbather lies on the beach, spread out so as much skin area as possible faces the sun. And just as the use of suncream is a compromise between staying in the shade and the risk of skin cancer, the coatings on high-technology glazing used in city office buildings are filters designed to transmit selectively from the spectrum of radiation.

The way that a single plant species modifies its shape in response to the local microclimate, to make the best possible use of sunlight, wind and water, is a guide to sustainable building design. But simply to mimic natural forms is usually wrong, because there are other physical laws which must be obeyed. For example, optimum form is related also to scale: the proportions of a structure depend on its absolute size – a small mammal is not the same shape as an elephant, nor is a garden plant the same shape as a mature tree. It is false reasoning to reproduce a natural form at a scale much larger or smaller than the original, or in quite different materials, with the expectation of achieving the optimum design. What natural forms and vernacular buildings do is indicate what is important.

4.1

Barns and winter shelters above Zermatt, Switzerland. By clustering together, the buildings give mutual shelter and minimise heat loss.

4.2

A tree canopy grows into a form that optimises the total exposure to light for photosynthesis.
King's Park, Perth, Australia

Cave, umbrella and greenhouse

Deep underground, the temperature is almost constant, day and night, summer and winter – desirable characteristics of buildings in a low-latitude desert, where burning sunshine and hot wind alternate with night-time cold. By contrast, in a warm humid climate, the need is just for an umbrella: it blocks heavy rain and direct sun, but allows the breeze to cool you. In a greenhouse, the rain and the breeze are blocked but sunlight can enter. On a clear night, the temperature is almost as low inside as out, but on a sunny day, the inside air temperature can be 20 degrees higher than outside. A greenhouse amplifies the daily temperature range.

Every building behaves thermally like some mixture of a cave, an umbrella and a greenhouse; Figures 4.3–4.5 are examples where one or other of these types dominates. A heavy masonry building is cave-like: it warms up and cools down slowly, with a lag between the time of the maximum temperature outside and the time of the inside maximum. The thicker the walls, the longer the delay and the smaller the internal temperature variation. Except, that is, in rooms that have large windows facing the sun. Then there is the heat-trapping greenhouse effect, and just a few minutes of sunshine can lift the air temperature (though not the deep fabric temperature) by several degrees.

The cave, the umbrella and the greenhouse are thermal models, but each implies an internal environment that differs in other ways: sound, air movement, light. Each, too, is associated with different structural principles and different materials: for example, buildings with thick masonry walls and a heavy roof act like caves, while lightweight framed structures with large windows have the characteristics of a greenhouse.

Daylighting cannot be considered in isolation. Design decisions on structural form and materials affect the form and layout of windows, and vice versa; and daylighting is related to other aspects of environmental performance: openings that are the best for daylight and view might be unsatisfactory acoustically or the cause of thermal discomfort. The optimum design is one in which the total of all measures of building performance is at its best; it is not necessarily the optimum design for daylighting, or any other individual requirement.

A great building gives something more on each revisit. It tells you of the people who built it, and of those who lived in it – their resources, their interests, what they held precious; it tells you, too, of its environment, the climate and the earth; and it tells of all that has happened to the place since the building was begun. Every part has meaning, and it gives its story at many scales, from the distant outline in the landscape to the close view of its materials and crafting.

So a concern that the building should be natural, and therefore that daylighting should influence its location, its basic form and every successive stage of design, is not just because this is necessary if the best possible lighting is to be achieved; nor just because this is required for high

4.3

Buildings with heavy masonry walls have cave-like thermal properties: cooler than outside during the day, warmer than outside at night. The diurnal temperature swing is lessened.

Isfahan, Iran, and Derbyshire, UK

4.4
If the air temperature is tolerable, only a roof is needed.
Bowali Visitor Centre, Kakadu, Australia, and Penzance, UK

4.5
Ordinary glass transmits the visible part of the solar spectrum and some infrared, but is opaque to the longer-wavelength radiant heat emitted by surfaces in a warm room. Large windows cause rapid temperature rise when in sunlight.
Glasshouse at Cragside, Northumberland, UK

sustainability; but because it adds to the subtlety and richness of the architecture.

Sunlight 1: shading and shape

What shape of building would minimise the total annual loss of sunlight on the ground from shadows cast by the building? A low and compact form? A very thin tall tower? A building with a courtyard?

On a winter morning in the Northern Hemisphere, even a low building throws a long shadow toward the north-west; shadows of trees can be hundreds of metres long. In the landscape, the shape of the ground is revealed by patterns of light and shade, its texture of hummocks and ditches emphasised by glancing illumination just as a sharply angled spotlight enhances the surface qualities of objects on display. The form of the ground is seen best of all when there is snow lying, as in Figure 4.6.

The diagrams in Figure 4.7 illustrate the shadows cast by a perfect cube on a flat surface by the sun, at latitude 50°. Note the shadow length in relation to the building height, which is equal to the distance between adjacent concentric circles. The shadows are drawn at 2-hourly intervals for mid-winter, mid-summer and the equinox in spring and autumn.

In December, the morning sun casts a long shadow towards north-west; it shortens at mid-day and lengthens again in the afternoon. The shaded area sweeps an angle of

4.6
Winter shadows. When the sun
is low in the sky, the length of a
shadow is much greater than the
height of the object that casts
the shadow.
Derbyshire, UK

about 90°. At the equinox, the sun's path from due east to due west throws a 180° sweep of shadow. On Midsummer's Day, the shadow from early morning sun falls south-west and the evening sun gives shadows to the south-east, an arc of shading of about 270°.

Figure 4.8, by contrast, shows the total length of time that sunlight falls on the ground. The contours mark relative exposure to the sun. Although shadows at low solar elevations are very long, they move quickly and obscure little of the annual sunlight from a distant point. The area with significant reduction of total annual sunshine is confined to a radius of about twice the building's height, measured from its centre of the plan, in this example of a cubic block.

If a calculation is made of the annual luminous energy received by the ground, instead of the duration of shading, the contours shrink inwards further, the maximum extent of the 90% line being about 1.8 times the height of the building. Ground illuminance is small at low solar elevations because the atmospheric attenuation of sunlight is greater and the

angle of incidence is large. A summation of lux-hours tends, therefore, to diminish the importance of long shadows.

A further emphasis on the relative importance of shadows at high solar elevations is noted when cloudiness is taken into account. To concentrate on the effects of geometry, the graphs here take the probability of sunlight on the ground to be equal across all solar elevations. Usually, though, the probability of sunshine is less when the sun is low; calculations on this basis result in a further small shrinking of the contours towards the centre of the plan.

Minimum total shadow area

Since the longest shadows occur when the sun is low in the sky, the way to minimise ground shading is to shape a building so that it projects as small an area as possible in the directions of sunrise and sunset. This means that if the building is rectangular in plan and section, the optimum form is a squat rectangle with the longer sides facing north and south.

North

Mid-winter

Equinox

Mid-summer

North

90%

70%

90%

1
2
3
4
5

4.8

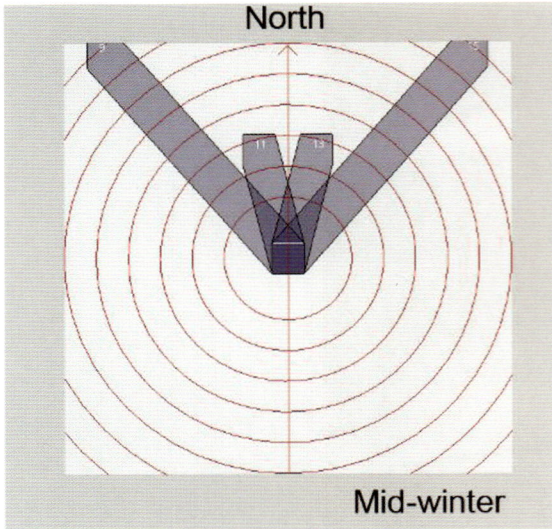

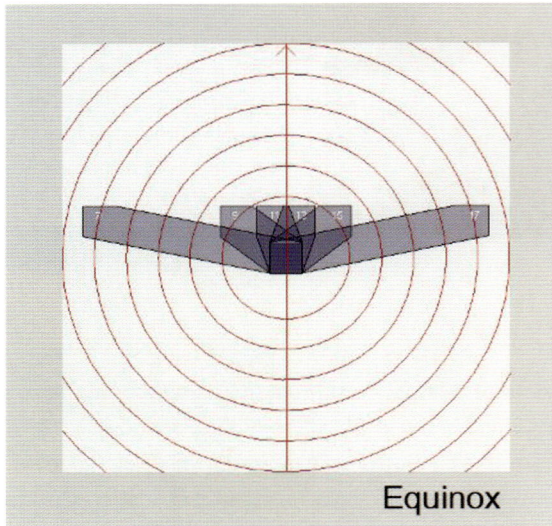

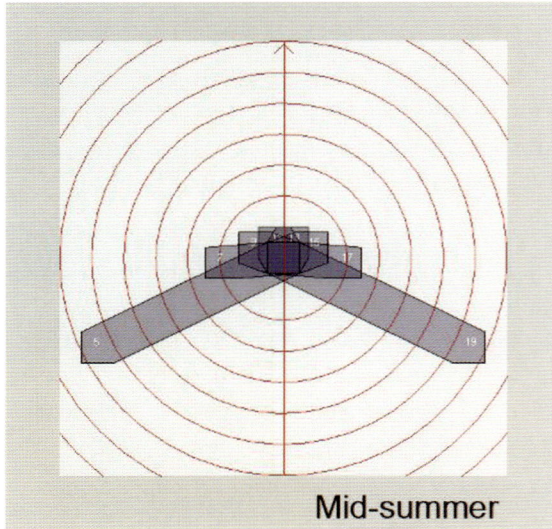

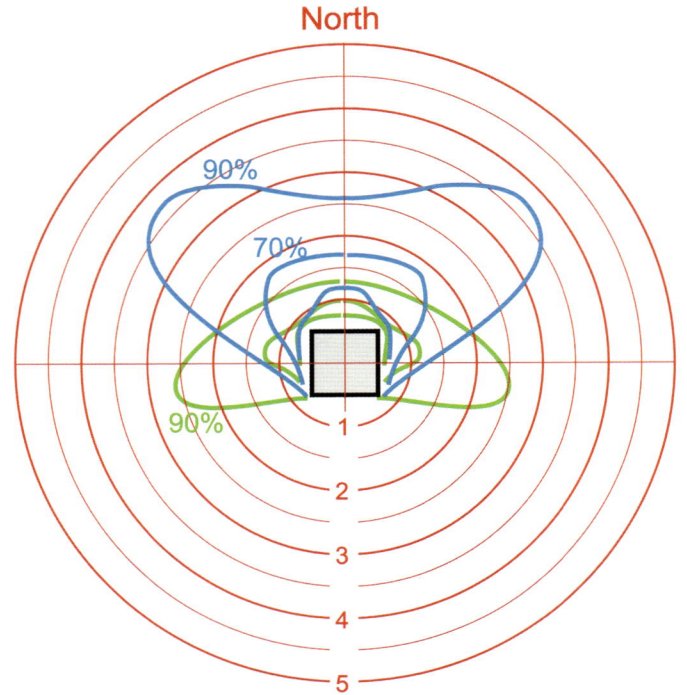

Hours of sunlight on ground. 50° N: blue, winter (autumn equinox to spring equinox); green, summer (spring to autumn). The contours give percentages of possible sunlight hours. The building is a cube and the concentric rings give distance from the centre of the building as a multiple of the height of the cube.

4.7

Shadows at 2-hour intervals through the day in mid-winter, spring and autumn equinox, and mid-summer at 50° latitude. The building is represented by a cube.

The upper graph in Figure 4.9 illustrates how the mean annual ground shadow area varies with plan ratio and height. The building is a rectangular block; the curves show the effect of changing the proportions while maintaining a constant volume. At 50° latitude, the average area of shaded ground is lowest when w/l is about 0.6, with the longer sides facing north and south. The curves are broad 'U' shapes, which implies that moderate deviation from the optimum plan ratio does not incur a significantly large increase in annual shading.

The shadow area is proportional to the square root of the building's height.

The lower graph shows that the proportions of the optimum rectangle depend on latitude. Near the Equator, the azimuth of sunrise and sunset is close to east and west throughout the year and the optimum w/l proportion is about 0.3. With increasing latitude, there is a greater difference between summer and winter directions of sunrise and sunset, a greater range of azimuth angles. The optimum plan fraction becomes greater, the more nearly square in plan is the building.

In the UK, the concept of 'probable sunlight hours' is used in town planning practice when assessing the likely impact of a proposed building on its surroundings. Worksheets 9 and 10 describe how this is done.

Sunlight 2: sunshades and solar collectors

The ideal sunshade obscures the sun and nothing else. Nearest to achieving this is a continuously moving device that tracks the sun. A disc sweeps across the sky during the day, casting a shadow on the area it is protecting. The disc follows the solar spiral, each daily path shifted slightly in altitude. Such a device is quite practicable for shielding a photocell in a meteorological station, but is usually impracticable for shielding a window in a building. Next best is a shading device that is static in relation to the time of day but is moved daily in response to the changing solar declination. This usually takes the form of a circular band that obscures the current daily sunpath – like the shade ring around the photocell in Figure 4.11. The ring is orientated so that the highest point is due south from the photocell (or due north in the Southern Hemisphere); its angle with the vertical is equal to the latitude of the site. When the centre of the ring lies on

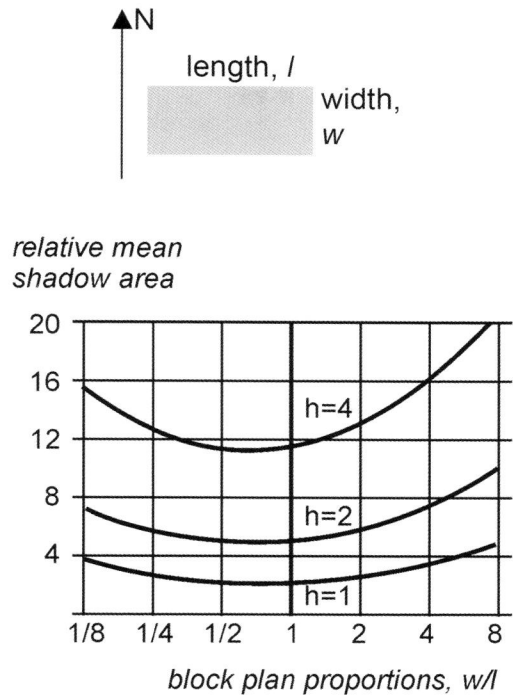

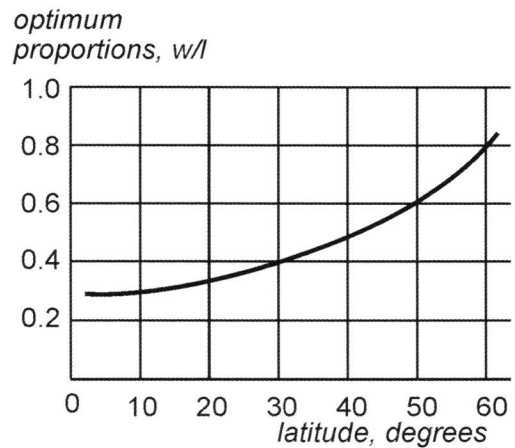

4.9

Proportions of a rectangular building for minimum ground shading. Upper graph: variation of shadow area with plan proportions at latitude 50° N. Lower graph: variation of optimum proportion with latitude.

4.10
A sun shade obscures the
solar spiral from the protected
opening.

the photocell, the equinox sunpath is covered. The upper and lower boundaries, for the mid-summer and mid-winter sunpath, are given by the shade ring positions that cover the noon sun 23.5° above and below the equinox position.

If a shading device must be static, the most efficient shape is a band that obscures exactly the solar spiral from every point to be shaded. It has been called the 'solar bracelet'. In Figure 4.12, the red rings that show the upper and lower limits of the adjustable shade ring also define the width of the solar bracelet that would shield the photocell. When the area to be shaded is larger in relation to the diameter of the ring, the bracelet (which need not be cylindrical in form) must be broader to screen every part of the protected area.

The higher the sun in the sky, the more easy it is to screen vertical windows from direct sunlight. In the tropics, north and south-facing façades are efficiently protected from the mid-day sun by horizontal shades such as overhanging eaves and projecting balconies. The sun falls at only a glancing incidence on these façades, so any small projection casts a long shadow.

Flat and low-pitched roofs, however, are perpendicular, or nearly so, to the high-elevation solar beam; and façades facing east and west face the sun directly at the beginning and end of the day. If sunlight must be excluded, these windows have to be covered completely: adjustable shading devices, such as louvres or blinds, are therefore needed if daylighting is to be maintained at other times. These can be a significant element in the architectural design of the building, as in Figure 4.13.

The importance of building orientation is greatest in the tropics. As latitude increases, with sites further and further from the Equator, the solar elevation at mid-day becomes correspondingly less: at 50° latitude, the maximum solar elevation is about 16°. The azimuth range of sunrise and sunset increases from the Equator to the Arctic (and Antarctic) Circles, so that at 66.5° latitude there is one day of the year when the sun is just visible on the southern horizon at mid-day and one day when the sun just dips below the northern horizon at midnight.

If the aim is to collect solar radiation rather than to exclude it, the receiving surface should face the solar spiral.

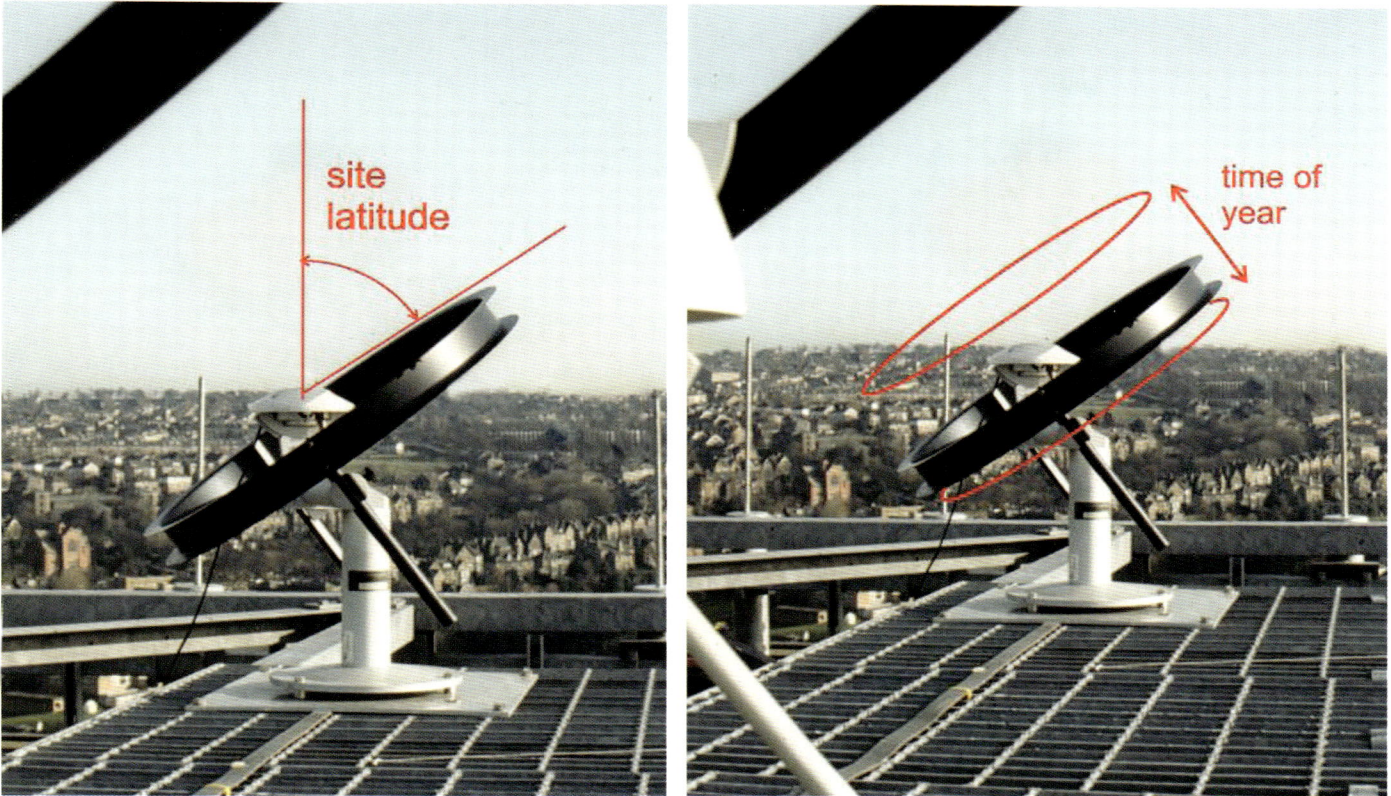

4.11

A shade ring screens the photocell from direct sunlight. It is orientated north–south and the ring is tilted by the latitude of the site. It is adjusted daily in response to the changing solar elevation through the year.

Many flower heads move to do this, as in Figure 4.15; so can solar collectors in advanced light-pipe systems, as shown in Chapter 9, Figure 9.10.

If a solar collector must be static, the optimum orientation and tile depends on two factors. Firstly, the intensity of the sun's beam depends on the length of its path through the earth's atmosphere. The longer the path, the more the beam is attenuated. Secondly, irradiance (the amount of radiation per square metre) is proportional to the cosine of the angle of incidence – Lambert's law again.

To maximise the energy received during the day, a static solar collector should face due south in the Northern Hemisphere and due north in the Southern Hemisphere.

Figure 4.14 shows growing beds in a historical garden designed to achieve early ripening of crops. In general, the optimum tilt of a collecting surface depends on the period for which energy gain is maximised: at a first approximation, the slope should be such that the surface is perpendicular to

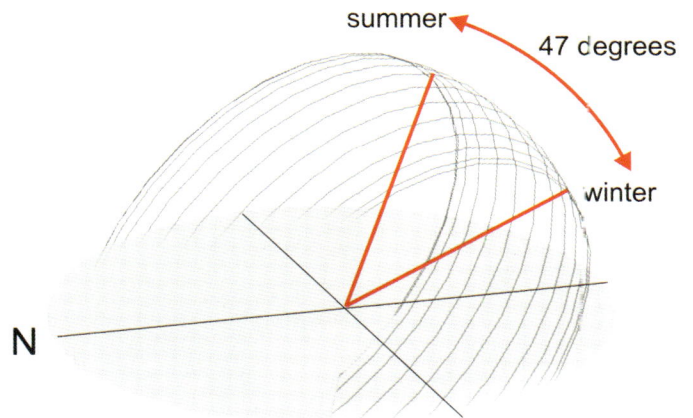

4.12

The solar spiral extends about 23.5° above and below the equinox sunpath.

4.13
As the solar beam approaches perpendicular incidence, a fixed solar shade must obscure increasingly more sky. To maintain daylighting, moveable louvres are better.
The Earth Centre, Rotherham UK

the average elevation of the noon sun during the period. If, therefore, the aim is to absorb the maximum solar energy during the winter months, a panel collector should be tilted though a zenith angle equal to the latitude plus about 13°. More accurate calculations take into account the variation of solar intensity with elevation and the angle of incidence throughout the day. Figure 4.16 gives the optimum slope for the 21st day of each month. It shows that if a solar panel can be adjusted in slope through the year, the energy gained is significantly greater than that from a fixed panel.

It is interesting to note that near the Equator, the optimum angle in mid-summer is more than 90° – the collector tilts slightly toward the north (in the Northern Hemisphere). This increases the energy received during the morning and afternoon.

Sunlight 3: using reflected sunlight to illuminate rooms

The beam of direct sunlight is too intense and too directional for normal task lighting. A white surface in strong sunlight is dazzlingly bright, and shadows are hard-edged and black. The aim in designing a room to be lit with sunlight is to create a strong field of interreflected light while avoiding excessive heat gain and glare. Overheating is minimised by excluding the direct beam from the room through the choice of orientation and the use of external shades; glare is prevented by ensuring that the beam does not fall on visual task areas in the room and by avoiding a view onto very bright external surfaces.

4.14
Sloping beds in a nineteenth-century walled garden, designed for early ripening of crops.
Trengwainton Garden, Cornwall, UK

4.15
This flower head increases its attractiveness to insects by turning towards the sun. The brightness in deep recesses is maximised and the solar warming strengthens the scent.

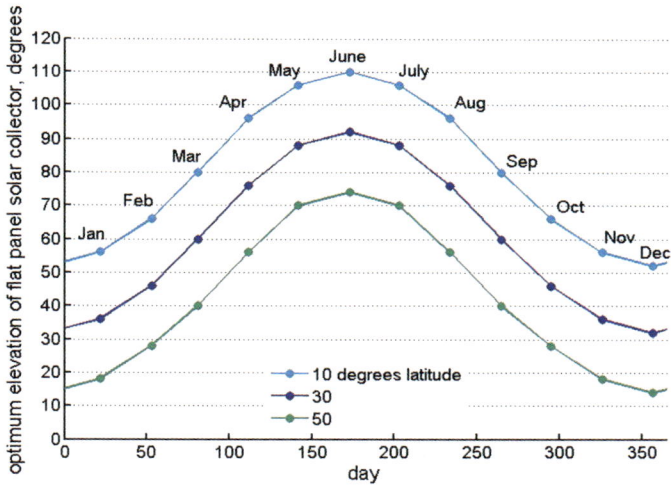

4.16
The optimum tilt for a flat solar collector to maximise the energy received on a particular day. The dots on the curve represent the 21st day of each month. The computed values take into account the angle of incidence through the day and the intensity of the solar beam, but not differences in cloudiness through the day.

Most urban buildings in warm sunny climates show little attempt to use sunlight for interior lighting. This makes thermal control easier, especially if the building is air-conditioned: windows can be heavily shaded or use low-transmittance glazing, and electric lighting can provide all the illumination needed. There is some subjective justification for this: a cool, almost windowless, enclosure can seem attractive when the external climate is harshly hot, although the same room in a cool climate might be judged artificial or gloomy. It is not sustainable architecture, though, and such a design strategy leads to buildings that give no indication of the climate and culture in which they stand.

A sophisticated vernacular architecture exists in many countries with climates dominated by clear skies and strong sunshine. This includes buildings which are dark inside, having small pierced openings in thick heavy walls: it is the basic way to provide shelter in a place where there is a great diurnal temperature swing, very hot days and cold nights. But where a classical architectural culture has developed, such as in the great cities of Iran, there can be found a design approach that combined building and garden, view and interior daylight and had sophisticated natural cooling and ventilation.

The daylighting strategy in this approach can be summarised by three aims:

1 Create a diffuse field of light outdoors

Plants do this best. Trees and other foliage outside the window provide shade from the direct beam, they create a complex three-dimensional field of light, and they are a chosen subject of view.

The optimum density of foliage depends on the climate: if tree crowns are dark-coloured and dense, too little light reaches lower surfaces; if the foliage is sparse, little light is scattered. In general, the nearer the site is to the Equator, the denser can be the crown. Deciduous trees are better than conifers, because their foliage is usually lighter in colour, and they have a special advantage if different degrees of shading are required in winter and summer. Windows should look into foliage, not totally beneath it, so the trees should be not much higher than the building. Figure 4.18 shows a recently planted courtyard garden in Yazd, Iran; the trees are beginning to transform a strong downward beam into a complex, low-brightness pattern that windows will overlook.

2 Reflect light upwards onto the ceiling of rooms

The effect of upwardly reflected sunlight can be seen in Figure 4.19. The bright sheen within two of the arches is due to the patch of sunlight visible through the openings. Sunlit ground can be much brighter than the sky: at a solar elevation of 60°, the luminance of a patch of light-coloured ground, reflectance 0.4, in full sunlight might be 12 kcd/m². The mean luminance of a blue sky is about 5 kcd/m². These are typical values: they depend on the turbidity of the atmosphere, and sky luminance varies significantly with the direction of view.

A bright surface beneath a window – the ground, a flat roof, a light-shelf or a balcony – can act as a source of light for

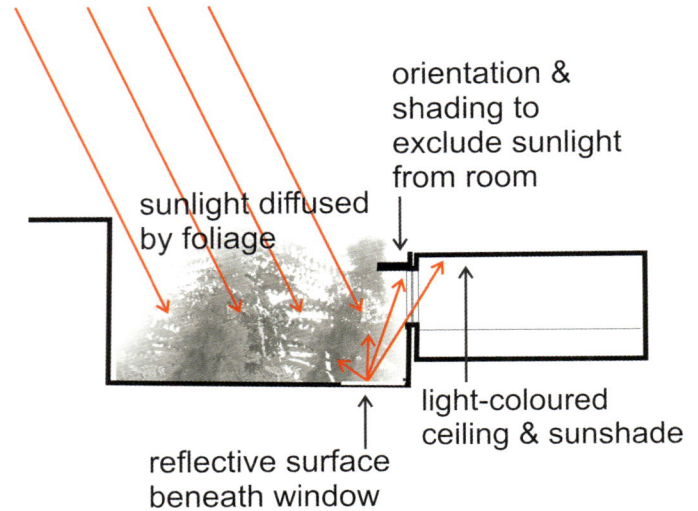

4.17
Strategy for using reflected sunlight as interior illumination.

4.18
Foliage creating a low-brightness field of diffuse light.
Yazd, Iran

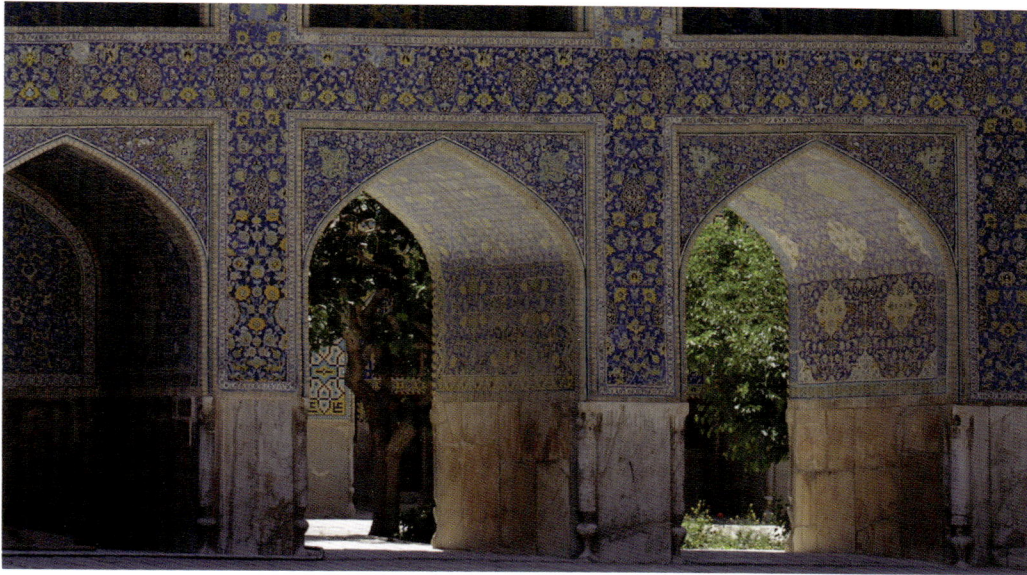

4.19

Ground-reflected sunlight visible on the soffits of the arches. Compare this image with the upper picture in Figure 4.3.

The Imam Mosque, Isfahan, Iran

a room. Figure 4.20 illustrates the contribution it can give. The curves give illuminance on the horizontal working plane at desk height for various depths of room and different amounts of glazing in the window wall. The vertical axis shows the desktop working plane illuminance when outside the illuminance in the patch of sunlight is 50 klx. Light that comes into the room from other parts of the sky or after reflection by foliage or other outside surfaces is not included.

The values shown in the graph are calculated based on the room shown in Figure 4.21. It is assumed that there is a patch of sunlight beneath the windows, extending to an angle 30° from the wall. The ground there is of light-coloured stone, reflectance 0.4. The ceiling is white and the interior as a whole has an average reflectance of 0.5. The window transmits 50% of the light incident on it from below.

The reference value of 50 klx is typically the illuminance on the ground from direct sunlight at 10.30am on a clear sunny day in Northern Europe, around latitude 50°. Nearer the Equator, at latitude 30°, there is 50 klx or more between 9am and 3pm during all the summer months on sunny days, mid-March to mid-September; in the dry tropics, a value of 50 klx from direct sunshine is exceeded between 9am and 3pm for most of the year.

With a single window wall, a deep room does not collect enough reflected sunshine to maintain a significant working

plane illuminance. Design strategies in this case include the use of windows in more than one side. Differing orientations and external obstructions imply that the optimum window form is not the same in the different elevations of a building.

In a deep room with a high ceiling, a series of windows with light shelves can be an element of the roof structure, as in Figure 4.22. Again, the exact shape depends on orientation and latitude: shading devices should allow the

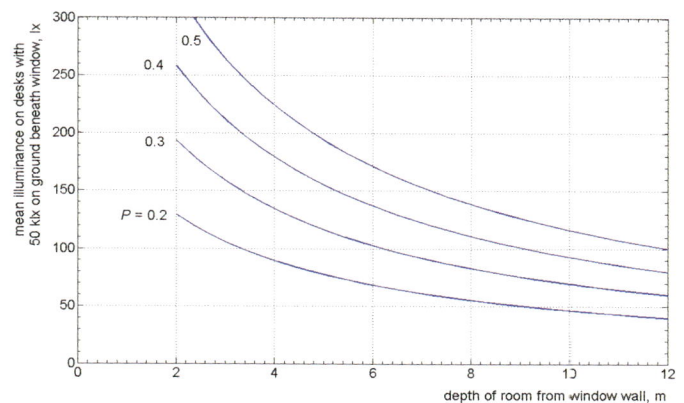

4.20

Mean working plane illuminance from reflected sunlight, calculated for the room shown in Figure 4.21. The value P is the fraction of the window wall that is glazed, seen from inside.

direct beam to fall on each light-shelf but not enter the window opening.

An alternative to the light-shelf is the use of a window system that is exposed to sunlight but redirects light towards the ceiling. This may employ external components (such as horizontal louvres), internal reflectors (Venetian blinds) or the glazing material itself (laser-cut acrylic sheets). Heat gain must be checked, especially in the latter two cases; so must the requirement of a view out.

3 Avoid bright surfaces near the horizontal line of view

When the sun is 70° or more above the horizon, its beam falls at only a glancing angle on vertical surfaces, so these are not illuminated strongly. At lower solar elevations, the brightness of sunlit walls can be unacceptably glaring if in the field of view of a person concentrating on a visual task. So can a window with glazing that diffuses a beam of light instead of transmitting it regularly or redirecting it away from users' view-lines.

In Figure 4.23, the window faces the afternoon sun, which shines into the room. Thermally, this is desirable in winter but not in summer, but the room is large in comparison with the window area, so the effect is mainly local to the window. Visually, the patterned glazing controls the brightness: at seated eye level, it permits a view into a garden, but, looking in the direction of the sky, the coloured panes reduce the luminance. The glass does not significantly diffuse the solar beam, so coloured patterns are cast on the wall. If the glass

did transmit light diffusely rather then regularly, the window luminance would be much higher.

Planning

The three aims in this strategy are interlinked in a balancing of light penetration against glare. Reflected light from nearby ground falls mainly on the area of ceiling closest to the window; this tends to give a noticeable illuminance gradient down the working plane. Penetration of light into the room increases as the area of sunlit ground is increased. For example, if the angle of bright surface below the window (as in Figure 4.21) is raised from 30° to 60°, the mean working plane illuminance is increased by a factor of more than three; but for most rooms this would be accompanied by a sense of harsh glare from the large area of brightly sunlit ground. As the extent of sunlit surrounding surfaces gets larger, the illuminance on the outside face of a window increases, and therefore (i) the window can be smaller for a given interior illuminance and (ii) considerations of glare lead to smaller openings. Traditional buildings in warm dry climates take one or other of the extremes: where there can be trees and gardens, the windows are large; where the site is bare and dry, windows reduce to pierced openings in thick walls.

The use of sunlight for interior lighting depends crucially on the fundamental form and orientation of a building. It depends, too, on more than mere illuminance calculations – view, glare, interior daylight and balancing electric lighting must be considered together. Perhaps that is why this form of daylighting is employed so little – why, in warm climates even more than in temperate zones, the windows of urban commercial buildings are closed to natural light; and despite

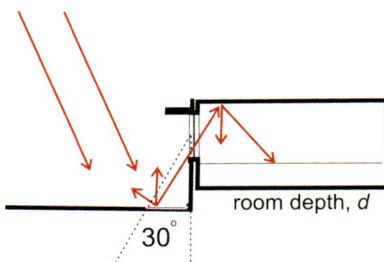

4.21
The room is 6 m wide and 3 m high, with mean reflectance 0.5 and window transmittance 0.5; ground reflectance is 0.4. The patch of sunlight extends to an angle of 30° from the window and the illuminance there is 50 klx.

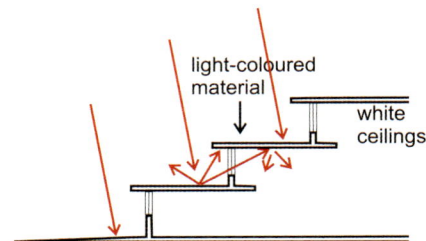

4.22
Stacked light-shelves.

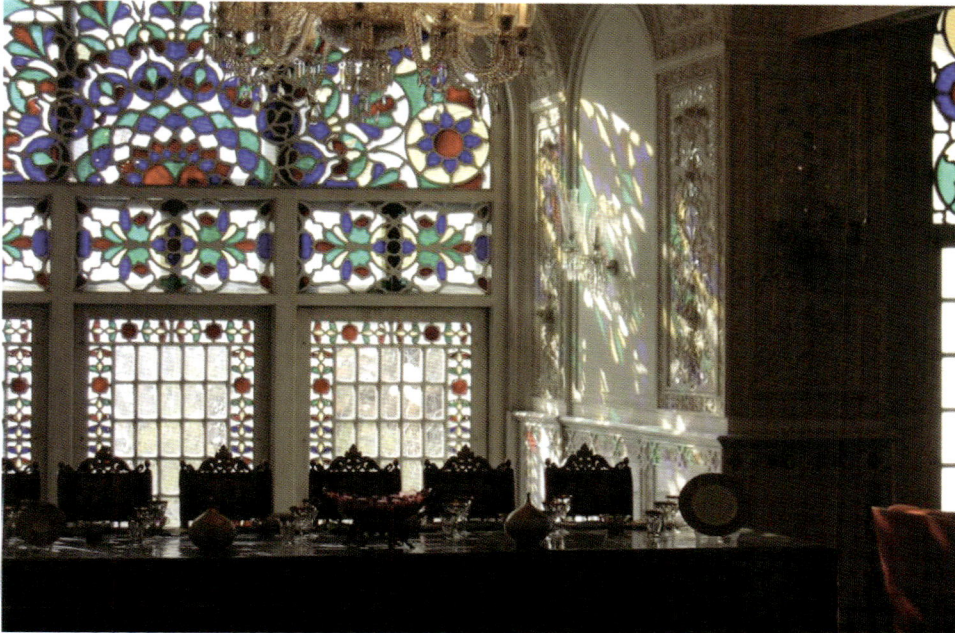

4.23
Window in the Green Palace, Tehran, Iran.

the availability of adequate daylight throughout the working year, electric lighting is used totally.

Light from the diffuse sky

This section is about buildings in cloudy climates where daylight is to be the sole source of illumination. The use of daylight and electric lighting together is covered in the next section.

If a room such as a classroom or office is to rely solely on light from windows, there are two basic requirements:

1   Every point in the room that needs strong daylighting must have a clear view of the sky.
2   The total area of windows must be sufficiently large and the reflectance of surfaces sufficiently high for there to be a significant amount of interreflected light in the room.

Examining these in more detail:

The no-sky line

Any part of the interior that has no view of the sky must be lit only by reflection. If this is a workplace, the level of reflected light will often seem unsatisfactorily low for reading and writing, and the room may seem harsh or gloomy, with a large brightness contrast between inside and outside.

The 'no-sky line' on a room surface is the boundary between the area that can receive direct skylight and that which is masked from the sky. It is a useful indicator of unsatisfactory daylight in rooms, and especially convenient in development control to assess whether the reduction of daylight by a proposed new building is likely to have a significant effect on rooms in existing buildings.

Figure 4.24 shows in principle how the no-sky line can be plotted. In the simple case of an unvarying external skyline,

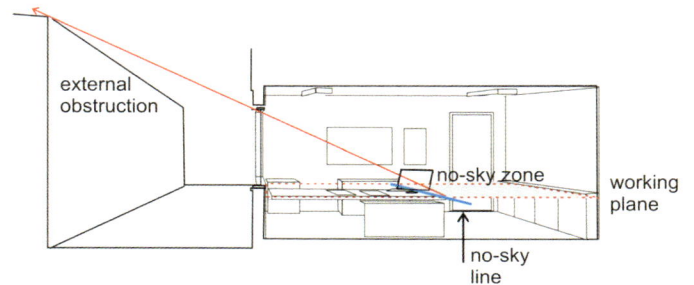

4.24
The no-sky line indicates which parts of a room receive only reflected daylight.

the no-sky line is a straight line parallel with the window wall. For a room with several windows looking out onto different external obstructions, it is necessary to work in three dimensions, testing whether oblique views of the sky exist. This is easy when evaluating an existing building on site, but in the office, working from drawings, it can be time-consuming and best done by computer.

Limit of strong daylight

In a side-lit room, the amount of daylight falling on desktops drops sharply with increasing distance from the windows. In an office or a school classroom, there is a point where daylight seems inadequate for the visual tasks: it is not necessarily a matter of illuminance: on a bright day, this might be easily adequate. It is that the room looks gloomy; there is harsh contrast between inside and outside. If there is electric lighting, users will tend to switch it on. This point of insufficient daylight usually occurs where the daylight factor on the desks drops below 2%. The research evidence supporting this is incomplete, but the rule has been in use for half a century, and it, or an equivalent measure, is to be found in codes and standards in many countries. In a cloudy climate, the average illuminance from the sky alone is about 25,000 lx when the solar elevation is 30°. The indoor illuminance would then be 500 lx, a commonly used value for the desk illuminance required in offices.

This leads to the following rules of thumb:

- In a room with one window wall, the area of strong daylight at desk top level extends into the room a distance 2d, where d is the height of the window above the desktop.
- A room with windows in two opposite walls has adequate daylight across the room when the depth is not more than 5d.

These are illustrated in Figure 4.25 and they apply where (i) external obstructions are not large – not higher than about 25° above the horizon, (ii) the windows have clear glazing, and (iii) the upper room surfaces are light-coloured. Broadly, they indicate the working plane area where the daylight factor at a point is at least 2%. For a single window, the distance 2*d* applies to a line through the centre of the window opening; if

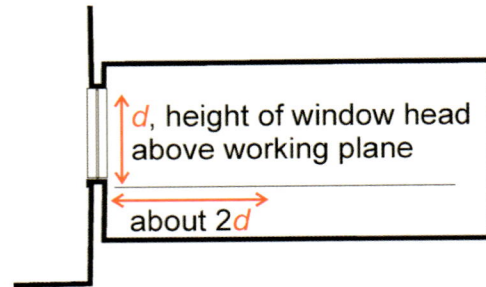

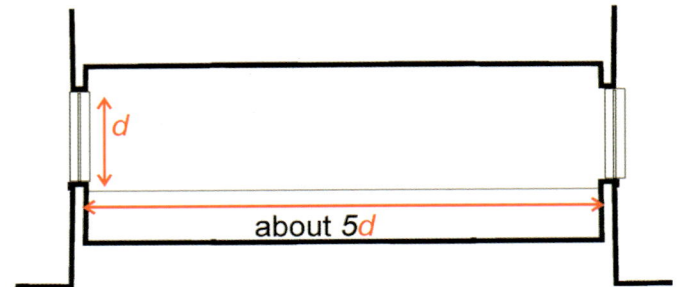

4.25
Rules of thumb for the extent of strong daylight from side windows.

windows fill more than one-third of the window wall area, as in Figure 4.20, the distance can be taken to apply to the full width of the window wall.

Two very different buildings – a village school in Figure 4.26 and the Divinity Schools of Oxford University in Figure 4.27 – show what such a daylight distribution looks like. Both have windows in opposite walls, and both were conceived as totally daylight buildings. In the Divinity Schools, the windows are higher than required by the rule of thumb, but this only partly compensates for light loss caused by mullions and glazing bars, and the low internal surface reflectances. In both cases, there are external obstructions. The two cases illustrate the minimum provision of daylight that we would now expect where the users may be engaged for periods of an hour or more on desk-based tasks. It is likely that, given this daylight level in an urban office building, the users would switch on the electric lighting.

To provide full daylighting in a medium-sized or large workplace, ceilings must be high and the required window area must be a substantial proportion of the façade area.

4.26
Village school in Zhejiang Province, China.

So daylight is not free: in both initial and lifetime costs, and especially in the use of energy for thermal control, the cost of a daylit room is greater than that of a less tall room with smaller windows, where electric lighting provides some of the required illumination.

Roof lights and other forms of window

The higher the window in a room, the greater the resulting illuminance on horizontal surfaces such as desktops. There are two reasons for this: the sky tends to be brighter at the zenith than just above the horizon, and the light falls more nearly perpendicular on horizontal surfaces in the room. Considering only desktop (or horizontal working plane) lighting, the required area of horizontal roof lights is about half the area of side windows needed to provide the same mean illuminance. But there is a disadvantage: much less light falls on walls and other vertical surfaces, so the room looks darker. To increase the amount of interreflected light, the floor and ceiling should be as high in reflectance as possible, but in heavily furnished rooms, such as offices, the combined reflectance of working plane and floor tends to be low. For this reason, recommended average daylight factors for rooms with roof lights are usually higher – up to double – the values recommended for side-lit rooms.

Whatever the opening, the same rule applies: to have a high level of daylight illuminance, a significant angle of sky must be visible. An easy test of the daylight potential of a building that is complex in section is to draw the no-sky lines for each window, then use these to estimate the amount of sky visible at key points. Figure 4.28 is an example: the shaded areas show where relatively low levels of daylight will be experienced.

Electric lighting during daytime

Much guidance on sustainable design argues for greater use of daylight but barely covers the crucial element of lighting control. Energy savings are proportional to the reduction in the use of electric lighting, not to the amount of daylight in a room. This may seem obvious, but it needs to be emphasised because if there is to be any saving of power, there must be a means of adjusting electric lighting in

4.27
The Divinity Schools, Oxford.

We have already noted that daylight is not free. Large windows and high ceilings increase initial costs; maintenance and additional heating and cooling increase running costs. Whether measured in the use of natural resources, or energy use, or as money, the lifetime costs of providing daylight are significant.

If several alternative designs are made for a building, ranging from full daylighting to windows that provide only a minimum view, and the lifetime costs are estimated for each of these, it is most commonly found that the relationship between cost and daylight provision tends to be a shallow U-shaped graph: costs tend to be higher with very large or very small windows, and there is a fairly flat intermediate region that represents minimum costs. When the construction and environmental costs associated with windows are balanced against the total costs of lamps and luminaires, the use of daylight and electric lighting together tends to be the most sustainable solution for daytime lighting. Under present-day costs, the optimum solution for all but the smallest interiors is usually a scheme using both types of source, where electric lighting and windows are planned and operated so that they complement each other.

Electric lighting and daylighting are components of a single scheme, not independent items to be designed by different people at different stages. They are complementary, because they have different characteristics as illuminants: Table 4.1 makes a comparison.

response to the changing daylight in a room. This may be manual control by the occupants – switching lights on and off, raising and lowering blinds – or it may be any of a range of mechanical and electronic systems, including central automatic management of all the building's environmental equipment.

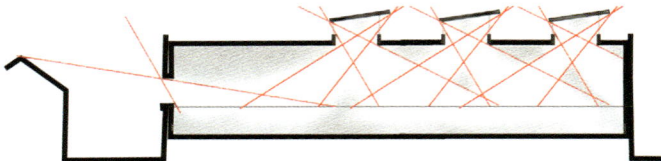

4.28
By sketching no-sky lines in plan or section, the spacing of rooflights can be checked.

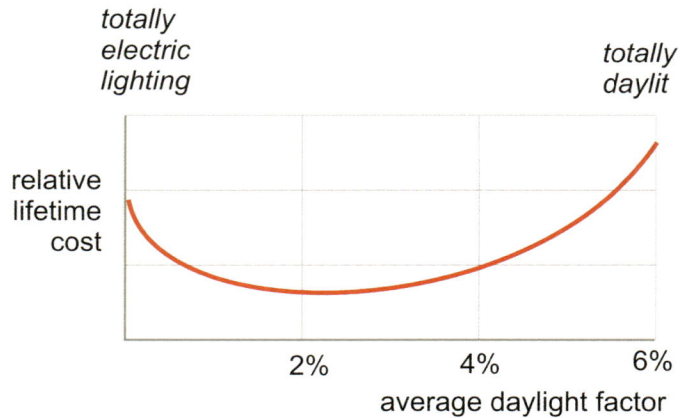

4.29
Typical curve showing the effect on lifetime costs of the balance between daylight and electric lighting.

Table 4.1: Characteristics of skylight and electric light as task illuminant

	Skylight (diffuse daylight)	Electric light
Source size and beam form	Windows act as large sources, giving a broad soft-edged directional beam. With side windows, there is a predominantly horizontal flow of light	Electric lamps and luminaires are available in a vast range of sizes and types. They can give pencil-like beams or an output that is, directionally, almost uniform; they can act as points of light, or linear sources, or broad luminous areas
Control	Usually only limited control with blinds and louvres	Optical control depends on source size: the smaller the lamp, the easier the optical control of the output
Colour	Varying colour appearance, excellent colour rendering	Depends on source. Wide choice of colour appearance and colour rendering

Electric lighting has three specific roles in an integrated, well-controlled lighting scheme:

1 *Establish place and character*. The daylight, the electric lighting and the surface finishes must be consistent with the architectural design of the room as a whole. They may of course play a major part in establishing the nature of the place.

2 *Maintain task illuminance*. Electric lighting must provide additional illuminance in the early morning and late afternoon, and where it is inadequate at other times in the parts of a room distant from a window. But good task lighting design goes beyond mere supplementing of illuminance. It uses the differing characteristics of the sources to best enhance the critical features of the tasks: From Table 4.1, we can conclude that in a workspace with a window to its side, the illumination for many tasks can be excellent, and it is a situation frequently preferred by users; it is not easy to achieve that broad flow of light with conventional electric lighting. But the versatility given by the vast range of lamps and luminaires available means that electric lighting can be designed very precisely to suit the requirements of particular tasks.

3 *Minimise excessive contrast within the room*. When window areas are less than those needed for full daylighting, the brightness of room surfaces can be low in comparison with the view to the outside, and the rear of the room can appear dark and gloomy compared with the area near the window. Electric lighting must therefore illuminate more than the tasks: it must brighten the walls and ceiling where these receive little daylight, and, if the wall areas surrounding windows receive little direct or reflected daylight, these too should have supplementary electric lighting. But the aim is not to achieve uniformity. Experiments in which subjects assessed luminance

patterns in office-like rooms suggest that (a) the brightness of the major vertical surfaces in a room should have diversity and (b) their mean brightness should be equivalent to an illuminance at least one-third of the horizontal illuminance at desktop level (assuming a mean wall reflectance of 0 5). This can be expressed in another way: maintain as far as possible the spatial variation of daylight in the room, using supplementary electric lighting to reduce harsh contrasts.

People in temperate regions generally prefer a room with a daylight appearance to one that seems to be entirely artificially lit. (This may well be true also in other climates, but we have insufficient evidence to generalise.) A naturally lit appearance does not, however, depend on the luminous energy on the room being predominantly daylight. A daylight appearance can be maintained even though a majority of the task lighting is electric. What is important is that both the spatial and the temporal variation of daylight should be evident. That is:

1 The pattern of brightness on room surfaces should be consistent with the brightness distribution due to the windows; and

2 The variation of daylight with time of day and with weather should be apparent.

To meet this requirement – to ensure that the daylight is not swamped by a flood of electric lighting – the quantity of daylight in the room must be at least the same order of magnitude as the flux from luminaires; furthermore, daylight must dominate on surfaces close to windows.

Consider an office-type room that requires a mean total working plane illuminance of 500 lx. In London, an external diffuse illuminance of 10 klx or more is achieved for about

70% of working hours (Chapter 3, Figure 3.20). If the room has an average daylight factor of 2% from side windows, the mean working plane illuminance from windows will be about 200 lx and the level near windows will exceed 1000 lx, when outside it is 10 klx.

These figures suggest that an average daylight factor of 2% may be a very useful guideline in establishing the balance between daylight and electric lighting in rooms such as offices. This is, in fact, a recommendation made in current codes of good practice in the UK. Comparable criteria have been used in other parts of Europe and in other temperate climates.

But it follows from the argument above that different average daylight factors would be appropriate in other building types and different climates. In dwellings and in rooms where the illuminance required is less than an equivalent amount of light to a horizontal illuminance of less than 500 lx, less daylight is required; similarly, in warm humid climates, the higher solar elevation gives greater external illuminance and therefore a smaller daylight factor. In these conditions, the appropriate recommendation might be an average daylight factor of 1.5% or even 1%. The lower limit is constrained by the following factors:

1   *Contrast with the exterior.* The lower the internal illuminance, the greater the contrast between the overall brightness of the interior and the view out through the window, and thus a higher probability that the room will look gloomy and the windows glaring.

2   *Variation within the room.* Although the mean interior illuminance might be low, patches of strong light (on tasks, for example) may cause the daylit surfaces to seem dull.
3   *The expectations of users.* People who use the building may be accustomed to a specific room brightness. In particular, there may be a systematic difference between users in cool and in warm climates. In tropical regions, there is the sense that 'bright' equals 'hot'. It is a topic needing research.

Worksheet 4 shows how the average daylight factor can be calculated. Tentative room dimensions and window areas may be checked at an early stage of design.

It is also possible to use the average daylight factor as a means of determining the limiting proportions of buildings. Figure 4.30 relates the proportion of glazing in a façade to depth of room and the height of external obstructions. It is based on an urban office with ceiling height 3 m and room width 6 m. Windows are double glazed with overall transmittance 0.5 and a mean room surface reflectance of 0.35. This is a fairly low value, but is realistic if an office is cluttered or wall finishes are dark. The glazing fraction P is the glazed area divided by the total area of the window wall, seen from inside.

The graph in Figure 4.30 shows that if the glazing proportion is only 0.2, the room can have a daylight character only if the room is less than 3 m deep and the external obstruction is negligible. With a glazing proportion of 0.5, a room depth of about 10 m is possible on an open site;

4.30

Low-reflectance room: limiting depth of a room with windows in one wall, for 2% average daylight factor and different values of the glazing fraction *P*. Room width 6 m, height 3 m, window transmittance 0.5 and mean interior surface reflectance 0.35.

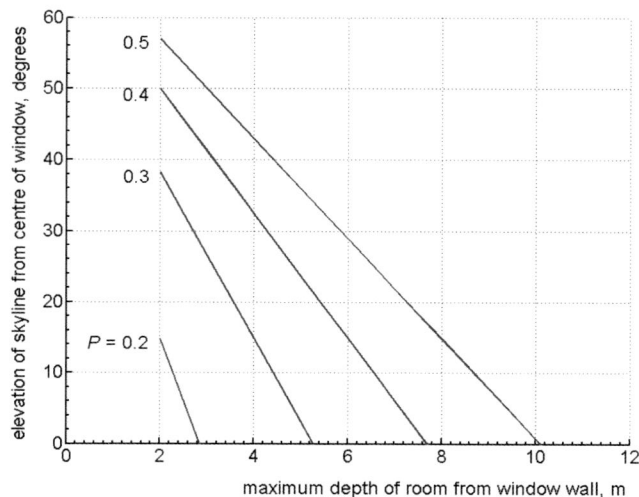

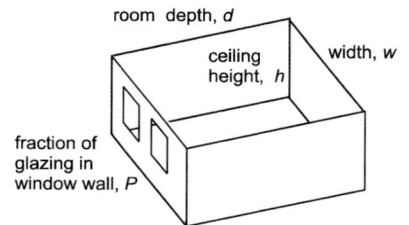

a heavily obstructed site with a skyline 50° above the horizon limits the depth to 3 m.

The aim in designing for daylight appearance is to maximise the amount of interreflected light within a room. This depends on the amount entering, and thus the window transmittance, and on the reflectance of the interior surfaces.

Figure 4.31 is based on the same room, but with 0.6 window transmittance and 0.5 mean room surface reflectance. The sensitivity of daylighting to glazing transmittance and room surface reflectance can be seen by comparison with the previous graph: for example, with a 25° angle of obstruction and a 0.4 glazing fraction, the maximum room depth increases from 5 m in the first case to about 7.5 m in the second. With relatively small increases in transmittance, the permissible room area becomes 50% larger.

When there are windows in two opposite walls, the graphs can be used to estimate the maximum distance between them by looking up the depth for each wall separately, then adding the two values.

Lower ceilings and smaller values of room width reduce the penetration of daylight. But it is room proportions not absolute dimensions that count; therefore, if width and

ceiling height are changed by the same factor, so too is the room depth.

We can now clarify the decisions to be made during the initial stages of design. These are set out in Table 4.2.

Later design stages must incorporate several checks, particularly in relation to the following:

- regulations on permissible glazed areas
- heat gain and loss
- solar penetration
- task illuminance
- direct and reflected glare.

There are two topics – lamp colour and lighting controls – that, though not strictly related to the form of the building, are usefully discussed in this chapter.

Lamp colour

No single lamp colour used in supplementary lighting can match the colour of the daylight in a room. The colour of daylight changes as the sun climbs and descends in the sky; and it varies with weather, with air pollution, and from one part of the sky to another. The difference in colour between diffused sunlight and light from the diffuse sky can be seen in Figure 4.32. Fortunately, it is not necessary for the electric light falling on a room surfaces to be indistinguishable from daylight, but users do have preferences about lamp colour. Where there is general electric lighting, the colour appearance should be intermediate – that is, a correlated colour temperature in the range 3300–5300 K – and the colour rendering quality should be high.

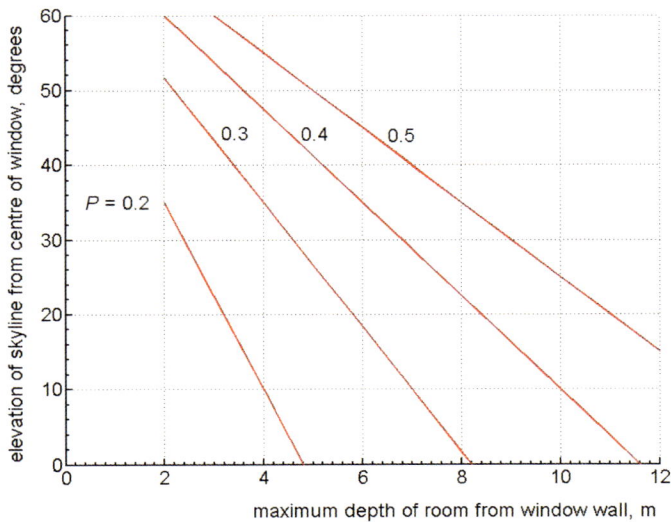

4.31
High-reflectance room: limiting depth for 2% average daylight factor: as Figure 4.30, but with window transmittance 0.6 and mean interior surface reflectance 0.5.

Table 4.2: Initial decisions on room dimensions with side windows

Question	If the answer is 'yes'
Is the room to be totally daylit?	Use Figure 4.25 to estimate maximum room depth
Is the room to be lit using electric lighting during daylight hours?	Use Figures 4.30 and 4.31 to estimate maximum room depth
	Use Figure 4.25 to find areas where daylight is adequate for tasks
Will people remain in fixed locations?	Check glazed area required for view (Table 6.2 in Chapter 6)

4.32
Differences in daylight colour in two rooms with opposite orientation. The room on the left is lit with reflected sunshine, the right-hand room by skylight only.

This can be taken also as a guide to lamps used for local task lighting, and for daytime electric lighting in the home, and in other informal situations.

The type of lamp and the colour of light it produces should be consistent with the overall design intentions. Consideration should be given to the colour appearance at night: lamps that seem a good match to daylight can appear too blue when the sky is not visible as a reference.

Control

The choice of control system is crucial to the performance of the lighting, and the people who use a building must be an integral element of the system. This is implied by the theory of control, because it is the response of the users that is the ultimate measure of performance.

But, even more importantly, people have clear expectations about their authority to control their immediate environment. These expectations are related to ownership and status. In your own home, you decide when electric lights should be switched on, or windows opened; the occupier of a personal office assumes the same. In a shared space, there are social rules to be followed.

If users, individually or collectively, believe that they should be able to alter their environment but cannot do so, they are dissatisfied. There can be resentment when lack of personal control is the result of social factors: if the employer, for instance, imposes restrictions that the worker considers unreasonable. The same can apply when there is an automatic system. If electric lighting is suddenly switched off (daylight having reached a pre-determined level) or automatic blinds obscure a view that is enjoyed, the normal response of users is to attempt to override the system.

Chapter 5 discusses the choice of control systems.

The view to outside

A piece of traditional advice to architecture students goes as follows: 'Visit the site, find the place where the view and daylight are best, sit down there and enjoy what you see.

4.33
Window in a house in Helsinki by Alvar Aalto. The design of the window
enhances the view.

Then imagine that you are in the building you are designing.
Picture in your mind the furniture, and all the people and
things that would surround you: then you can decide where
the windows should be placed and how big they must be.'

Sometimes there is a special view that becomes the
dominant generator of a building's form: the resort hotel
where every bedroom looks out over the sea, the airfield
control room. But external views are necessary from almost
every building, and optimising the balance between provision
of view and all the other factors in window design involves
decisions all through the process of design – site layout, block
form and orientation; interior planning and the form of rooms;

the design of detail, the layout of workspaces and the
detailing of shading devices.

The further a person is from a window, the larger the
window must be to maintain a satisfactory view; this is
especially important in workplaces where freedom to move
around is constrained. Research in offices in South-East
England during the 1980s led to recommendations such as
those listed in Chapter 6, Table 6.2.

Maintenance

Atmospheric dirt is deposited on glazing. The dirt can be
small solid small particles – soot, dust, sand, for instance –
and it can be droplets of oil or acid water. It is anything that
can be carried by air movements and it may come from
sources hundreds of kilometres away: dust from the Gobi
Desert falls on a large area of western China, and motorists
in Britain grumble about the dust film of Sahara sand that
sometimes coats their windscreens.

If windows are vertical and exposed to heavy rain, the
quantity of deposited dirt builds up to some moderate value
and remains approximately constant: new deposition is
balanced by the amount washed off. Conversely, in
sheltered situations, depositions accumulate.

In more detail, the amount of dirt on a window
depends on:

1 The angle of glazing. The closer the window plane is to
   vertical, the faster the flow of water down the surface
   and the more efficient the removal of dirt.
2 The exposure of the window to driving rain. High windows
   exposed to wind and rain are scoured vigorously; those
   under a large canopy or behind shading devices
   accumulate dirt.
3 The type of glazing. Old glass in industrial cities becomes
   etched by polluted rainfall that creates a rough pitted
   surface that holds onto deposited particles. At the other
   extreme, 'self-cleaning glass', float glass with a thin film
   of titanium dioxide, actively sheds deposited dirt as
   rainwater runs across it.
4 The cleaning regime. With exposed vertical glazing,
   window cleaning at intervals of a few weeks or more may
   have little effect on the transmission of light because the

equilibrium conditions of deposition develop rapidly and cause only a minor reduction of transmittance. Cleaning is essential to prevent an indefinite accumulation of dirt when glazing is sheltered.

In some circumstances, dirt on the inside face of windows can absorb more light than deposition on the outside surface does. If there is a warm moist atmosphere inside, the condensation that forms on the interior face of the window tends to carry polluting elements such as smoke particles, and fats and odours from cooking. A noticeable light-absorbing layer can rapidly build up. Especially prone to this are swimming pool buildings, gymnasia and health clubs, and restaurants.

Deposited dirt on glass is apparent even though light transmission is barely affected and windows are normally cleaned to preserve their appearance. Accumulated dirt is unsightly even when the window is not in the normal direction of view, like the roof light illustrated in Figure 4.34. It should be a normal assumption in design that all glazing be accessible for maintenance – for cleaning and for replacement of damaged glass – and that access to both the external and internal faces of the window is necessary.

Window cleaning contractors have a range of techniques available: cleaning by hand from portable ladders; the use of extending probes with pressurised water; 'cherry pickers' (vehicles with extending platforms), rope access (abseil), and the use of gantries installed on the building.

Again, it is the basic form of the building that first determines both whether any glazing will be naturally scoured by wind and rain and whether it can be easily accessible so that regular maintenance is economical. High glazing beneath an overhang is difficult to reach; large inclined surfaces of glass may need a moveable gantry on rails to be built as part of the window system; shading devices may interfere with window washing or make access to the glazing impossible. Establishing that there can be access to the internal and external surfaces of all glazing is part of the early design procedure. At the detailed design stage, there follows the need to incorporate the requirements of safety: these include features such as handholds, fixing of anchors, openings for access, and footings for ladders; they also include means of

4.34
Glazing that is difficult to reach for maintenance and sheltered from scouring by rainwater. Its attractiveness as a roost to birds aggravates the problem.

ensuring that general users of the building, and those who would enter the building illicitly, are not able to use or interfere with the access and equipment provided for maintenance. Data sheet 16 lists recommended values of dirt transmittance to use in calculations.

Imagination

This chapter presents an analytical approach to the choice of building form. Topic by topic, it sets boundaries around the field of possible designs so that the search for the best solution becomes increasingly focused. This might imply that creative design is a linear process, but it is not. Analysis is necessary, but not adequate on its own. Invention is

essential, and the subject of light and colour has a power to stimulate the visual imagination. It seems possible to go beyond architecture that is merely satisfying, to create places that give joy, excitement or deep content.

The visual opportunities of daylighting have been described by many, but the exploration of architectural form in daylight is more than a visual activity. It is a route into the creative imagination, a way of bringing together all the factors reviewed in this chapter.

Images are valuable in stimulating inventiveness. Especially while learning to design, it is helpful to keep a steadily growing notebook that records not just the visual forms but also a technical understanding of them. Some examples are shown in Figures 4.35–4.43.

4.35
Diffuse daylight: soft-
edged shadows, the
rich decoration looking
subdued.
Telfes, Austria

4.36

Direct sunlight: sharp edges and strong contrasts. Note the reflected light on the ceiling of the arcade opposite.
Toledo, Spain

4.37
The flower is illuminated by diffuse daylight. Interreflection within the cavity creates a
quite even illuminance, but there is sufficient variation to reveal the geometric forms.
Convulvulus

4.38
A similar form to that in Figure
4.37 but at a very different scale.
Innsbruck Cathedral

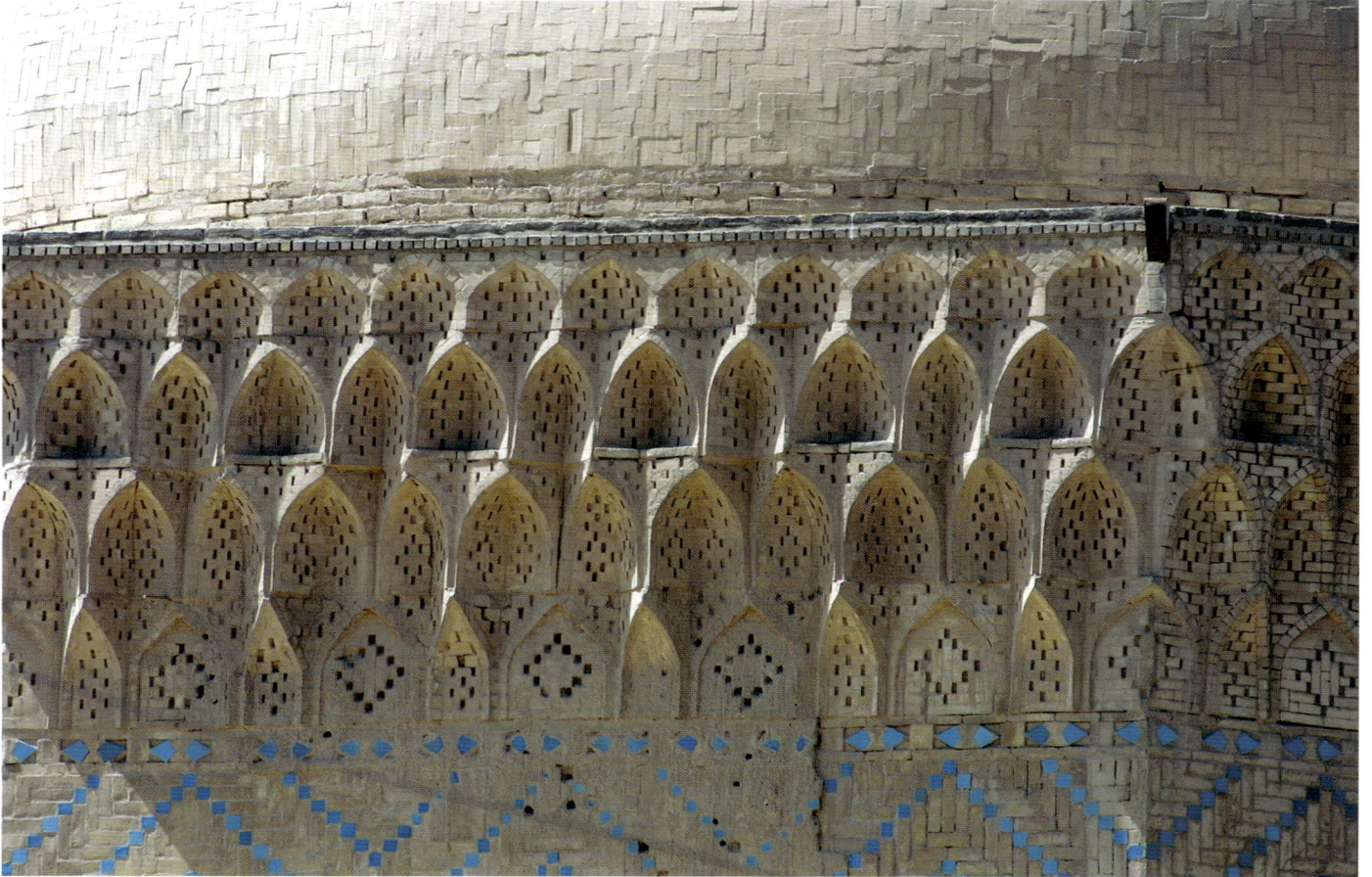

4.39

Sunlight at glancing incidence emphasising texture. Note particularly the scalloped
forms – direct light making bright lines along the rims; reflected sunlight from below
shining on the undersides.

Yazd, Iran

4.40

The form of a translucent material emphasised by sunlight on the reverse side. The shadows of other leaves are visible.

4.41

Strong colours on a white background in hazy sunlight. Compare the saturated pigments of the flowers with the painted window surround. The shadows are also painted.

Telfes, Austria

4.42
Shadows and strong
sunlight. Shadows can be
complex and subtle, and are
valuable enhancers of visible
form at all scales, from
the overall shape of a large
building to the fine detail of
materials and fittings.
Santiago de Compostela, Spain

4.43

When the wind touches foliage and shadows move, a new perceptual dimension is added.

The Chinese Garden, Sydney, Australia

## five

Energy and control

Electricity used for artificial lighting is a significant cause of a building's CO_2 cost: in offices, it can be 30% of the total. This is why good daylighting is so important to a sustainable architecture. In domestic buildings, the requirements of health suggest that higher levels of daylight than are currently used are desirable. This gives scope for energy savings.

The key to a sustainable use of energy in buildings is the control of electric lighting and of window transmittance by shading devices and internal screens such as window blinds.

This chapter summarises the background to energy-efficient design, then goes on to describe control systems and how they affect the energy impact of a building.

Daylight and energy

In climate-sensitive design, the inherent physical properties of the building's form and materials are used to transform the external climate into the conditions that the users need and want inside a building. This does not mean that the environmental control of the building must be entirely passive – that no energy must be used in creating the desired internal conditions: it means that the use of energy during the building's lifetime must be minimised, and that the overall effect of the built world of which it is part must be neutral. Climate-sensitive design is a concern both for the environment of the people who use the building and for conservation of natural resources.

Lighting is a central component of sustainable architecture, and, for the designer, a sustainable use of daylight depends on two things:

1 Recognition of the balance of sunlight and skylight that determines the daylight climate of a place;
2 Finding the balance between daylight and electric lighting in the interior environment of the building that both minimises the lifetime energy cost and gives user satisfaction.

The two ratios, between sunlight and skylight and between daylight and electric lighting, determine a building's sustainable performance.

Sunlight and skylight

In a cloudy climate, the diffuse sky has to be the source of useful daylight. To achieve the maximum interior illuminance for a given glazed area, windows must face the sky, with the constraint that discomfort from sunlight and sky glare must be avoided. In Europe, the levels of diffuse radiation differ little across the entire region. Cumulative graphs of daylight availability such as Figure 3.20 show that a horizontal illuminance of 10 klx might be available for 70% of working hours and 20 klx for 40% of working hours. For school hours the percentages are greater.

5.1

Drying mud bricks. When the sun is overhead, about 1 kW of radiant energy falls on each square metre of ground.
Iran

By contrast, global illuminance, the total of sunlight and skylight, varies greatly with latitude. A global horizontal illuminance of 30 klx is exceeded for 30% of working hours in Northern Europe, but 70% of the time in the south. The relative uniformity of the diffuse sky should not lead us to believe that the total daylight coming through, say, a north-facing window will be similar throughout Europe. The predominance of sunny skies in the south means that, even if the sun is not on the window façade, the ground and the faces of other buildings may be sunlit, and the luminance of the landscape may exceed that of the sky. Where sunshine is reliable, the primary aim in design is to optimise the use of reflected sunlight, so windows must face the reflecting surfaces. Upward light falling on a white ceiling from bright areas below the horizontal – the ground and the lower parts of buildings – can give a better distribution of daylight in the room than is achieved with skylight. Again, there is the constraint of avoiding discomfort, although the main cause of

this tends to be glare from sunlight on light-coloured external surfaces. Sunlit snow is an extreme case: it can have a much greater luminance than the sky.

Daylight and electric lighting: a summary of energy implications

About half of the total energy of solar radiation at the earth's surface is in the visible spectrum. The amount of visible light for each watt of total solar radiation varies according to sky conditions, but roughly 100 lumens is contained within 1 watt: a patch of sunlight with irradiance 1 kW/m^2 thus has an illuminance of about 100 klx. Chapter 2 described luminous efficacy, the ratio of visible radiation to total radiation. The value of about 100 lm/W for the average luminous efficacy of daylight compares with approximately 12 lm/W for incandescent lamps and 80–90 lm/W for the best fluorescents. This means that, considering only the light itself, less total energy is required to achieve a given illuminance in a room with daylight than with most electric light sources.

This, however, is only part of the story. The energy used by electric lighting is primarily a direct cost: it consists of the actual energy consumed in the building and of the background losses incurred in generating electricity and distributing it. There are, in addition, the energy costs of manufacturing and installing the equipment and ultimately of disposing or recycling it. The energy expenditure with daylight is primarily indirect: it consists firstly of the additional building costs (because higher storey heights, larger window areas, and increased heating and cooling capacity might be required) and the costs of the additional energy needed to compensate for the effect of large windows on the internal environment.

Chapter 4 discussed the optimum balance between daylight and electric lighting. Rooms can be designed so that daylight alone is adequate except during dawn and dusk and on gloomy winter days. Such spaces, in cool climates, are likely to have average daylight factors exceeding 5% and, with side windows, a layout in which task areas lie within a distance from the window about 2½ times the desk-to-window head height. But the large area of windows needed can cause unwanted thermal gain and loss, and the need for daylight penetration into deep rooms can make higher ceilings necessary.

The optimum balance of electric lighting to daylight in workplaces depends on the size and function of the building, the availability of daylight during the operating hours of the building, and the financial background. It is influenced also by the quality of the environmental control: the better the control of thermal gain and loss, sound transmittance, and ventilation, the more daylight can be introduced without penalties of discomfort. The walls and roof of the building act as an envelope that is transparent to daylight but limits the entry of energy in other forms. Until recent years, the poor thermal characteristics of this envelope undermined potential energy savings by losing heat in winter and gaining heat in summer. High-performance glazing with multiple layers and spectra-selective coatings has greatly improved both wintertime and summertime energy performance of glazing with little loss of visible transparency. Glazing systems are described in Chapter 9.

The U-shaped graph showing lifetime energy costs as a function of the daylight/electric lighting balance was described in the previous chapter (Figure 4.29). In temperate climates and with moderate thermal control, the optimum has tended to be equivalent to an average daylight factor of about 2%, but with advanced glazing and good building environment control, the most effective quantity of daylight may lie in the range of 2–4% average daylight factor.

Where large savings are potentially available, the control systems of the electric lighting, window shading and blinds play a critical role. In open plan offices, good control is essential if there is be any saving at all. But successful implementation of automatic controls is not proving easy: too often, control systems are installed so that high scores on environmental rating scales are achieved, only for these systems to lie unused owing to poor design or failure to commission properly.

Control systems

Lights can be switched on and off by users, or they may be controlled automatically. Automatic controls can be linked to daylight sensors and occupancy detectors; they normally have time settings and they can – and for most interiors should – have user over-ride controls. Shading devices such as blinds can similarly be left to user control or operated automatically. In Chapter 4, we noted the importance of user satisfaction in achieving sustainability, especially that people have clear expectations about their authority to control their immediate environment. These expectations depend both on the nature of the place and on social factors, such as ownership and status. The performance of a control system depends not only on its efficiency in maintaining specified physical conditions but also on its acceptability.

For manual operation to be effective, two conditions must apply. Firstly, the means of control must be convenient. The electric lighting for an area in the building and the blinds on the windows that provide illumination and view must be controllable from within the area. Furthermore, operating these should have a minimal effect on adjacent spaces. The second requirement is that the users should want to save energy. The ethos that prevails among, for example,

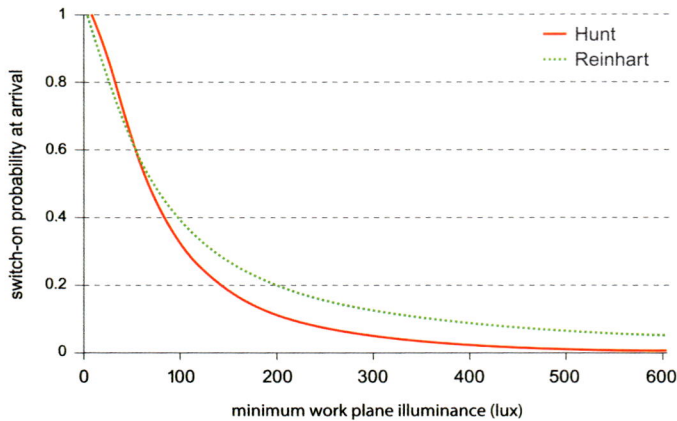

5.2

Manual switching of electric lighting: probability of users switching on upon arrival. The probability is strongly related to the minimum illuminance in the workplace.

After Reinhart and Voss [98].

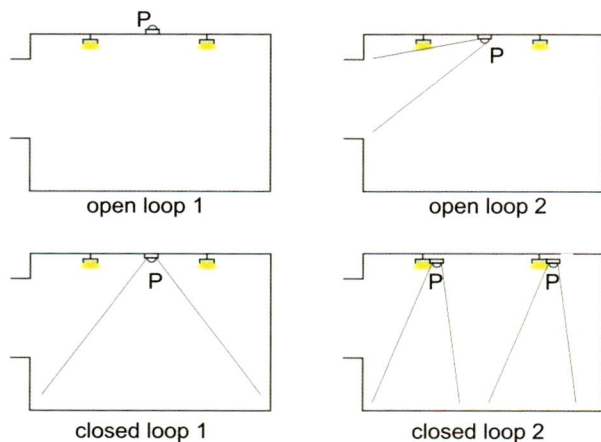

5.3

Types of daylight-responsive electric lighting control ('P' indicates the photocell position):
• open loop 1: a cell measures external illuminance;
• open loop 2: a cell measures window luminance;
• closed loop 1: a cell measures working plane luminance;
• closed loop 2: cells measure luminance of individual areas.

the workers in an office has a huge effect on the sustainable performance of the place. People must be satisfied with the conditions and they must be habitually economical with energy. The two conditions are related: a condition of satisfaction is an ability to control one's personal environment.

With manual switching, as the number of people in a workplace becomes greater, the probability increases that all the lighting will be switched on. In small to medium rooms, simple manual switching can achieve substantial energy savings over the continuous use of electric lighting. Hunt's studies in the UK in the 1970s and those in Germany by Reinhart in the 2000s showed that the probability of a person switching on lights where the daylight level was 100 lx was about 35%; this dropped to about 15% at 200 lx and to almost zero at 500 lx. Paradoxically, an automatic system working at 500 lx would use more energy.

Automatic lighting controls take two forms:

1 *Open loop systems*. The electric lighting is controlled by a photocell, either outside or inside the building (where it is masked from the electric lighting). Open loop systems tend to be used for small offices, atria, and sets or rooms that have the same exposure to the daylight – that is, of similar orientation and similar obstruction of the sky. Normally, the photocell is roof-mounted. Some systems employ several photocells with different orientations; from these, a measure of the sky luminance distribution can be obtained and rooms of different orientations can be managed. In some cases, a single vertically mounted photocell is used; this is normally for the control of a single room. Alternatively, an open loop system may be controlled by sensing the window luminance.

2 *Closed loop systems*. These use a photocell that is in the room and is exposed to both daylight and electric lighting. The cell is in a feedback loop with the controller, enabling a pre-set internal illuminance to be maintained. Some forms of closed loop allow an increase in the set point internal illuminance to permit higher levels of internal illuminance under brighter skies. Closed loop systems are more complex, especially if the artificial lighting is zoned. They are regarded as more appropriate in larger spaces with multiple orientations.

Both types may operate simple on/off switching or dimming, which is more satisfactory if it functions correctly.

Window blinds and other forms of shading can also be controlled automatically. They can be linked with the electric lighting controls, but if there is an integrated system serving two or more functions, this reaches a higher level of complexity. Blinds operated by the user, either manually or with remote control, can cause open loop automatic lighting controls to fail if there is no way in which the status of the blinds is recognised by the system. Automatic blind controls can fail if they are not linked with lighting controls or if the systems are mismatched (for example, if they are from different manufacturers). Blind use is related both to sun position and to the brightness of the diffuse sky. Some research has suggested that blind use in offices is more determined by VDU reflections than direct sky glare. A study in a German office buliding where blinds had both manual and automatic control showed that 47% of all blind movements were automatic. Nearly half of these were corrected manually: the majority were manual opening after automatic closing; the remainder were mainly manual closing after blinds had opened in the presence of weak low-angle sun.

Surveys of lighting control systems in buildings in use suggest that very few work as intended. There are physical causes of this. For example, the relationships between consumed power, control voltage and light output vary widely for different ballasts (Figure 5.4). This has an impact especially on open loop systems and tends to result in inadequate levels of artificial light. In closed loop systems, there is often inconsistency in the installation of photocells. These are usually ceiling-mounted and record the light emitted by a section of the working plane. But the area viewed depends on the acceptance angle of the cell and its angular sensitivity; the cell receives a weighted average of the light reflected towards it, and this can be very sensitive to the characteristics of the cell and of its exact location. In a room with side windows, there is a steep, non-linear gradient of daylight illuminance on the working plane, and daytime electric lighting may also be asymmetric: a small variation of sensor position can cause a significant change in the light falling on the cell. Furthermore, the distribution of the light in a room varies with the sky luminance distribution, with possible sun patches; and also with the settings of blinds, which may direct light onto the sensor. The spectral sensitivity of the photocell may skew the detected signal, responding differently to light from an overcast sky, reflected sunlight, blind-modified sunlight, electric light and light reflected by surfaces of strong chroma within the room.

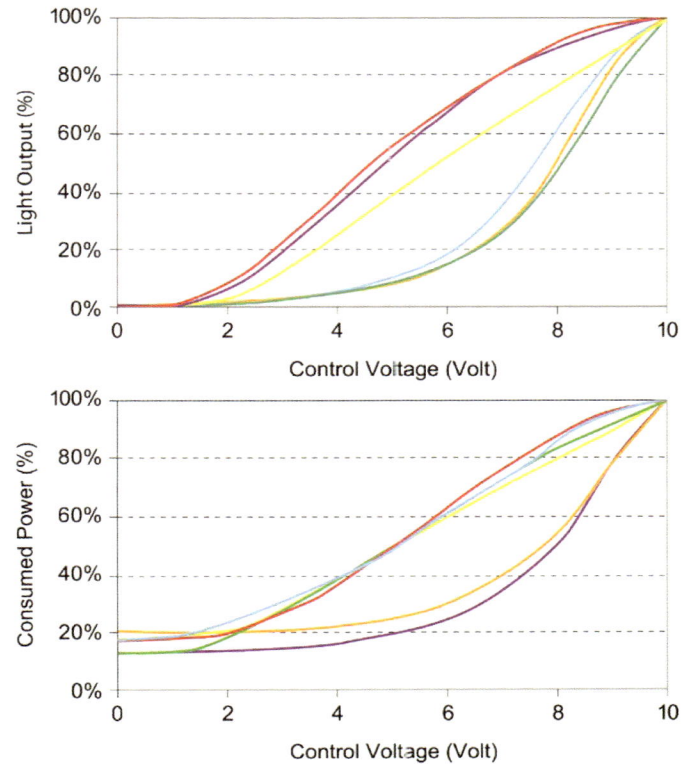

5.4

Light output, consumed power and control voltage for a variety of ballasts. *After Doulos, Tsangrassoulis & Topalis [103].*

Most current daylight-responsive control systems use horizontal illuminance as the quantity to be maintained. The control criterion is usually working plane illuminance. The arguments for this are that it correlates to quite a large extent with other measures of light in a room and that it is consistent with the assumptions on which electric lighting is usually calculated. There are several contrary arguments:

- Illuminance is only a weak predictor of user satisfaction and of task performance.
- There is no reason to assume that either the optimum illuminance or the plane of measurement is the same for screen-based work as for the original desk-based tasks from which the standard office criteria were derived.
- No account is taken of directionality and modelling for three-dimensional tasks.
- The luminance distribution of the room is not preserved and the essential variability of daylight may be lost.

We have seen that people's response to daylight depends on several physical factors as well as subjective characteristics, so control of a single measure of light quantity is not likely to provide a preferred environment. The fact that users consider it important to control their own environment is an advantage, not a hindrance, to the design of a system, because feedback from users can be more direct and more precisely aimed than automatic sensing. With some notable exceptions, control systems for electric lighting and for window shading do not have the sophistication of controls in many other fields; the deficiencies are found not in the inner procedures of the luminaire operation but in the incomplete sensing of the room environment and in the absence of clarity and simplicity in the management and operation of the equipment in practice.

Calculating energy use

The need for more detailed measures of daylight has arisen from methods of predicting energy use. A simple calculation may be performed to estimate the potential energy savings from daylight. For instance a horizontal illuminance of 10 klx is available in the UK for 70% of the year during typical office hours (09.00–17.30). This is available for an even higher percentage of time if school opening hours are considered. A daylight factor of 2% would provide 200 lx for this time. The environmental assessment method for offices (BREEAM) at present gives credit for a daylight factor of 2% covering 80% of the office space.

Climate Based Daylight Modelling is a computer technique in which natural lighting is simulated over a whole year using real daylight data (either radiation converted with luminous efficacy or actual daylight measurements). Most software designed for the simulation is based on radiance. For instance, DAYSIM uses daylight coefficients to simulate conditions at hourly (or other) intervals to produce a variety of information, including lux-hours (annual daylight exposure), which is particularly useful in galleries and museums. Some other measures of daylight performance are listed in Table 5.1.

BS EN 15193:2007 *Energy Performance of Buildings – Energy Requirements for Lighting* provides a manual method

Table 5.1: Measures of daylighting performance

Measure	Acronym	What it indicates
Daylight autonomy	DA	The percentage of the year where illuminance levels may be satisfied by daylight alone. This may be adjusted for working hours. Does not consider levels lower than full daylight autonomy and is not useful for daylight-linked dimmable artificial light
Useful daylight illuminance	UDI	The number of hours with working plane illuminance between 100 and 2000 lx. Above 2000 lx, it is assumed that blinds are likely to be used to permit VDU use
Continuous daylight autonomy	DA_{com}	DA adapted to take into account levels below full daylight autonomy
Maximum daylight autonomy	DA_{max}	Adopts a similar approach to UDI in the sense that an upper limit is introduced where blinds are likely to be used. This is based on an upper limit of 10 times the design illuminance, e.g. 5000 lx for 500 lx design illuminance

for calculating the potential contribution of daylighting to reducing the artificial lighting energy consumption of buildings. The actual energy performance of the artificial lighting system is determined by the potential of using daylight substitution and of realising savings with the use of occupancy detectors.

The calculation uses a form of daylight factor together with a measure of availability of daylight (taken to be related to latitude) to produce a daylight supply factor. Finally, a control factor is applied; this depends on room size and on what daylight-related lighting controls are installed. In the final energy calculation, parasitic load on the system of any automatic controls must be taken into account.

With vertical glazing, the concept of a daylight factor across the centre axis (parallel to the window) is used. With roof lights, a utilisation factor method is used to give a mean daylight factor somewhat analogous to the conventional average daylight factor. The standard provides manual calculation techniques for the daylight factors, although, of course, physical model or computer simulations could be used (and may be necessary for complicated spaces). Standard reflectances are used. No tables or calculation techniques are used to take account of varying reflectance.

Worksheet 7 gives a step-by-step description of the method.

Closed loop control algorithms

At present, the most commonly used closed loop system is the integral reset. The rate of change to the output of the controller is measured by the magnitude of the input.

In a basic integral reset system, the task illuminance is given by

$$E_T(t) = E_D(t) + E_{Em} \left[1 - S_D(t) / S_{Em}\right] \qquad (5.1)$$

where

$E_T(t)$ is the total illuminance

$E_D(t)$ is the daylight contribution to that illuminance

E_{Em} is the illuminance when the electric lights are fully on and there is no daylight

$S_D(t)$ is the daylight component of the signal produced by the sensor

S_{Em} is the signal produced by the sensor when electric lights are fully on and there is no daylight

and

$$\frac{E_D(t)}{S_D(t)} = \frac{E_{Em}}{S_{Em}} \qquad (5.2)$$

In other words, the photosensor should produce the same signal whether produced from daylight alone or electric light alone.

The disadvantage with this algorithm is that the total illuminance can fall below the reference level, as in Figure 5.5. This dip in output is avoided by the following alternative algorithm, at the cost of increased energy use.

$$E_T(t) = E_D(t) + E_{Em} \left(\frac{1 + M[S_D(t) - S_{Em}]}{1 - MS_{Em}} \right)$$

where

$$M = \frac{E_D(t_{cal})}{E_D(t_{cal}) \, S_{Em} - E_{Em} \, S_D(t_{cal})} \qquad (5.3)$$

and

$$\frac{E_D(t)}{S_D(t)} = \frac{E_D(t_{cal})}{S_D(t_{cal})}$$

t_{cal} represents the chosen calibration values for the ratio between daylight level and signal, evaluated at times when the daylight level is below the design illuminance level.

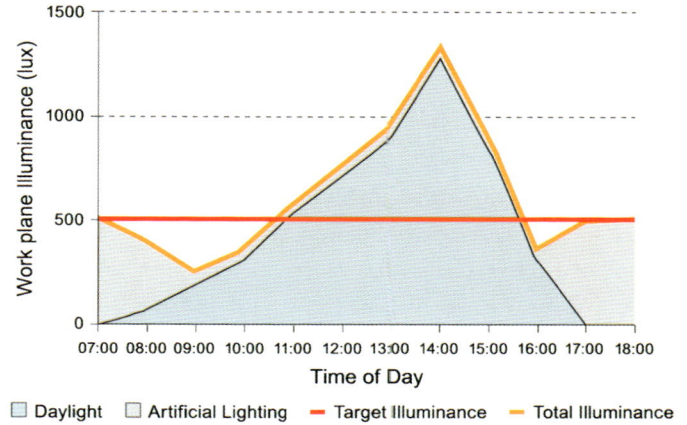

5.5

Performance of a simple closed loop control algorithm based on Equations (5.1) and (5.2).

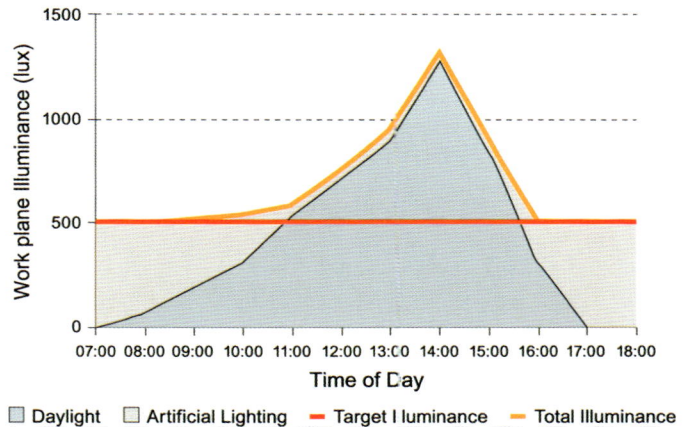

5.6

Performance of an algorithm based on Equation (5.2). The dip in total output is avoided, at the cost of greater energy use.

Three variables that may be measured as a control for the lighting in a room are the luminance of the working plane, the luminance of the walls (or other vertical surfaces in the field of view) and the window luminance. In the absence of artificial light they are quite highly correlated, because variation between them is caused only by differences in the sky distribution and by changes in the façade and blind systems. Sunlight penetration clearly disturbs the correlation significantly, but direct sunlight tends to be excluded when the façade illuminance is high. The relationship between the luminances of different surfaces depends greatly on room shape, size and reflectance, window position, and window area. The location and sensitivity of photosensors must be chosen with an understanding of the way electric lighting and daylight are distributed in the space.

Intelligent systems that adapt to user behaviour can be employed, but usually require user interaction. In a simple closed loop installation, the reference level is not necessarily the target working plane illuminance.

Automatic closing of blinds is usually controlled by detecting illuminance above 5000 lx from direct sunlight on the working plane or diffuse irradiance of 450 W/m^2 at the orientation of the window. Blinds are raised when the irradiance falls below 280 W/m^2. Low-angle sun is often unwanted in a workplace: it is glaring and contributes little to horizontal illuminance; it is also difficult to recognise automatically.

## six

Standards, design guidance and development control

This chapter examines the requirements of daylighting standards. It begins by describing the nature of design standards, then reviews the criteria given in Chapter 1 to derive minimum acceptable daylighting standards for dwellings and for workplaces. It then examines the implications of these for development control.

Current criteria in the UK are discussed in Worksheet 17.

What standards must do

The design of a new building is constrained by a large number of mandatory requirements, probably hundreds in all. These requirements are concerned with the health and safety of those people who will use the building and those who construct it, with the materials and quality of the building fabric, with the environmental qualities of the interior, with the effect of the development on nearby existing buildings, with energy expenditure, and with various other factors. They come in various forms and various degrees of legal standing: there are codes of practice, some mandatory, others advisory; there are national and local regulations; there are national and international standards, which may or may not be locally applied.

This chapter examines the function of standards that are intended to ensure that good daylighting is provided in building. We begin by listing attributes that every design standard should possess. (For the moment, we will use 'standard' as a general term, whatever the legal framework, and use 'mandatory' or 'advisory' to indicate its standing.)

To be effective, a standard must:

1   Have a clear and beneficial purpose.
2   Define the domain of its applicability – where and when it does and does not apply.
3   Set out requirements that are few in number, meaningful and simple to test.

Now consider criteria of good lighting and how they match these requirements of an effective standard. The quality of lighting in a school classroom, for instance, is the outcome of many factors: they include the geometry of the room, the control of sunlight, the layout of luminaires, the absence of direct glare and of bright reflections, the illuminance on tasks, and the control of windows and electric lighting. Most of these are difficult to express in numerical terms and, at the design stage, difficult to assess with simple tests.

Lighting is not unique in this. The same problem exists with other environmental characteristics, such as noise, ventilation, or thermal comfort; it occurs also with purely physical requirements of a building, such as structural stability. The first conclusion to draw is that:

• A standard can include only few of the criteria of good design.

This has the corollary that

• Meeting the requirements of a standard does not mean that a lighting scheme is good.

6.1
The urban canyon. The
microclimate of a city street
differs from the environment
at roof level. To a large extent,
the daylight in the canyon
is determined by building
regulations and by criteria used
in urban planning.
Tallinn, Estonia

The challenge for the author of a standard is to develop simple tests that are good predictors not only of particular requirements but of the success of the whole scheme.

Evidence and judgement

Good standards are founded on good research. Their requirements can be little more than guesswork unless it is known how people respond to lighting and of how light behaves in buildings. But scientific evidence alone is not enough to determine design criteria.

Consider this case. The aim is to have sufficient illumination in a workplace for good visual performance. The graph in Figure 6.2 shows how task performance is related to the illuminance on the task. This example is hypothetical, but is typical of real results. What it shows is that performance is poor at low levels of light. The curve relating performance to illuminance rises steeply at first, then flattens off so that a further increase of illuminance has no measurable advantage. The three dots on the curve show that at 10 lx the performance is 0.8 of the maximum, at 100 lx it is 0.9 and at 1000 lx it is 0.95: in this hypothetical example, an increase from 0.8 to 0.95 in performance requires a hundred-fold increase in illuminance.

This is the evidence. Now suppose that you are responsible for recommending the value that would be set in a mandatory standard: what level of task illuminance do you set? The graph itself gives no guidance. To decide, you would take other factors into account: the cost of failure, for example, and the costs of providing lighting. Research results such as graphs of performance against illuminance are literally data – reference points – on which judgements are made.

The second conclusion to be drawn is that:

- All criteria in standards are human judgements.

This applies universally: standards of structural safety are based on statistics of loading and of material failure, but some finite probability of collapse has to be adopted. Traffic speed limits are based on data relating speed to the frequency of accidents, but whether to set the limit in an urban area at 20, 30 or 40 mph remains a necessary judgement.

Real data are much less clear than the hypothetical example of Figure 6.2. The visual tasks used in subjective experiments are simplifications of real tasks, and a normal workplace accommodates a variety of different activities. Furthermore, the curve on the graph is merely the best-fit line to a broad scatter of individual responses: not only do people vary in ability, but each person varies from day to day.

No matter how detailed and realistic they are, empirical experimental results and survey data are merely examples. Good standards depend on sensitive and informed judgements that use the research evidence; but every proposed criterion is a 'line that has to be drawn somewhere'.

This applies to international standards and to national regulations, and it applies to the criteria given in this book. Numerical requirements such as recommended levels of illuminance and minimum daylight factors need to be related to their context, recognising that these criteria reflect the social and physical environment of the time and the place where they were written.

A spectrum of design guidance

Regulations and mandatory standards may be a necessary part of a campaign to achieve good lighting, but what they can achieve is limited. They are valuable in assuring that a minimum acceptable level is reached, but, alone, are not appropriate for propagating good practice.

It is useful to consider three levels of guidance publications: see Table 6.1.

It is a serious fault that many existing codes of practice do not explicitly state the categories in which their requirements fall. In particular, daylighting standards tend not to distinguish the minimum acceptable level from the level of good practice. An ideal framework of regulation and guidance would include every level and be consistent between them. Regulations governing minimum standards should be part of a broader propagation of information at the appropriate technical level to the design professions, the developers and clientele, and the planning authorities.

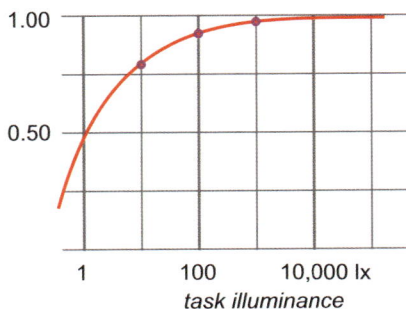

fraction of optimum performance

6.2
Simplified graph showing the typical relationship between task illuminance and performance.

Table 6.1: Categories of design guidance

I	Standards that define the lowest acceptable level of provision. Usually, these are mandatory regulations produced on the assumption that, in their absence, insufficient attention or resources would be devoted to this element of a building.
II	Codes or guides that describe good current practice – the standard expected of a high-quality building at the present time. To promote good practice, there must be dissemination of new techniques and solutions from research and practice – essentially, this is education for the professional and for all involved in the building procurement team.
III	Publications describing innovation and the creative work of the best designers. This is the seedbed of tomorrow's good practice. It depends on experimentation and review, on analysis and criticism, and it is the duty of the research journals and the professional societies to provide this.

Daylight criteria 1: minimum acceptable conditions in dwellings

Chapter 1 listed design aims. The task now is to identify criteria on which a standard could be based. We begin by considering minimum acceptable conditions in individual dwellings. The conclusions may then be extended to other places where people might be living for long periods: care homes, prisons, student housing and military accommodation.

Three major requirements emerge from Chapter 1:

1 For health

(a) exposure to a 24-hour cycle of light and darkness;

(b) exposure to sufficient illumination during winter months to minimise seasonally related depression;

(c) contact with the outside world: a view.

Virtually all dwellings and institutional residential buildings except those for specific groups such as military personnel may at some time be used by people who, handicapped by illness, physical disability or extreme age, are rarely able to go outside. Such buildings must therefore have the potential to provide the cycle of darkness and strong light required for health. The importance of this is greatest in regions at the latitude of Northern Europe and higher.

A good view tends to be ranked by users as more important than good interior daylight illumination. At present, there is insufficient research evidence on housing to quantify this (as opposed to hospitals, for instance, where the effect of an external view has been correlated against measures of patient recovery).

2 Task lighting

Many activities in a dwelling can be classified as visual tasks – examples are food preparation, reading and writing, nursing care, applying cosmetics, and using computers; there are considerations of safety, such as the use of stairs. It is to be noted that some users will have poor eyesight. Daylight is not necessarily the most appropriate illuminant, but it is best for some tasks. The disadvantages of illuminance as a

criterion are, firstly, that people are relatively insensitive to the absolute level of light and, secondly, that calculations of daylight illuminance are complex.

3 Expectations about daylighting

Users' satisfaction depends on their expectations, which depend, in turn, on their experiences. This is a crucial factor in the acceptability of a standard, but a difficult factor to incorporate.

In summary, there is very strong evidence, firstly, that daylighting in a dwelling is important to the health and well-being of the people who live there, and, secondly, that people's responses to daylight depend on climate and culture. A universal criterion of good daylighting probably does not exist, and, even when considering a single region, it is hard to find an obvious rule that defines the minimum acceptable standard.

The approach to take is to isolate the most important factors, as we have just done; then, with knowledge of the local context, to search for simple, testable criteria. Here, then, are three requirements that could apply to dwellings in the UK:

Daylight in dwellings: minimum acceptable conditions

1 Every new dwelling should include a space with strong daylight in winter. In private houses, this requirement is taken to be satisfied if at least one of the following conditions applies:
- There is a window of at least 1 m² in a habitable room that receives direct sunlight for one half-hour per day of probable sunlight during the period 1 November to 31 January.
- There is an enclosed space of at least 5 m² floor area, such as a conservatory or balcony, with an average daylight factor of at least 5%.
- There is an average daylight factor of at least 2% in one habitable room.

2 In all other habitable rooms, the average daylight factor should not be less than 1%. 'Habitable' should be taken to include living rooms, kitchens and bedrooms, but not bathrooms, WCs or circulation areas.

3 Every window that receives direct sunlight should have a means by which the occupants can control the entry of sunlight.

Comment

The aim is to ensure that everyone has access in the home to a level of natural light that could reduce health problems associated with low daylight. It is clear that this demands a greater quantity of daylight than specified by most current standards applicable in the UK; for this reason, its applicability is limited here to new buildings.

At the beginning of the twentieth century in the UK, regulations such as local byelaws and the provisions of the London Building Acts required minimum window areas and minimum spacing of buildings that would be equivalent to average daylight factors in the range 0.5–1.0% in habitable rooms. These criteria, intended to ensure adequate conditions of light and ventilation in the poorest dwellings, had developed over half a century of debate and experience. For us, they indicate the level of natural light that our experience associates with the lowest standard of housing – hence the proposal to adopt a value at the top of this range as the minimum acceptable provision of daylight now.

The sunlight requirement is, slightly more demanding that the current British Standard recommendation of 5% of probable annual sunlight hours over the winter half-year.

In the post-World War II years, recommendations for high levels of daylight led to rooms with excessive solar heat gain. Current practice in the UK is to install less solar control than used in comparable buildings in continental Europe, particularly in residential buildings. Inadequate sunlight control is so widespread that a mandatory requirement is suggested. The present climatic trend towards greater fluctuation in weather conditions associated with global temperature rise suggests that the importance of shading devices and other window controls may increase.

View and its converse, visual privacy, are highly desirable in dwellings, but are difficult to specify in a concise testable way. For that reason, it is not included among the requirements of minimum acceptable conditions.

Daylight criteria 2: minimum acceptable conditions for desk-based workspaces

Offices, classrooms, small-scale manufacturing assembly, call-centres, and study areas in the home are all examples of desk-based workplaces. What characterises them is, firstly, the need to carry out a range of visual tasks in two and three dimensions, usually with a focus on reading and writing on VDUs and keyboards or on paper; and, secondly, that the people working in these spaces may remain static for periods of an hour or more. Users may be restricted in their ability to change the position or orientation of their workplace.

From Chapter 1 it is clear that there are four critical factors:

- adequate task illuminance
- a balance between electric lighting and daylight that maintains a daylit appearance; in particular, electric lighting that does not mask the temporal and spatial variability of daylight
- view to the outside world
- avoidance of direct and reflected glare.

Daylit rooms are preferred over those with entirely electric lighting. Considerations of energy use require as much daylight as possible without thermal or visual discomfort, and without increasing the volume of the building with ceiling heights greater than is otherwise necessary. This implies that full daylighting is often not the most sustainable solution.

Daylight in desk-based workspaces

1 There should be adequate illuminance on tasks. This requirement is taken to be satisfied if the illuminance from daylight and electric lighting together achieve the values set out in the British and European Standard BS EN 12464.

2 During daytime working hours, all people in a workplace should have access to daylight. This should be provided in the workplace itself, unless the activity requires daylight to be excluded, in which case there must be a daylit space within the building to which people have free access.

3 The daylit space should:
(a) have an average daylight factor of at least 2% on a horizontal working plane at desktop height;
(b) have a view to the outside; in a deep room with windows in only one wall, the requirement is taken to be satisfied if the area of glazing is at least that given in Table 5.2.

4 Occupants of the workplace should have the means of:
(a) preventing the entry of sunlight;
(b) reducing the entry of skylight when the external brightness is high;
(c) reducing the use of electric lighting when there is adequate daylight.

So the basis of a specification for minimum acceptable conditions could be:

Table 6.2: Desk-based workplaces: minimum glazed areas for view when windows are restricted to one wall

Depth of room from outside wall, m	Percentage of window wall when seen from inside
< 8	20
8–11	25
11–14	30
> 14	35

Comment

The point has been made that people are relatively insensitive to the absolute level of light in a room, and that task brightness does not correlate very highly with people's performance. But the advantages of using illuminance as a criterion are (a) that it has an obvious physical meaning; (b) that for electric lighting, it is easily calculated and measured; and (c) that it has been widely used for many years.

Probably the majority of desk-based workplaces in the UK have an average daylight factor that is less than 2%, so this requirement would lead to slightly increased fenestration generally which is supported by the evidence on the grounds of both energy economy and user satisfaction.

Clause 4 of the workplace criteria, should not be necessary in a mandatory standard, but experience suggests that it is. When construction of a building is over-running its budget, savings in costs have to be drawn from the last stages of work on the building, such as the fittings, decoration and furnishings. Among these are blinds and lighting controls, and the commissioning of building management systems. It is not unusual to find that these components, essential to the quality of the users' environment, have been omitted or replaced in the specification by inferior items.

Daylight standards in urban planning

Redevelopment of an urban site usually reduces the daylight on existing buildings. In the centre of any city that is economically successful, there is a long-term tendency towards taller buildings and higher plot ratios (plot ratio is the total floor area of a building divided by the site area it occupies). The usual reason for commercial redevelopment is to increase the area of profitable floor space on the site. As a consequence, from decade to decade, the level of daylight on city streets and on the lower windows of the buildings that surround them becomes steadily lower.

Many individuals and groups have an interest in a redevelopment project. Table 6.3 gives some examples.

In the UK, planning control is made on the basis of broad public interest in accordance with policies set out in local development plans (now 'frameworks'). It is not concerned with benefit or loss to individuals, and the rules about what might be taken into account are the outcome of a large number of court decisions. It often occurs that a development that would benefit the area as a whole conflicts with the interests of those who use or own nearby existing buildings. Planning decisions can then be difficult, with strong consequences: construction costs are large and a developer's margin of profit volatile; local residents and users of existing buildings present strong opinions, and political bodies can be involved.

Table 6.3: Some of the interests in commercial redevelopment of an urban site

Party	Interest
Public authority	Health and safety; energy use; environmental standards generally Preservation and enhancement of architectural and historical qualities Economic viability of the town; rates or taxes from the site; the costs of administering development control Public support
Users of adjoining property	Maintaining or improving the environment in and around existing buildings
Owners of adjoining property	Maintaining existing property value; sharing general economic gain
Users of new building	Working conditions; enjoyment of special qualities of the place; privacy
Client or operator of the new building	Initial cost; development time; rental, operating and maintenance costs
Developer	Profit, development time; goodwill

Daylighting requirements are effectively constraints on the form and size of buildings and therefore limits on the profitability of an investment: planning decisions based on daylighting criteria are often challenged. Prolonged negotiation is expensive, especially when a refusal of planning consent is followed by an appeal, but it is worthwhile for the developer to persist with a proposal for as long as the financial expectation of the outcome (the probability of success multiplied by the benefit if successful) is greater than the cost. If there is potentially a large additional profit, it is worthwhile for the developer to press an application even when the probability of success is not large. To achieve a situation in which abortive work by the developer and the costs of implementation by the planning authority are minimised, it is necessary for daylighting requirements to be applied rigorously and consistently. For this to happen, the criteria used must be unchallengeable, and therefore be (a) clearly related to the stated aims of the authority and (b) appropriate to the specific location.

It is useful to consider urban daylight under three headings:

1 Sunshine

In cool weather, direct sunlight is almost always welcome in streets and other urban spaces. It gives warmth and brightness, and enhances enjoyment of the architecture. When the air temperature is such that additional warmth from sunlight increases discomfort, shading is needed, but the brightness of sunlight and the way that it enhances architectural form remains attractive. Sunlight is desirable and often essential in gardens, parks and other areas where there is planting.

The criteria for acceptable exposure to sunlight need to take into account:

(a) winter sunlight on residential buildings where this is required for the health of occupants;

(b) sunlight on planting;

(c) provision of shading where sunlight could cause thermal discomfort;

(d) sunlight on buildings of architectural importance and in outdoor areas where its presence enhances people's enjoyment of the place.

There is also the need to check whether a sudden view of the sun, either direct or reflected from glazing, could be a handicap to drivers.

2 Daylight for illumination

The aim in development control is to ensure that both new and existing buildings are exposed to sufficient sunlight and skylight to enable the criteria of adequate room lighting (such as given above for dwellings and workplaces) to be met. Energy use must be taken into account: it is not to the public benefit for new developments to reduce the daylight on existing buildings to a degree that their use of electric lighting increases.

3 Daylight as information

Earlier in the book, we emphasised that 'view' and 'daylight' are not separate attributes of a window: view is just one of the ways in which we respond to daylight, an ability we have to make use of the information implicit in natural light's variation in direction and time.

The quantity of daylight, whether measured in lux or expressed as a daylight factor, is not a good predictor of view. It comes predominantly from the sky, so it informs about time and weather; and it indicates the level of light within the interior, which, in turn, determines what we might see of whatever is inside the room. But a window that gives only a view of the sky is not usually satisfactory. Generally, it is a broadly horizontal line of sight that gives the most information: looking out through a window, we focus on the distant skyline and the buildings and landscape at about eye level. The upper sky and the ground close below the window are valued parts of a comprehensive view, but the density of information is usually greatest in a zone a few degrees above and below the horizon. A measure of the nearness of obstructing buildings and of the extent of distant view is the horizon factor, which is described in Chapter 7.

Measures and criteria

In development control, tests of whether a proposal meets daylight requirements must be simple and robust: few of

those who submit proposals for development, and few
of those who approve or reject them, have expertise in
daylighting. Every criterion should be paired with a
test that:

1 Can be done manually by a person without advanced
   technical knowledge;
2 Can be done by computer for complex or large
   development proposals;
3 Is consistent – that is, it must give similar results
   for similar situations, and when applied by different
   people;
4 Requires no information outside the project itself that
   is not publicly available – specifically in site
   development, it should not need data on the interior
   of existing buildings.

These are difficult to achieve, and, to a large extent, it is
the choice of the method of testing that determines the type
of criteria set, rather than the other way round. Table 6.4
suggests measures for the three criteria headings.

Vertical sky component, sky factor and horizon factor are
explained in Chapter 7, and probable sunlight hours in
Chapter 3. The measures chosen for the purposes of urban
planning and development control are not necessarily those
that are the best predictors of interior daylight. Their purpose
is to compare alternative development schemes and to
assess the impact of proposed development.

Daylight and street form

Table 6.5 illustrates the essential relationship between the
form and character of a street and the level of daylight there.
It shows nine streets: for each is given a photograph, the
vertical sky component, D_{sv}, and the horizon factor (horizon
index) values, Hi_{30} and Hi_{100}. Also given is the percentage of
the horizontal plane at 2 m above the ground that is covered
by buildings and other constructed objects. This is labelled
the plan fraction, A_p. It applies to an area 100 m × 150 m
centred on the viewpoint.

The sky component and horizon factor values are the
means of three points in each case, calculated for an eye
level 2 m above ground level.

Note how sensitively the vertical sky component varies
with the width : height proportions of the streets. In areas
that are to be conserved, a regulation that requires a higher
value of D_{sv}, the vertical sky component, than that on existing
buildings leads inevitably to built forms that are untypical
architecture. Note also how sunlight is an essential element in
a narrow canyon of a street. A conclusion that might be
drawn from these examples is that narrower streets are more
acceptable in warm sunny climates than in temperate regions.
Considerations of thermal comfort lead to a similar
conclusion.

The horizon factor depends on absolute dimensions,
not ratios. Hi_{30}, the proportion of views less than 30 m,

Table 6.4: Measures of daylight for development control purposes

Requirement	Situation	Measure	Notes
Sunshine	Windows of residential buildings	Probable sunlight hours during November, December and January (in the Northern Hemisphere)	Alternatives are (a) possible sunlight hours and (b) a given duration of possible sunlight on a given day (such as the winter solstice or the equinox).
	Gardens, public open spaces	Annual probable sunlight hours	Probable sunlight hours has the advantage that the criterion can be linked directly with user needs
Daylight for illumination	Cloudy climates and climates with cloudy seasons	Sky component on a vertical plane at window positions	In cloudy climates, skylight is the principal source of illumination
	Sunny climates	(a) Probable sunlight hours on the ground below window (b) Sky factor on a vertical plane at window positions	In dry climates, reflected sunlight can be the principal source, but this might not be applicable to all orientations or in obstructed situations. In that case, an alternative skylight criterion is necessary and the assumption of a uniform sky is probably no less appropriate than a standard overcast sky
Daylight and information: view and proximity		Horizon factor	The horizon factor measures obstructions at eye level

Table 6.5: Daylight and street form. D_{sv}, sky component on vertical surface; Hi, horizon factor; A_p, plan fraction

D_{sv}: 34% without trees
Hi_{30}: 63%
Hi_{100}: 2%
A_p: 29%

Kew, London, UK. A suburban street. Trees reduce the daylight falling on windows more than other buildings do. The street is less than 30 m wide and the buildings on either side are close to each other, so the majority of views are less than 30 m and practically all are less than 10 m.

D_{sv}: 24% without trees
Hi_{30}: 4%
Hi_{100}: 11%
A_p: 25%

Tufnell Park, London, UK. The daylight on the face of buildings is less than in the case above because the skyline is at a higher angle and it is more nearly continuous.

Where the street width approaches 30 m, most views from windows lie in the central zone, but views down crossing roads and wider gaps between buildings yield some long views.

D_{sv}: 17–24%
Hi_{30}: 95%
Hi_{100}: 0%
A_p: 40%

Rye, UK. Small buildings with a relatively narrow street width. The variation in the sky component is caused by the differing roof heights and varying distance between façades.

Note how the use of white paint on facades enhances the brightness appearance of the street.

D_{sv}: 16%
Hi_{30}: 48%
Hi_{100}: 3%
A_p: 59%

Bloomsbury, London, UK. A much larger scale of building than the previous example. In canyon-like streets, the sky component depends on the height/width proportion, while the horizon factor is determined by the absolute width.

Table 6.5: Continued

D_{sv}: 16%
Hi_{30}: 96%
Hi_{100}: 2%
A_p: 47%

Kirkby Lonsdale, UK. A small traditional town often has narrow streets in the centre but buildings on the periphery with extensive views into open landscape. The horizon factor therefore varies greatly, and this is a characteristic that needs to be maintained in conservation projects.

D_{sv}: 14%
Hi_{30}: 98%
Hi_{100}: 0%
A_p: 75%

Spitalfields, London, UK. Eighteenth-century speculative housing. Note the large windows on the left-hand terrace, compensating for low levels of incident daylight.

D_{sv}: 11%
Hi_{30}: 89%
Hi_{100}: 2%
A_p: 67%

Tallinn, Estonia. The sunlight, painted walls and the presence of people give a greater sense of liveliness than the daylight factor suggests.

Table 6.5: Continued

D_{sv}: 9%
Hi_{30}: 96%
Hi_{100}: 2%
A_p: 73%

Florence, Italy. The street activity is here, and so is hazy sunlight. On hot days, the shading is welcome, but in dull winter weather, the street can look dull.

D_{sv}: 2%
Hi_{30}: 99%
Hi_{100}: 0%
A_p: 64%

Santiago de Compostela, Spain. This again illustrates that if there is sunlight and thermal comfort, a street with little skylight can be attractive. Inside the buildings, the lower stories have little daylight. The top storey, though, is well lit and used as dwellings.

is sensitive to street width and changes abruptly as the distance between opposite façades increases from below 30 m to just above. The value of Hi_{100} is sensitive to the spacing of blocks. Where there are significant gaps between adjacent buildings, the proportion of long views is much higher than where street façades are largely continuous.

Conclusions

This chapter examines the implications of the daylight criteria set out in Chapter 1. We have taken two building types and used the criteria to derive the minimum acceptable conditions of daylight. These apply to the design of a new building. We now examine the implications of the criteria for development control, looking in particular at the effect of a new building on the daylight received by nearby existing buildings.

The problem is one of selection: which of the many measures of daylight should be used in assessing the impact of a new building? The formal requirements must be few, clearly relevant and simple to test. The discussion in the last few pages and a critical review of the urban areas illustrated in Table 6.5 suggest two requirements that could form a basis for determining the acceptability of a proposed building.

1 The requirement of health

This is the need to ensure that there is sufficient daylight for the long-term health of building users. It applies to any building where people are not freely able to go outside: care homes, some types of institutional residential building, hospitals and health care buildings with inpatients. It applies to dwellings where a person might be confined indoors through disability or age. With the aim in current policy of enabling those people to remain at home rather than in institutional care, this includes most types of housing.

Taking the list given earlier of minimum acceptable conditions of daylighting in dwellings, a proposed development should ensure that the windows of habitable rooms in existing dwellings continue to receive *either* adequate sunlight *or* adequate skylight. Possible criteria at the minimum acceptable level in the UK are a vertical sky

component on the window of 27% and probable sunlight hours of one half-hour per day through the period 1 November to 28 February. The sunlight criterion is equivalent to about 4% of annual total probable sunlight hours, slightly more demanding than the present criterion of 5% during the winter 6 months.

2 The requirement of local consistency

Table 6.5 shows that daylight varies greatly over the range of common street forms; so do the nature of the architecture, the economic values and the expectations of users. Daylight criteria should do so also.

This implies that the level of daylight to be maintained as a site is redeveloped must be that typical of the locality, unless (a) there are higher values required for health, or (b) the planning authority sets higher values in a planned improvement of the environment of the locality. Particular buildings, or building types, may be given individual criteria, especially where high architectural and historical qualities are to be conserved.

At the stage of local development planning, numerical daylighting criteria should be established – values that are to be the minimum acceptable conditions of daylighting on existing buildings when a site is redeveloped. Normally the criteria of sunlight hours, and vertical sky component would be included. The horizon factor Hi_{30} would be included as a measure of encroachment and loss of privacy where there is to be housing, and the horizon factor Hi_{100} would be included in places where clear open spaces are to be maintained.

Discussion

This approach to development control is motivated by the need to minimise the cost to the planning authority of development control and the cost to the developer of delay and abortive work. It was noted above that this requires criteria to be stated clearly and applied consistently. It also requires that standards be relevant to the place and the conditions. Disputes arise if ad hoc criteria are applied and if there is no consistency; and also in the opposite situation, if blanket criteria are applied in differing circumstances.

The way in which the requirements are stated above implies that if an existing building at present has an exposure to daylight that is above the level defined by the criteria, a new building may reduce it to that level. There is the question, though, whether it is equitable that a building that now enjoys a high level of daylight should have that reduced to the minimum standard for the locality. In present UK practice, it is taken that a loss of 20% of skylight or sunlight is a noticeable reduction.

There are three responses to this. Firstly, the aim is a clear and unchallengeable procedure. Secondly, a reduction in daylight exposure is a general characteristic of city growth and therefore to be anticipated; if there is a reasonable probability that an adjacent site may be redeveloped, this should be a factor in the purchase price of the building. Thirdly, there exist methods in law of gaining damages from the developer; the Rights of Light procedure in the UK is an example,

although legal action is limited in scope and it is not in any case desirable as a part of the normal development process.

It would be possible to adopt the rule that the daylight incident on an existing building may be reduced to whichever of these is the highest: 80% of its present value, the criteria defined by the health requirement and those defined by the local consistency criteria. This would maintain a higher quantity of daylight after development but reduce the potential size of new buildings. An alternative is to state that large and noticeable reductions in daylight are not desirable, even though the final value is above the minimum, and that these will be taken into account in assessing the overall impact of the proposed building on its surroundings.

## seven

Daylight factors

The daylight factor is a way of quantifying the daylight in a room. It was invented before computers were available, and so incorporates several simplifying assumptions to make manual calculation practicable. It remains, however, a very useful tool and is used as a criterion in many daylighting standards.

The worksheets present practical examples: this chapter gives the background. It explains the differences between the different types of daylight factor, and what they mean,

and how the formulae are derived. It then describes the horizon factor which is a measure of the proximity of adjacent buildings.

A daylight factor is the ratio of the daylight illuminance on a given surface to the simultaneous illuminance from the whole sky, expressed as a percentage. It is approximately the ratio between the daylight in a room and the amount on the ground outside. More precisely, as in Figure 7.1, it can be pictured as the illuminance on a desk expressed as a percentage of the illuminance that would be measured there if all the building above the height of the desk, and everything outside, were lifted off. It is assumed, unless specifically stated otherwise, that the sky is cloud-covered with a luminance distribution defined by the CIE Standard Overcast Sky (this was described in Chapter 4). Sunlight is always excluded from the calculation.

This idea of evaluating daylight as a ratio between inside and outside was developed as a way of quantifying daylight when, in the 1930s, only slide rules, books of tables and graphical methods were available for calculations. To reduce the complex varying nature of daylight to useable formulae, some broad simplifying assumptions were made: that there was no sunlight, that the sky was overcast with a simple luminance pattern, that all surfaces inside and outside were diffuse reflectors, and that the room was empty. With the increasing use of daylight factors in practice, the approach became formalised: the sky luminance distribution was formalised as a mathematical function, calculation methods were developed for use in practice, and daylight factor criteria for the lighting of schools and other buildings were embodied in regulations.

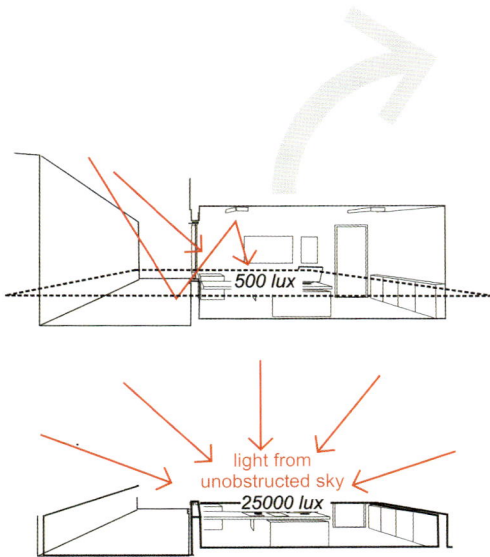

7.1

The daylight factor can be visualised as the illuminance on a room surface expressed as a percentage of the illuminance with all the upper part of the building sliced away. With a desk illuminance of 500 lx and a reference illuminance of 25 klx, the daylight factor at the desk would be 2%.

The use of the daylight factor has persisted to the present day. A procedure used in official standards and codes of practice acquires considerable inertia and continues in practice even though alternatives are available. But the daylight factor has an important characteristic: it is a good indicator of the overall appearance of a room. This is because the brightness appearance of a place depends at least as much on the relative luminance of surfaces within the field of vision as on absolute values: and, by definition, the daylight factor is a measure of the contrast between inside and outside.

Daylight factors take two forms: the daylight factor at a point and the average daylight factor over a surface. The point value was the original form: it is more cumbersome to calculate manually, and it is now usually confined to software applications where the computer evaluates the distribution of daylight across a room. The average daylight factor is an easier calculation and usually a better indicator of the overall appearance of a room.

The average daylight factor

The formulae for average daylight factors are called *total flux* methods. They work by calculating the total amount of light (luminous flux) falling on a surface, then finding the fraction transmitted to the next surface, and so on. Surface illuminance is obtained by dividing the flux received by the surface area. This gives the mean value, but no information about the distribution of light across the surface.

So, to find the average daylight factor in a room, we first find the daylight factor on the outer face of the window – the illuminance on the window surface divided by the simultaneous illuminance on unobstructed ground. There are several ways of estimating this.

1 A rule of thumb

If θ is the angle of visible sky measured in section through the window, as in Figure 7.2, then the average daylight factor on the vertical outside window surface is

$$D_w \approx \frac{\theta}{2}, \text{ where } \theta \text{ is measured in degrees.} \qquad (7.1)$$

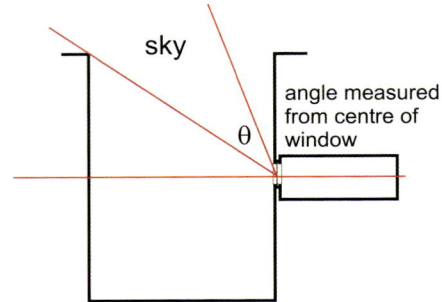

7.2
Angle of visible sky.

The basis for this is twofold: firstly, from an unobstructed sky, the direct illuminance on the vertical surface is about 40% of that on open ground, and reflected light from the ground adds typically about 5%. Secondly, the sky gets brighter towards the zenith but the angle of incidence on the window gets larger, so the contribution from a given value of θ tends to be independent of the elevation.

The daylight factor includes both direct light from the sky and light reflected from the ground, from other buildings and from landscape features such as trees and hills. Some planning regulations use only the direct part as a criterion: this is called the sky component.

2 Sky component with a horizontal skyline

When a window looks out onto a street where the roofline of the opposite buildings is level, the sky component is directly related to the angle of the roofline above the horizon, as in Figure 7.3: see Table 7.1.

This is plotted in Worksheet 3, which gives an example of its use, and the formula is in Section 6.4 of Algorithms and Equations.

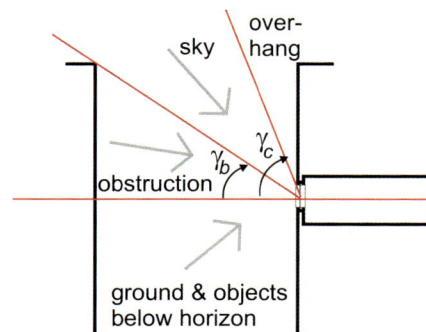

7.3
Angles of obstruction.

Table 7.1: Vertical sky components for a window facing a continuous skyline

Height of skyline above horizon, γ_b, degrees	Sky component on vertical surface, with 20° overhang above ($\gamma_c = 70°$), %	Sky component on plane vertical surface ($\gamma_c = 90°$), %
0	38.51	39.62
10	32.98	34.09
20	26.27	27.38
30	19.09	20.19
40	12.26	13.36
50	6.53	7.64
60	2.40	3.51
70	0	1.11
80	0	0.14

3 Vertical sky component: graphical methods

Graphical techniques were the main means of daylighting evaluation before computers were commonplace. By plotting the window on a scaled chart, or by superimposing overlays or special protractors on architectural drawings, it was possible to estimate levels of daylight with the minimum of calculation. Several ingenious tools were developed for the practitioner: notable are the Waldram diagram and the BRS protractors and nomograms.

Graphical methods are still useful. They permit a relatively quick analysis of situations where the geometry is not compatible with the simplifying assumptions inherent in the methods just described, but, above all, they can be very efficiently adapted for use with images from digital cameras.

Worksheet 3 shows how the sky component on the face of a window can be obtained from a fish-eye photograph.

4 Daylight factor on the window

The sky component is usually the largest part of the incident daylight, but there are other paths by which light reaches the window. A formula to calculate this is Equation (7.9), below. The next few pages show how the formula is derived; you can skip these if you wish and go straight to the next section.

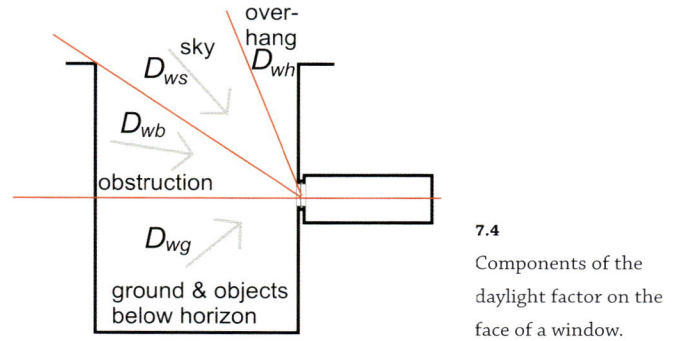

7.4 Components of the daylight factor on the face of a window.

The total daylight factor on the window incorporates the light from four zones. These are shown in Figure 7.4:

D_{wh} — reflection from the head of the window, or projections such as balconies

D_{ws} — sky component

D_{wb} — light reflected from buildings and other objects obscuring the sky

D_{wg} — light reflected from the ground and other surfaces below the window.

The figure shows the zones as parallel bands, as when there is a horizontal roofline, but they may be any shape: an obstruction may be a tall tower or an indeterminate shape such as a tree canopy.

It is necessary now to make some simplifying assumptions so that the calculation remains feasible as a manual method. We are looking for a level of precision consistent with that of finding the sky component. This is what we assume:

1 The sky illuminance on the face of the obstructing building is the same as on the window being studied, and the surface is matt with reflectance ρ_b.

2 The illuminance on an external horizontal plane level below the centre of the window is twice the illuminance on the window, and the effective reflectance of this plane is ρ_g.

3 The amount of light reaching the window after two or more reflections is negligible.

The last of these is a reasonable assumption with an overcast sky unless external reflectances are very high. When there is external sunlight, though, interreflection can be a significant contribution.

So, taking the four components:

The value of D_{wh}, light from an overhang or the soffit of the window opening is usually negligible. Not only is the light falling at glancing incidence on the window, but it has been twice-reflected (upwards by lower surfaces, and then by the underside of the balcony or window soffit).

D_{ws} is the sky component, obtained with a dot diagram or from Table 7.1.

D_{wb} is found as follows. Let D_{wsb} be the additional sky component if there were no obstructions above the horizon. This can be found in the same way as the sky component by taking the obstruction to be visible sky. If, however, the overhead obstruction is small, with γ_c greater than 70° or so, it is adequate to take

$$D_{wsb} = D_{wo} - D_{wh} - D_{ws} \qquad (7.2)$$

where D_{wo} is the vertical sky component from an unobstructed sky (given in Table 7.1 as 39.62%).

The obstruction-reflected component is then D_{wsb} scaled by the ratio of the obstruction luminance to the sky luminance that it obscures.

Let L_b be the luminance of the building and L_h the luminance of the sky just above the horizon. Following the assumptions above, we take the illuminance on the obstruction to equal that from direct skylight on the window. This sky component is, by definition, a percentage of the horizontal unobstructed illuminance, E_{dh}:

$$D_{ws} = \frac{E_{ws}}{E_{dh}} \times 100 \qquad (7.3)$$

The luminance of the obstruction is

$$L_b = \frac{E_{ws}\rho_b}{\pi} \qquad (7.4)$$

But, from the definition of the CIE Overcast Sky, there is a fixed relationship between sky luminance just above the horizon and E_{dh}:

$$E_{dh} = \frac{7\pi}{3}L_h \qquad (7.5)$$

Then, substituting back into Equation (7.3) and rearranging,

$$\frac{L_b}{L_h} = \frac{7\rho_b D_{ws}}{300} \qquad (7.6)$$

So the obstruction-reflected component is

$$D_{wb} = (D_{wo} - D_{ws})\frac{7\rho_b D_{ws}}{300} \qquad (7.7)$$

The light reflected from the ground plane is found in a similar way. From the assumption above, the illuminance on the ground plane is twice that of the adjacent vertical surface. Its luminance is the illuminance multiplied by the reflectance, divided by π. Treating this as a half-infinite plane, the illuminance back onto the window by reflection is the ground plane luminance multiplied by $\pi/2$, so, very simply,

$$D_{wg} = D_{ws}\,\rho_g \qquad (7.8)$$

The daylight factor on the vertical surface of a window is therefore

$$D_w = D_{ws}\left(1 + D_{wsb}\frac{7\rho_b}{300} + \rho_g\right) \qquad (7.9)$$

The value of D_{wsb} is given by Equation (7.2), but if the window head overhang is not greater than about 20° the approximation $D_{wsb} \simeq (39.62 - D_{ws})$ is adequate.

Chapter 8 continues the analysis of light reflection in a street.

The average daylight factor in a room

The interior daylight illuminance is found by multiplying the illuminance on the window by the window area, then dividing it by the interior surface area. This is the application of the total flux principle: it does not matter that we are working with daylight factors, which are relative values, not lumens and lux directly. So, if all of the light falling on the window passed through the glazing onto the room surfaces, the average daylight factor on these surfaces would be

$$\bar{D} = D_w \frac{a_w}{a_r} \qquad (7.10)$$

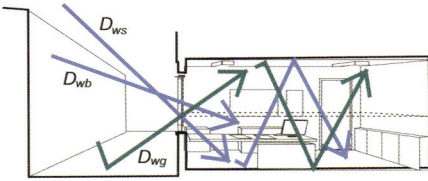

7.5
The split-flux method. Light falling downwards on the
window is assessed separately from upward light.

where a_w is the area of glazing and a_r the total room surface
area (walls, ceiling and floor).

Two things affect the outcome, though: firstly, some of
the light is lost because the glazing and the dirt on it absorbs
some of the light – the proportion passing through is referred
to as the transmittance, τ. Secondly, there is interreflection
within the room, which increases the amount of light energy
falling on surfaces. As a first approximation, the room can be
treated as an integrating sphere and Sumpner's formula
applied (see Chapter 2). The equation for the average
daylight factor thus becomes

$$\bar{D} = D_w \frac{a_w \, \tau}{a_r \, (1-\rho)} \tag{7.11}$$

where ρ is the mean reflectance of the enclosing
room surfaces – ceiling, walls (including windows) and
floor.

Equation (7.11) gives the average daylight factor across
all the room surfaces. It would be useful, though, to
know how much light falls on the ceiling and upper walls –
which subjectively is a good indicator of the brightness
appearance of the room – and on the working plane and
lower surfaces, so comparisons can be made with
electric lighting.

We therefore split the room at mid-height, to get an upper
and a lower part, as in Figure 7.5, and we make that further
assumption, that all downward light falls initially on the lower
surfaces and all upward light initially on the upper part of
the room.

The final illuminance over all the lower surfaces is the
initial illuminance from downward light, the first reflection
from the upper part of the upward light on the window,

plus the effect of interreflection. The daylight factor on the
lower surfaces is thus

$$\bar{D}_{\text{lower}} = \frac{2\tau(D_{ws} + D_{wb} + D_{wg}\rho_u) \, a_w}{(1 - \rho_u\rho_l) \, a_r} \tag{7.12}$$

And, equivalently, for the upper part of the room,

$$\bar{D}_{\text{upper}} = \frac{2\tau[D_{wg} + (D_{ws} + D_{wg})\rho_l] \, a_w}{(1 - \rho_u\rho_l) \, a_r} \tag{7.13}$$

ρ_u and ρ_l are the average reflectances of the upper and lower
parts, and each part is taken to have an area $a_r/2$.

If the window has a shading device over it, or horizontal
louvred blinds inside, the transmittance may vary with
direction. This is discussed in Chapter 9.

Equation (7.12) can be simplified firstly by substituting $\theta/2$
for $(D_{ws} + D_{wb} + D_{wg}\rho_u)$ and secondly by using ρ^2 instead of
$\rho_u\rho_l$, where ρ is the overall mean reflectance. The equation
then becomes

$$\bar{D}_{\text{BRE}} = \frac{\theta \, \tau \, a_w}{(1 - \rho^2) \, a_r} \tag{7.14}$$

This formula was developed at the Building Research
Establishment and is used extensively in the UK in daylighting
regulations and codes of practice. The BRE formula was
developed theoretically for the average daylight factor on a
horizontal working plane at desktop height, and was tested
and found to agree well with measurements in a model room.

Equations (7.12) and (7.14) produce very similar results.
Figure 7.6 shows the correlation between them when applied
to two samples of 41 rooms varying randomly in length,
width and height, in window area and in external obstruction
angle. The split-flux values are slightly below the BRE daylight
factors when the obstruction is large, but the agreement is
very good otherwise.

These forms of the split-flux formula and the BRE equation
can therefore be taken to be interchangeable in most practical
contexts. The shorter BRE equation is appropriate when the
obstruction creates a skyline parallel with the horizon; the
split-flux method should be used with vertical or complex
obstructions when it is necessary to first obtain the daylight
factor on the face of the window.

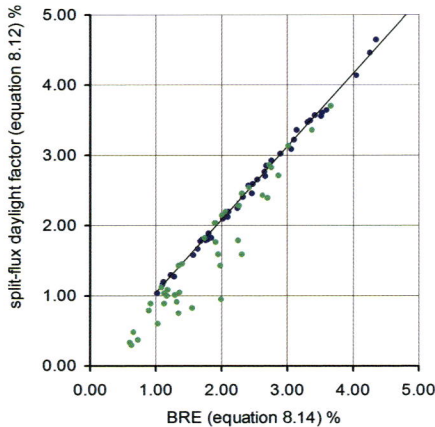

7.6

Comparison between the split-flux formula and the BRE formula for the average daylight factor. This was calculated by randomly allocating width, depth and ceiling height to 41 rectilinear rooms, then applying both formulae.

Two cases were examined. In the first, the external obstructions were limited to a skyline height randomly selected in the range 10° to 25° (blue dots). In the second, the obstructions could be much larger, from 10° up to 60° (green dots).

Parameters were window transmittance 0.5; upper and lower reflectances 0.7 and 0.3; width range 3–6 m; depth 3–8 m; ceiling 2.8–4 m; glazed fraction of window wall 0.2–0.7.

The 'correct' daylight factor doesn't exist!

Every daylight factor formula is based on simple assumptions that are taken to be models of a real situation: that the CIE Overcast Sky formula describes a real sky; that internal and external surfaces are matt, with uniform reflectance; that the room is empty; and so on. Furthermore, even the few simple parameters that most formulae use can rarely be better than fair estimates; and quantities such as the reflectance of surfaces and the transmittance of windows can rarely be other than informed guesses, because it is just not known what will happen in the building during its lifetime. Unfortunately, the final calculated daylight factor is very sensitive to these parameters: for example, taking glazing transmittance to be 0.6 instead of 0.5 leads to a 20% increase in the result of the calculation using Equation (7.14).

A calculated daylight factor is best considered an indicator of room performance when the sky is overcast. It does not exist in the real world, and it can never be measured, because real buildings never match the assumptions embodied in the formula. What then is the usefulness of these calculations? The answer is that they are valuable in three ways:

Firstly, the average daylight factor is an indicator of the appearance of a room. Chapter 1 showed that people's satisfaction with their environment depended on their expectations, which depended, in turn, on their experiences. Although a given value of average daylight factor is most unlikely to have the same subjective connotations everywhere in the world, in temperate climates, and particularly in rooms such as offices and classrooms, there appears to be a good consistency in the relationship between average daylight factor and subjective appraisal of daylighting. It is summed up in Table 7.2.

Secondly, the average daylight factor is a robust basis for architectural decisions. It can be calculated at an early design stage: the formulae can be inverted, so, by adopting a particular daylight factor, such as 2%, the required window area can be calculated. This then informs the design of façades and the overall nature of the building.

Thirdly, under some circumstances, daylight factors can produce accurate predictions of available daylight in a room. This is described in the next chapter.

Table 7.2: Average daylight factor in offices compared with visual character of the room: temperate climates, side windows

Average daylight factor from side windows	Rooms without electric lighting	Rooms with daytime electric lighting
1%	Gloomy appearance, harsh contrast with view out	Electric lighting may mask daylight variation
2%	Areas distant from a window may seem underlit	Appearance of daylit room even if electric lighting is the main task illumination
5%	The room looks brightly daylit. Visual and thermal discomfort may occur with large window areas	Electric lighting rarely needed
10%	The character of a semi-outdoor space, such as a conservatory. Visual and thermal conditions may be unsuitable for office-type tasks	

It is important that the presentation of daylight factor as a number indicates the confidence limits of the calculation. Look again at the series of percentages in the left-hand column of Table 7.2. Each number is double, or more, the previous value. We can say that there is a significant difference, in both the subjective character and the physical environment, between a room with an average daylight factor of 2% and one with an average daylight factor of 5%. There may be a noticeable difference between rooms with daylight factors of 2% and 3%. However, not only would a difference between 2% and 2.1% be almost certainly subjectively unnoticeable, but such a distinction would be completely unjustified scientifically. The level of uncertainty in the parameters and the simplifying assumptions in the models preclude such pretensions to precision. Average daylight factor calculations have little absolute meaning beyond the decimal place. The percentage values should be rounded off to the nearest whole number except in very controlled situations, such as when alternative designs are being compared and calculations are made with the same formula and with matching parameters.

Daylight factors are used in regulations to ensure that a specific level of natural light is achieved in buildings. It should be clear from the last few paragraphs that if a requirement is for a particular average daylight factor, the formula for calculating this must also be specified. It is also important to specify the criterion in a way that takes rounding into account. A figure written as '2%' implies some number equal to or greater than 1.5% and less than 2.5%; a minimum requirement of '2.0%' has the meaning that a value of 1.95% obtained by the specified type of calculation would be acceptable. In regulations, it is therefore normal to find a required level of numerical precision one level greater than justified by the basis of the calculation. The accuracy of daylight measurements and calculations in general is discussed in the last section of Chapter 8.

Correlations and variations

An average daylight factor is largely a geometrical calculation: no lighting units appear in the formulae; the only values that are not areas or angles are reflectance and transmittance,

and these are non-dimensional ratios. It is not surprising that values calculated with equations such as (7.12) correlate with other geometrical measures. There is a very strong relationship between the average daylight factor and the ratio of window to total surface area. This is not surprising, because this ratio is a key part of the daylight factor equation. Parameters of room shape, reflectance, transmittance and sky angles tend in practice to lie within a small range, so the ratio of areas is a valid and convenient predictor of average daylight factor. Figure 7.7 shows this.

The ratio of window to floor area was long used as a means of specifying the daylight required in a room. There is justification for this, as can be seen in Figure 7.8. These results suggest that for simple robust standards, such ratios may be more appropriate that the longer formulae of daylight factor calculations.

In some countries, the point daylight factor in the centre of the room is used as a criterion. Figure 7.9 compares this with the average daylight factor. With low to moderate angles of obstruction by a horizontal skyline, the two measures are close. When a high obstruction blocks more of the sky, the point value in the centre tends to be lower than the average across the room.

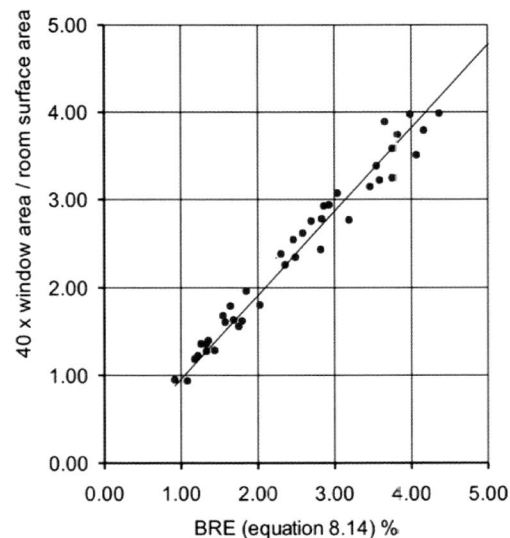

7.7

Comparison between the BRE equation and the window area/room surface area fraction. Calculated as for Figure 7.6 with external obstruction angle 10–25°.

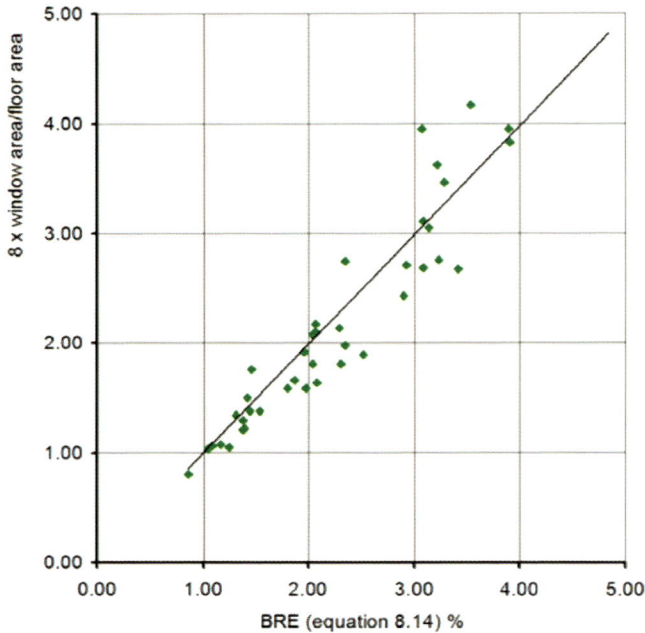

7.8

Comparison between the BRE equation and the window area/floor area fraction. Calculated as for Figure 7.6 with external obstruction angle 10°–25°.

The internally reflected component

The daylight falling on a room surface consists of light that has come directly through the window and light that has been reflected by another interior surface. These can be separated in the average daylight factor formulae. In the BRE formula, Equation (7.14), the term $(1 - \rho^2)^{-1}$ is the sum of the series

$$1+ \rho^2 + (\rho^2)^2 + (\rho^2)^3 + (\rho^2)^4 + \dots$$

which represents the direct light on the surface plus light that has bounced off the surface, then off another surface back to the original, then light that has undergone two pairs of reflections, and so on. If the direct light is excluded, we get

$$[\rho^2 + (\rho^2)^2 + (\rho^2)^3 + (\rho^2)^4 + \dots] = \frac{\rho^2}{1- \rho^2}, \text{ provided } \rho^2 < 1$$

which leads to the rule that the internally reflected component equals the average daylight factor multiplied by the reflectances involved in each bounce. That is, for the formulae given,

$$\bar{D}_{irc} = \rho\, \bar{D}$$
$$\bar{D}_{irc\ lower} = \rho_u\rho_l\, \bar{D}_{lower}$$
$$\bar{D}_{irc\ upper} = \rho_u\rho_l\, \bar{D}_{upper}$$
$$\bar{D}_{irc\ BRE} = \rho^2\bar{D}_{BRE} \qquad\qquad (7.15)$$

The second and third of these use the split-flux formula. In these, the initial illuminance is taken to include the first reflection of upward light by the ceiling and of downward light by the floor. The first equation gives the mean component over all room surfaces, the second and third apply to the upper and lower halves of a room, and the fourth to interreflection on the working plane.

Secondary spaces

Figure 7.10 shows an L-shaped room. Interiors like this should be treated as two separate spaces, because the daylight can vary significantly between the two parts.

The procedure is to find first the average daylight factor in the main space, treating this as a simple rectangular room, then

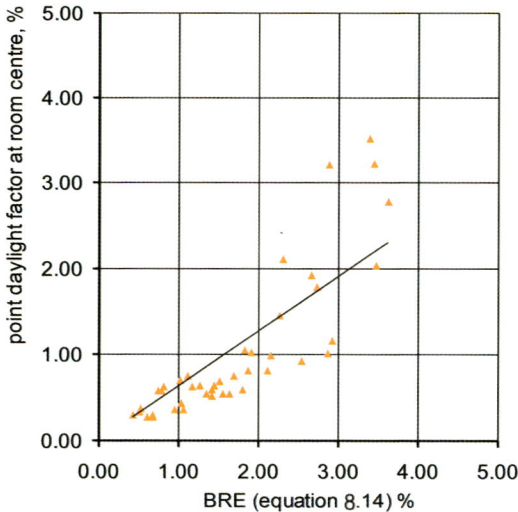

7.9

Comparison between the BRE equation and the point daylight factor at desktop height in the centre of a room. Calculated as for Figure 7.6 with external obstruction angle 10–60°.

With low obstruction angles (high daylight factors), the two values agree well. When the obstruction angle is large, the point value is lower than the average. The trend line shows the best linear fit overall.

7.10

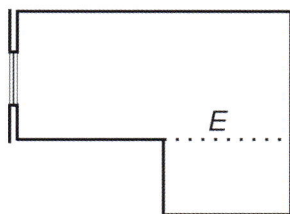

Primary and secondary spaces in an L-shaped room.

7.11

Sky angles with rooflights.

to treat the opening, *E*, between the two as a window through which daylight flows to the secondary space.

To find the daylight factor on *E*, Equation (7.11) is usually the most appropriate, because it gives the mean over all the surfaces of the room. If, however, the main window is obscured from *E*, the interreflected component should be used. We need the following values:

a_e area of *E*

a_{r1} surface area of main space (walls, including *E*), floor, ceiling

a_{r2} surface area of secondary space (including *E*)

ρ_1, ρ_2 mean reflectance of main and secondary spaces (taking into account that the opening *E* has in effect a reflectance close to zero).

The mean daylight over the enclosing surfaces of the secondary space is given by

$$\bar{D}_2 = D_E \frac{a_E}{a_{r2}\,(1-\rho_2)}$$

$$= D_w \frac{a_w\,a_E\,\tau}{a_{r1}\,a_{r2}(1-\rho_1)(1-\rho_2)} \qquad (7.16)$$

This uses the form of daylight factor defined by Equation (7.11) because to find D_E, we are concerned with the light falling on the vertical surfaces of the main space, not the horizontal working plane.

Windows in other planes

All the formulae that we have considered up to now have been to find the daylight obtained by a vertical window. The BRE equation (7.12), is, however applicable to horizontal rooflights and to sloping glazing. The sky angle θ is measured in the centre of the opening, in the plane of the inside face, as in Figure 7.11. If the skyline, the top of the obstructions,

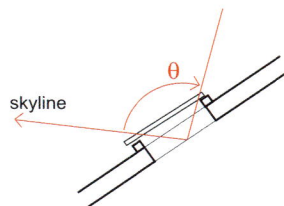

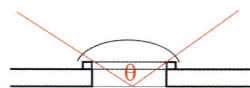

is visible, this forms the lower limit to the sky angle; it is never below the horizon. The upper limit may be given by the window reveal, as in the upper diagram. Horizontal rooflight angles are normally determined by the depth of the reveal, as in the lower.

The angle θ may be greater than 90°. This implies that rooflights give greater illuminance than side windows of the same area. This is true, but it is usually the working plane or the floor of the room that is more strongly illuminated: the walls and the ceiling receive less, so the room may appear relatively dark. A common recommendation is that if a room is lit with horizontal rooflights, the average daylight factor should be twice the value required for such a space with side windows.

Rooflights in general have a lower glazing transmittance, τ, than side windows. They tend to be dirtier, of heavier glazing, and more obstructed by frames and supports.

More than one window in the room

Illuminance is additive: if two lamps shine on a surface, the combined illuminance is the sum of their individual illuminances. They do not interact. The average daylight factor in a room with several windows is the sum of the daylight factors calculated separately from each. If there are two or more windows in a wall, of the same construction and with the same view of the sky, all can be treated as one window with the total glazed area.

There is one proviso: all windows must be taken into account when assessing the mean reflectance of interior surfaces. Since most light falling on a window, from either side, passes through it, the effective reflectance of glazing is low, typically about 0.1. If one-third of a wall is glazed, and the reflectance of the non-glazed area is 0.5, the area-weighted mean reflectance would be

$$\frac{2 \times 0.5 + 0.1}{3} \simeq 0.37$$

Glazing below the working plane

The BRE equation embodies the assumption that all downward light falls on the working plane. If a significant area of the glazing is below working plane height, the equation over-estimates the average daylight factor. The following modification is based on the assumption that the light entering through the low glazing is reflected twice before reaching the working plane:

$$\bar{D}_{BRE'} = \frac{\theta \, \tau \, (a_{wa} + \rho^2 a_{wb})}{(1 - \rho^2) \, a_r} \tag{7.17}$$

where a_{wa} and a_{wb} are, respectively, the areas of glazing above and below the working plane.

The same assumption cannot, strictly, be made about the split-flux equation, because the downward light is taken to fall on all of the lower half of the room. But, numerically, the split-flux and the BRE formulae are close, and, so that they can be used interchangeably, the following amendment could be made pragmatically:

$$\bar{D}_{lower'} = \frac{2\tau \left[\left(D_{ws} + D_{wb} \right) \left(a_{wa} + \rho_u \rho_l \, a_{wb} \right) + D_{wg} \rho_u \, a_w \right]}{(1 - \rho_u \rho_l) \, a_r} \tag{7.18}$$

Equation (7.13) for light on the upper surface of the room remains unchanged.

Rooms with balconies

If a balcony is largely enclosed, it behaves as a separate room. The procedure is then to treat the balcony as a main space and the room itself as a secondary area. Equation (7.16) is then applied. If the balcony is glazed, another transmittance factor should be included; then the mean daylight factor in the room is

$$\bar{D}_{room} = D_{bw} \frac{a_{bw} \, a_{rw} \, \tau_{bw} \tau_{rw}}{a_b \, a_r (1 - \rho_b)(1 - \rho_r)} \tag{7.19}$$

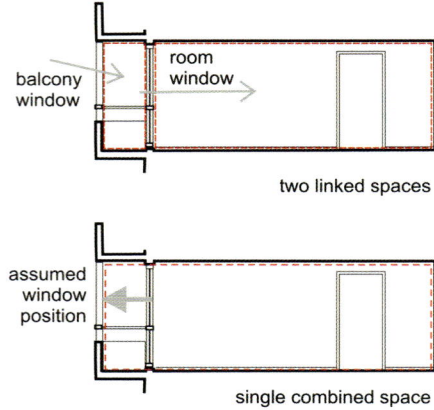

7.12
Alternative methods for rooms with balconies.

where D_{bw} is the daylight factor on the face of the balcony window; a_{bw} and τ_{bw} are the area and transmittance of the balcony window; a_{rw} and τ_{rw} are the corresponding values for the glazing between balcony and room; a_b is the surface area of the balcony (including openings) and a_r is the surface area of the room; and ρ_b and ρ_r are the mean surface reflectances.

An alternative is to treat the balcony and room as a single space with the combined dimensions, as in Figure 7.12. All the glazing is assumed to be in the balcony windows; this is given transmittance $\tau_{bw} \times \tau_{rw} \times b_{rw}$, where b_{rw} is the fraction of the cross-section of the room that is blocked by window and doorframes between balcony and room.

Inserting the dimensions into Equation (7.12), the daylight factor in the lower half of the room is therefore

$$\bar{D}_{room \, lower} = \frac{2\tau_{bw} \, \tau_{rw} \, b_{rw} (D_{bws} + D_{bwb} + D_{bwg} \rho_u) \, a_{bw}}{(1 - \rho_u \rho_l) \, (a_r + a_b)} \tag{7.20}$$

Atria, arcades and greenhouses

Daylight in the atrium space

An atrium, which in the modern sense is a large well-glazed internal space, is no different in principle to any other room. It is often the major volume in the building, though, intended to be a prestigious space, perhaps a grand entrance, with a size and geometry that suggest that daylight analysis could be difficult. Often it isn't.

7.13

Shopping arcade in Norwich, UK.

7.14

Shopping arcade, Great Torrington, Devon, UK.

1 A quick and dirty method for spaces with a high proportion of glazing

Imagine that you are standing on the open site, and the walls and framework of the building, by magic or by helicopter, suddenly appear around you. What fraction of the sky is now blocked from your view?

Now glass is installed in the windows and the rooflights. How bright is the sky seen through the glass, compared with the clear opening?

Time passes. Climbing plants now grow within the space, people have hung banners from the roof and the glazing doesn't seem to have been cleaned very much. How much daylight is there now, compared with the level when the building was new?

The daylight factor on open ground is, by definition, 100%. The daylight factor at the point you were standing is

100% × (fraction of sky visible) × (transmittance of glazing) × (light loss factor)

or

$$D = 100 f_s \tau_g f_m \qquad (7.21)$$

Two major approximations are embedded in this calculation: no account is taken of the luminance distribution of the sky and internal interreflection is ignored. The more evenly the windows are distributed over the hemisphere of sky, the less the sky distribution matters. And if there is a large amount of glazing, interreflection is small by comparison with the sky component.

In the early design stages of a building, Equation (7.21) can be inverted to obtain an estimate of the glazing fraction required. For example, suppose that a daylight factor of 10% is needed in a conservatory space. Assuming a glazing transmittance of 0.5 and a maintenance factor of 0.7, the fraction of the building envelope that should be glazed is

$$f_s = \frac{D}{100\,\tau_g f_m}$$

$$= \frac{10}{100 \times 0.5 \times 0.7} = 0.29 \qquad (7.22)$$

Something between one-quarter and one-third of the surface area of walls and roof need to be glazed.

2 Using dot diagrams

If a fish-eye photograph looking upwards at the interior of the atrium is available or a stereographic image of the walls and roof can be drawn, the overlays given in the data sheets can be used to estimate the sky component. Worksheet 8 tells you how to plot stereographic projections.

Figure 7.15 shows a site photograph taken with a fish-eye lens looking upward in a central city area. Superimposed is a proposed atrium with just the outlines plotted on a stereographic diagram from a point 2 m below the ceiling of the room, which is rectangular in plan and has four glazed openings in the ceiling. Tall buildings nearby partly block the sky. Laid on top of both images is a daylight diagram. The number of dots on unobstructed sky is proportional to the sky component on an external horizontal surface. An alternative overlay gives the sky component on a vertical surface.

Each dot is worth 0.1% sky component; there are 281 that lie on the sky visible through the glazing. If the glazing transmittance is 0.5 and the light loss factor (which accounts for dirt) is 0.6, the sky component on a horizontal surface 2 m below one of the openings would be 281 × 0.1% × 0.5 × 0.6 = 8.43%, which should be rounded to 8%.

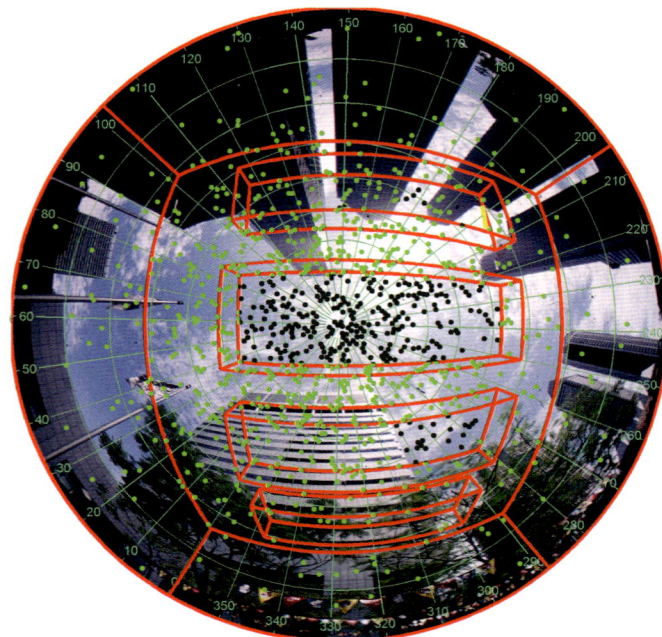

7.15

Dot diagram overlay used to assess sky component.

The interreflected light can be found by using Sumpner's formula again:

$$\overline{D_{irc}} = \frac{D_{hr\,roof}\, a_{window}\, \tau_g\, \rho_{well}}{a_{well}(1 - \rho_{well})} \qquad (7.23)$$

This gives the mean interreflected component on the interior surfaces of the well. In a deep well with light-coloured surfaces, the reflected light can be a large fraction of the total illuminance on the walls near the base. The symbols a_{window} and a_{well} are the glazed area and the total internal surface area. D_{hr} is the daylight factor on the outside of the window and ρ_{well} the mean well reflectance.

The direct and reflected components are added, and the result rounded to the nearest integer. See the final section of Chapter 8, which discusses accuracy and presentation of calculations.

3 BRE average daylight factor formula

Suitable for shallow spaces, such as the arcade in Figure 7.14, and where roof lights are simple in form, the BRE formula,

7.16
A makeshift covered market.
The canopies shade goods from
sunlight and offer some shelter
from tropical rain.
Singapore

Equation (7.14), gives the mean daylight factor on a horizontal surface. In all but the shallowest spaces, this can be taken as the floor. Figure 7.11 illustrates how the angle of view can be estimated.

Deep spaces

The proportions of an atrium space are characterised by the well index

$$k_{wi} = \frac{h(w+l)}{2wl}$$

where *l*, *w* and *h* are the length, width and height of the well.

As the well index increases the distribution of light becomes increasingly sensitive to the shape of the space in plan and section, the surface reflectances, and whether these are diffuse or specular. Ultimately, it becomes a light pipe (which is discussed in Chapter 9). Atrium spaces make an excellent subject for theoretical lighting analysis, and several good abstract models have been developed. RADIANCE and other lighting simulation software has been used to evaluate complex atrium forms, but, because the light distribution is very sensitive to changes in parameters, care must be taken in setting up the model and ensuring that check calculations are made.

For the designer, the design of an atrium or of another type of highly glazed space is straightforward because the important decisions are the obvious ones:

- How much glazing is needed?
- How will direct sunlight be controlled?
- How will heating, cooling and ventilation be managed?

These are strategic decisions, made at an early stage of a project, and when an atrium fails – by overheating, perhaps – it is usually because obvious design questions have not been answered.

One of the reasons for planning buildings around atria is to incorporate planting, especially varieties too large to be normal indoor plants. Illumination is essential to their survival, and both daylight and electric light can contribute. Lamps are available with a spectral output more efficient for photosynthesis than those with spectra aimed at optimum luminous efficacy.

The illuminance required depends not just on the species, but also on their prior cultivation. Plants from nurseries in warm climates tend to require more light than those adapted to the smaller levels of daylight in cool regions. Broadly the range of required illuminances extends from 200 lx to over 2000 lx, but specialist local knowledge is needed for specific guidance. With large specimens, light is required not only on the upper canopy, but also on lower parts of the plant. Just as in their natural habitat, species of plants indoors tend to colonise the microclimates best suited to them, and indoor landscape design should begin with mapping physical conditions throughout the atrium – light, temperature, humidity – and using this analysis to select the planting.

Secondary rooms

The daylight in rooms with windows looking out into atria can be estimated using the approach for secondary spaces described above.

For offices, it is usually in buildings with deep plan form that windows looking into an atrium are found. They are a substitute for windows to the outside, and often less satisfactory, because most, if not all, of the secondary room tends to be behind the no-sky line, and an internal view is less liked by users than one to the outside world. An atrium view is, however, preferred to an entirely windowless space.

If, however, the atrium space is a circulation route – a shopping mall, an enclosed walking area within a care home, or the means of linking classrooms in a school – secondary spaces, as well as being the shops or classrooms, can be rest areas, places for social interaction, coffee shops or private study areas; and, if these are designed to have windows giving special views and patches of bright daylight, an atrium can be a complex and interesting place.

Atria give scope for an architecture that changes through the cycle of day and night. It is possible, in tall atria, to maintain a daylit appearance after dark with the use of high-colour-temperature lamps mounted near roof lights to simulate skylight and high-pressure sodium lamps giving patches of apparent sunlight. Glass surfaces are black, though, and the illusion is never complete. Usually, as in Figure 7.17, dusk triggers a completely different character of

7.17

A shopping mall by day and by night.

Sha Tin, Hong Kong, China

place, and lighting that reinforces our sense of time is inherently desirable.

Daylight at a point

The *sky factor* is the simplest and oldest measure of the daylight at a point in a building. It is the illuminance on a surface from direct skylight, expressed as a percentage of the illuminance from the unobstructed sky. It differs from the sky component of the daylight factor in two ways: it is based on a sky of uniform luminance, and it is calculated on the assumption that windows are unglazed.

The sky factor is thus a dimensionless quantity (being a ratio) and it is calculated from purely geometric parameters (since reflectance of surfaces and transmittance of glazing are both excluded). There are advantages to this: it depends solely on the dimensions of buildings, not on their colours and materials, which can change; and it is the most easily calculated of daylight illuminance indicators.

The sky factor is still used as a criterion in Rights of Light cases in English law and is discussed in Worksheet 17.

The sky component of the daylight factor

The sky factor was succeeded, in all but Right of Light cases, by the sky component. This is a more realistic approach: it assumes that the sky has the luminance distribution of an overcast sky and that the windows are glazed. Figure 7.18 shows the path of light from sky to room. The formulae for calculating the sky component take four factors into account:

1   The luminance pattern of the sky. Unless otherwise stated, this is the CIE Standard Overcast Sky.
2   Dirt on the window. This is normally assumed to be a constant, such as 0.8.
3   The transmittance of the glazing. This varies with the angle at which light strikes the surface. The transmittance of glass is greatest when a beam is perpendicular to the plane of the glass, but approaches zero with light that just skims the surface.
4   The angle of incidence at the room surface.

The sky component formulae are obtained by combining equations for the four factors, then mathematically integrating over the angles that define the view of the sky from the room surface.

This results in some long equations, but it is not normally necessary to evaluate these directly. In the 1950s and 60s, tables of sky components were published and various

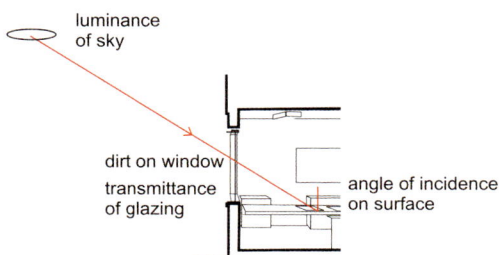

7.18
Calculating the sky component.

graphical methods were invented; sometimes these are still useful. For everyday practice, there is software, usually part of larger applications, that produces daylight contours across room surfaces.

External and internal reflection

In the conventional approach to daylight factor calculation, the other pathways of light between sky and room surface are collected together in the *externally reflected component (ERC)* and the *internally reflected component (IRC)*. The first includes only light reflected from buildings and other objects above the horizon; typically, this is found by assuming that the obstructing surfaces are 0.2 times the luminance of the sky they obscure. The IRC deals with the interreflection within the room, and includes light that has been reflected from the ground. Equations (7.15) can be used to find the average value of the IRC.

In a side-lit room, the IRC decreases with distance into the room; however, usually the maximum is not immediately beside the window, but a short distance into the room – this is because some of the light falling on the window goes outwards through the window. When assessing the minimum daylight factor in a room, usually at the greatest distance from a window, an estimate of the minimum IRC is used; there is an equation for this in Algorithms and Equations.

Daylight factor contours

The distribution of daylight across a room is depicted well by contours of equal daylight factor; they give far more information than the average daylight factor. Several software packages include routines for producing such contours. Manual calculations, though, can be useful, and contours can be sketched if the daylight factor is estimated or calculated at two or three points in a room. Figure 7.19 is an example; it shows daylight factor contours on a horizontal surface at desktop level. Worksheet 5 shows how point daylight factors are calculated.

The horizon factor

The horizon factor (also known as the horizon index) is not a measure of light but an indicator of the proximity to a window of buildings and other obstructions. It provides a measure of

7.19

Daylight factor contours in a general office.

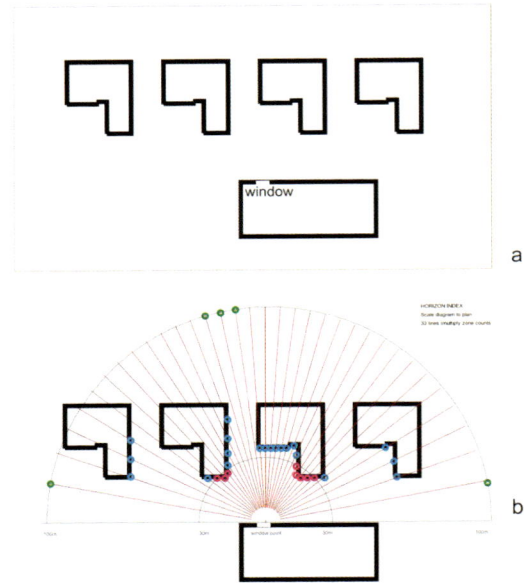

7.20

Using the *Hi* overlay: here, 8 lines (24%) are blocked within 30 m, 5 lines (15%) reach 100 m.

encroachment and potential loss of privacy; it is also an indicator of the extent of the view from a window. In another form, the horizon factor can be used also as a measure of apparent urban density.

It is a complement to the daylight factor, because it takes into account the angle above the horizon of an external obstruction but not its nearness.

This is what the horizon factor is: imagine taking a horizontal slice through a window at eye level, forming a horizontal plane over the whole site. Projecting upwards through the plane are the obstructions that are higher than eye level at the window – buildings, trees, hills. They all obscure some of the horizon. Now measure two things:

1   The fraction of the horizon that is blocked by obstructions nearer than 30 m
2   The fraction of the horizon that is either unobstructed or obstructed by objects more than 100 m away.

The horizon factor can be calculated by drawing a number of radial lines on a site plan and then counting the number of intersecting obstructions. An overlay that does this is included in Worksheet 18.

Figure 7.20 illustrates this. The overlay is located on the plan with the centre of the semicircle on the window being studied, and it is orientated to a line of sight perpendicular to the window wall. The faces of all buildings within the semicircle that are higher than the viewpoint are marked, and

the points where the radiating lines intersect these façades within the 30 m arc are counted; so are the lines that are not blocked within 100 m. The horizon factor is presented as a pair of percentages, Hi_{30} and Hi_{100}. Using this overlay, the line counts are multiplied by three to obtain percentages. In the example, $Hi_{30} = 24\%$ and $Hi_{100} = 15\%$.

In the context of European expectations, an interpretation of the horizon factor could be as shown in Table 7.3.

In the example of Figure 7.20, the values of 24% and 15% indicate that, should the larger block be a residential building, its users would have glimpses of a far view but might find the other blocks too close. Almost certainly, any further intrusion into the 30 m zone would be unwelcome.

Table 7.3: Proximity zones

Zone	Distance of obstruction from window	
Hi_{30}	Less than 30 m	Intrusion within this zone threatens privacy because at this range it is possible to see into facing windows. An extension or a new building in this zone is likely to be resented even if it has a blank façade
Hi_{100}	More than 100 m	Long views into this zone tend to be highly valued, especially if complemented by nearby views of activities

The horizon factor is weighted so that sightlines perpendicular to the window are more important than those at a skewed angle of view; the number of lines in a segment of view centred on an angle θ from the perpendicular is proportional to cos θ, the same relationship as illuminance from an oblique angle of light.

Only obstruction by buildings and other elements of the built environment are normally taken into account: the value of Hi should not be affected by obstruction due to trees, hillsides and the natural world in general. This reflects the preferences for the content of a view. There are some instances where this might not apply, such as when a neighbour's view is blocked by fast-growing conifers.

There is scope also to use this aspect of the Hi to negotiate over landscaping in association with new development. Trees planted in front of a new building could reduce its measured impact by the extent to which they mask it from sight.

The horizon factor can be used also to assess the extent of views and the degree of enclosure from a specific urban open space and from the streets and open areas of a defined area of a city. This is done by superimposing on a site plan lines that, instead of radiating from a point, have their starting points randomly assigned in the area being studied, and have random directions. It is an operation that is possible by hand but is particularly suited to computer use.

eight

Daylight illuminance

This chapter shows how the daylight inside a building is calculated from the exterior daylight climate described in Chapter 4. It begins by describing how illuminance can be calculated from daylight factors, showing the limitations of this approach and also the conditions in which the use of daylight factors is valuable. The chapter then shows how reflected sunlight can be analysed. It then considers some special cases – distant obstructions, trees and shiny façades – and concludes by discussing accuracy in daylight calculations and measurements.

8.1

Sometimes it is necessary to have numerical values of illuminance. But calculating is not designing: at best, it is only a small part of the process, just as lighting design is itself part of the creation of an architectural space. Here, structure and daylight and decoration are inseparable elements of the place.

Dolat-Abad Garden, Yazd, Iran

Illuminance and daylight factors

The daylight factor is, by definition, the illuminance on a surface expressed as a percentage of the external diffuse illuminance.

Therefore,

$$E_{\text{surface}} = \frac{E_{dh}\, D}{100} \qquad (8.1)$$

The definition of daylight factor also states that the calculation is based on a standard sky luminance distribution, usually the CIE Overcast Sky. But real skies vary, and the pattern of the Overcast Sky, where the luminance just above the horizon is only one-third of the zenith value, occurs infrequently, even in predominantly cloudy climates.

The outcome is that, under real skies, the ratio of indoor to outdoor illuminance is not constant. Figure 8.2 shows just how large this variation is: the ratio ranges from about half the daylight factor to more than twice its value.

A further source of error lies in the orientation of the room. Even excluding sunlight, south-facing windows receive

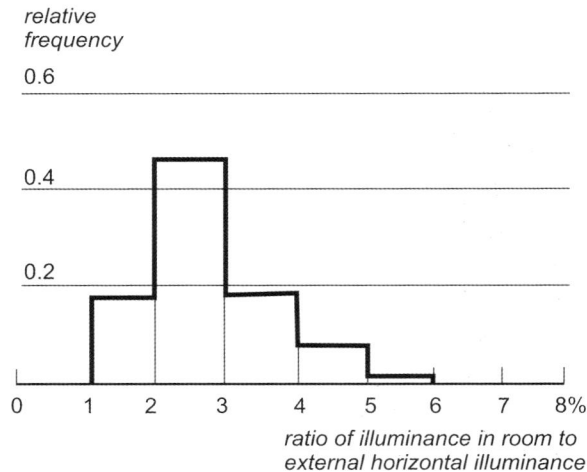

relative frequency

8.2
Effect of a variation in the sky luminance distribution. Daylight at a point in a room given as a percentage of external horizontal diffuse illuminance. Measurements were taken May–July in a north-facing room; sunny conditions were excluded.
Nottingham, UK

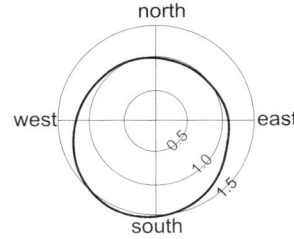

8.3
Orientation factor, f_o, for London. This is used in association with daylight factors to compensate for the variation with orientation of the daylight falling on windows.

more light than those in other orientations (in the Northern Hemisphere). This can be taken into account by multiplying the daylight factor by an orientation factor, f_o. Figure 8.3 illustrates this for London. The equation for daylight illuminance therefore becomes

$$E_{\text{surface}} = \frac{E_{dh}\, D\, f_o}{100} \qquad (8.2)$$

Chapter 3 showed that illuminance from sky depends on the height of the sun, but, in a cloudy climate, the light falling on the ground varies greatly either side of the mean for any particular solar elevation. We have just seen that the daylight illuminance in a room varies as the sky's luminance pattern changes. There are thus two major sources of uncertainty in the use of a daylight factor to predict interior illuminance: fluctuation in the total amount of light penetrating a cloudy atmosphere and fluctuation in the sky's brightness pattern. The conclusion has to be that a daylight factor is not a good predictor of instantaneous illuminance in a room.

It is an entirely different situation, though, when the need is to predict annual hours of daylight availability. Fluctuations of internal illuminance due to variation in the sky brightness pattern must be seen in the context of the very much greater variation in external illuminance with time of day, time of year and weather. Figure 8.4 illustrates the annual illuminance in a room calculated firstly on the basis of a constant sky luminance distribution and secondly by assuming that the interior-to-exterior illuminance ratio varies with the distribution shown in Figure 8.2. The curves are very close: the changing sky luminance distribution acts as an additional variance that spreads the cumulative curve only a small amount.

Statistical results about the long-term occurrence of daylight in a room are much more robust than estimates of instantaneous illuminance. Used in this way, the daylight factor becomes a powerful tool.

% of working year

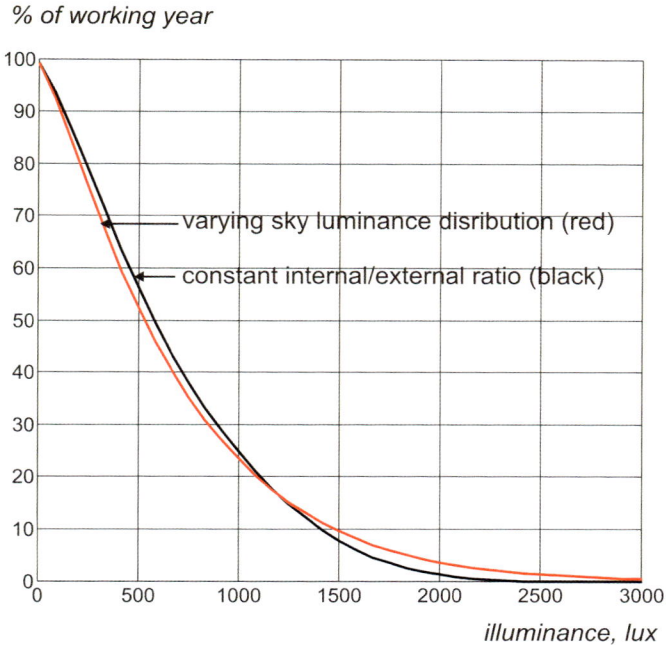

8.4

Illuminance at a point in a room. Cumulative graph showing the percentage of a complete working year between 09.00 and 17.00 that daylight illuminance exceeded the values given. The curves were calculated using data from Nottingham, UK (Chapter 3, Figure 3.20). The black curve shows the effect of a constant internal-to-external illuminance ratio of about 2.8%; the red curve is the distribution of illuminance with a ratio varying as in Figure 8.2. The difference between the curves is small – the additional variance tending to extend the tail of the curve and reduce slightly the frequency of occurrence at lower illuminance values.

Look at Figure 8.5: if we adopt a required interior illuminance, such as 500 lx, the horizontal axis can be marked with the daylight factor that gives this illuminance across the range of exterior illuminances. Then the vertical axis indicates the fraction of annual hours that a given daylight factor gives the required interior illuminance.

This could be plotted as a separate graph, as in Figure 8.6. Moreover, if the total number of hours that lie within the calculation period is found (such as 2000 hours 09.00–17.00 Monday–Friday for 50 weeks), the hours of adequate daylight can be found directly. The vertical axis in Figure 8.6 is labelled in that way. The daylight factor contours can thus be redrawn as contours of available daylight, either as percentages, as in Figure 8.7, or as the absolute number of hours.

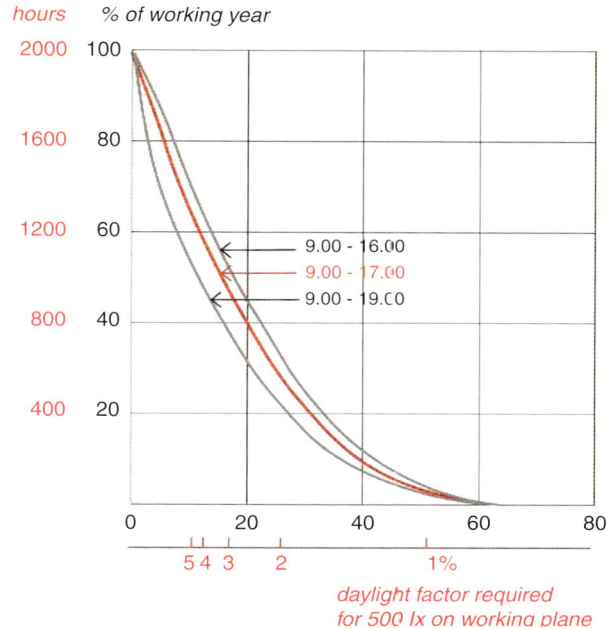

8.5

Frequency at which a given diffuse illuminance is exceeded during the working year (Monday–Friday). British Summer Time (daylight saving time) is taken into account.
Based on data from Nottingham, UK

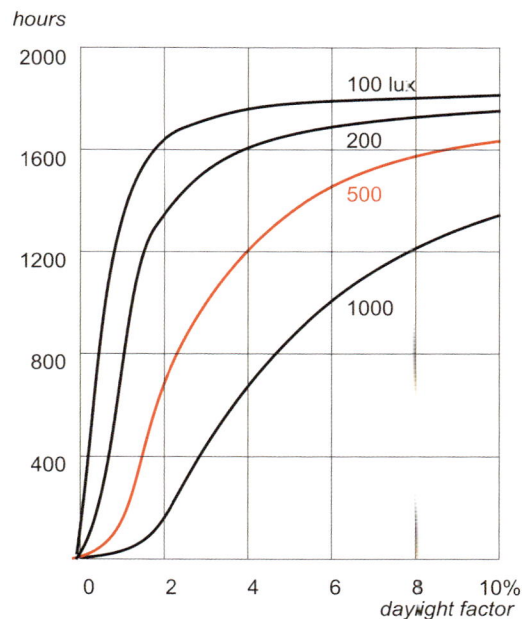

8.6

Hours and daylight factors for which the given illuminance is exceeded. Based on Figure 8.5, 09.00–17.00 curve.

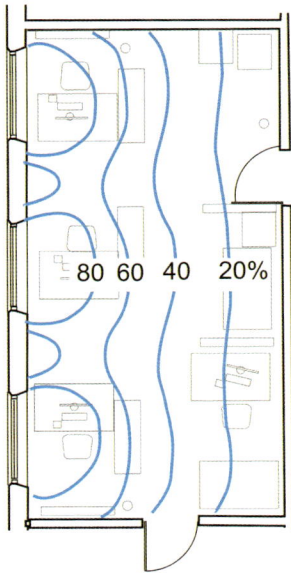

80 60 40 20%

8.7
Percentages of the time that daylight
illuminance would exceed 500 lx
between 9.00 and 17.00 during the
year. Based on Figure 8.6, 500 lx curve.

This is a very clear guide to the planning of daytime electric lighting. At the desks near the windows, daylight alone would be adequate for most of the time. At the back of the room, 500 lx would be available during less than one-fifth of working hours and occupants would tend to leave electric lighting permanently switched on.

These contours of daylight availability do not themselves produce an estimate of the likely electricity use. Other factors must be taken into account: the most important is the response of the lighting control to changes in daylight; another is occupant behaviour, such as drawing blinds to exclude sunlight. These are discussed in Chapter 5.

The value of daylight factors

The average daylight factor over the plan area of a room is a good indicator of the brightness appearance of the space and of its thermal characteristics, but any spatial mean is a poor predictor of electric lighting use. For example if 500 lx is required and the average daylight factor is 2%, it is not true that electric lighting would be unnecessary when the external diffuse illuminance reaches 25 klx: about half the room would then be still less than 500 lx.

The daylight factor around a single point indicates less about the overall appearance of a room than does the average daylight factor. Nor is it a good predictor of the absolute illuminance there, because the ratio of internal to external illuminance is not constant. It is, though, a very useful way of estimating daylight availability in a room, the number of hours in which a given illuminance is exceeded during an arbitrary period, such as office working hours during the course of a year.

Illuminance from reflected sunlight

Daylight factors are based on the assumption that there is no sunshine. They are useful because they convey the character of a room on a dull overcast day and can be used to predict interior illuminance if the external diffuse illuminance is known. This approach is unrealistic for sunny climates and is incomplete even in cloudy maritime regions.

Advanced software can predict the distribution of luminance and colour in a room under virtually any lighting conditions (the basis for this is given in the next chapter). But it is often expensive in time to carry out detailed simulation, and there remains a need for quick calculations that aid design decisions.

The remainder of this chapter shows how the principles applied in the average daylight factor formulae can be used to give estimates of the illuminance within a room from reflected sunlight.

This is easily done, but it is helpful first to introduce a bit of theory. You can skip this section if you are allergic to mathematics.

Two computational tools

(a) Configuration factor and form factor

These describe the flow of light from large sources. The first deals with light flowing from a large source to a small area around a point on another surface, as in the upper diagram in Figure 8.8:

Configuration factor, $cf_{a,b} = \dfrac{\text{illuminance on } a}{\pi \times \text{luminance of } b}$

$\qquad\qquad\qquad = \dfrac{\text{illuminance on } a}{\text{reflectance of } b \times \text{illuminance on } b}$

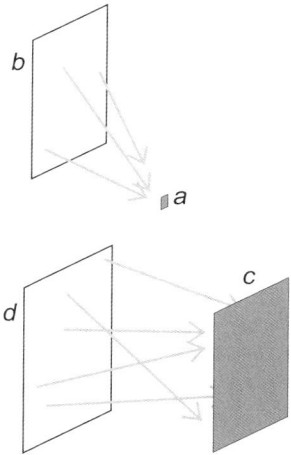

8.8

Configuration factor and form factor.

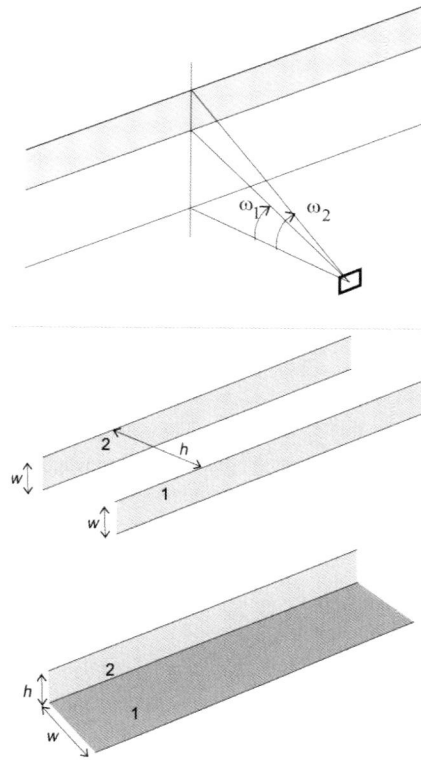

where illuminance is measured in lux and luminance in candelas per square metre, with the assumption that the surfaces are perfectly reflecting and diffusing.

The second gives the average illuminance over a finite surface area, as in the lower diagram of Figure 8.8:

$$\text{Form factor, } F_{c,d} = \frac{\text{mean illuminance on } c}{\pi \times \text{ luminance of } d}$$
$$= \frac{\text{mean illuminance on } c}{\text{reflectance of } d \times \text{illuminance of } d}$$

The configuration factor and the form factor can be defined in other ways, and they have many applications in other topics, such as radiant heat transfer. Two very useful and simple relationships that we shall use are shown in Figure 8.9. The configuration factor from an infinitely long strip, n, to a point, m, on a plane parallel to the strip is

$$cf_{mn} = \frac{\sin\omega_2 - \sin\omega_1}{2} \qquad (8.3)$$

The form factor between two infinitely long parallel strips, of width w, directly facing each other, a distance h apart, is

$$F_{1,2} = \sqrt{1+\left(\frac{h}{w}\right)^2} - \frac{h}{w} \qquad (8.4)$$

Between two perpendicular strips,

$$F_{1,2} = \frac{1}{2}\left(1 + \frac{h}{w} - \sqrt{1+\left(\frac{h}{w}\right)^2}\right) \qquad (8.5)$$

8.9

Top: Configuration factor of an infinitely long strip and a point on a parallel plane.

Centre: Form factor between two infinitely long parallel strips, facing.

Bottom: Form factor between two infinitely long parallel strips, perpendicular.

(b) Direction cosines

To calculate the effect of sunshine, it is necessary to deal with the orientation of the building and the position of the sun in the sky. This is easily done by converting the angles involved to *direction cosines*, which can be imagined as the coordinates of arrows pointing in the direction of the object, as in Figure 8.10. If α_s and α_a are the azimuth and elevation of the sun, the corresponding direction cosines are

$$c_1 = \cos\alpha_s \cos\gamma_s$$
$$c_2 = \sin\alpha_s \cos\gamma_s$$
$$c_3 = \sin\gamma_s \qquad (8.6)$$

Similarly, if the vertical façade of a building faces a direction α_b, the cosines of a line perpendicular to the façade are

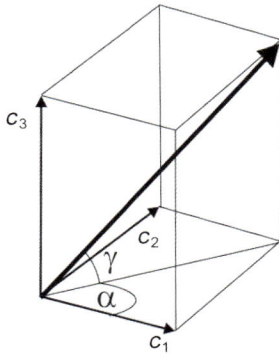

8.10
Direction cosines are the coordinates of the tip of an arrow of unit length.

$$b_1 = \cos a_b$$
$$b_2 = \sin a_b$$
$$b_3 = 0 \qquad (8.7)$$

It is convenient to use different letters to denote different sets of direction cosines, such as b_1, b_2, b_3 for building surfaces and s_1, s_2, s_3 for the solar beam.

Once calculated, direction cosines greatly simplify subsequent computation. For example, if sunlight falls on the façade, the angle of incidence, θ, is given by

$$\cos\theta = -(s_1 b_1 + s_2 b_2 + s_3 b_3) \qquad (8.8)$$

So the solar illuminance there is

$$E_b = -E_{sn}(s_1 b_1 + s_2 b_2 + s_3 b_3)$$
$$\text{provided } (s_1 b_1 + s_2 b_2 + s_3 b_3) < 0 \qquad (8.9)$$

This can be generalised into a general equation for the illuminance on a plane. If the sum of the cosines multiplied together is positive, the light would fall on the back of the plane.

The illuminance on a horizontal surface from the sun is simply

$$E_{sh} = E_{sn} s_3 \qquad (8.10)$$

Ground-reflected sunlight

If there is a patch of sunlit ground near a window, the reflected illuminance on the centre of the window is

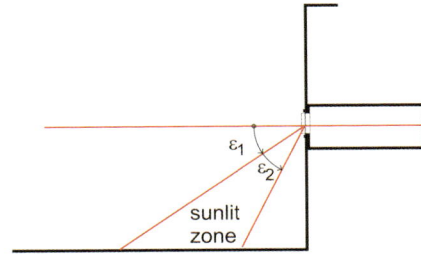

8.11
Illuminance on a window from a strip of sunlit ground.

$$E_{gw} = E_g \rho_g cf_{wg} \qquad (8.11)$$

where E_g is the illuminance on the sunlit ground, ρ_g the ground reflectance and cf_{wg} the configuration factor between the ground and a point on the window.

If the ground surface extends a large distance away from the window in all directions, the illuminance is close to that from a diffuse semi-infinite plane:

$$E_w = \frac{E_g \rho_g}{2} \qquad (8.12)$$

If the sunlit zone is a strip parallel with the window and stretching towards infinity, as in Figure 8.11, the illuminance on the window from reflected sunlight is

$$E_w = \frac{E_g \rho_g (\sin\varepsilon_2 - \sin\varepsilon_1)}{2} \qquad (8.13)$$

Skylight and sunlight in the urban canyon

Calculations of daylight illuminance differ from daylight factor analyses in one important aspect: they have to be made for a specific date and time, and for a particular place – or, at least, for a specific solar elevation and azimuth. It is necessary to know the direction of the sun in relation to the built form, and also the solar normal illuminance and diffuse sky illuminance.

This implies that calculations have to be repeated for different daylight conditions and, to minimise work, these conditions need to be chosen to be crucial to design decisions. It is the critical cases that should be analysed: where there is low elevation sunlight, where conditions when sunlight on the window might cause discomfort, and where the external illuminance is very low, the sun obscured or the sky very cloudy.

Worksheet 10 gives a step-by-step procedure for calculating the illuminance from sunlight and skylight in a room overlooking a street. The procedure follows the same stages as the split-flux average daylight factor calculation: first, the illuminance on the outside face of the window is estimated; then this light is distributed over the interior surface. It assumes that the street approximates to a long straight urban canyon, with buildings of equal height on either side. The method is based on some general formulae, which can be used to develop numerical models of many lighting situations.

Shadows

Figure 8.12 shows sunlight falling on some street surfaces. The solar elevation and azimuth, and the orientation and dimensions of the street, determine which surfaces receive sunlight. If the sun shines exactly down the street, the ground alone is illuminated. But this is a momentary occurrence; at all other times, part of one façade or the other will receive sunlight and, if the sun is high in the sky, so will the ground. In that case, as in the upper diagram of Figure 8.12, the length of the shadow from the wall is

$$w_{sh} = \frac{(h_u + h_d)}{w} \frac{\cos|\alpha_b - \alpha_s|}{\tan\gamma_s} \qquad (8.14)$$

where α_s and γ_s are the azimuth and elevation of the sun, and α_b is the direction the building faces. If w_{sh} is greater than the street width w, the shadow line must occur on a façade. The height of this above the ground is

$$h_{sh} = \frac{(h_u + h_d)(w_{sh} - w)}{w_{sh}} \qquad (8.15)$$

Mean illuminance over an area, from area sources

In the urban canyon, this occurs in two ways: illuminance on street surfaces from the sky, and light reflected between major elements, such as from one wall of the canyon to another.

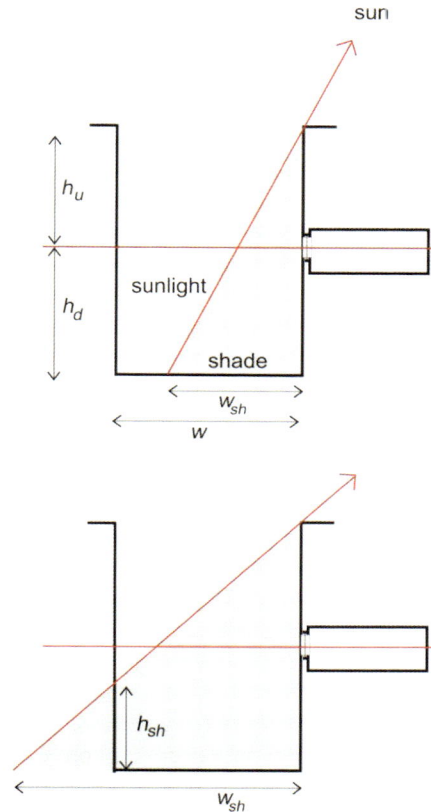

8.12
Shadow in an urban canyon.

Illuminance from sunlight is usually much greater than that from the diffuse sky, so the result of a daylight calculation involving both sun and sky tends to be insensitive to the sky luminance distribution. It is therefore valid to take the sky as being uniform in brightness. This is justified also by the fact that sunshine can be associated with many different sky brightness patterns.

The assumption of a uniform sky makes it very easy to calculate the mean sky illuminance on a surface: it is just the horizontal sky illuminance multiplied by the form factor:

$$\bar{E}_{sky} = E_{hd}F_{surface-sky}$$

So, using Equation (8.5), the mean sky illuminance on the facade opposite to the window and above window level (marked h_u) is

$$\bar{E}_{skyu} = E_{hd}\frac{1+H_3 - \sqrt{1+H_3{}^2}}{2} \qquad (8.16)$$

where

$$H_3 = \frac{w}{h_u}$$

The mean skylight illuminance of all that façade would be

$$\bar{E}_{skyud} = E_{hd}\left(\frac{1+H_4 - \sqrt{1+H_4{}^2}}{2}\right) \qquad (8.17)$$

where

$$H_4 = \frac{w}{h_u + h_d}$$

The mean illuminance on the lower façade, h_d, is not given directly by Equation (8.5), but can be obtained from the two above:

$$\bar{E}_{skyd} = \frac{\bar{E}_{skyud}(h_u + h_d) - \bar{E}_{skyu}h_u}{h_d} \qquad (8.18)$$

The mean sky illuminance on the ground is similarly found by multiplying the unobstructed sky illuminance by the form factor, this time using Equation (8.4)

$$\bar{E}_{skyg} = E_{hd}\left(\sqrt{1+H_g{}^2} - H_g\right) \qquad (8.19)$$

where

$$H_g = \frac{w}{h_u + h_d}$$

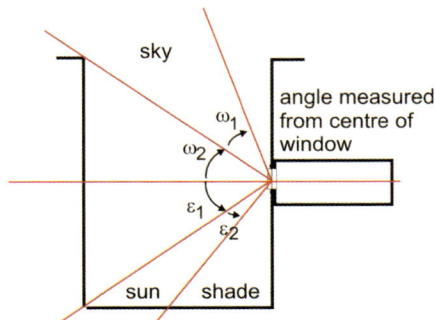

8.13
Angles used in calculation.

The same procedures – using the form factor equations for perpendicular and parallel facing surfaces, and subdividing and subdividing areas – can be used to estimate light reflected between street surfaces.

Illuminance at a point from area sources

Form factors are used to find the mean illuminance from an area source onto another area, as above. *Configuration factors* are used where the illuminance around a point from an area source is required. Equation (8.5) is applicable to sky illuminance on a window and to reflected illuminance from the facade opposite.

The illuminance on the window from the diffuse sky is thus

$$\bar{E}_{skyw} = \frac{E_{hd}(\sin\omega_1 - \sin\omega_2)}{2} \qquad (8.20)$$

From sunlight and skylight reflected by the opposite façade above the level of the centre of the window,

$$\bar{E}_{ruw} = \frac{\rho_b(E_{sunu} + \bar{E}_{skyu})\sin\omega_2}{2} \qquad (8.21)$$

where ρ_b is the reflectance of the opposite building and E_{sunud} is the solar illuminance on it.

From sunlight and skylight reflected by the opposite façade below the level of the centre of the window,

$$\bar{E}_{rdw} = \frac{\rho_b(E_{sund} + \bar{E}_{skyd})\sin\varepsilon_1}{2} \qquad (8.22)$$

From sunlight and skylight reflected by the sunlit area of ground,

$$\bar{E}_{rgw} = \frac{\rho_b(E_{sung} + \bar{E}_{skyg})(\sin\varepsilon_2 - \sin\varepsilon_1)}{2} \qquad (8.23)$$

where ρ_g is the ground reflectance
And, finally, from the shaded area of ground,

$$\bar{E}_{rg2w} = \frac{\rho_g\bar{E}_{skyg}(1 - \sin\varepsilon_2)}{2} \qquad (8.24)$$

Interreflected light

Light falling initially on the ground is reflected back to the sky and onto the two façades. There are two common ways of dealing with this. The more advanced method is to use form factors in a set of simultaneous equations; this is described under 'Finite area methods' in Chapter 10. The second, which we shall now develop, is to adapt Sumpner's equation (described in Chapter 2).

The equations listed up to now in this chapter take into account the direct light on the window and the first-reflected light. If the street is visualised as a cavity into which sunlight and skylight fall, the mean illuminance on the interior surfaces of the cavity will be

$$\bar{E}_w \approx \frac{w(E_{dg} + E_{sh})}{2(w+h)(1-\rho_c)} \quad (8.25)$$

where the illuminance on the cavity opening is $E_{sh} + E_{dh}$ and the internal reflectance of the cavity is the weighted average of wall and ground reflectance, taking into account the opening:

$$\rho_c = \frac{\rho_g w + 2\rho_b h}{2(w+h)} \quad (8.26)$$

The term $(1 - \rho_c)^{-1}$ is the sum of $(1 + \rho_c + \rho_c^2 + \rho_c^3 + \ldots)$, which represents the initial illuminance plus the successively smaller quantities from successive bounces. The direct light and the first reflection are already taken into account, so the series needed is $(\rho_c^2 + \rho_c^3 + \rho_c^4 + \ldots)$, which is equivalent to $\rho_c^2(1 + \rho_c + \rho_c^2 + \ldots)$, giving the final equation

$$\bar{E}_{wr} \approx \frac{w(E_{dg} + E_{sh})\rho_c^2}{2(w+h)(1-\rho_c)} \quad (8.27)$$

Interior illuminance

The light on the interior surfaces of the room is calculated in the same way as the split-flux average daylight factor. First, the upward and downward illuminance on the window are separated: the upward light, illuminance, E_{wu}, is that reflected by the ground, the lower façade opposite, plus half the total from later reflections; the downward light, E_{wu}, is

from the sky, the upper opposite façade and the other half from interreflection.

The illuminance on the lower surfaces of the room is

$$E_{lower} = \frac{2a_w \left[\left(E_{wd}\tau_{dd} + E_{wu}\tau_{ud} \right) - \left(E_{wu}\tau_{uu} + E_{wd}\tau_{du} \right) \right]}{a_r(1 - \rho_l\rho_l)} \quad (8.28)$$

And similarly for the upper room surfaces:

$$E_{upper} = \frac{2a_w \left[\rho_l \left(E_{wd}\tau_{dd} + E_{wu}\tau_{ud} \right) + \left(E_{wu}\tau_{uu} + E_{wd}\tau_{du} \right) \right]}{a_r(1 - \rho_u\rho_l)} \quad (8.29)$$

Configuration factors more generally

Given the configuration factor of an exterior object, the reflected illuminance from it onto the window, and hence its contribution to the mean interior illuminance, is given by

$$E_{window} = E_{object}\rho_{object}\, cf_{window-object}$$

Configuration factors can be obtained from fish-eye images.

Figure 8.14 shows a dot diagram superimposed on a vertical fish-eye photograph of a site. The number of dots in a particular zone is proportional to the configuration factor between a diffusing surface in that zone and a point on a surface at the camera position and in the plane of the camera's sensor. There are 500 dots in total, so each is equivalent to a 0.02 configuration factor.

Sunlight reflected from the path in the foreground can be estimated: 134 dots lie on this path, so the configuration factor to the camera position is about 0.268. If the path had reflectance 0.25 and was in bright sunshine, with illuminance 85 klx, the reflected illuminance from the window would be

$$E_w = 85000 \times 0.25 \times 0.268$$
$$= 5695 \text{ lx}$$

This can be compared with the value using Equation (8.13). The far edge of the path lies 27° below the horizon; the near edge is directly beneath the camera, 90° below the horizon. The configuration factor from Equation (8.26) is

8.14

Using a dot diagram to obtain configuration factors.

$$cf = \frac{\sin 90° - \sin 27°}{2} = 0.273$$

which would give an illuminance of about 5800 lx.

Using a dot diagram is equivalent to taking samples, and the same mathematical guidelines apply. In particular, the confidence interval – the range of values within which the true value lies – is inversely proportional to the square root of the number of dots. Comparison of the two answers indicates the degree of uncertainty.

This must be put into the context of uncertainty in the adoption of other parameters: typically, these cause greater error. For example, if the path reflectance had been estimated to be 0.20 instead of 0.25, the calculated illuminance would be 20% lower. Similarly, in interior daylight calculations, the window transmittance and room reflectance values are often no better than informed estimates. It is essential that, for presentation, final illuminances be rounded off to a figure that indicates the degree of uncertainty in the values inserted in the calculation. In the case above, a fair presentation of the result might be to state that a path illuminance of 85 klx gives 6 klx on the window surface.

The sky factor is, in effect, a configuration factor between the sky and a horizontal surface in a room. It can be estimated as above from fish-eye images taken with the camera pointing upwards. The configuration factor dot diagram is superimposed and the dots overlying the sky seen through a window are counted. This method is not sufficiently precise for legal work, but it is useful for initial assessments of the daylight in a room.

Trees, distant surfaces and shiny façades

We look now at three common situations that do not fit easily into the normal calculation procedures.

The transmittance of trees

Trees are important to daylight: they enhance a view, they scatter and block sunlight and skylight, and they modify other aspects of the microclimate. The comfort and visual enjoyment that foliage can create in warm sunny climates is shown well in Figure 8.15. The importance of the presence of trees has been discussed in earlier chapters, firstly in relation to the therapeutic value of a view and secondly as a means of diffusing sunlight.

They are not, however, easy to incorporate in calculations: they are complex and changeable in shape and in the way they transmit and scatter light.

In winter, the effect of a deciduous tree is a partial obscuring of the sky. The surface of the tree trunk and branches is usually low, and thus the light reflected from it is normally negligible in daylight calculations. The transmittance can be derived from luminance measurements on site of the luminance of the tree crown compared with the sky behind it, taking the mean of several readings. It can be estimated also from photographs by superimposing a random dot pattern over the image, and counting the numbers of dots covering points on the tree and the number on the background sky; the mean transmittance is then

$$\tau_t = \frac{\text{number of dots on sky}}{\text{number on sky} + \text{number on tree}} \qquad (8.30)$$

3.15
Urban trees creating a bright
diffuse light under strong
sunlight.
Bellingen, NSW, Australia

If the photograph is a fish-eye image, the configuration factor dot-diagram described earlier may be used.

Tree crown transmittance, τ_t, depends on species, on climate and on the direction of view. It varies between different examples of a species. If values for a particular specimen are not available, the values listed in Table 8.1 are reasonable assumptions for daylighting calculations.

A more difficult quantity to measure is the overall reflectance of a tree canopy to skylight and sunlight. There is a need for more research here, especially practical measurements of the luminance of trees seen from the side. The literature on plant science and on remote sensing tends to concentrate on upwards and downwards light – the obstruction of tree canopies and plant foliage to light on lower vegetation, and overall reflectance of crops and forests seen from satellites.

We can make an estimate of the light reaching a window from a tree by splitting it into three components, assuming a uniform sky that gives a horizontal illuminance E_{hd}, with a solar normal illuminance E_{sn}. The configuration factor from the tree to the centre of the window is cf_{wt}. So the components are as follows:

1 The *illuminance from the area behind the tree* is $cf_{wt}\,\tau_t\,E_{hd}$ if the sky is visible through the canopy or $cf_{wt}\,\tau_t\,E_s\rho_s$ if a surface of illuminance E_s and reflectance ρ_s is behind the canopy.

2 The *illuminance from reflected skylight* is

$$cf_{wt}\left(1-\tau_t\right)\frac{E_{hd}\rho_f}{2}$$

This assumes that, under diffuse light, the tree acts like a vertical surface of reflectance ρ_f.

3 The *illuminance from reflected sunlight* is

$$cf_{wt}\left(1-\tau_t\right)E_{sn}\rho_f\,\frac{1}{2}\left(1+\cos\left(\frac{\beta}{2}\right)\right)$$

Table 8.1: Approximate transmittance of the canopies of individual trees

	Winter	Summer
Urban trees such as common lime, silver birch and London plane	0.55	0.15
Small decorative trees and immature specimens	0.75	0.25
Evergreen conifers	0.15	0.05

8.16

In winter, the deciduous tree acts primarily as an obstruction to skylight.

This takes into account sunlight if it is incident on the canopy from any direction. β is the angle between the direction of sunlight and a line drawn from the centre of the tree canopy to the centre of the window.

Adding these up produces the rather cumbersome equation

$$E_w = cf_{wt} \left\{ \tau_t E_{hd} + (1-\tau_t)\frac{\rho_t}{2}\left[E_{hd} + \left(1+\cos\left(\frac{\beta}{2}\right)\right)E_{sn}\right]\right\} \quad (8.31)$$

The components are illustrated in Figures 8.17 and 8.18.

If, instead of the diffuse sky, there is a wall or other surface behind the tree, the first bracketed term is changed from $\tau_t E_{hd}$ to $\tau_t E_s \rho_s$, as above.

It is necessary to estimate the tree reflectance, ρ_f. This is a weighted average of branch and foliage reflectances, and it incorporates the effect of cavities. Typical values for daylighting calculations are shown in Table 8.2.

Table 8.2: Approximate reflectance, ρ_f, of trees seen from the side

	Winter	Summer
Trees with dense light-coloured foliage in summer	0.1	0.4
Trees with open foliage	0.1	0.2
Evergreen conifers	0.1	0.1

Distant objects

Distant hills look lighter and bluer than those nearby. Chapter 2 explains how this is due to scattering in the atmosphere along the line of sight. Light from the distant hillside is diffused and some light from the sky and from the ground is scattered towards the viewer. This is shown in Figure 8.19.

Where obstructions to daylight are large but distant, it is necessary to take into account their relatively high luminance. Assuming that the sky is overcast, the ratio of the luminance of the distant object, L_x, to the sky luminance just above the horizon, L_s, is

$$\frac{L_x}{L_s} = 1-(1-\rho k_w)e^{-\sigma x}$$

$$(8.32)$$

where ρ is the reflectance of the object, k_w is a factor that takes into account the slope of the object (Table 8.3), σ is an extinction coefficient (Table 8.4) and x is the distance away of the object. Figure 8.20 illustrates this equation.

Shiny façades

The reflectance of a glazed curtain wall changes with the direction of view. Looking directly at the wall with a sightline perpendicular to the glass, it is possible to see through windows into the interior. Just how far inside you can see

Table 8.3: Slope factor, k_w

Slope	0° (horizontal)	30°	60°	90° (vertical)
k_w	2.3	2.1	1.6	1.3

Table 8.4: Approximate extinction coefficient, σ

	Clear weather	Moderate visibility	Mist, light rain	Fog
Maximum visibility distance, km	40	10	4	1
Extinction coefficient, σ, km^{-1}	0.1	0.3	1	3

8.17
In summer, the branches and foliage in silhouette indicate how much light is blocked; but the sunlit leaves are translucent and increase the brightness of the tree.

depends on the balance between interior brightness and the brightness outside, and on the type of glazing. But if the line of sight is at a glancing angle to the glass, there is almost total reflection. The line of sight just bounces off the façade. Looking upwards towards a tall building, what is seen is the reflection of the sky, as in Figure 8.21.

A specular façade will often be brighter than it would be if finished with a matt material such as light-coloured stone. It has a lesser effect on the daylight falling on lower buildings. For calculation, the approach is to treat the obstructing building as a mirror, as in Figure 8.22.

For example, to obtain the daylight factor on the face of the small existing building, first the near façade is drawn a distance away twice that between the buildings. Then the view is divided into three zones: a sky zone, *A*; a modified sky zone, *B*, which is treated as sky but the value multiplied by the estimated specular reflectance of the curtain wall; and an external obstruction, *C*. If any other buildings would be reflected, more zones might be necessary.

The reflectance depends on the nature of the glazing, the frame and protruding obstructions such as balconies, and the direction of view. For quick exploratory calculations, a flat glazed façade might be assumed to take a mean specular reflectance of about 0.5 at low angles of view,

increasing to about 0.8 near the top of a high building with only a glancing angle of incidence.

Figure 8.23 shows different areas of sky reflected in glazing in various planes. Figure 8.24 shows a building reflecting a view that makes it appear transparent.

The accuracy of lighting measurements and calculations

Does it matter if the overall amount of light in a room falls by 10%? How accurate is it possible to be when measuring light? And what margin of error is to be expected in a lighting calculation?

The answers to these three questions are crucial, not just to design decisions but also to the way in which lighting is specified in contract documents or standards.

Taking them separately, the first question could be stated more generally as follows:

* How precisely is the eye sensitive to small differences in brightness?

Look at Table 8.5. Outdoors at night, a clear full moon provides enough light for us to walk safely along a country

8.18

The light passing from the tree in the direction of the arrow is taken to be the sum of three components: light from the background, passing directly through the tree (green arrow); sunlight reflected and scattered (yellow); and reflected skylight (white).

road. With only the light of stars, we can recognise the broad shapes of trees and buildings. Sitting indoors, with illumination from a single candle, we can read a book, but we can also read comfortably on a bright cloudy day outdoors. We find it dazzling when strong sunlight falls on the white page, but being on a beach in fine summer weather is one of the pleasures in life.

The highest illuminance in Table 8.5 is one hundred million times greater than the lowest. This is the range in which the eye operates, and this vast extent is achieved through the various processes of light adaptation: having two sets of visual photoreceptors in the retina; the automatic adjustment of these cells by bleaching and regeneration; our behavioural responses to light; and the narrowing and enlargement of the iris.

Adaptation blunts our sensitivity to absolute levels of light for the benefit of increased sensitivity to immediate spatial

and temporal changes. But our ability to notice relative differences between levels of light depends also on the transition between them, both spatially and temporally. If two patches of light are side-by-side, with a hard edge between them, we can discriminate between small differences in brightness. The difference has to be greater if there is a gradual transition. For example, we tend not to notice that the luminance of a wall close to a window is many times greater than its value 3 m away if there is a smooth brightness gradient.

The same applies to variation of light with time. If there is a sudden change in brightness of something in our field of vision, we are immediately aware, especially if it occurs on the periphery of the visual field. If, though, we were sitting by a window reading a book in the afternoon, we probably would not notice the daylight falling to one-fifth of the illuminance it gave an hour earlier. If a spatial or a temporal variation is gradual, there must be a relatively great change before it is perceived. Splayed window reveals that provide an area of intermediate luminance between the sky outside and the dark interior window wall reduce the apparent inside–outside contrast.

In general, Weber's law applies: the minimum perceptible difference is proportional to the absolute luminance. The brighter the situation, the larger the difference must be if it is to be perceived. Symbolically,

$$\frac{L_t - L_b}{L_b} = \text{a constant}$$

L_t is the luminance of a target seen against a background luminance L_b.

Vision is akin to human hearing in range. In audibility, the sound pressure at the threshold of pain is 13 orders of magnitude greater than that at the threshold of awareness – a difference that tends to be masked by the practice of expressing sound pressure in decibels, a logarithmic scale.

Vision and hearing, in both sensitivity range and the meaning of comfort, are fundamentally different from our perception of warmth. Table 8.6 lists some temperatures in everyday experience. The range of temperatures at which a person is comfortable is even smaller than the range on this list: sitting outdoors wearing light clothing can be uncomfortably cool when the air temperature is 5 °C, and

8.19
Hills silhouetted against each other: they increase in brightness with distance. In mist or in a strongly polluted atmosphere, the effect of distance is enhanced.

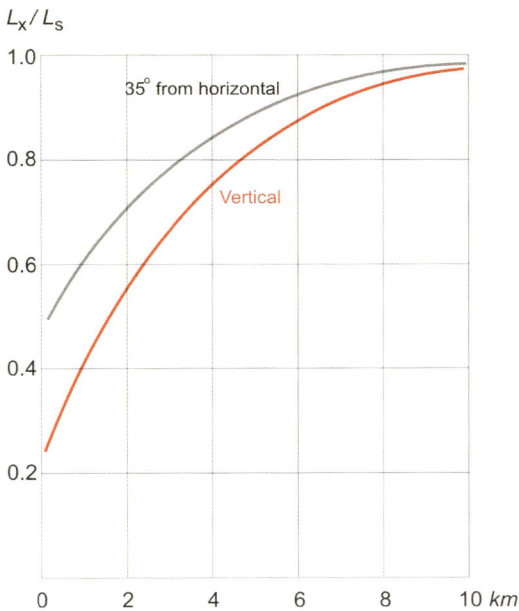

8.20
How luminance changes with distance: surface luminance at distances up to 10 km away, divided by horizon sky luminance. Overcast sky, $\sigma = 0.3$, $r = 0.2$.

uncomfortably warm at 35 °C – an increase of about 10% in absolute temperature (K).

By comparison, an increase of 10% in the daylight outdoors is normally unnoticeable. It would not affect comfort and it would have a negligible effect on task performance.

Significant numerical differences are an order of magnitude greater in lighting than in the thermal environment. For this reason, a schedule of the illuminances recommended for various activities is usually based on the series 50, 100, 150, 200, 300, 500, 700, 1000 lx. Each level is between 1.4 and 2.0 times the previous level, and such intervals are about the lowest meaningful differences in room illuminance.

The next question is this:

• How precisely can light be measured?

The absolute accuracy of illuminance meters used in most practical applications is seldom better than ±10% (digital displays on instruments often imply a greater precision and this is misleading). This uncertainty has several causes, such as calibration error, dirt and imprecise colour correction; but most commonly the largest source of uncertainty is poor

8.21

Reflection of the sky in a glazed curtain wall.

Sydney, Australia

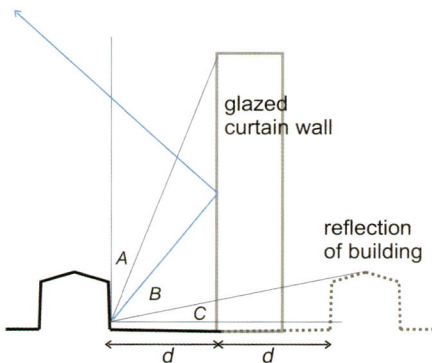

8.22

Estimating the daylight factor when the obstruction is glazed.

8.23

Windows at different angles reflecting different patches of sky.

Tallinn, Estonia

cosine correction – ensuring that the response of the sensor in relation to the angle of incidence is Lambertian.

When measuring light on-site rather than in the laboratory, there is further uncertainty: levelling error, fluctuating illumination, false reflections and shading of sensors. The outcome is that the absolute value of a single illuminance reading made on site may be 20% above or below the true value. Relative values, where readings of a single meter are compared, can be more accurate, typically ±5% with good measurement practice; but a ratio of readings from two independent photocells, indoors and outdoors, for example, compounds the individual variations.

In the laboratory, a high-quality instrument, well maintained and frequently re-calibrated, may approach an

Table 8.6: Typical temperatures

	°C	K
Outdoor air on a winter night	–10	263
Ice in a cool drink	0	273
Air in a living room	20	293
Hot but drinkable cup of coffee	65	338
Uncomfortably hot water	75	348
Air temperature in a hot oven	200	473

error range of ±1%, but ±5% is a reasonable assumption for good practice in an applied laboratory.

Scale models of buildings are used to predict daylight in situations for which calculations are difficult. They are used also in research as a physical check on new theory. When light is measured in scale models, the main cause of uncertainty is imprecision in the model. This can be dimensional error: for example, a 1 mm error at a scale of 1 : 500 represents a 0.5 m difference at the real scale; in a sunlight assessment, this could imply an error of several minutes in the duration of a site shadow. Error can also be due to the use of materials that differ from the real case in the way they transmit or reflect light: for example, the interreflected light in a room could be several times greater than the true value if the model is made of white card instead of realistic materials (see Figure 2.28 in Chapter 2); and the use of shiny instead of matt surfaces, or vice versa, can give seriously misleading results.

The third question is:

• How accurate are lighting calculations?

A calculation is a numerical model, an abstracted representation of a physical process. Numbers represent quantities of light or the properties of a material. How the physical state changes as these numbers vary is represented by rules for combining these numbers, rules written as formulae, equations or algorithms. These may be simple, mere rules of thumb, or they may be computer programs with several hundred lines of instructions and thousands of repetitions of each operation.

Short calculation or long, the same conditions hold. The accuracy of a computation – that is, how well a numerical result predicts the outcome of a real process – depends on two things.

8.24

This building looks transparent because it is reflecting a view very similar to the view it obscures.

Tallinn, Estonia

Table 8.5: Typical illuminances

On open ground at night, with stars but no moon	0.001 lx
On open ground, with stars and a half-moon	0.04 lx
On a surface facing the full moon in clear weather	0.4 lx
On the page of a book, facing a candle 1 m away	1 lx
On desks from electric lighting in an office	400 lx
On an office desk near a window on a bright spring morning	1 klx
On open ground outdoors on a slightly cloudy summer morning in Northern Europe	40 klx
On the ground from sun and blue sky on a summer day in a Mediterranean climate	100 klx

The first of these is the extent to which the rules represent the real world. Practical calculations are based on simplifying assumptions, and the more compact the calculation, the bolder the assumptions. We have already noted some that are found in most daylighting calculations:

- The sky varies smoothly in brightness.
- The sun is not shining.
- The ground and the external surfaces of buildings are matt surfaces of uniform reflectance.
- The skyline is horizontal.
- Surfaces are uniformly illuminated, matt and of uniform reflectance.
- The room behaves in interreflection like a hollow sphere.

These are not substitutes for more precise methods or a by-product of lazy computer programming: they are valid assumptions in given conditions. The art of good calculation lies in choosing the model, the symbolic analogy to a physical process, that gives sufficiently accurate results for minimum cost – the measure of 'cost' being the use of time or of any other relevant resource.

As a project moves from stage to stage, there is a different balance to be made between the costs of calculating and the required quantity and precision of results: at the early stages of design, quick estimates of the major implications of alternative schemes are needed; later stages require robust calculations of dimensions and performance; and finally, when a scheme has to be presented or defended, realistic simulations and very good graphics are required. A simple calculation that yields an approximate result is not wrong, but it can be used inappropriately.

The second factor that determines the accuracy of a computation is the validity of its input values. The saying 'rubbish in, rubbish out', or one of its many variants, applies not only to computers: it is a warning about any calculation. Data entered into a lighting calculation are not exact: the luminance of the sky, the amount of dirt on the windows, the colour of the walls – at best during the design stage of a building, such parameters are careful estimates. The problem is not how to avoid rubbish; it is how to interpret calculated results knowing that nothing can be considered precise.

Specifying and presenting lighting quantities

We have seen that the processes of adaptation constrain our awareness of absolute levels of light, and that both measurements and calculations give results with a significant level of uncertainty. This should be in mind when interpreting data, and the presentation of results should indicate the degree of uncertainty. In construction practice, rather than research or laboratory work, error bounds are not given explicitly but indicated by the number of significant figures in the value presented.

With measuring instruments such as illuminance meters, it is useful to distinguish between the absolute accuracy of the instrument and its discrimination, which is often an order of magnitude more precise. For example if the true values of two illuminances are 2000 lx and 2200 lx, and a portable meter gives measurements of 1800 lx and 1980 lx, the absolute values are approximately 10% low, but the relative values are much more reliable. There is an analogy with calculations: repeated computation with the same parameters, varying only one factor, might yield quite inaccurate estimates of the true value but a good assessment of the influence of the factor that was varied.

Table 8.7 suggests some conventions.

Rounding is done, of course, at the end of a calculation, not before. The aim of good scientific practice is to present the best estimate of a value and the bounds of likely error in the estimate.

Table 8.7: Presentation of lighting measurements and calculations

	Suggested presentation	Examples	
		Raw value from measurement or calculation	Presented value
Site measurement of daylight illuminance with hand-held meter	Two significant figures	35,123 lx 827 lx	35 klx 830 lx
Daylight factor calculated with assumed values of reflectance and window transmittance	One significant figure below 10%, two above 10%	6.45% 0.31% 17.36%	6% 0.3% 17%
Interior daylight illuminance, calculated with daylight factor and mean external diffuse illuminance	From 0.5 value to twice value, rounded	486 lx	'Between 240 and 1000 lx'
Interior daylight illuminance, calculated with daylight coefficients and measured sky luminance values	Round to nearest 10 lx	1056.7 lx	1060 lx
Model measurement of daylight factor (large model in artificial sky)	Round to whole number	3.78% 0.45%	4% 'Below 1%'
Sunshine duration, measured with model on heliodon	Round to nearest 5 minutes, use 24-hour clock	'From 9.43 am until 2.21 pm'	'From 09.45 until 14.20'
Annual hours of electricity use calculated with point daylight factors and cumulative external illuminance data	*Absolute value:* rounded to nearest 100 hours	2345 hours	2300 hours
	Comparing values (e.g. different controls) calculated with the same parameters: round each to nearest 20 hours	2349 hours and 2331 hours	2340 hours and 2340 hours, 'no significant difference'

## nine

Collecting daylight: windows, light pipes and other devices

The original meaning of 'window' was an opening in a wall or roof, but even in simple buildings a window has several components. The amount of light transmitted depends on many factors: outside, there are roof overhangs, deep reveals and shading devices; there is the glazing material itself, the dirt on it, the frame supporting it; inside, there may be blinds, curtains, window decorations and all sorts of other objects that partially block the light.

The first part of this chapter sets up a general approach to methods of conveying daylight to the interior of a building – not just conventional windows, but light pipes, light shelves, solar tracking devices and other innovative technology. It focuses on the need to estimate the transmittance of the system for daylight calculations. The second part of the chapter is an overview of daylight technologies.

9.1

A window in a traditional Estonian house seen from outside and inside.

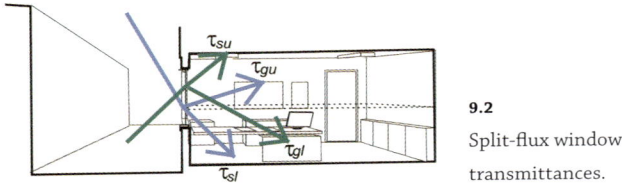

9.2

Split-flux window transmittances.

Transmittance

Every device for carrying daylight into a building has three components: a collector, on which daylight falls and which may be designed to receive light from specific directions; a channel, which carries the light through the fabric of the building; and a distributor, which emits the light in the interior. A light pipe clearly has these components, but a conventional window can also be analysed in this way: the collector incorporates the shading devices and other external fixtures; the channel is the glazing itself, with its inherent transmission properties; the distributor incorporates internal blinds and anything else that affects the distribution of the transmitted light. The advantage of this generalisation is that the performance of the window, characterised by its transmittance, becomes easy to calculate.

Values of transmittance must be qualified by the spectral range to which they apply: when we are discussing buildings, the range is either that of total solar radiation or that of light, the visible wavelengths. In this book, we refer to the visible range unless specifically stated otherwise.

Transmittance is denoted conventionally by the symbol τ (the Greek letter *tau*). It is the luminous flux entering the room divided by the luminous flux falling on the window. It can be a single number, representing the overall performance of the window, or an array of values that are the transmittance values at different directions. The BRE average daylight equation (Equation (7.14) in Chapter 7, and Worksheet 4) uses a single value. The split-flux methods divide the light into upward and downward components. It is acceptable to use a single transmittance value here if the window is a simple opening, but if there are shading devices externally or blinds inside, separate transmittances are needed, four numbers in all, as in Table 9.1.

For example, if 20,000 lm falls on a window, 15,000 lm from above and 5,000 lm from below, and the transmittance values are

Table 9.1: Split-flux transmittance

		Luminous flux emitted into the room by the window	
		On the upper part of the room	On the lower part of the room
luminous flux falling on the window externally	from ground and lower surfaces	τ_{gu}	τ_{gl}
	from sky and upper surfaces	τ_{su}	τ_{sl}

$$\tau_{gu} = 0.4, \quad \tau_{gl} = 0.1$$
$$\tau_{su} = 0.2, \quad \tau_{sl} = 0.5$$

then the luminous flux falling on the upper and lower room surfaces is

$$F_{upper} = 5000 \times 0.4 + 15000 \times 0.2 = 5000 \text{ lm}$$
$$F_{lower} = 5000 \times 0.1 + 15000 \times 0.5 = 8000 \text{ lm}$$

To incorporate separate transmittances, the average daylight factor equations (7.12) and (7.13) have to be expanded:

$$D_{il} = D_{ws}\tau_{sl} + D_{wb}\tau_{sl} + D_{wg}\tau_{gl}$$
$$D_{iu} = D_{ws}\tau_{su} + D_{wb}\tau_{su} + D_{wg}\tau_{gu}$$

then

$$\bar{D}_{lower} = \frac{2a_w(D_{il} + D_{iu}\rho_u)}{a_r(1 - \rho_u\rho_l)}$$
$$\bar{D}_{upper} = \frac{2a_w(D_{iu} + D_{il}\rho_l)}{a_r(1 - \rho_u\rho_l)}$$

$$(9.1)$$

D_{il} and D_{iu} represent the fractions of light falling initially on the lower and upper parts of the room.

We began by taking τ to be a single number representing the transmittance of a window; then, for increased precision, divided the input and output each into two zones. The clear progression is to split the incoming and outgoing light into many zones. Imagine, as in Figure 9.3, a window placed in the centre of a very large sphere. The sphere is divided into zones and the transmittance is now defined by a table of values, a matrix in which each element is the fraction of incident light from an external zone that reaches a particular internal zone. The zones are normally subdivisions of a hemisphere by azimuth and elevation, but finite zones can be used, as in Figure 9.3. An alternative is for the interior hemisphere to be

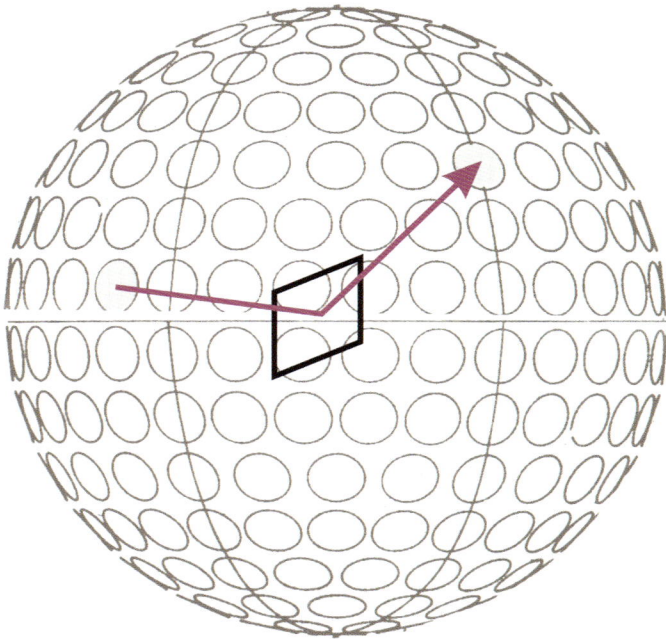

9.3

Bi-directional transmission coefficients using discrete sky zones.

divided into zones projected from a subdivision of the room. In effect, the matrix associates external zones with defined patches of interior surface. This loses generality because the transmittance matrix must be derived for every room, but after that the computation is very efficient. And, just as a single transmittance value is the heart of an average daylight factor calculation, and the up–down matrix is the basis of the split-flux method, so the exterior-zone–room-patch matrix is central to the calculation of daylight coefficients.

The numbers in the matrix are called bi-directional transmission coefficients. Hypothetically, these could be replaced by an equation, a mathematical function mapping a hemisphere onto a hemisphere, but a real window would require this to be a complicated discontinuous function.

Estimating transmittance

To put a numerical value on the transmittance of a window or other device, analyse its three components separately. Then

overall transmittance = transmittance of collector
× transmittance of channel
× transmittance of distributor

Note that transmittance is different from transmittivity, which is sometimes given in data on properties of materials. Transmittivity is the fraction of flux transmitted by unit distance of the material. It excludes surface effects.

Shading devices and window reveals

In a conventional window, the collector comprises all the building elements that affect the light falling on the window. In Figure 9.4, a set of horizontal louvres partly shade the glazing. Now consider a horizontal beam exactly framed by the edges of the glazing. The transmittance of this horizontal beam is equal to the fraction of the beam striking the glazing plus the proportion of the blocked light that is reflected on to the glazing. A visual estimate suggests that the direct fraction is about 0.5 and that with matt white louvres about one-fifth of the remainder is reflected inwards, giving a transmittance at this stage of 0.6.

But more than this is needed: sunlight falls at different incident angles, and for diffuse light we need the mean transmittance over a range of angles. This is much more difficult to estimate: for accuracy, real measured values are required, or the results from computer simulation. Some typical numbers are given in the data pages of the Worksheets. However, for initial estimates of daylighting, a reasoned estimate from a drawing such as Figure 9.4 is inevitably better than a quick guess.

When light falls at an oblique angle onto an opening in a thick wall, some of the light falls on the sides of the opening. The fraction passing directly through depends on the

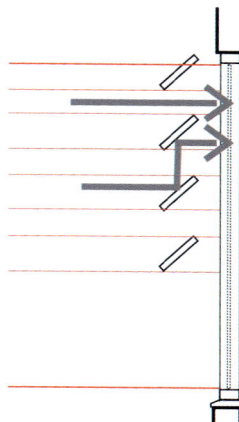

9.4

Estimating the transmittance of shading devices: fraction of a beam falling directly on glazing and fraction reflected on to it. For diffuse light, the average transmittance at all angles of incident light is required.

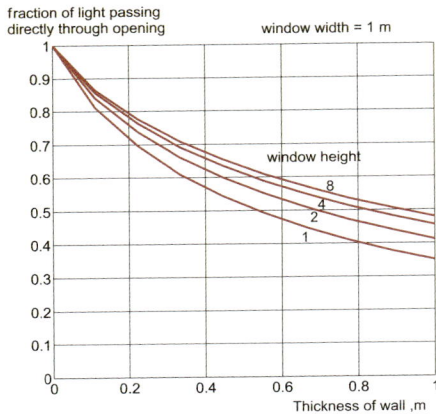

9.5

The fraction of diffuse light passing directly through a rectangular opening in a thick wall. The opening is 1 m wide; the curves indicate openings 1, 2, 4 and 8 m high. The wall thickness varies from zero to 1 m. The faces of the reveal are black.

dimensions of the opening and the direction of the incident light. Figure 9.5 shows the mean transmittance of an unglazed rectangular opening over all angles of incidence. It will be seen that with a square window (height 1 m) and a wall thickness of 0.2 m, the fraction of light passing through is just over 0.7. If the inside faces of the reveal were painted matt white, light reflected from the faces of the reveal would increase the fraction of light passing through to about 0.8. This example has window reveals that are rectilinear. When window reveals are splayed so that the inner opening is larger than the outer, two things happen: more light comes through directly and the faces of the reveals provide areas of intermediate brightness between inside and outside, reducing contrast and therefore lessening glare.

Glazing transmittance

The transmittance of a sheet of glass depends on the angle of incidence. If a beam is normal to the face of the glass, most is transmitted; if it falls on the glass at a glancing angle, it is almost entirely reflected. A formula for this is given in Algorithms and Equations, Sections 5.6 and 5.7, and approximate transmittances are listed in Worksheet 15. In daylight calculations, the direct transmittance is used for a beam of light striking the glass. Where the incident light is a diffuse field, it is the average transmittance over all angles

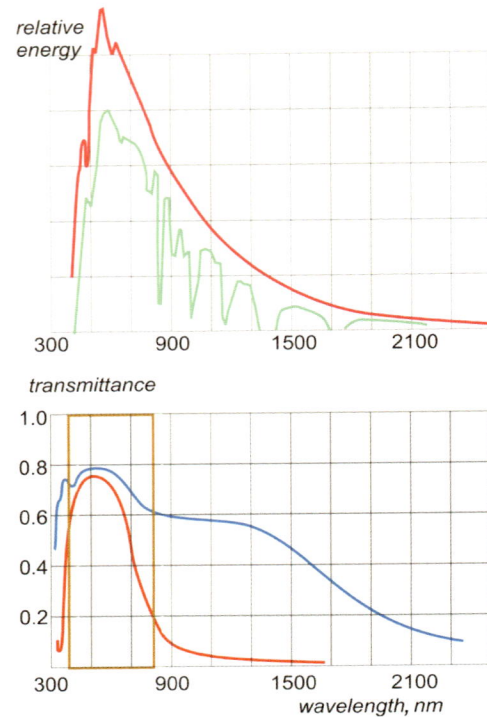

9.6

The solar spectrum and glazing transmittance.
Upper: Smoothed graph of the extraterrestrial solar spectrum and the spectrum at the earth's surface.
Lower: The blue curve shows the transmittance of low-emittance coated glass for high thermal gain and low thermal loss. The red curve shows the transmittance of double silver glass for low thermal gain.

that is required. The diffuse transmittance of glass is about 0.91 of the value for a beam perpendicular to the surface.

The transmittances of low-e and double silver glazing are shown in Figure 9.6. The transmittance of the assembly must also take into account the frames and glazing bars of the window. These typically occupy at least 10% of the total area of the window aperture. The glazed roofs of atria usually have a greater percentage of blocking elements: a substantial amount of structure, air-conditioning ducts and exhausts, luminaires, and controls. Looking directly upward, their obstruction to light may not be large but seen from upper floors looking into the atrium a large proportion of the sky is often covered.

Internal elements

The effect on transmittance of blinds, curtains and other obstructions is the most difficult part of the window to estimate, because they are dependent on the users. These internal components serve several purposes: they redirect the light, they reduce the brightness of the view to the outside and they are used to increase privacy; consequently, they are adjusted in response to changes in daylight, to changed activities in the room and to different users.

How people respond to changing daylight – to glare, sunlight penetration and unsatisfactory illuminances – is the topic most in need of research in the whole area of daylighting. In the absence of detailed knowledge, it is necessary to make simple rules. One is that when the illuminance on the task exceeds a given level, such as 2000 lx, users close the blinds and exclude the daylight almost entirely – a practice that is unsatisfactory on the grounds of energy efficiency, and problematic in larger workplaces, where lighting conditions change significantly with distance from the window. It is not just because such assumptions reduce the predictive power of computer simulation that more knowledge is needed: it is because we cannot design the lighting and its controls well if we have only crude models of behaviour. We know that user decisions tend to be made on the brightness of the whole space, rather than the illuminance of a small area, and on glare and reflections, and that there is interaction between users: but we do not know enough to predict how people might behave in any particular circumstance.

To find the transmittance of the internal element of a window, the procedure is the same as for the external elements: assess the fraction of the glazing that is visible from within the room from the relevant directions, and add to this an estimate of the amount of blocked light that reaches the interior after reflection. The transmittance of blinds is given in the data sheet, Worksheet 15.

The overall transmittance of a window is the product of the component reflectances:

$$\tau = \tau_1 \times \tau_2 \times \tau_3$$
where
τ_1 is the transmittance of the collector (the external elements)
τ_2 is the transmittance of the channel (the glazing and frame)
τ_3 is the transmittance of the distributor (the internal elements)

If a single value of the overall transmittance is required, the three terms are the component transmittances multiplied together. If the transmittance is to be represented by a table of values for different input–output directions, such as Table 9.1, the three terms become tables, or matrices, of the component transmittance combined by matrix multiplication. Interreflection between components, such as between the inner face of the glazing and blinds, can be incorporated using formulae such as in Section 5.8 of Algorithms and Equations.

Glass and glazing

Glass is the subject of highly competitive industrial research and development. Consequently, manufacturing techniques are sophisticated; techniques used include the coating of glass with very thin metallic films, adding small quantities of other substances to the glass itself, and forming sandwiches of glass with other materials and sealed units in which a glass envelope contains gases such as argon.

Spectrally selective glasses

Half of the solar radiation is in the visible spectrum, so that cutting the solar transmittance uniformly over all wavelengths reduces daylight proportionally. This was a problem with earlier solar glasses because it was found that building users do not like heavily tinted glazing: in surveys evaluating user response to glazing of different types, the fraction of people dissatisfied was found to increase sharply as transmittance dropped below about 0.4. In addition, the colours of the resulting glass caused colour adaptation: this was particularly noticeable when a window was opened and the chromatic distortion of the glass revealed by comparison with the true view.

What was required was the development of spectrally selective transmitting glazing that reduces transmittance of the infrared (IR) but with little attenuation in the visible spectrum. In addition, insulating properties of glass are improved if emissivity in the far-IR is reduced. Normal float glass transmits strongly in the visible spectrum and in the near-IR (radiation with wavelengths close to the visible); in the far-IR (long-wavelength radiation emitted by surfaces at about normal room temperature), glass transmittance is low. This is the reason a greenhouse is warmer than the air outside: solar radiation in the visible and near-IR falls on the glazed walls and roof and passes through, warming the air and the internal surfaces. These re-radiate, but at much longer wavelengths to which the glass is almost opaque, so the heat is trapped. In the earth's atmosphere, certain gases – water vapour, CO_2, methane and others – act in the same way, so this mechanism in the earth's energy balance is called the greenhouse effect by analogy.

The aim of glazing with a low transmittance of total solar energy coupled with a high visible transmittance is achieved by coating the glass with a single or double layer of silver. The double layer gives a better cut-off at the limits of the visible but a lower light transmittance. The total solar energy transmittance (sometimes referred to as the TSET or *g*-value) is the sum of the solar energy transmittance of the glazing and the solar energy absorbed by the glazing and re-radiated inward. The silver coating has very low emissivity (0.03), which reduces the far-IR re-radiation from the warm glass to the interior if correctly placed. Figure 9.7 shows how the position of the coated surface is related to the function of the glazing.

Used in colder climates where heat loss is the main problem, low-e glass has coatings such as fluorine-doped tin oxide that give a low emissivity, which reduces radiation losses to the outside while maintaining a high value of solar transmittance.

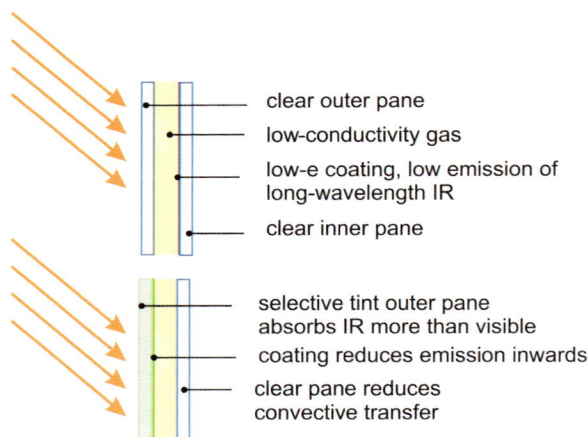

9.7
Upper: Sandwich construction of glazing panels for maximising heat gain and thermal insulation in cool climates. Note that the coating is on the cavity face of the inner pane.
Lower: For minimising solar gain in warm climates, the coating is on the cavity face of the outer pane. It is optional whether the outer pane is tinted; clear glass is more frequently used.

Switchable glazing

'Smart' windows, that is, windows whose transmission can be changed to suit the prevailing external environment, have yet to have a major market impact. Present glasses are reliant on absorption rather than reflection. Absorbing radiation rather than reflecting it causes the glass to become hot, and this will provide a heat gain to the room, a particular problem in warm climates. Limiting solar transmittance during hot, high-radiation conditions while allowing penetration of that radiation during cold, low-radiation conditions is clearly very desirable in energy terms. Under the latter conditions, the window would be in a clear state; under other conditions, the window will have a variable transmission optimised for thermal and visual comfort.

Electrochromic devices use a multilayer thin film where the cycled electric charge that causes the change of state commonly uses the properties of tungsten oxide or other transition metal oxides. Lithium ions are injected into the tungsten oxide in a reversible reaction promoted by the application of an electrical field:

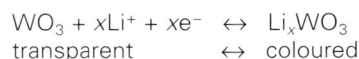

$$WO_3 + xLi^+ + xe^- \leftrightarrow Li_xWO_3$$
$$\text{transparent} \qquad \leftrightarrow \qquad \text{coloured}$$

Other types of glazing that have important and immediate practical applications are *self-cleaning glass*, which has coatings to reduce the adherence of dirt particles and enhance washing by rainwater, and *light-directing glazing*, in which miniature louvres or laser-cut acrylic panels are sandwiched between glass sheets.

The choice of components when designing a window depends on the functional requirements. Table 9.2 is a guide.

Light pipes

The components of a mirror light pipe (MLP) – or tubular daylight guidance system (TDGS) – are:

1   An external collector on the roof of the building. In most cases, this is a clear polycarbonate dome removing ultraviolet radiation and excluding rain and dust.
2   A hollow tube with a highly reflective inner surface, typically of anodized aluminium or laminated silver film.

Table 9.2: Window requirements

To reduce	Solution
Solar heat gain	In order of efficacy: 1 Orientation of building 2 External shading 3 Solar-reflective glazing 4 Body-tinted glazing 5 Blinds and other internal shading
Conducted heat loss and radiant heat loss externally	Multiple layers of glazing, low-emissivity glazing, insulated window frame
Sound transmission	Widely spaced multiple layers of glazing with minimum coupling, absorbing materials in reveal
Inwards view (increased privacy)	1 Layout of building 2 Mesh curtains, adjustable blinds 3 Patterned or diffusing glass 4 External screens
Glare from the sky	1 Orientation and planning of windows in relation to task areas 2 Internal or external blinds 3 Low-transmittance glazing

3   A diffuser on the interior. This converts the strongly directional light emitted from the pipe to a more even distribution on room surfaces.

Light pipes are widely available across the market in different sizes and are produced by several manufacturers. They may have rigid or flexible walls and include bends or elbows. Most are designed to be used vertically, but horizontal light pipes carrying light deep into the building from a window wall are possible.

The transmittance of the actual pipe is determined by the reflectance of the coating material, the number of bounces, and the number and type of bends. Manufacturers have concentrated on increasing the reflectance of the internal surface (values above 99% have been claimed). Increasing the diameter of the pipe reduces the number of bounces; bends cause difficulties with optical control and increase the number of bounces. Most systems are not hermetically sealed, because adjustments may be required during installation. Dust tends to accumulate, which adversely affects pipe reflectance and the transmittance of the system as a whole.

The transmission of a light pipe with an arbitrary cross-section is given by

$$\tau_{pipe} = \rho_{pipe}^{\,L\tan\theta/d_{eff}} \tag{9.2}$$

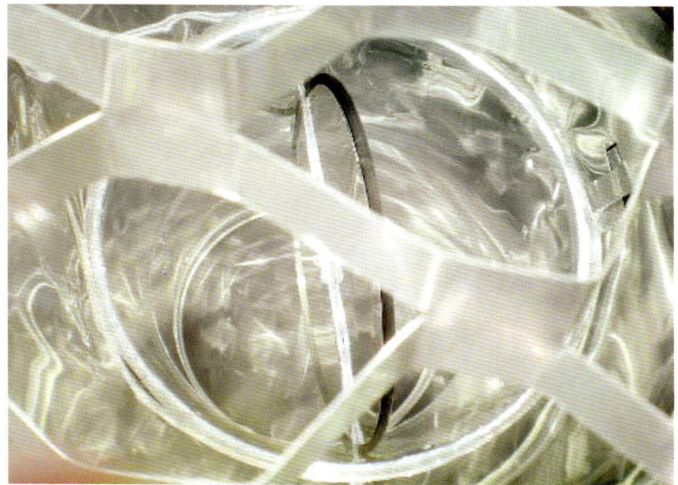

9.8

Light pipe collectors. The top of a light pipe must be robust and weatherproof. A high quality of maintenance is needed to avoid major reduction of light transmittance.

where ρ_p is the reflectivity of the pipe, L is the length of the pipe, θ is the angle between the direction of incident light from the pipe's axis, and d_{eff} is the effective diameter of the entrance aperture. For a cylindrical pipe of actual diameter d, $d_{eff} = \pi d/4$.

Under low angles of incidence of the light (θ close to 90°), or high values of the aspect ratio, L/d_{eff}, or low reflectance, ρ_p, the transmission is low.

It has been estimated that a 30° bend causes a 20% loss of light.

The efficiency of a light pipe may be measured using an integrating sphere on the termination of the pipe.

Using Sumpner's formula (described in Chapter 2), the efficiency of a pipe with a horizontal collector is given by

$$\eta = \frac{4\pi r_s^2}{s_{coll}} \frac{(1-\rho_s)}{\rho_s} \frac{E_s}{E_{hext}} \qquad (9.3)$$

where r_s and ρ_s are the radius and reflectance of the integrating sphere, s_{coll} is the area of the collector, and E_s and E_{hext} are the measured illuminance on the sphere and the simultaneous illuminance on an external horizontal surface.

The efficiency is the ratio of the luminous flux falling on the collector to the flux emitted by the distributor. It varies with the directionality of the incident light. For a flat collector aperture, the efficiency under diffuse light can be about $1/\pi$ the value for a beam on the axis of the pipe.

If η is known, interior illuminances can be calculated. If a light pipe system has a collector area s_{coll} and in the building the light is distributed over a room surface area s_{int} then, when the daylight illuminance on the collector is E_{ext}, the mean direct illuminance on the room surface is

$$E_{int} = E_{ext} \frac{\eta s_{coll}}{s_{int}} \qquad (9.4)$$

For example, if $s_{coll} = 0.1$ m^2, $s_{int} = 5$ m^2, $E_{ext} = 25$ klx and $\eta = 0.3$,

$$E_{int} = 25,000 \times \frac{0.3 \times 0.1}{6} = 125 \text{ lx}$$

There have been some suggestions to improve the performance of light pipes. Most non-imaging collectors or concentrators fail because, although a greater collection area is provided, the light reaches the tube at an increased angle to the axis, leading to an increased number of bounces down the tube. An alternative method for climates that are mainly sunny is to use an adjustable light deflector to align the sun's rays closer to the pipe axis. This deflector may be a laser-cut panel.

The results from this are good, particularly with low-angle sun, so wintertime light penetration is significantly improved. In a test in Florence, Italy, the angle of elevation of the sheet was changed only monthly, but the increase in accumulated light (lux-hours) was sixfold under sunny skies in winter but

with little change in summer. Under overcast conditions, however, the deflecting sheet reduced transmission by about 13% if held vertical over the pipe and 23% if horizontal. It is necessary in design to balance the needs of overcast and sunny conditions. There is an analogy here with the choice of window size. Generally, smaller windows are found in warmer, sunnier climates. These provide good daylight under clear skies, whether by direct sun or ground- and façade-reflected sunlight; but rooms can seem gloomier than in comparable colder cloudier locations, where window sizes have been designed to compensate for low daylight levels.

Light pipes are useful where daylight needs to be brought to deep interior spaces, and they can be used to create an unexpected bright area where the general daylight level is low. Particularly noticeable with light pipes is the change in the apparent colour of the light when sunlight is added to diffuse light outside. Light from overcast or blue skies invariably lends a high colour temperature to the space; the presence of sunlight shifts the colour appearance from the blue towards the yellow–red.

The light output of a tubular daylight guidance system may be calculated from the tube transmission efficiency (TTE), the transmission of the transparent covering and diffuser, and a maintenance factor. The TTE is calculated as a function of the reflectance and aspect ratio of the tube. Information and tables may be found in CIE 173:2006 Appendix C.

Light shelves

A light shelf is a canopy set within the window opening instead of above the window head. It serves three purposes: a sunshade, a screen that blocks the view of the sky at high elevations, and a means of lessening the contrast within the room by reducing illuminance in the area near the window. Unless it is reflecting sunlight, a conventional light shelf does not increase the amount of light delivered towards the back of the room. A disadvantage of the light shelf is that a higher ceiling tends to be necessary.

In effect, it creates two separate windows. The lower behaves as a conventional window under a projecting canopy; the upper acts like a window above a reflecting ground surface. The performance of both parts under sunlight and skylight can be assessed using the methods of Chapter 8.

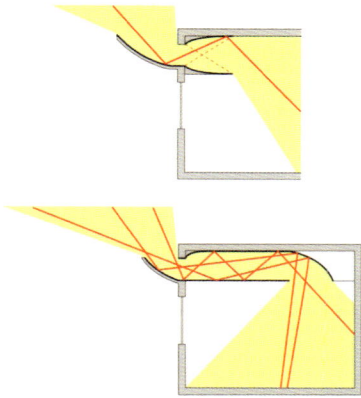

9.9
Anidolic light shelves.

Transmission of light into the interior is improved if the upper surface of the shelf is glossy; it is increased further if the shelf and the ceiling immediately above are anidolic specular surfaces. These are compound parabolic reflectors that concentrate diffuse light but do not produce an image. The light is deflected towards a line perpendicular to the axis of the concentrator. This implies that a zenithal collector is ideal for redirecting light down a horizontal tube, and a collector used in reverse can be an efficient method of diffusing light within the building.

A shiny ceiling over all the room conveys a greater amount of light from a light shelf to the back of the room than one that is matt white, but it looks dark. Looking upwards within the room, the floor and dark lower surfaces are reflected; light falling on the ceiling from the window is not scattered towards the eye.

Light shelves suffer serious light loss from dirt accumulation. The upper side of a shelf is usually hidden from view and awkward to clean. It is important to consider maintenance when designing a light shelf system and to use realistic estimates of long-term reflectance when predicting performance.

Heliostats

Direct sunlight on the ground can produce an illuminance of 100 klx. Assuming the sunlight can be properly transmitted and diffused within a building, and ignoring for a moment system losses, the flux from 1 m² of direct sunlight could

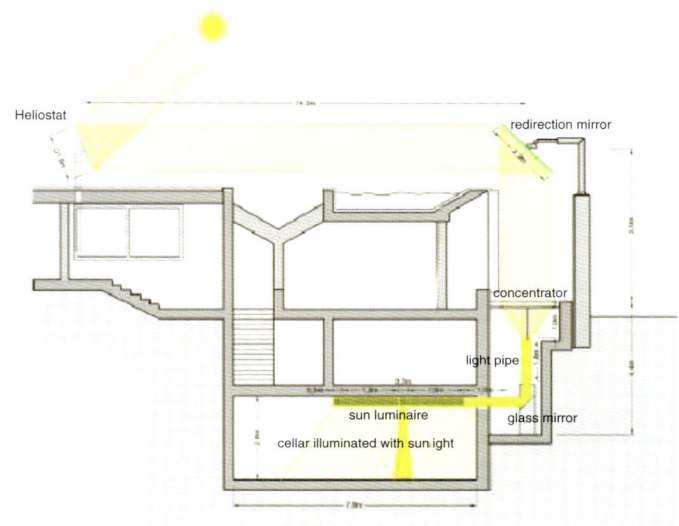

9.10
A mirror heliostat: the collecting mirror and the layout of the system.
Near Innsbruck, Austria

illuminate 200 m² of internal space to 500 lx. With optical systems, sunlight has one great advantage over diffuse light: the rays are almost parallel and can therefore be concentrated into a narrow beam. Unfortunately, the heat is also concentrated.

Heliostats are devices that track the sun and concentrate its light, but thermal problems place a practical limit on that concentration. The tracking device is either a mirror or a lens. Typically, a 1 m diameter Fresnel lens focuses the beam to a minimum patch about 10 mm across, but not all heliostats concentrate to such levels. Figure 9.10 shows a mirror heliostat at Bartenbach Lichtlabor that concentrates the beam on a mirror tube in the manner of a light pipe. It illuminates a basement room with a quality of light that is highly appreciated. The 1 m diameter Fresnel lens system on the roof of The University of Athens (Figure 9.11) concentrates sunlight into a liquid optic light guide 11 mm in diameter. As with glass and fibre optics, the maximum angle of acceptance of a liquid optic device depends on the critical angle within the system. The enclosing material needs to be of a lower refractive index than the liquid. The entrance to the liquid fibre optic requires a cooling system, but thermal problems would be greater in bundles of glass or acrylic fibres with a bonding material.

Flexible fibre optic tubes may be fed easily into buildings where cables might go. Special care needs to be taken when bending the tubes, to avoid miniscule cracks in the retaining material, which destroys the light transmission. In the room, the light can be distributed by several methods. One is to couple the fibre optic tube to

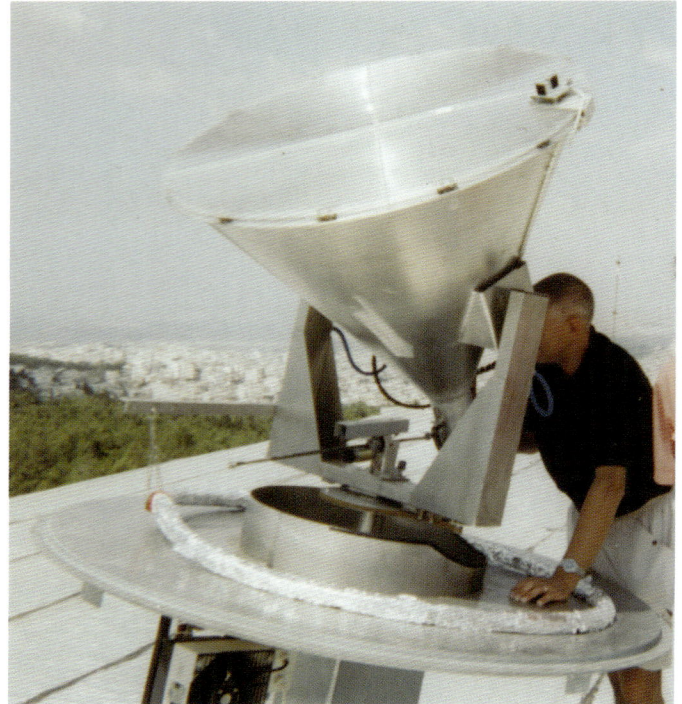

9.11
A Fresnel lens as the collector of a heliostat.
Athens, Greece

an acrylic material screen-printed with diffusing dots. LEDs may also be linked to this system to provide artificial light when sunlight is unavailable. Practical estimates of light transmission through the liquid optic guide from a 1 m diameter Fresnel lens are 32,000 lm with a guide 2 m long and 16,000 lm with a guide 50 m in length. These estimates include all losses.

ten

Daylight coefficients and numerical models

This chapter describes techniques used in computer programs for daylight modelling. It introduces the concept of daylight coefficients and shows how they can be computed using radiosity methods and Monte Carlo simulation.

The fundamental equation

One equation is the foundation of every daylighting calculation. It links the luminance of a patch of sky to the illuminance it gives on a surface:

$$E_{ki} = L_i s_i d_{ki} \qquad (10.1)$$

This equation states that the desktop illuminance (at k in Figure 10.1) depends on three factors: the luminance of the

sky zone, L_i; its angular size, s_i; and the daylight coefficient, d_{ki}, the fraction of the emitted light that finds its way to the desktop.

As a sky patch is made smaller and smaller, the three factors on the right-hand side of Equation (10.1) become increasingly independent of each other. This has important implications. It means, in particular, that once the daylight coefficients have been calculated, they can be used to find the surface illumination from any sky luminance distribution.

Stating this formally: the daylight coefficient is the limiting ratio of illuminance to the product of luminance and size as the solid angle s_i shrinks to zero around a sky point (γ, α):

$$d_k(\gamma, \alpha) = \frac{E_{ki}}{L_i s_i}, \ \lim s_i \to 0 \qquad (10.2)$$

The daylight coefficient embodies the total effect on daylight of a building's form and materials. It can apply to any surface, inside or outside, and it can apply to the illuminance around a point or the mean illuminance over an area. Every method of calculating daylight illuminance or daylight factor is, in essence, a way of solving the fundamental equation for a specific case.

If the sky is subdivided into n zones, the total illuminance from the sky is simply the sum of the illuminances from individual zones:

$$E_k = \sum_{i=1}^{n} L_i s_i d_{ik} \qquad (10.3)$$

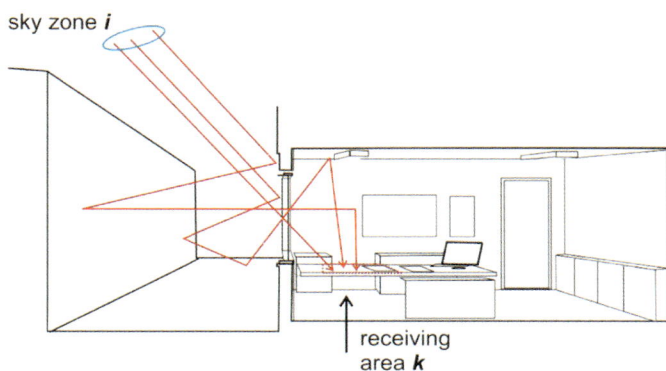

10.1

The fundamental equation of daylighting links the luminance of a sky patch with the resulting illuminance on a surface.

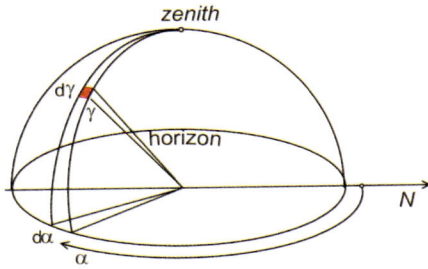

10.2

Sky angles.

The sky can be treated as a continuous surface. Then, provided luminance, size and daylight coefficient can be written as analytic functions of azimuth and elevation, the total illuminance at some point k is

$$E_k = \int_0^{\pi/2} \int_0^{2\pi} L(\gamma, a) \, d_k(\gamma, a) \cos\gamma \, \mathrm{d}a \, \mathrm{d}\gamma \qquad (10.4)$$

Translating from the mathematics, this says, 'Divide the sky dome into a mesh of tiny zones, with a grid size of δa in azimuth and $\delta\gamma$ in elevation. The area of each zone is $\cos\gamma \, \delta a \, \delta\gamma$ (the $\cos\gamma$ is there because the zones become narrower as γ increases). Then multiply every area by the luminance of its zone and its daylight coefficient, and add up the results.'

For example, the daylight coefficient for illuminance on a horizontal surface is

$$d_h(\gamma, a) = \sin\gamma \qquad (10.5)$$

Then, if the sky is uniformly bright, with luminance L,

$$E_h = \int_0^{\pi/2} \int_0^{2\pi} L \sin\gamma \cos\gamma \, \mathrm{d}a \, \mathrm{d}\gamma$$
$$= \pi L \qquad (10.6)$$

E_h is the illuminance in lux if luminance is given in cd/m².

With a CIE Overcast Sky of zenith luminance L_z, where

$$L(\gamma, a) = L_z \frac{1 + 2\sin\gamma}{3} \qquad (10.7)$$

the integral evaluates to $E_{hoc} = (7\pi/9) L_z$.

The horizontal diffuse illuminance from the sky is, in effect, a weighted average of sky luminance. Conversely,

the luminance of a sky patch can be written as a function of horizontal illuminance. For a standard overcast sky, it would be

$$L(\gamma, a) = E_{hoc} \frac{9}{7\pi} \frac{1 + 2\sin\gamma}{3}$$
$$= E_{hoc} \frac{3}{7\pi} (1 + 2\sin\gamma) \qquad (10.8)$$

The illuminance on an interior surface is the daylight factor at that surface multiplied by the horizontal illuminance from an unobstructed sky:

$$E_k = E_{hoc} D_k$$
but
$$E_k = \int_0^{\pi/2} \int_0^{2\pi} L(a, \gamma) \, s(a, \gamma) \, d(a, \gamma) \, \mathrm{d}a \, \mathrm{d}\gamma$$
$$= E_{hoc} \frac{3}{7\pi} \int_0^{\pi/2} \int_0^{2\pi} (1 + 2\sin\gamma) \cos\gamma \, d(a, \gamma) \, \mathrm{d}a \, \mathrm{d}\gamma$$
$$D_k = \frac{3}{7\pi} \int_0^{\pi/2} \int_0^{2\pi} (1 + 2\sin\gamma) \cos\gamma \, d(a, \gamma) \, \mathrm{d}a \, \mathrm{d}\gamma \qquad (10.9)$$

So the daylight factor is simply a weighted integral of the daylight coefficients.

Subdivision of the sky

A sky scanner is an instrument for measuring the luminance distribution of the sky. Its sensor is a photocell set in a tube with optics that limit its field of view to a small zone of the sky. The width of the zone, the acceptance angle, is typically about 11° across. Electric motors turn the sensor in elevation and azimuth so that it tracks across the sky.

The pattern of scanning is governed by several constraints: the patches should not overlap, they should be distributed evenly across the sky, and in total they should contain a high proportion of the total sky area. Preferably, the pattern should be symmetrical across the sky and be defined by a simple formula.

Figure 10.3 shows the subdivision adopted by the CIE for the International Daylight Measurement Project. The hemisphere is divided into seven horizontal bands 12° high plus a zenith zone 12° across. Each band is split into intervals

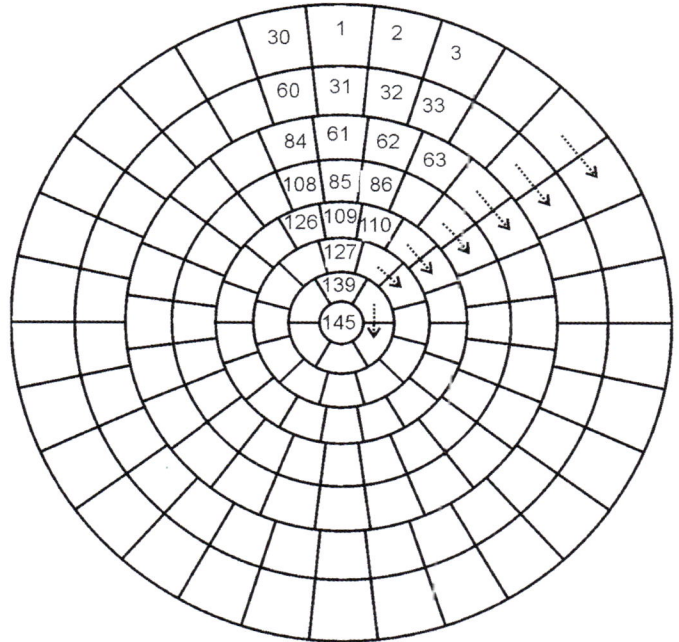

10.4

Subdivision of the complete sky. The angular sizes of the patches vary slightly; they are listed in Table 10.1.

Sky, sun and point sources

The choice of 11° as the acceptance angle for the scanning luminance meter is not arbitrary. Recall from Chapter 2 that the inverse square law, which strictly applies only to point sources, can be used with only minor error for finite sources when the maximum dimension of the source is not greater than about one-fifth the distance from source to receiver. With a circular aperture, this is equivalent to an acceptance

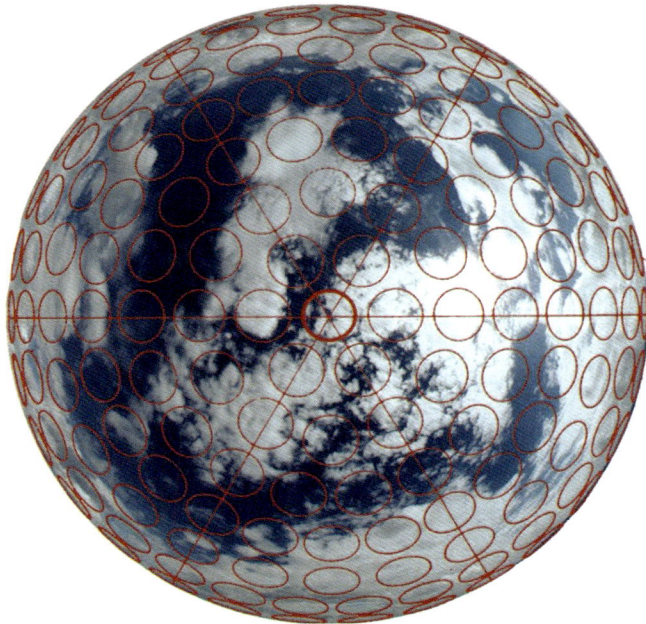

10.3

Subdivision of the sky for luminance scanning.

of about 12°; this varies with elevation, but is chosen to give a three-way symmetry in azimuth. The scanning points lie at the centre of each zone. There are 145 points in all, giving a sky coverage of 67% with zones 11° in diameter and 46% with 10° zones.

For calculations, rather than scanning measurements, the zones do not have to be of constant size. Subdividing the sky with the same angles but using the whole mesh instead of a fixed aperture centred in the subdivisions means that the whole sky is covered, but at the cost of small differences between bands. This is shown in Figure 10.4 and Table 10.1.

Table 10.1: Angles of sky subdivision

Zone numbers	Elevation of band centre, degrees	Number in band	Azimuth increment, degrees	Solid angle subtended by zone, steradians
1–30	6	30	12	0.0435
31–60	18	30	12	0.0416
61–84	30	24	15	0.0474
85–108	42	24	15	0.0407
109–126	54	18	20	0.0429
127–138	66	12	30	0.0445
139–144	78	6	60	0.0455
145	90	1	360	0.0344

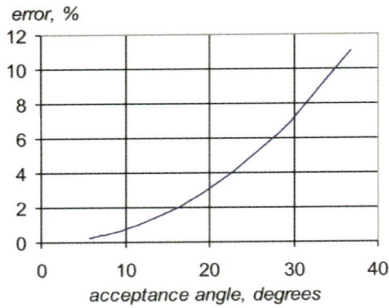

10.5

Error in applying the inverse square formula to an area source. Taking the source in the form of a circular disc, the graph shows the percentage error when a point source assumption is used in place of a configuration factor.

angle of just below 11°. Figure 10.5 shows that the error in the assumption of a point source is then about 1%.

The luminance of the sky could be written as $L = E_n/s$; the luminance of a small patch is equal to the normal illuminance from that patch divided by its angular size. The fundamental equation could therefore be written as

$$E_{ki} = (E_n)_i\, d_{ki} \tag{10.10}$$

Illuminance from a sky patch is equal to the normal illuminance from the sky patch multiplied by the daylight coefficient. This means that the source does not have to be a patch of diffuse sky. It can be the sun: the product of solar normal illuminance and the daylight coefficient at the solar position gives illuminance from sunlight. The fundamental equation of daylighting ties together illuminance from the diffuse sky, illuminance from sunlight and the inverse square law.

Daylight coefficients can be measured using scale models lit by a spotlight that is moved around the model. Two photocells are used, one measuring illuminance on a plane perpendicular to the beam, the other at the position in the model for which the daylight coefficients are required. The coefficient is just the internal illuminance divided by the normal illuminance. An early piece of equipment for doing this is shown in Figure 10.6. The model sits on a table that can rotate in steps under computer control. Lamps, set in a quadrant, are also under computer control and can be switched individually or in groups. A photocell records incident light on the model, and this has been calibrated to give normal illuminance from whichever lamps are lit; an array

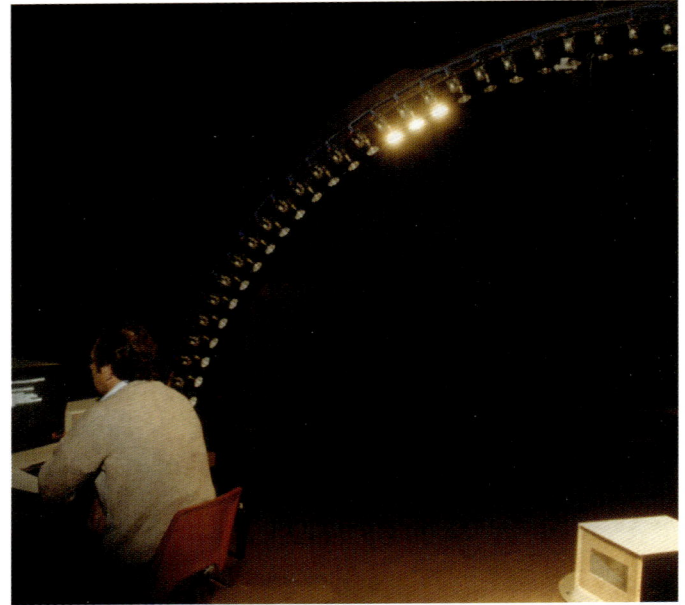

10.6

Measuring daylight coefficients in a scale model.

of photocells records illuminance in the model. The computer program switches the lamps and rotates the table so that a set of daylight coefficients is collected automatically.

Calculating daylight coefficients: finite area methods

For a single point in a building, the set of daylight coefficients is a list of n numbers, where n is the number of sky zones. Now, imagine a room in which a grid has been drawn on all the enclosing surfaces – floor, windows, walls and ceiling. Suppose there to be m cells in all. The daylight coefficients for all of those cells would form m lists of n numbers.

These could be written as a table, or matrix:

$$\mathbf{d} = \begin{pmatrix} d_{11} & \cdots & d_{1n} \\ \vdots & \ddots & \vdots \\ d_{m1} & \cdots & d_{mn} \end{pmatrix} \tag{10.11}$$

where d_{ki} is the daylight coefficient for surface point k from sky zone i.

The list of final illuminances on the room surfaces could then be written as the totals of the respective daylight coefficients multiplied by the normal illuminance from each sky zone.

$$E_1 = d_{11}(E_n)_1 + d_{12}(E_n)_2 + \ldots + d_{1i}(E_n)_i + \ldots + d_{1n}(E_n)_n$$
$$E_2 = d_{21}(E_n)_1 + d_{22}(E_n)_2 + \ldots + d_{2i}(E_n)_i + \ldots + d_{2n}(E_n)_n$$
$$\vdots$$
$$E_k = d_{k1}(E_n)_1 + d_{k2}(E_n)_2 + \ldots + d_{ki}(E_n)_i + \ldots + d_{kn}(E_n)_n$$
$$\vdots$$
$$E_m = d_{m1}(E_n)_1 + d_{m2}(E_n)_2 + \ldots + d_{mi}(E_n)_i + \ldots + d_{mn}(E_n)_n$$

This is far more compact in matrix notation:

$$\mathbf{E} = \mathbf{dE}_n \qquad (10.12)$$

It can be written with the product of sky zone size and luminance instead of normal illuminance:

$$\mathbf{E} = \mathbf{dsL}$$
where
$$\mathbf{s} = \begin{pmatrix} s_1 & 0 & \cdots & 0 \\ 0 & s_2 & \cdots & 0 \\ \vdots & \vdots & s_i & \vdots \\ 0 & 0 & 0 & s_n \end{pmatrix} \qquad (10.13)$$

The daylight coefficient matrix, **d**, embodies all the transformations that the field of light undergoes between the sky and the interior of the building.

It is calculated in stages, from the room surfaces outwards. Imagine, first, the enclosing surfaces of a room subdivided into a mesh of m elements. Enclosing all is a vast sphere, many times larger in diameter than any dimension of the room; this is subdivided into n zones. The room is suspended in space – no ground, no external obstructions. There is 'sky' all round, and we can write daylight coefficients between the zones of sky and the centre of every mesh element in the room, as a matrix, $\mathbf{d}_2$, which has m rows representing room points and n columns representing sky zones. Figure 10.7 illustrates the concept.

Each number in this matrix is either

$d_{1ki} = 0$ if zone i is blocked from point k, or
$\qquad = \cos \omega_{ki} \tau_{ki}$ if k is visible to i through a window $\quad (10.14)$

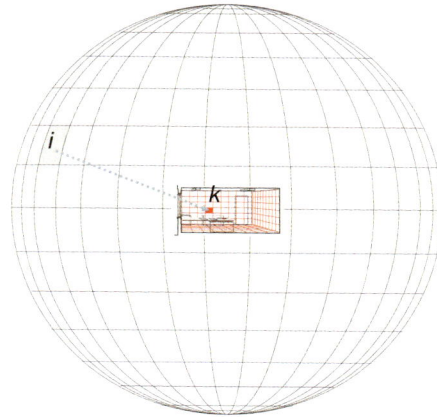

10.7
Sky zones and interior surface subdivision.

where ω_{ki} is the angle of incidence of light from i onto the surface at k, and τ_{ki} is the transmittance of the window in the direction of i to k. Assume for the moment that it is a simple glazed opening.

There is interreflection between the elements of the room. The final illuminance on each element is its initial illuminance plus the illuminance due to light reflected from every other element. This can be written as a set of simultaneous equations:

$$E_1 = E_{d1} + E_2\rho_2 F_{12} + E_3\rho_3 F_{13} + \ldots + E_m\rho_m F_{1m}$$
$$E_2 = E_1\rho_1 F_{21} + E_{d2} + E_3\rho_3 F_{23} + \ldots + E_m\rho_m F_{2m}$$
$$\vdots$$
$$E_m = E_1\rho_1 F_{m1} + E_2\rho_2 F_{m2} + E_3\rho_3 F_{m3} + \ldots + E_{dm} \qquad (10.15)$$

where E_{dk} is the initial illuminance at surface point k, ρ_k is the diffuse reflectance at k and F_{kj} is the form factor between k and j. Form factors are described in Chapter 8, and listed in Algorithms and Equations.

Solving the simultaneous equations is trivial in computation if there are a few tens of patches but, if their number is very large, more advanced numerical methods are required.

Equation (10.15) can be rewritten as

$$\mathbf{E} = \mathbf{d}_1\mathbf{E}_d$$
where
$$d_1 = \begin{pmatrix} 1-\rho_1 F_{11} & -\rho_1 F_{12} & \cdots & -\rho_1 F_{1m} \\ -\rho_2 F_{21} & 1-\rho_2 F_{22} & \cdots & -\rho_2 F_{2m} \\ \vdots & \vdots & 1-\rho_k F_{kk} & \vdots \\ -\rho_m F_{m1} & -\rho_m F_{m2} & \cdots & 1-\rho_m F_{mm} \end{pmatrix} \qquad (10.16)$$

This approach to the interreflection of light between finite elements is called the radiosity method. It is used extensively in computer graphics and in engineering calculations of radiant heat transfer. In its original formulation, it is applicable only to situations where reflected light is totally diffuse: that is, where all surfaces act as Lambertian reflectors. Hybrid procedures have been developed, and there exist many algorithms for faster computation of complex situations.

The next stage is to involve the outside world in the computation, to include the effect of ground reflection and the blocking of the sky by buildings and other obstructions. This will produce a pair of matrices, $\mathbf{d}_3$ and $\mathbf{d}_4$, which transform the original luminance distribution of a hemisphere of sky into a sphere of brightness, the visual environment of a site on the earth's surface.

The matrix $\mathbf{d}_4$ describes the initial luminance of the external surfaces from light from sun and sky. It is based on the daylight coefficients of the external surfaces. For instance, the illuminance at point a on the tall obstruction in Figure 10.8 is

$$E_a = d_{a1}s_1L_1 + d_{a2}s_2L_2 + \ldots + d_{an}s_nL_n$$
where
$$d_{ai} = \cos\gamma_i \cos(a_a - a_1) \tag{10.17}$$

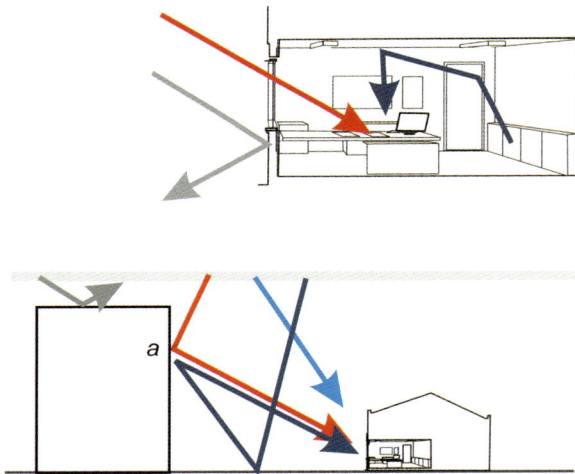

10.8
Upper: Stages 1 and 2: direct and reflected interior light.
Lower: Stages 3 and 4: direct and reflected exterior light.

and its luminance is

$$L_a = \frac{E_a \rho_a}{\pi} \tag{10.18}$$

where ρ_a is the reflectance of the surface at a.

We have already met the formulae for the illuminance and luminance of external surfaces in Chapter 8. For calculating daylight coefficients, interreflection between external surfaces can be treated in the same way as in Chapter 8, and included in the matrix $\mathbf{d}_4$. Alternatively, an interreflection matrix, $\mathbf{d}_3$, could be set up by subdividing the external surfaces, as was done with the internal surfaces.

We are creating a transformed sky that can be acted on by the partial daylight coefficients $\mathbf{d}_1$ and $\mathbf{d}_2$. To complete the chain, it is necessary to include the zone angular sizes, as with $\mathbf{s}$ in Equation (10.13). It is convenient to link this with the conversion from illuminance to luminance, as in Equation (10.18), so we define a matrix $\mathbf{t}$ that, like $\mathbf{s}$, has non-zero elements only on the leading diagonal, which are

$$t_i = \frac{s_i \rho_i}{\pi} \tag{10.19}$$

The final interior surface illuminances are then

$$\mathbf{E}_{room} = \mathbf{dsL}_{sky}$$
where
$$\mathbf{d} = \mathbf{d}_1\mathbf{d}_2\mathbf{t}\mathbf{d}_3\mathbf{d}_4 \tag{10.20}$$

The component matrices do not have to be the same size: the different stages could consist of different numbers of elements. $\mathbf{L}_{sky}$ covers a hemisphere; this could be mirrored to give the luminance of the ground and other elements below the horizon, or a different subdivision could be used. Similarly, the room subdivision need not be the same as the enclosing sphere. All that is essential is that the matrices have the dimensions required for matrix multiplication, that is, for $\mathbf{ab}$ to have meaning, the number of columns in $\mathbf{a}$ must equal the number of rows in $\mathbf{b}$.

Inherent in the computation is the assumption of linear independence – that the transformation from sky to the luminance pattern of the built environment is completely unaffected by the transformation by the window and internal reflection. This could not be said about the effect of louvres, for instance, or of the window reveal. There could be light flowing between the window glazing and these other elements; and the apparent size and shape of these elements would differ from place to place within the room.

It is useful to separate 'near' objects from 'distant' objects, those for which the luminance of every patch is independent of later transformations. Shading devices and the various components of a window system are 'near' to each other and to the grid of room surfaces: they cannot easily be broken down into a series of independent linear transformations. For radiosity calculations, they must, at the least, be reduced to very small zones. It is easiest to treat a complex window as a single component, defined by bidirectional transmittance data (as described in Chapter 9). These data form the basis of the transformation matrix, $\mathbf{d}_1$.

Samples of rays: the Monte Carlo method

Figure 10.9 is a snooker table. There is one ball on it, which has been struck firmly and is bouncing from cushion to cushion, losing some momentum at each impact. The figure could, though, be a diagram showing the first five reflections of a narrow beam of light in a mirror-lined box: the rules that describe specular reflection of light can mimic a bouncing snooker ball.

The path of the ball can be calculated, bounce-by-bounce, and this procedure could be written as a set of instructions:
Requirements:

- The dimensions of the table; the weight and size of the ball.
- The rule for reflections – how the direction and velocity of the ball are changed on impact.

Algorithm:

1 Choose the initial position of the ball and its direction and speed after being struck with a cue.
2 Calculate where and when the ball will hit the edge. Record this.
3 Is there a pocket where the ball would meet the edge? If 'yes', record which pocket and how long the ball took to reach it, then stop.
   If 'no', continue to the next step.
4 Assume the ball to be at the collision point and calculate the new direction and velocity.
5 Go back to Step 2.

This set of instructions is the typical structure of computer programs for simulating physical events, not only of moving objects but also light and sound. The aim is to use them experimentally just as physical scale models, or laboratory replications of the real world could be used. The snooker ball model could be used to investigate questions such as 'Is there anywhere on the table from which a ball will never go into a pocket, whatever its initial direction and speed?'.

But all that has been described up to now has limited applicability: it works with an idealised snooker table and could be used to study a mirror-lined box. It cannot, though, be applied to lighting in buildings, because no real material is a perfect mirror and many are highly diffusing. A ray striking a Lambertian surface does not bounce off as a reflected ray: it becomes a diffuse spread of light.

The solution to this is to repeat the simulation many times, assuming that a reflected ray exists but choosing a different angle of reflectance each time. The eventual results are

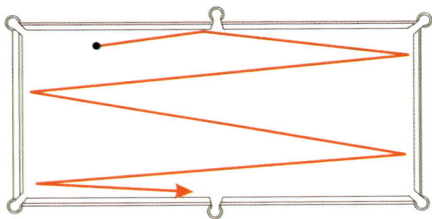

10.9

A ball on a snooker table, or a ray of light in a mirror-lined box.

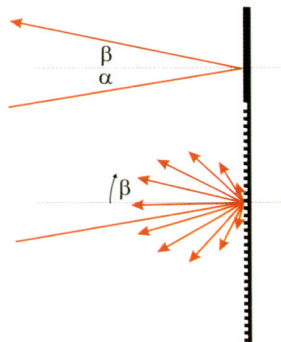

10.10

Rules of reflection:
specular: $\beta = \alpha$.
Lambertian: probability of β is proportional to $\cos \beta$.

combined: for example, the areas of the enclosure that receive most hits by rays could be determined.

The use of chance

The choice of the angle of reflection is not usually decided by systematically assigning values in advance. A ray might undergo many reflections: if there are *f* possible angles of reflection (a few hundred perhaps) and *n* reflections, there will be n^f possible paths of a single ray. The list of alternative paths can be not only impracticably great but also incomplete, because all paths involving intermediate angles are excluded.

The procedure adopted is one of sampling. Random numbers are used to assign the subsequent path of a ray after a diffusing process. This is mathematically equivalent to taking samples in any investigation, and the results have to be treated statistically in the same way. Such mathematical techniques that rely on chance in the calculation are called Monte Carlo methods.

The rules of reflection must model the physical process. If, for example, the reflection is specular, the angle of reflection is equal to the angle of incidence. If it is Lambertian, the new direction is independent of the initial direction, and the probability of the ray returning at an angle β from the perpendicular to the surface is proportional to cos β.

Programming languages contain commands for generating random numbers. If the reflection rule is a simple function, it can be converted into a formula that scales random numbers to the distribution required. For example, to obtain a list of numbers scaled for a Lambertian distribution,

$$\beta = \arcsin \sqrt{\mathbf{R}} \qquad (10.21)$$

where **R** is a list of random numbers between 0 and 1. Other formulae are listed in Equations and Algorithms.

Forwards and backwards

Consider again the snooker table model. If you wanted to know the ultimate distribution around the table of balls that commenced from a certain spot, then the procedure described above would work well. Suppose, though, that the question was about the way that shots from anywhere on the

table ended in one particular pocket; in that case, the program would be very inefficient because most of the repetitions would be of no interest. It would be much quicker to begin at the pocket, and trace the balls backwards, recording their routes over the table. This is, in fact, entirely valid. With light, it can be formalised by the principle of reciprocity.

So, if the purpose of the computation is to find the luminance distribution in a room from light emitted by a luminaire, forward simulation is best: rays are tracked in the direction that light is flowing. If, alternatively, the question concerns the illuminance at a small number of points in a complex luminance field, it is more efficient to treat rays as being emitted at those positions and track them until they intersect one of the real sources.

The huge advantage of the Monte Carlo method is the ease with which different physical characteristics can be modelled. A surface can be perfectly diffuse, perfectly specular, or have some empirically determined reflectance curve. The space between surfaces can be filled with a scattering and absorbing medium such as smoke. The disadvantage of the method is that, compared with radiosity computations, the computation time can be long. The scope for entering many parameters and building up a realistic picture also implies that the process of setting up a model can be slow, whether an advanced software package or a purpose-written program is being used.

An outline of a program

The elements set out in the snooker table algorithm are those of a practical Monte Carlo procedure. We will now develop it into a simple program for finding daylight coefficients. It refers to formulae listed in Algorithms and Equations and could be realised in a high-level language such as MATLAB.

Figure 10.11 illustrates the procedure. It is backward ray-tracing: we imagine that particles are being emitted from the room surface for which we want a table of daylight coefficients. These particles bounce around the room, some go through the window, and are reflected between external surfaces and pass eventually upwards to the sky, which is divided into zones.

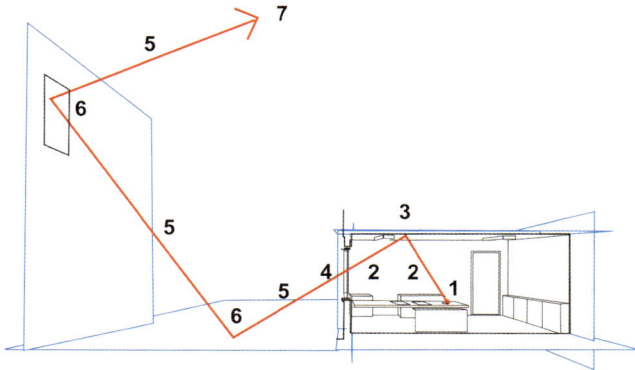

10.11

Stages in the simulation of a particle.

Each particle is given a 'weight' on emission. This is modified by each interaction and, on arrival at a particular sky zone, is added to the total received by the zone. The weight could be a single number – unity on emission and multiplied by the surface reflectance at each bounce and the glazing transmittance as it passes through a window – or it could be a series of values such as colour coordinates, spectral values or polarisation.

The simulation is completed by a statistical analysis of the results.

(a) Data structure

The organisation of the data – the way in which parameters and working variables in the program are allocated and stored – is crucial to the ease of writing a program and the efficiency with which it runs.

A general-purpose light simulation package of commercial quality is modular in construction, which means that it is divided into blocks of code that can operate, and be written and tested, autonomously; and it is object-oriented, so the data are treated as abstract data types to which general rules apply. There is also a great increase in program speed when with a matrix-based language allows a simulation program to be written in terms of parallel operations on lists of values or 'vectors' rather than repetitive operations on single quantities.

It is, though, easiest to understand the nature of simulation by imagining individual particles whose tracks can be interpreted as rays of light, so we will discuss it in those terms.

Data structure of the geometrical form

For this example, we shall assume that the shape and dimensions of a room and of external blocks are stored in a hierarchy of *points*, *planes* and *patches*: each point is defined by three numbers, its *xyz* coordinates in given axes; each plane by three points; and each patch by three or more points lying on a plane. The patches carry attributes such as transmittance and reflectance. The advantage of this structure lies in its simplicity; other hierarchies are available and may be found in CAD and in computer games.

It is convenient, though not necessary, to distinguish between internal surfaces and external objects, because the level of detail that is required often differs. There can be other separate sets of geometrical data. If a complex window system is being modelled, this can be treated as a distinct case. When there are independent parameter sets, each is defined by reference to a separate zone in three-dimensional space. A particle entering this zone is handled by the rules that apply there.

In the example given below, there are two zones, the interior of the room and outside the window.

Particle data

Each individual particle is defined by its *position* at a given moment, its *direction* and its *weight*. The direction is defined by three direction cosines (which were introduced in Chapter 8). Planes can also be allocated direction cosines; these define the direction of a line perpendicular to the surface, and their use simplifies calculations.

Collection of results

A record is kept of the total number of particles emitted and of their weights. Each sky zone has a bin, an array that receives the weight of every particle reaching the zone.

Simulation parameters

It is necessary to specify the positions for which daylight coefficients are required in the room. We term these *reference positions*. They might be points or areas. One technique is to take a large area or even several areas of the room as reference positions, then label each particle with the point of its origin and sort these into appropriate bins on arrival in a sky zone.

The simulation must also have stopping rules. An individual particle may bounce around the system indefinitely, extending run time towards infinity, so it is necessary to specify a maximum number of iterations or a minimum weight; when this is reached, the particle is abandoned. When daylight coefficients are calculated from the simulation results, the weight of abandoned particles must be taken into account.

It is also necessary to specify the number of particles that are to be emitted. Like many sampling processes, the uncertainty in the results is inversely proportional to the square root of the number of samples taken – that is, to the number of particles emitted. Taking a number of separate runs with, say, ten thousand particles enables the error range to be calculated. The variance in the results depends on the parameters of the simulation. If the room being modelled has very low daylight, the daylight coefficients will be small, and in simulation relative few of the emitted particles would reach the sky. For a given level of confidence, more repetitions are needed when daylight levels are low than when a room is strongly lit.

It is efficient in the use of computer time to maintain a continual calculation of variance during the simulation, stopping when a given confidence range has been reached.

(b) Procedure

Formulae for the procedure are listed in Algorithms and Equations.

Input: Dimensions and form of the building and external objects; surface characteristics; reference positions; number of iterations.

Calculate planes: direction cosines and distance from origin.

Main loop:

1   Emit particle in a random direction from a random point in the reference area.

2   Calculate which enclosing plane is nearest. Calculate the position of the intercept and in which patch it lies. Record the intercept as the new position of the particle.

3   Find the surface characteristics of the patch. Does the particle pass through the surface? If 'yes', multiply the particle weight by the transmittance of the patch. Is the particle reflected by the surface? If 'yes', multiply the weight by the reflectance.
    Is the particle weight less than the minimum permitted? If 'yes', record the weight and return to Step 1.

4   Has the particle passed through a window to the exterior? If 'no', go to Step 2.
    Determine the new direction of the particle.

5   Would the particle intercept an external surface? If 'no', go to Step 7.
    Otherwise, calculate which external plane is nearest. Calculate the position of the intercept and in which patch it lies. Record the intercept as the new position of the particle.

6   Find the surface characteristics of the patch. Multiply the weight by the reflectance.
    Is the particle weight less than the minimum permitted? If 'yes', record the weight and return to Step 1.

7   Calculate which sky zone the particle has reached. Add the weight to the bin for the zone.

8   Is the number of repetitions less than the stopping rule? If 'yes', return to Step 1.

Calculate the daylight coefficients.

The use of daylight coefficients

Daylight coefficients describe how individual parts of the sky affect the daylight on a surface. They can be found for any surface, inside a room or outdoors. Figure 10.12 plots the coefficients for unobstructed ground, for a vertical surface and for a point in the centre of a room. This room has a single window: over the range of angles of sky visible from the reference point, the graph follows the shape of that for an unobstructed surface; over all the other angles, the daylight coefficient indicates light that has been reflected. The graphs are plotted by taking a stereographic diagram of the sky and drawing it in perspective. The daylight coefficient is then shown by the height of the plotted surface above this.

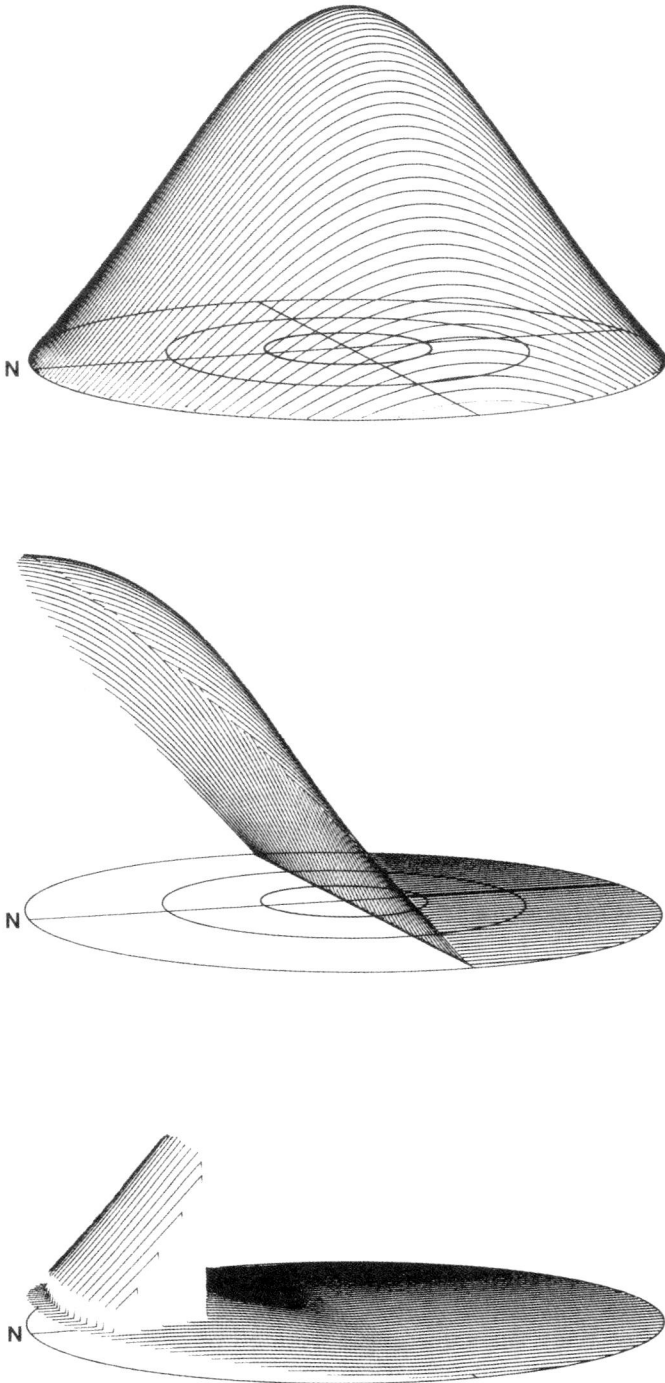

Coefficient values can be interpolated. It is useful to do this along the sunpath, because the interior illuminance from direct and reflected sunlight can then be obtained immediately by multiplying solar normal illuminance by the coefficient on the sunpath for the particular time.

Daylight coefficients provide a means of evaluating the daylight in a room at a specific moment or at intervals of time over a complete year. This makes it possible to develop statistics of the illuminance on a desk or any other room surface over a given period, and then to find simple summaries of the statistics to characterise the daylight performance of a room as an alternative to the daylight factor. The difference between this approach and the use of cumulative illuminance described in Chapter 8 is that daylight coefficient simulation can produce an instantaneous picture – exactly when, for example, particular extreme values occur – while the cumulative distribution gives only the overall statistics. The importance of the daylight coefficient approach is that, within a simulation program, models of user behaviour or of the performance of a lighting control system can be incorporated. This can become a dynamic adaptive modelling of energy use or of the luminous environment of the workplace. An application for which it is valuable to assess the effect of external daylight fluctuations is the art gallery display. The visual impact of daylight variation can be assessed, but so also can the luminous energy incident on paintings, in relation to conservation.

But the discussion on errors in Chapter 8 remains relevant: the accuracy of a computation depends on the validity of the data and the appropriateness of the model. If a simulation is based on the assumption of an empty room, with uncertain estimates of the colour and reflectance of internal and external surfaces, and of window transmittance, and if it assumes that surfaces are matt and that the sky has a smoothly varying luminance distribution, then daylight in the real building is likely to be very different from the image on the computer screen.

At the present time, the topic most in need of further research is the response of people and of automatic control systems to daylight fluctuation, and in particular to the interaction of the two. Despite many excellent case studies, there is a great gap in our knowledge, and this limits our ability to make accurate predictions.

10.12

Graphs of daylight coefficients.

Upper: On an unobstructed horizontal surface.

Middle: On a vertical surface (with no ground reflection).

Lower: At a point in a room with one rectangular window.

Daylight coefficients and dot diagrams

The dot diagram is a graphical way of taking random samples. It would be possible to estimate the total daylight illuminance on a surface by taking a number of points on the sky hemisphere, calculating the illuminance due to the sky around each point and then taking the average. The points should be random, to avoid any bias in the selection or any spurious results that might arise if rows of points happened to coincide with the geometry of the building, but they would have to be evenly distributed over the hemisphere. There is, however, an ingenious alternative: if the sample points are distributed so that the probability of a small patch of sky containing a point is proportional to the fraction of the total illuminance that is due to that small patch then the illuminance is, in effect, pre-calculated. The illuminance due to any area of sky is proportional to the number of dots in that area. The same reasoning applies for diagrams giving probable sunlight hours or configuration factors.

With sky illuminance diagrams, there is clearly a link with daylight coefficients. The density of dots over a small patch of sky is then proportional to the daylight coefficient multiplied by the sky luminance there. Figure 10.13 illustrates this in a different way: it is an image of the sky hemisphere in which the lightness of each pixel is proportional to the contribution of the corresponding spot in the sky to the illuminance on a vertical surface. This can be compared with the middle diagram of Figure 10.12, which shows the daylight coefficient before multiplication with the overcast sky luminance distribution. If Figure 10.13 is inverted, black for white, and then coarsely pixellated, it becomes a dot diagram.

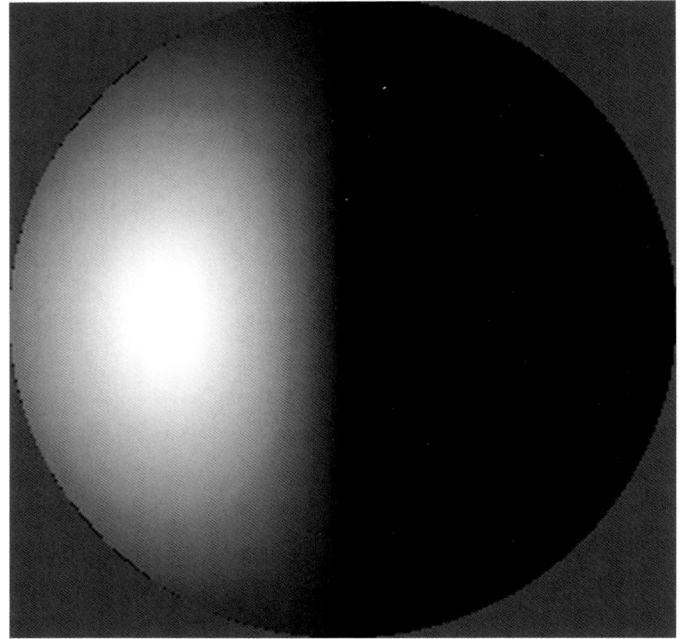

10.13

The lightness of any small area of the disc is proportional to the illuminance on a vertical surface due to that patch, the daylight coefficient multiplied by the sky luminance. The image could be transformed into a dot diagram. Compare this with the middle diagram in Figure 10.12.

Finally ...

Natural lighting is complex and interesting, and making models – physical or theoretical – is fun. It is just necessary to remember that, in practice, the purpose of calculations is to aid decision-making. For the designer, a complex, more precise or realistic, computation is not better than one done quickly: provided that the result is sufficiently accurate to guide the decision, the easier the calculation the better.

## eleven

Notes and references

This chapter suggests places where more information might be found, particularly on topics only lightly covered in the book. It also contains references and discussion supporting arguments advanced in the main text.

Further reading: general books

In *How to use this book*, we noted that daylighting crosses boundaries of subject disciplines and professions. Publications about daylighting are correspondingly diverse.

1 Books about the delight of daylight in architectural spaces

There are many of these. Some are collections of beautiful images to which the text is secondary, but especially useful are those that give enough technical material for the examples illustrated to be adoptable as practical solutions. A classic is W. M. C. Lam's *Sunlight as a formgiver for architecture* [1]. Derek Phillips, an architect who became internationally known as a lighting designer, presents an authoritative survey [2].

2 Technical books written before computers were widely available

The foundations of our present approach to daylighting were laid during the first part of the twentieth century. Daylight became an accepted factor in city planning; methods for quantifying daylight for planning and for legal purposes were invented, notably by P. J. and J. M. Waldram. The need to replace slum housing in the 1930s and then to rebuild after World War II stimulated government-sponsored research that led to important publications such as the *Post-war buildings study: The lighting of buildings* [3]. In the UK, research at the Building Research Station produced new tools for practitioners and added greatly to daylighting theory and analysis. Research supported by government funding and by glass and lighting manufacturers became established in some university departments. The state of knowledge was summed up by Hopkinson *et al.* [4], Walsh [5] and Lynes [6]. These books remain valuable.

3 Publications for professional guidance by official organisations

Guides to good practice by government bodies exist in many countries, and take several forms. Examples of long-established research units that have produced a substantial literature for practitioners are the US Lawrence Berkeley National Laboratory and the UK Building Research Establishment (the successor to the Building Research Station). In some regions, electricity supply companies offer advice on lighting and have useful publications. The main working references for practitioners tend, though, to be the codes and guides prepared by professional institutions, such as the IESNA *Lighting handbook* [7] and CIBSE Society of Light and Lighting publications [8–10]. Useful introductions to the use of daylight are *Tips for daylighting* [11] and *Daylighting design in architecture* [12].

4 Books and other resources related to international research projects

Collaborative research within the European Community has involved daylight researchers throughout Europe and has produced books that give a thorough overview of daylighting practice [13–15], and multimedia teaching packages such as [16]. Task 21 of the International Energy Agency included a systematic review of daylighting resources [17].

5 Books on lighting theory

Parry Moon's *The scientific basis of illuminating,* published in 1936, was of fundamental importance to establishing illumination theory. It was republished in 1961 [18] and Moon and Spencer generalised the theory in [19]. Useful later books are *Lamps and lighting* [20] and *Lighting engineering: applied calculations [21]*. A delightful book that everyone curious about natural light should possess is *The nature of light and colour in the open air* by the Flemish astronomer Marcel Minnaert [22].

General notes

Two hypotheses

Much of Chapter 1 is based on two hypotheses. They are stated assertively in the text in order to develop practical recommendations, but they are hypotheses nevertheless, and it is necessary to provide some evidence and reasoning to support them.

They are:

1   Each of us has expectations about the form, the materials and the image of rooms and buildings, and the way in which people behave in them. We have, that is, a conception of what is 'normal' in a place, a range of conditions that for us define 'a bedroom', 'a church', 'a classroom' and every other place to which we attach a generic name.
2   Daylight in a room is valued because it carries information about the world outside.

The first is easily justified: a concept of what is 'normal' must exist because we are aware when a place is not normal.

Statements such as 'a very big bedroom' would be meaningless if either the speaker or the hearer had no expectation of the usual size of a bedroom, or if their expectations differed significantly.

The second is supported by the evidence that a view from a room to the outside is not only highly valued but can be therapeutic; and furthermore that the nature of the view affects the outcome. This indicates that information, not just luminous energy, is a factor. Consistent with this is the general finding that, unless the function of the space precludes it, a daylit room is preferred to one that is totally electrically lit.

Next, it is known that spatial and temporal variation of light on room surfaces is valued. This has been found in experiments in which subjects in windowless laboratory test rooms are required to adjust the lighting to their preference. They tend to choose brightness patterns that have the characteristics of a daylight space. They are found to prefer levels of illuminance that could be those on a desk near a window; and, in particular, they value 'interest' in the lighting of vertical surfaces, defined by temporal and spatial variation of brightness. See, for example, [23]. We have findings from other research that links the object of view with a physiological response, for example, that a very bright video screen with an interesting image is experienced as less glaring than a screen displaying a random pattern with the same photometric characteristics [24].

The essence of the second hypothesis, therefore, is that variation of room brightness caused by physical effects in which a person has interest is preferred over random variation. Despite the evidence being only circumstantial, we take this emphatically to be the case: that in a daylit room this natural variation of light on room surfaces provides awareness of changing weather and the progress of time. It is a link with the outside world even when no direct view exists.

Having made this assumption, much else falls into place, such as the apparently inconsistent findings from the 1960s onward about the optimum quantity of supplementary electric lighting. The most important outcome is that this hypothesis can form the basis of a rational approach to the optimum balance of daylight and electric lighting in a room.

Three rules

Chapter 1 begins by stating three rules that encapsulate daylighting design:

1   Make the building appropriate to the climate.
2   Preserve the natural variation of daylight.
3   Give users control of their own environment.

The first is justified by the aim of sustainability and, we would argue, the scope it gives for an architecture that is subtle and rich in its attachment to its place. This rule guides the choice of materials, and it refers to the structural form, the achieving of comfort and, because climate and human culture are intertwined, to the values and expectations of those who construct and use a building. But, concerning daylight, it has a very specific meaning: it is to recognise the balance between sunlight and skylight. That balance is the most important characteristic of a daylight climate, and it dictates the strategy for achieving the best daylighting.

We have argued that people need and enjoy the inherent variability of daylight. The way the daylight climate changes from place to place at a geographical scale is covered by the first rule. The second rule applies to urban spaces and to the interior of buildings. It is an instruction to leave recognisable the changes of brightness from one part of a room to another and from one moment to the next. And this, too, has a precise implication for design: it determines the balance between electric lighting and daylighting in a room. The quantity of electric lighting in a daylit room, and its distribution, should be such that people using the room can remain aware of the daylight's spatial and temporal variability.

The third rule could be justified by one factor alone: the aim to satisfy the wishes of users. But it is necessary because we know that sustainability depends on the satisfaction of users, and also that people's tolerance of a changing environment depends on the extent to which they are able to adapt themselves. It is also worth noting that an environmental control system that involves the response of the people in the space is likely to be better than one that does not.

Illustrations

Unless noted otherwise, photographs are by Peter Tregenza. We are indebted to several people or organisations for permission to use copyright material in the text and illustrations; these are acknowledged in the individual chapter references.

Chapter notes

Chapter 1: references on health

The standard work is *Human factors in lighting* [25]. This is a key reference that summarises with great clarity our present knowledge of the way people respond to their luminous environment. Reference [26] is a useful overall review of daylight benefits by Boyce and others. There is a substantial literature on SAD (seasonal affective disorder) [25, 27]. Dislocation of diurnal rhythms is common in people with dementia, and controlled exposure to bright light can ameliorate these symptoms. This has been demonstrated experimentally, for example in [25, 28, 29]. An increase in light exposure during daytime lessened sleep disturbances of patients with dementia and of older people generally. Some have reported amelioration of agitated or aggressive behaviour, but this was not found in other studies [30, 31]. Figueiro [32] has presented a 24-hour lighting scheme, considering especially people with Alzheimer's disease. Lighting in general for people with dementia is discussed by Torrington and Tregenza [33].

In a comprehensive literature review, Farley and Veitch [34] reported that windows with views onto nature may enhance working and well-being in a number of ways, including life satisfaction. They conclude also that a view outside is important not only for its restorative quality, but also as a means of enhancing control over the environment.

As instances of individual studies, Wilson [35] found a significantly lower incidence of patients with post-operative depression in rooms with windows compared with those in windowless rooms. Ulrich [36] showed that patients recovering from surgery in a ward with a window overlooking trees required less powerful analgesic drugs and had shorter recovery times than matched groups of patients in a ward with a view only of a brick wall. From observations in care homes, Chalfont [37] reported that the presence of view windows can trigger social interactions: people tend to group in seats around an attractive window and the view itself provides an easy opening for conversation. Recommendations for immediate implementation made by Ulrich *et al.* [38] in a review of the role of the physical environment in hospital buildings included the provision for patients of stress-reducing views of nature, and improvement of lighting, especially natural lighting. Farley and Veitch [39] present a good literature review. Roessler [40] has argued that communication, not illumination, is the primary function of windows.

Chapter 1: place

The term 'schema' was used by Piaget [41] in describing how children learn to understand the world. Development theory was advanced by Anderson [42], while Bartlett [43] showed that long-term memory could be seen as changing schemata. Brewer and Treyens [44] described the role of schemata in the memory of places. Barker [45] introduced the term 'behavioural setting' and showed the importance of social factors in perception of place.

Lawson [46] gives a lucid introduction to the psychology of place. Perceptual illusions and the characteristics of vision are covered in many introductory books on visual perception. Gregory's *Eye and brain* [47] remains a very attractive simple introduction to the subject.

Useful historical reviews of daylight standards are given by Lukman and Hayman [48] and by Wu and Ng [49].

Chapter 1: work, comfort and display

Boyce [25] gives an authoritative discussion on visual performance. Figure 1.15 is based on work by Weston [50]. Figure 1.18 is based on Arden and Weale [51].

Galasiu and Veitch [52] review research on user preference and behaviour in offices. In a study of windowless simulated open-plan offices, Veitch *et al.* [53] found that people who perceived their lighting to be of higher quality showed greater well-being at the end of the day. Keighley [54] examined window shape in offices.

Hopkinson *et al.* [4] established the basis of the current approach to glare. An overall view was provided by Chauvel and more recently by Nazzal and Chutarat [55].

Different approaches are described by Lynes [56], Tuaycharoen and Tregenza [57] and Stone [58].

The use of daylight for people with impaired vision is well reviewed by Littlefair [59]. Display as a general purpose in lighting is introduced in *The design of lighting* [60]. Light as a medium for display is enthusiastically described by Turner [61] and illustrated by the Lyon Festival of Light [62]. Cannon-Brookes [63] analyses the scope and problems of daylighting in museums and galleries. Wilson *et al.* [64, 65] describe recent European work.

Chapter 2

This chapter is a general introduction to the physical concepts of illuminating engineering; these are covered by general textbooks on lighting, though usually with less emphasis on daylighting processes. The transmission of light through the atmosphere is a standard topic in atmospheric science: attractive texts are by Frederick [66] and Kaler [67]. Sumpner's original paper is [68].

Chapter 3

Books on climate and meteorology tend to discuss solar radiation as a whole, rather than that part of it which we term 'light'. They do provide, however, some good references for further reading. General works such as that by Iqbal [69] give a clear introduction, including solar geometry. Regional studies are useful; examples are the *European solar radiation atlas* [70], *Solar radiation and daylight models* [71] and the *Climatic data handbook for Europe* [72]. Data collected during the International Daylight Measurement Project and subsequent studies are to be found on the internet: an example is [E1]. Substantial research has examined the derivation of daylight illuminances from weather satellite data. Examples are [73, 74].

The CIE standard skies are defined in the General Sky standard [75]. Seminal papers that formed the basis of the luminance distributions are [76–78]. Important contributions to the international collaboration were [79–83].

Solar normal illuminance outside the atmosphere is known as the luminous solar constant; it can be derived by integrating the product of the extraterrestrial solar spectrum and the V_λ curve, the sensitivity function of the human eye. The best current estimate is given by Darula *et al.* [84] . The solar spectrum is described by McCartney and Unsworth [85, 86]. Littlefair [87] is among several authors on the luminous efficacy of daylight. Muneer [71] reviews solar radiation and daylight models.

Figure 3.29 is by Michael Wilson.

Chapter 4

Daylighting as an element of design for sustainability is recognised by many authors. Books by Olgyay and Olgyay [88, 89] and Givoni [90] have been influential since they were first published. Examples of more recent publications taking differing approaches to the topic are those by Hyde [91], Hawkes and Forster [92], Szokolay [93] and Wilson *et al.* [94]. Lynes and Cuttle [95] give the theory of efficient solar shading. Hopkinson [96] and Morris [97] describe ground-reflected light. Littlefair [98] describes solar dazzle from sloping facades. *Reset* is a book on renewable energy sources in settlements planned to be constructed in Europe. It integrates the results and conclusions into a set of design guidelines for managers and designers of settlements, urban sites and utilities. It was developed within a EU-funded project and is available at [E2].

Chapter 5

Offices have been the most studied of building types, and several important surveys have examined occupants' preferences for task and background illuminance and their behaviour in switching lights and operating blinds. See papers by Hunt [99], Roche *et al.* [100], Christoffersen *et al.* [101], Littlefair [102], Reinhart and Voss [103] (the German study quoted on p. 115), Boyce *et al.* [104] and Nicol *et al.* [105]. Parys *et al.* [106] have investigated the impact of occupant behaviour on energy use. A study of energy use in housing is described in [107].

Figure 5.2 is based on [103], Figure 5.4 is from Doulos *et al.* [108], with permission from Elsevier. The lighting simulation software RADIANCE is at [E3], and relevant articles are [109–111]. DAYSIM is at [E4]. The British and European Standard is BS EN 15193:2007 [112].

Chapter 6

Guidance on the drafting of standards is given in BS 0–1 [113]. The current UK standard on daylighting is BS 8206–2:2008[114]. In the UK, the guide most widely adopted for daylight in development control is by Littlefair [115]. Table 6.2 is based on [116] and is quoted in BS 8206–2.

Chapter 7

Key papers in the development of daylight factors were [6, 76, 117–120]. Important evidence for the correlation between average daylight factor and satisfaction with daylight includes Roche *et al.* *[100],* Christoffersen *et al.* [101], Veitch and Newsham [121] and Escuyer and Fontoynont [122]. Reinhart and LoVerso [123] have proposed a design sequence based on average daylight factor and room depth formula. Brotas and Wilson [124] describe an extension of the daylight factor concept.

There is a large literature on daylight in atria. Aizlewood [125], Littlefair [126] and Samant and Yang [127] give an overview of methods; Sharples and Lash [128] provide an excellent critical review, and Sharples and co-workers have published a number of studies examining the effect of atrium form, reflectance and other parameters on daylight distribution in atria, for example [129] and [130]. Planting in atria is discussed in [E5].

Chapter 8

The measurements showing that the daylight factor at a point is a poor predictor of instantaneous illuminance are described in [131]. This had been observed earlier by Ives and Knowles [132] (quoted in [133]). Littlefair [134] developed the orientation factor.

Many formulae for form and configuration factors are given by Siegel and Howell [135]. Practical applications of reflected sunlight are described in several papers by Maitreya (e.g. [136]) and by Morris [97], Tsangrassoulis *et al.* [137], Cabus [138], Chaiyakul [139] and Brotas and Wilson [140]. Littlefair [98] gives a method for calculating reflection from sloping glazed façades.

Tree crown reflection and transmittance has been the subject of several research projects: examples are Yates and

McKennan [141], Canton *et al.* [142], Wilkinson [143] and Al-Sallal and Abu-Obeid [144]. Attenuation of light in the atmosphere is described in *Vision through the atmosphere* [145] and by Tregenza [146].

Many books on scientific methods and experiments discuss error and presentation of results. Good examples are [147, 148]. Bodart *et al.* [149] and Cannon-Brookes [150] describe the use of scale models for daylight measurements.

Chapter 9

The glass manufacturers are the most up-to-date source of information on current products.

Button and Pye [151] give a good general review of the use of glass in buildings. Hutchins [152–154] and Littlefair and Roche [155, 156] discuss advanced glazing systems and their implications. Kristensen [157] reviews daylight technology in non-domestic buildings. A book reviewing solar thermal technologies is [158]. Research on the properties of glass exposed to weather and pollution is described in [159–161].

Boyce [162] describes the acceptability of tinted glazing, Foster and Oreszczyn [163] Venetian blinds, Edmunds [164] laser-cut deflecting panels and Scartezzini and Courret [165] anidolic daylighting systems. Sutter *et al.* [166] examine solar shading in offices. There is a large literature on the performance of light pipes, for example by Venturi *et al.* [167], Carter [168], Jenkins and Muneer [169], Paroncini *et al.* [170] and Robertson *et al.* [171]; the CIE publication *Tubular daylight guidance systems* [172] gives a broad review and includes calculation methods. Tsangrassoulis *et al.* [173] describe a heliostat system. A case study of glazing systems in office refurbishment is [174].

The photographs in Figures 9.8, 9.10 and 9.11 are by Michael Wilson.

Chapter 10

The original papers on daylight coefficients are [175, 176]. Radiosity and Monte Carlo techniques are described by Siegel and Howell [135]. Radiance [110] is an advanced application of ray-tracing computation in lighting. Mardaljevic and co-workers [177, 178] have made notable use of Radiance in advancing daylighting prediction.

Worksheet 7

Permission to reproduce extracts from BE EN 15193:2007 is granted by BSI. British Standards can be obtained in PDF or hard copy formats from the BSI online shop at http://www.bsigroup.com/Shop or by contacting BSI Customer Services for hard copies only: Tel: +44 (0)20 8996 9001, Email: cservices@bsigroup.com.

Worksheet 11

Web-based HDR tools are available at [E6].

References

Web pages

E1 http://www.satel-light.com/core.htm
E2 http://new-learn.info/learn/packages/reset/index.html
E3 http://radsite.lbl.gov/radiance/HOME.html
E4 http://www.daysim.com
E5 http://www.new-learn.info/learn/packages/clear/thermal/buildings/micro_climate/vegetation/greenery.html
E6 http://www.luxal.eu/resources/hdr/webhdr.shtml

Publications

1. Lam, W.M.C., *Sunlight as formgiver for architecture*. 1986, New York: Van Nostrand Reinhold.
2. Phillips, D., *Daylighting: natural light in architecture*. 2004, Oxford: Architectural Press/Elsevier.
3. DSIR, *The lighting of buildings*, in *Post-war building studies*. 1944, London: Lighting Committee of the Building Research Board of the Department of Scientific and Industrial Research, HMSO.
4. Hopkinson, R.G., P. Petherbridge and J. Longmore, *Daylighting*. 1966, London: Heinemann.
5. Walsh, J.W.T., *The science of daylight*. 1961, London: Macdonald. p. 285.
6. Lynes, J.A., *Principles of natural lighting*. 1968, London: Elsevier.
7. Rea, M.S., ed. *Lighting handbook,* 9th ed. 2000, New York: Illuminating Engineering Society of North America.

8. CIBSE, *SLL Lighting guide 10: Daylighting and window design*. 1999, London: Chartered Institution of Building Services Engineers.

9. CIBSE, *The SLL lighting handbook*. 2009, London: Chartered Institution of Building Services Engineers.

10. CIBSE, *Code for lighting*. 2009, London: Chartered Institution of Building Services Engineers.

11. O'Connor, J. *et al.*, *Tips for daylighting*. 1997, Berkeley, CA: Lawrence Berkeley National Laboratory.

12. Loe, D. and K. Mansfield, *Daylighting design in architecture: making the most of a natural resource*. 1998, Garston, Watford, UK: Building Research Establishment.

13. Baker, N. and K. Steemers, eds. *Daylight design of buildings – a handbook for architects and engineers*. 2002, London: James & James.

14. Baker, N.V., A. Fanchiotti and K.A. Steemers, eds. *Daylighting in architecture: a European reference book*. 1993, Brussels & Luxembourg: James & James.

15. Fontoynont, M., ed. *Daylight performance of buildings*. 1999, London: James & James.

16. Wilson, M., ed., *SynthLight*. 2002, London: LEARN.

17. Aschehoug, O.E.A., ed. *Daylight in buildings: a source book on daylighting systems and components. Report of IEA SHC Task 21. NBNL Report-47493*. 2000, Berkeley, CA: Lawrence Berkeley National Laboratory.

18. Moon, P., *The scientific basis of illuminating engineering*. revised ed. 1961, New York: Dover.

19. Moon, P. and D.E. Spencer, *The photic field*. 1981, Cambridge, MA: MIT Press.

20. Henderson, S.T.M. and A.M. Marsden, eds, *Lamps and lighting*. 1972, London: Edward Arnold.

21. Simons, R.H. and A.R. Bean, *Lighting engineering: applied calculations*. 2001, Oxford: Architectural Press.

22. Minnaert, M., *The nature of light and colour in the open air*. 1940, London: G. Bell.

23. Loe, D.L. and E. Rowlands, *The art and science of lighting: a strategy for lighting design*. Lighting Research and Technology, 1996. **28**: p. 153–164.

24. Tuaycharoen, N. and P.R. Tregenza, *Discomfort glare from interesting images*. Lighting Research and Technology, 2005. **37**(4): p. 329–341.

25. Boyce, P., *Human Factors in Lighting*, 2nd ed. 2003, London: Taylor & Francis. 584.

26. Boyce, P., C. Hunter and O. Howell, *The benefit of daylight through windows*. 2003, New York: Lighting Research Centre, Rensselaer Polytechnic Institute.

27. Lam, R.W. and A.J. Levitt, eds. *Canadian consensus guidelines for the treatment of seasonal affective disorder: a summary of the report of the Canadian Consensus Group on SAD*. Apollo Light Research Archives. 1999, Vancouver: Clinical & Academic Publishing.

28. Lyketsos, C.G. *et al.*, *A randomized, controlled trial of bright light therapy for agitated behaviours in dementia patients residing in long-term care*. International Journal of Geriatric Psychiatry, 1999. **14**(7): p. 520–525.

29. Forbes, D.A., S. Peacock and D. Morgan, *Nonpharmacological management of agitated behaviours associated with dementia*. Geriatrics Aging, 2005. **8**(4): p. 26–30.

30. Mishima, K. *et al.*, *Morning bright light therapy for sleep and behaviour disorders in elderly patients with dementia*. Acta Psychiatry Scandinavia, 1994. **89**: p. 1–7.

31. Fetveit, A., A. Skjerve and B. Bjorvatn, *Bright light treatment improves sleep in institutionalised elderly – an open trial*. International Journal of Geriatric Psychiatry, 2003. **18**(6): p. 520–526.

32. Figueiro, M., *A proposed 24 h lighting scheme for older adults*. Lighting Research and Technology, 2008. **40**(2): p. 153–180.

33. Torrington, J.M. and P.R. Tregenza, *Lighting for people with dementia*. Lighting Research and Technology, 2007. **39**(1): p. 81–97.

34. Farley, K. and J. Veitch, *A room with a view: a review of the effects of windows on work and well-being*. 2001, Ottawa: National Research Council Canada, Institute for Research in Construction. p. 33.

35. Wilson, L., *Intensive care delirium: the effect of outside deprivation in a windowless unit*. Archives of Internal Medicine, 1972. **130**: p. 225–226.

36. Ulrich, R.S., *View through a window may influence recovery from surgery*. Science, 1984. **224**(42): p. 421.

37. Chalfont, G.E., *Design of care environments for frail old people*, PhD thesis. 2006, University of Sheffield.

38. Ulrich, R. *et al.*, *The role of the physical environment in the hospital of the 21st century: a once-in-a-lifetime opportunity*. 2004, Center for Health Systems and Design, College of Architecture, Texas A&M University. p. 69.

39. Farley, K. and J. Veitch, *A room with a view: a review of the effects of windows on work and well-being*. 2001, Ottawa: National Research Council Canada, Institute for Research Construction.

40. Roessler, G., *The psychological function of windows for the visual communication between the interior of rooms with permanent supplementary artificial lighting and the exterior*. Lighting Research and Technology, 1980. **12**(3): p. 160–168.

41. Piaget, J., *Naissance de l'intelligence chez L'enfant [The origins of intelligence in children]*. 1952, New York: International Universities Press. p. 419.

42. Anderson, R.C., *Some Reflections on the Acquisition of Knowledge.* Educational Researcher, 1984. **13**(9): p. 5–10.

43. Bartlett, F.C., *Remembering: an experimental and social study.* 1932, Cambridge: Cambridge University Press.

44. Brewer, W.F. and J.C. Treyens, *Role of schemata in memory for places.* Cognitive Psychology, 1981. **13**: p. 207–230.

45. Barker, R.G., *Ecological psychology: concepts and methods for studying the environment of human behaviour.* 1968, Oxford: Oxford University Press.

46. Lawson, B.R., *The language of space.* 2001, Oxford: Architectural Press.

47. Gregory, R.L. *et al., Eye and Brain: The Psychology of Seeing,* 5th ed. 1997, Princeton, NJ: Princeton University Press.

48. Lukman, N. and S. Hayman. *Daylight design rules of thumb,* in *36th ANZAScA Conference.* 2002, Deakin University.

49. Wu, W. and E. Ng, *A review of the development of daylighting in schools.* Lighting Research and Technology, 2003. **35**(2): p. 111–124.

50. Weston, H.C., *The relationship between illumination and visual efficiency: the effect of size of work,* in *Industrial Health Research Board.* 1945, London: His Majesty's Stationery Office.

51. Arden, G. and R. Weale, *Nervous mechanisms and dark adaptation.* Journal of Physiology, 1954. **125**: p. 417–426.

52. Galasiu, A.D. and J.A. Veitch, *Occupant preferences and satisfaction with the luminous environment and control systems in daylit offices: a literature review.* Energy and Buildings, 2006. **38**(7): p. 728–742.

53. Veitch, J., G. Newsham, and P. Boyce, *Lighting appraisal, well-being and performance in open-plan offices: a linked mechanisms approach.* Lighting Research and Technology, 2008. **40**(2): p. 133–151.

54. Keighley, E.C., *Visual requirements and reduced fenestration in office buildings – a study of multiple apertures and window area.* Building Science, 1973. **8**: p. 321–333.

55. Nazzal, A.A. and A. Chutarat, *A new daylighting glare evaluation method; a comparison of the existing glare index and the proposed method, an exploration of daylighting control strategies.* Architectural Science Review, 2001. **444**(1): p. 71–82.

56. Lynes, J.A., *Discomfort glare and visual distraction.* Lighting Research and Technology, 1977. **9**(1): p. 51–52.

57. Tuaycharoen, N. and P.R. Tregenza, *View and discomfort glare from windows.* Lighting and Technology, 2007. **38**(2): p. 185–200.

58. Stone, P.T., *A model for the explanation of discomfort and pain in the eye caused by light.* Lighting Research and Technology, 2009. **41**(2): p. 109–121.

59. Littlefair, P.J., *Daylighting in homes of partially sighted people: a review.* Submitted for publication in Lighting Research and Technology, 2010.

60. Tregenza, P.R. and D.L. Loe, *The design of lighting.* 1998, London: E. & F.N. Spon.

61. Turner, J., *Lighting: an introduction to light, lighting and light use.* 1994, London: Batsford.

62. Public, E., ed. *Lyon 8 Decembre: fetes des lumières.* 2002, Lyon: Esprit Public.

63. Cannon-Brookes, S., *Daylighting museum galleries: a review of performance criteria.* Lighting Research and Technology, 2000. **32**(3): p. 161–168.

64. Wilson, M., *Lighting in museums: lighting interventions during the European demonstration project 'Energy efficiency and sustainability in retrofitted and new museum buildings' (NNES-1999-20).* International Journal of Sustainable Energy, 2006. **25**(3–4): p. 153–169.

65. Wilson, M., A. Viljoen and J. Nicol, *Environments in archaeological museums in the Mediterranean region,* in *Renewable energy, WREC special edition, Part 1.* 2000, Oxford: Pergamon. p. 412–419.

66. Frederick, J.L., *Principles of atmospheric science.* 2008, Sudbury, MA: Jones and Bartlett.

67. Kaler, J.B., *The ever-changing sky: a guide to the celestial sphere.* 1996, Cambridge: Cambridge University Press.

68. Sumpner, W.E., *XII. The diffusion of light.* The London, Edinburgh and Dublin Philosophical Magazine and Journal of Science (Fifth Series), 1893. **35**: p. 81–97.

69. Iqbal, M., *An introduction to solar radiation.* 1983, Toronto: Academic Press.

70. Scharmer, K. and J. Greif, eds. *The European solar radiation atlas. Volume 1: Fundamentals and maps.* 2000, Paris: Les Presses de l'École des Mines.

71. Muneer, T., *Solar radiation and daylight models for the energy efficient design of buildings,* 2nd ed. 2004. Oxford: Architectural Press.

72. Bourges, B., ed. *Climatic data handbook for Europe.* 1992, Dordrecht: Kluwer Academic Publishers.

73. Dumortier, D., *Satellight: la base de données européenne de rayonnement solaire et de lumière naturelle disponible sur Internet,* Lux – Cahier Technique, 2000(206): p. VI–VIII.

74. He, J. and E. Ng, *Using satellite-based methods to predict daylight illuminance for subtropical Hong Kong.* Lighting Research and Technology, 2010. **42**(2): p. 135–147.

75. Commission Internationale de l'Eclairage, *Spatial Distribution of daylight – CIE Standard General Sky.* 2003, Vienna: Commission Internationale de l'Eclairage.

76. Moon, P. and D.E. Spencer, *Illumination from a non-uniform sky.* Illuminating Engineering, 1942. **37**: p. 707–726.

77. Kittler, R. *Standardisation of the outdoor conditions for the calculation of the Daylight Factor with clear skies,* in *Sunlight*

in buildings. 1967. Rotterdam: Commission Internationale de l'Eclairage.

78. Kittler, R., R. Perez and S. Darula. *A new generation of sky standards*, in *The 8th European Lighting Conference Lux Europa.* 1997, Amsterdam: NSVV (Netherlands Institution of Illuminating Engineering).

79. Perez, R., R. Seals and J. Michalsky, *All-weather model for sky luminance distribution– preliminary configuration and validation.* Solar Energy, 1993. **50**(3): p. 235–245.

80. Nagata, T., *Luminance distribution of clear skies, part 1: measurements of the luminance distribution.* Transactions of the Architectural Institute of Japan, 1971(185): p. 65–70.

81. Nagata, T., *Luminance distribution of clear skies, part 2: theoretical considerations.* Transactions of the Architectural Institute of Japan, 1971(186): p. 41–48.

82. Nagata, T., *Luminance distribution of clear sky and the resulting horizontal illuminance.* Journal of Light and Visual Environment, 1983. **7**(1): p. 23–27.

83. Tregenza, P.R., *Standard skies for maritime climates.* Lighting Research and Technology, 1999. **31**(3): p. 97–106.

84. Darula, S., R. Kittler and C.A. Gueymard, *Reference luminous solar constant and solar luminance for illuminance calculations.* Solar Energy, 2005. **79**: p. 559–565.

85. McCartney, H.A. and M.H. Unsworth, *Spectral distribution of solar radiation I: direct radiation.* Quarterly Journal of the Royal Meteorological Society, 1978. **104**(441): p. 699–718.

86. McCartney, H.A. and M.H. Unsworth, *Spectral distribution of solar radiation II: global and diffuse.* Quarterly Journal of the Royal Meteorological Society, 1978. **104**(442): p. 921–926.

87. Littlefair, P.J., *The luminous efficacy of daylight: a review.* Lighting Research and Technology, 1985. **17**(4): p. 162–181.

88. Olgyay, A. and V. Olgyay, *Solar control and shading devices.* 1957, Princeton, NJ: Princeton University Press.

89. Olgyay, V., *Design with climate: bioclimatic approach to architectural regionalism.* 1973, Princeton, NJ: Princeton University Press.

90. Givoni, B., *Man, climate and architecture.* 1969, Amsterdam: Elsevier.

91. Hyde, R., *Climate responsive design.* 2000, London: E. & F.N. Spon.

92. Hawkes, D. and Forster, W., *Energy efficient buildings: architecture, engineering and environment.* 2002, New York: W.W. Norton.

93. Szokolay, S., *Introduction to architectural science: the basis of sustainable design*, 2nd ed. 2008, Oxford: Architectural Press.

94. Wilson, M. *et al. Creating sunlit rooms in non-daylit spaces*, in *RightLight.* 2002, Nice.

95. Lynes, J.A. and K. Cuttle, *Bracelet for total solar shading.* Lighting Research and Technology, 1988. **20**(3): p. 105–113.

96. Hopkinson, R.G., *The natural lighting of buildings in sunny climates by sunlight reflected from the ground and from opposing facades*, in *Architectural physics: lighting.* 1963, London: HMSO. p. 174–181.

97. Morris, E., *The influence of light coloured foreground in daylight design.* Building Science, 1966. **1**: p. 309–313.

98. Littlefair, P.J., *Prediction of reflected solar dazzle from sloping façades.* Building and Environment, 1987. **22**(4): p. 285–291.

99. Hunt, D.R.G., *Predicting artificial lighting use – a method based on observed patterns of behaviour.* Lighting Research and Technology, 1980. **12**(1): p. 7–14.

100. Roche, L., E. Dewey and P.J. Littlefair, *Occupant reaction to lighting in offices.* Lighting Research and Technology, 2000. **32**(3): p. 119–126.

101. Christoffersen, J. and K. Johnsen, *Windows and daylight – a post-occupancy evaluation of Danish offices*, in *CIBSE National Lighting Conference.* 2000, York.

102. Littlefair, P.J., *Predicting the annual lighting use in daylit buildings.* Building and Environment, 1990. 25(1): p. 43–53.

103. Reinhart, C. and K. Voss, *Monitoring manual control of electric lighting and blinds.* Lighting Research and Technology, 2003. **35**(3): p. 243–260.

104. Boyce, P., et al., *Occupant use of switching and dimming controls in offices.* Lighting Research and Technology, 2006. **38**(4): p. 358–378.

105. Nicol, F., M. Wilson and C. Chiancarella, *Using field measurements of desktop illuminance in European offices to investigate its dependence on outdoor conditions and its effect on occupant satisfaction, and the use of lights and blinds.* Energy and Buildings, 2006. **38**: p. 802–813.

106. Parys, W., D. Saelens and H. Hens, *Impact of occupant behaviour on lighting energy use*, in *Building Simulation 2009: 11th International IBPSA Conference.* 2009, Glasgow.

107. Wilson, M., O.B. Jorgensen and G. Johannesen, *Daylighting, energy and glazed balconies: a study of a refurbishment project in Engelsby, nr Flensberg, Germany.* Lighting Research and Technology, 2000. **32**(3): p. 127–132.

108. Doulos, L., A. Tsangrassoulis, and F. Topalis, *Quantifying energy savings in daylight responsive systems: the role of dimming electronic ballasts.* Energy and Buildings, 2008. **40**: p. 36–50.

109. Ward, G., *Real pixels*, in *Graphic gems II*, J. Arvo, er. 1991, Boston: Academic Press. p. 80–83.

110. Ward Larson, G. and R.A. Shakespeare, *Rendering with Radiance: the art and science of lighting visualization.* 1998, San Francisco: Morgan Kaufmann.

111. Reinhart, C., J. Mardaljevic and Z. Rogers, *Dynamic daylight performance metrics for sustainable building design*. Leukos, 2006. **3**(1): p. 1–25.

112. British Standards Institution, *BS EN 15193:2007 Energy performance of buildings. Energy requirements for lighting*. 2007.

113. British Standards Institution, *BS 0-1:2005. A standard for standards. Development of standards. Specification*. 2005.

114. British Standards Institution, *BS 8206–2:2008. Lighting for buildings. Code of practice for daylighting*. 2008.

115. Littlefair, P.J., *Site layout planning for daylight and sunlight: a guide to good practice. BRE report BR 209*. 1991, Garston, Watford, UK: Building Research Establishment.

116. Ne'eman, E. and R.G. Hopkinson, *Critical minimum acceptable window size: a study of window design and provision of a view*. Lighting Research and Technology, 1970. **2**(1): p. 17–27.

117. Dresler, A., *The 'reflected component' in daylighting design*. Transactions of the Illuminating Engineering Society (London), 1954. **19**(7): p. 50–60.

118. Hopkinson, R.G., J. Longmore and P. Petherbridge, *An empirical formula for the computation of the indirect component of daylight factor*. Transactions of the Illuminating Engineering Society (London), 1954. **19**(7): p. 201–218.

119. Seshadri, T.N., *Equations of sky component with a CIE Standard Overcast Sky*. Proceedings of the Indian Academy of Science, 1960. Paper 57A. p. 233–242.

120. Crisp, V.H.C. and P.J. Littlefair. *Average daylight factor prediction*, in *National Lighting Conference*. 1984, Nottingham.

121. Veitch, J.A. and G.R. Newsham, *Preferred luminous conditions in open-plan offices*. Lighting Research and Technology, 2000. **32**(4): p. 199–212.

122. Escuyer, S. and M. Fontoynont. *Testing in situ of automatic ambient lighting plus manually controlled task lighting: office occupants' reactions*, in *Proceedings of the 9th European Lighting Conference (Lux Europa)*. 2001, Reykjavik, Iceland.

123. Reinhart, C. and V. LoVerso, *A rules of thumb-based design sequence for diffuse daylight*. Lighting Research and Technology, 2010. **42**(1): p. 7–31.

124. Brotas, L. and M. Wilson, *The average total daylight factor*. Light and Engineering (Svetotekhnika), 2008. **16**(2): p. 52–57.

125. Aizlewood, M.E., *The daylight of atria: a critical review*. ASHRAE Transactions, 1995. **101**: Pt 2.

126. Littlefair, P.J., *Daylight prediction in atrium buildings*. Solar Energy, 202. **73**: p. 105–109.

127. Samant, S. and F. Yang, *Daylighting in atria: The effect of atrium geometry and reflectance distribution*. Lighting Research and Technology, 2007. **39**(2): p. 147–157.

128. Sharples, S. and D. Lash, *Daylight in atrium buildings: a critical review*. Architectural Science Review, 2007. **50**(4): p. 301–312.

129. Sharples, S. and T.J. Neal. *A model study of the influence of roof structure on daylight levels in atria type buildings*, in *3rd European Conference on Architecture*. 1993, Florence, Italy.

130. Sharples, S. and D. Lash, *Reflectance distributions and vertical daylight illuminances in atria*. Lighting Research and Technology, 2004. **36**(1): p. 45–57.

131. Tregenza, P.R., *The daylight factor and actual illuminance ratios*. Lighting Research and Technology, 1980. **12**(2): p. 64–68.

132. Ives, J.E. and F.L. Knowles, *The sill ratio method of measuring daylight in the interior of buildings*. Transactions of the Illuminating Engineering Society (New York), 1930. 34.

133. Phillips, R. *An historical outline of the concepts and terminology of natural lighting. Appendix 1 to Secretariat report 3.2: natural daylight*, in *13th Session of the CIE*. 1955, Paris: Commission Internationale de l'Eclairage.

134. Littlefair, P., *Daylight for lighting PD 58/83*, in *BRE Seminar 'Design and Selection of Lighting Controls'*. 1983, Garston, Watford, UK: Building Research Establishment.

135. Siegel, R. and J.R. Howell, *Thermal Radiation Heat Transfer, 3rd ed*. 1992, Washington, DC: Hemisphere.

136. Narasimhan, V. and V.K. Maitreya, *The reflected component of daylight in multi-storeyed buildings in the tropics*. Building Science, 1969. **4**(2): p. 93–97.

137. Tsangrassoulis, A., *et al.*, *A method for the estimation of illuminances on surfaces of urban canyons with balconies in sunlit areas*. Lighting Research and Technology, 1999. **31**(1): p. 5–12.

138. Cabus, R., *Tropical daylighting: predicting sky types and interior illuminance in north-east Brazil*, PhD thesis. 2002, University of Sheffield.

139. Chaiyakul, Y., *Urban daylighting in Bangkok*, PhD thesis. 2005, University of Sheffield.

140. Brotas, L. and M. Wilson. *Daylight in urban canyons*, in *Planning in Europe, PLEA2006 – 23rd Conference on Passive and Low Energy Architecture*. 2006, Geneva.

141. Yates, D. and G. McKennan, *Solar architecture and light attenuation by trees: conflict or compromise?* Arboricultural Journal, 1989. **13**: p. 7–16.

142. Canton, M.A., J.L. Cortegoso and C. de Rosa, *Solar permeability of urban trees in cities of western Argentina*. Energy and Buildings, 1994. **20**: p. 219–230.

143. Wilkinson, D.M., *Modelling tree crowns as geometric solids*. Arboricultural Journal, 1995. **19**: p. 387–393.

144. Al-Sallal, K.A. and N. Abu-Obeid, *Effects of shade trees on illuminance in classrooms in the United Arab Emirates*. Architectural Science Review, 2009. **52**(4): p. 295–311.

145. Knowles Middleton, W.E., *Vision through the atmosphere, 2nd ed*. 1952, Toronto: University of Toronto Press.

146. Tregenza, P.R., *Luminance of distant objects under overcast skies*. Lighting Research and Technology, 1992. **24**(3): p. 155–159.

147. Taylor, J., *An introduction to error analysis*. 1982, Mill Valley CA: University Science Books.

148. Gibbings, J., ed. *The systematic experiment*. 1986, Cambridge: Cambridge University Press.

149. Bodart, M. *et al.*, *A guide for building daylight scale models*. Architectural Science Review, 2007. **50**(1): p. 31–36.

150. Cannon-Brookes, S., *Simple scale models for daylighting design: analysis of sources of error in illuminance prediction*. Lighting Research and Technology, 1997. **29**(3): p. 135–142.

151. Button, D. and B. Pye, eds. *Glass in building*. 1993, Oxford: Butterworth Architecture.

152. Hutchins, M., *Glazing materials for advanced thermal performance and solar gain control*. Japan Journal of Solar Energy, 1997. **23**(5): p. 3–21.

153. Hutchins, M., *Modern glazing systems*, in *Proceedings of CEN/STAR Workshop Daylight and Glazing, Paris, October 2000*. Rivista della Stazione Sperimentale del Vetro, 2001. **31**(1): p. 5–12.

154. Hutchins, M., *Spectrally selective materials for efficient visible, solar and thermal radiation control*, in *Solar thermal technologies for buildings*, M. Santamouris, ed. 2003, London: James & James. p. 37–64.

155. Littlefair, P.J. and L. Roche, *The lighting implications of advanced glazing systems*. 1997, Garston, Watford, UK: Building Research Establishment.

156. Littlefair, P.J., *Innovative daylight: review of systems and evaluation methods*. Lighting Research and Technology, 1990. **22**(1): p. 1–17.

157. Kristensen, P.E., *Daylighting technologies in non-domestic buildings*. International Journal of Sustainable Energy, 1994. **15**(1–4): p. 55–67.

158. Santamouris, M., ed., *Solar thermal technologies for buildings: the state of the art*. 2003, London: James & James.

159. Pollet, I. and J. Peiters, *Daylighting properties of dry and wet glazing materials*, in *Clima 2000 Napoli 2001 World Congress*. 2001, Naples.

160. Tregenza, P., L. Stewart and S. Sharples, *Reduction of glazing transmittance by atmospheric pollutants*. Lighting Research and Technology, 1999. **31**(4): p. 135–138.

161. Ullah, M. *et al.*, *Attenuation of diffuse daylight due to dust deposition on glazing in a tropical urban environment*. Lighting Research and Technology, 2003. **35**(1): p. 19–29.

162. Boyce, P., *Minimum acceptable transmittance of glazing*. Lighting Research and Technology, 1995. **27**(3): p. 145–152.

163. Foster, M. and T. Oreszczyn, *Occupant control of passive systems: the use of Venetian blinds*. Building and Environment, 2001. **36**: p. 149–155.

164. Edmonds, I.R., *Performance of laser cut light deflecting panels in daylighting applications*. Solar Energy Materials and Solar Cells, 1993. **29**(1): p. 1–26.

165. Scartezzini, J.-L. and G. Courret, *Anidolic daylighting systems*. Solar Energy, 2002. **73**(2): p. 123–135.

166. Sutter, Y., D. Dumortier and M. Fontoynont, *The use of shading systems in VDU task offices: a pilot study*. Energy and Buildings, 2005. **38**(7): p. 780–789.

167. Venturi, L. *et al.*, *Light piping performance enhancement using a deflecting sheet*. Lighting Research and Technology, 2006. **38**(3): p. 167–179.

168. Carter, D., *Tubular guidance systems for daylight*. Building Research and Technology, 2008. **36**(5): p. 520–535.

169. Jenkins, D. and T. Muneer, *Modelling light-pipe performances – a natural daylighting solution*. Building and Environment, 2003. **38**(7): p. 965–972.

170. Paroncini, M., B. Calcagni and F. Corvaro, *Monitoring of a light-pipe system*. Solar Energy, 2007. **81**(9): p. 1180–1186.

171. Robertson, A., R. Hedges and N. Rideout, *Optimisation and design of ducted daylight systems*. Lighting Research and Technology, 2010. **42**(2): p. 161–181.

172. CIE, *Tubular daylight guidance systems*. 2006, Vienna: Commission Internationale de l'Eclairage.

173. Tsangrassoulis, A. *et al.*, *On the energy efficiency of a prototype hybrid daylighting system*. Solar Energy and Buildings, 2005. **79**(56–64).

174. Viljoen, A. *et al.*, *Investigations for improving the daylighting potential of double-skinned office buildings*. Solar Energy, 1997. **59**(4–6): p. 179–194.

175. Tregenza, P.R. and I.M. Waters, *Daylight coefficients*. Lighting Research and Technology, 1983. **15**(2): p. 65–72.

176. Tregenza, P.R., *Subdivision of the sky hemisphere for luminance measurements*. Lighting Research and Technology, 1987. **19**(1): p. 13–14.

177. Mardaljevic, J., *Validation of a lighting simulation program under real sky conditions*. Lighting Research and Technology, 1995. **27**(4): p. 181–188.

178. Nabil, A. and J. Mardaljevic, *Useful daylight illuminance: a new paradigm for assessing daylight in buildings*. Lighting Research and Technology, 2005. **37**(1): p. 41–57.

Worksheets

1 Worksheets

These sheets are stand-alone guides to practical tasks and calculations.

HOW TO ...

1 Make quick decisions: rules of thumb for cloudy climates
2 Make quick decisions: rules of thumb for sunny regions
3 Calculate the vertical sky component and vertical daylight factor
4 Calculate the average daylight factor in a room
5 Calculate the daylight factor at a point in a room
6 Calculate the number of luminaires needed
7 Calculate the energy used when daylight and electric lighting are used together
8 Use sky diagrams
9 Use sunpath diagrams
10 Calculate sunlight and skylight in the urban canyon

11 Measure light
12 Identify faults in workplace lighting
13 Use the right word

DATA

14 Typical reflectance of materials under diffuse daylight
15 Light transmittance of glazing
16 Reduction of glazing transmittance due to dirt
17 Current daylight criteria in the UK
18 Sky diagrams
19 Typical recommended task illuminances

1 *How to* make quick decisions: rules of thumb for cloudy climates

In most situations, good daylighting is easy to achieve. Used with professional intelligence, the following rules of thumb lead almost inevitably to satisfactory solutions. They apply directly to desk-based workplaces, but can be adapted for comparable building types.

The rules are not appropriate if the site for a new building is seriously overshadowed or if rooms inside the building have to be very deep or complex in shape.

THE MAIN PROBLEMS TO BE SOLVED

• Balance of daylight and electric lighting
• Direct and reflected glare

RULES OF THUMB

1 Use a combination of daylight and electric lighting during daylight hours unless the room is less than about 2.4 m deep.

2 Keep the average height of external obstructions below a line 25° above the horizon, measured from the centre of the window.
3 Make the glazed area of windows about 1/25 of the room's enclosing surface area (walls, including windows; ceiling; floor).
4 Plan the layout of the room so that people's sightlines are parallel with the window wall.
5 Plan electric lighting so that any luminaires close to windows can be switched off during daytime. The zone of strong daylight extends to a distance about 2h from a window; h is the height of the window head above desktop level.

Ensure that people working in the room:

(a) have a view to outside;
(b) can block any direct sunlight;
(c) can screen any sources of glare;
(d) can control electric lighting that affects their own workplaces.

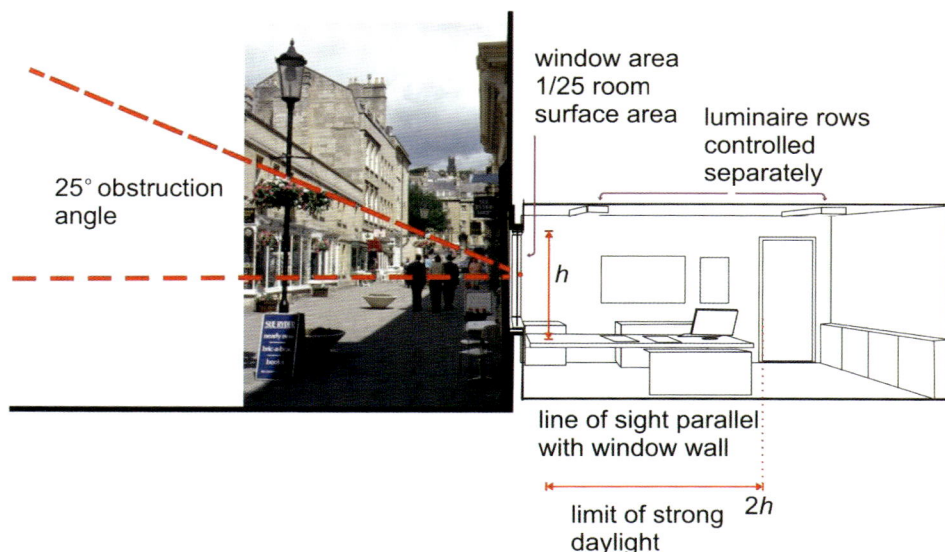

window area
1/25 room
surface area

luminaire rows
controlled
separately

25° obstruction
angle

h

line of sight parallel
with window wall

limit of strong   2*h*
daylight

W1.1
A small office overlooking a pedestrian street.

EXAMPLE

Figure W1.1 shows a section through the room and the adjacent outside space. The dashed red line shows the maximum external obstruction angle; the size of the window (which, in plan, would occupy about half the length of the window wall) shows what the 1/25th rule implies.

Rule 5 indicates that there should be strong daylight – that is, adequate illuminance for office tasks – as far back into the room as the edge of the desk. Beyond that, in the area of room most distant from the window, supplementary electric light would be needed to enhance the general brightness and to aid performance of visually difficult tasks. The VDUs and the desktops are orientated so that reflections of the sky and of the electric lighting fittings are not visible in shiny surfaces.

The illustration shows also that windows must have blinds or some other means of preventing direct sunlight falling on users or in the area of their visual tasks. The electric lighting must be controllable to prevent unnecessary energy use during the daylight hours. In a small office, it may be necessary only to ensure that separate marked switches are provided for daytime and night-time lighting.

2 *How to* make quick decisions: rules of thumb for sunny regions

The key to good daylighting in a sunny climate is the design of the space outside the windows. The solar beam needs to be scattered to create a diffuse field of light that is sufficiently bright to illuminate the room but not glaring. Foliage can do this attractively.

THE MAIN PROBLEMS TO BE SOLVED

- Reflecting light into the room without glare
- Excluding direct sunlight

RULES OF THUMB

1 Orientate buildings so that windows face north or south. When the sun is high in the sky, a small overhang is enough to shade a window. Large or adjustable shading devices are required when windows face the sun early or late in the day.

2 Reflect sunlight onto the ceiling. It is important that users do not look out onto light-coloured surfaces in strong sunlight. A strip of high-reflectance ground immediately below the windows is effective. Its width depends on the layout, but 1.5–2 m is typical.

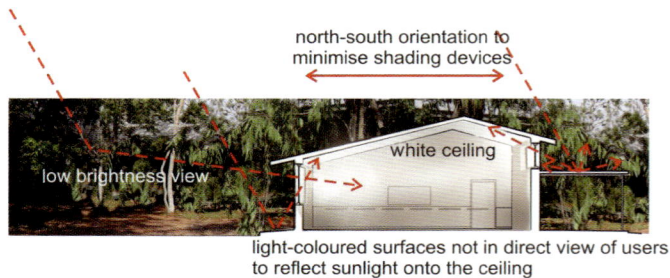

W2.1

A small office overlooking a pedestrian street.

3   Let sunlight fall on small trees and other vegetation outside the window. An alternative is to reflect sunlight from medium-reflectance walls facing the window. Natural earth colours, reflectance about 0.2, are appropriate. White surfaces in sunlight can be uncomfortably glaring; so can glossy surfaces.

4   Check the sun's path. The solar elevation, γ_s (the angle of the sun above the horizon), at noon is given by

$$\gamma_s = 90° - \lambda + \delta$$

where λ is the latitude of the place (e.g. London, 51°; Sydney, −35°) and δ is the solar declination (e.g. 21 December, −23.5°; 23 March and 23 September, 0°; 22 June, +23.5°).

5   Provide a view of the sky where possible – that is, where glare and direct sunlight can be avoided.

EXAMPLE: A RURAL SCHOOL CLASSROOM IN A WARM SUNNY CLIMATE

The advantages of shady woodland are substantial: it is cooler than open terrain, and views from the windows are attractive and interesting. However, because of the obstruction, relatively large windows are required. The proportion of openings shown in Figure W2.1 – about 40% of the area of the two window walls – is about the minimum needed if there is to be no daytime electric lighting. The more open the site, the smaller the windows may be, but account must be taken of users' expectations. In a desert environment, low levels of light are often associated with coolness.

In open terrain under clear skies, the air temperature measured near the ground surface oscillates between very cold in the early morning and very warm in the afternoon. Traditional buildings, especially in hot desert regions, maintain an interior temperature that approaches the 24-hour average by being massive in construction – built of thick masonry or compacted earth, with small windows. In large structures, especially public buildings such as markets, small roof openings make patches of bright sunshine, which, in turn, create an overall reflected illumination.

In the example, the planting outside is the native vegetation of the region. The nearby trees are too tall to be ideal: the foliage partly obscures the sky; and, because most of it is above window level, relatively little light is reflected into the room. The room daylight is enhanced by reflected sunlight from the light-coloured surfaces below the windows.

A clear blue sky is often less bright than a partly cloudy sky because less of the solar beam is scattered by the atmosphere. Coupled with this is the need to shade windows from direct sunlight to reduce unwanted heat gain. In warm dry climates, the combination of low sky brightness and obstruction by shading devices often means that the diffuse sky can make only a small contribution to interior daylight. But skylight should be used if orientation and shading permit: the most reliable daylight occurs when skylight, diffused sunlight and ground-reflected sunlight are all present.

3 *How to* calculate the vertical sky component and vertical daylight factor

The vertical sky component is the light from the sky falling directly on the vertical face of a wall or window. It excludes sunlight and light reflected from the ground or other surfaces. It is written as the percentage of the daylight illuminance on unobstructed ground. It is used in urban planning, particularly development control. The vertical daylight factor is the vertical sky component plus the illuminance due to interreflection.

METHOD 1: ESTIMATE THE SKY ANGLE

This gives an estimate of the daylight factor on a window facing a skyline of approximately constant height.

Draw a section through the window and the obstruction. Estimate in degrees the vertical angle of sky visible between the top of the obstruction and the window head (or overhang). The daylight factor on the vertical face of the window is approximately equal to half the number of degrees:

$$D_v \approx \frac{\theta}{2}\%$$ (W3.1)

where θ is the angle in degrees.

Table W3.1 Conversion from vertical daylight factor, D_v, to vertical sky component, D_{sv}

D_v	5.0	10.0	15.0	20.0	25.0	30.0	35.0	40.0	43.5
D_{sv}/D_v	0.77	0.79	0.81	0.82	0.84	0.86	0.88	0.89	0.91

Table W3.2 Conversion from vertical sky component, D_{sv}, to vertical daylight factor, D_v

D_{sv}	5.0	10.0	15.0	20.0	25.0	30.0	35.0	39.6
D_v/D_{sv}	1.27	1.24	1.22	1.20	1.17	1.15	1.12	1.10

The ratio of the sky component to the total daylight factor on a vertical surface depends on the sky angle θ and the reflectance. It can be estimated from Tables W3.1 and W3.2.

These tables are based on a street with buildings of similar height on each side. The façade reflectance is taken to be 0.2 and the ground cavity reflectance (the effective total reflectance of everything outside below window level) is taken to be 0.1.

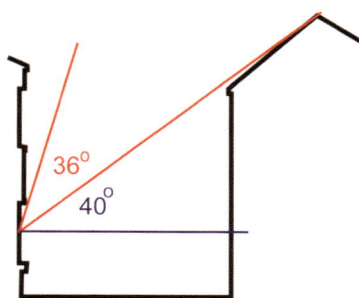

W3.1

Red: the angle of visible sky measured in section from the skyline of the obstructing buildings to the window head. Blue: the obstruction angle.

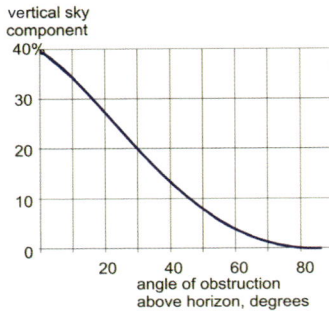

W3.2
Vertical sky component and angle of obstruction, ω. The equation for this graph is given in Algorithms and Equations, Section 4.2.

Example

In Figure W3.1, the sky angle is 36° (shown in red). Using the rule of thumb given as Equation (W3.1), the vertical daylight factor is approximately 18%. To find the corresponding sky component, Table W3.1 is used: it gives a conversion factor, D_{sv}/D_v, of 0.81 for a daylight factor of 15% and 0.82 for a daylight factor of 20%. Interpolating, we find the conversion factor is about 0.81, which gives a vertical sky component of 14.67%, which should be rounded off to the nearest whole number, 15%.

METHOD 2: ESTIMATE THE OBSTRUCTION ANGLE

This method also assumes that the roofline is horizontal and that the light obstructed by the window head or any overhang above the window is negligible. It uses only the angle of the roofline above the horizon, ω.

Read the vertical sky component from the graph in Figure W3.2. In the example above, the obstruction angle is 40°, giving a vertical sky component of 13%. It is no surprise that this is not exactly the same as the value found in the first example. Figure W3.2 is plotted from an exact mathematical formula while Equation (W3.1) is a numerical rule of thumb. Neither is necessarily a better approximation to a complex real situation than the other.

METHOD 3: TAKE A FISH-EYE IMAGE AND USE A DOT DIAGRAM

This method can be used to assess the daylight available to an existing building; it is useful in 'before-and-after' studies in the redevelopment of a site. It can be used also with drawings. Worksheet 8 describes how to plot a building on a sky projection.

Take a photograph looking upwards with a fish-eye lens at the centre of the window in the plane of the glazing. Figure W3.4 was taken with the window open; the line of the

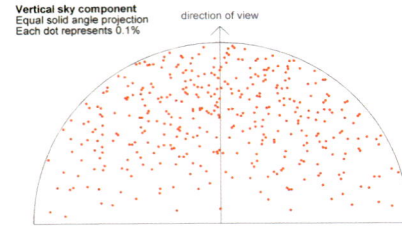

W3.3
Dot diagram from the data sheets.

window runs horizontally across the centre of the image. Below this is the view outward; above it is the interior of the room.

Select a vertical sky component overlay from the data sheets. The choice of stereographic or equal solid angle projection depends on the camera lens. Use the equal solid angle projection if in doubt: more of the currently available lenses are closer to this than to the stereographic. There are two versions, with differing number of dots. Ideally, at least 30 dots should lie on the area of visible sky in the photograph, so use the diagram with many dots for cases where little sky is visible.

Enlarge the overlay so that it is the same scale as the photograph, then rotate it so that the arrow points in the direction of view, with the base of the semicircle lying on the glass line.

Count the number of dots lying on the sky and multiply this by the dot value given on the diagram.

In the example, 103 dots lie on the sky. Each is worth 0.1% sky component, so

$$D_{sv} = 103 \times 0.1 = 10.3\%$$

which should be rounded to 10% for presentation.

Using Table W3.2, the vertical daylight factor would be 10.3 × 1.24 = 12.77, rounded to 13%.

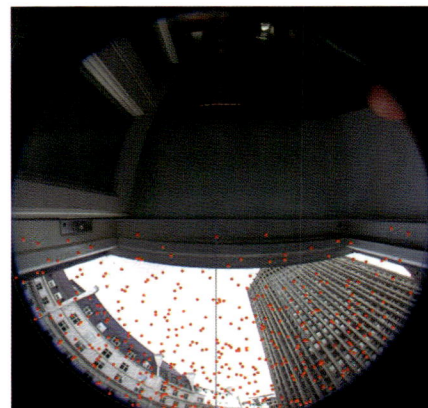

W3.4
The fish-eye photograph is taken at the centre of the window looking upwards. The dot diagram is scaled to the diameter of the photograph and aligned so that its baseline is in the plane of the glass. The dots lying on the sky are then counted.

4 *How to* calculate the average daylight factor in a room

The average daylight factor, $\overline{D}$ (pronounced dee-bar), gives a general impression of the daylighting in a space. In a temperate climate, it can be interpreted as follows:

Average daylight factor in rooms with side windows	Room character
Less than 1%	The place often looks gloomy; windows may be glaring. If it is a workplace, electric lighting is needed both to carry out visual tasks and to brighten the room generally. When the lights are switched on, the room does not have a daylit appearance
2–4%	Electric lights are needed during daytime hours to supplement the illumination of most visual tasks, but daylighting can provide the general lighting of the room surfaces and the room will look predominately daylit when there is supplementary electric lighting
5%	Strong daylighting. Supplementary daytime lighting is not normally needed
More than 5%	Thermal discomfort is likely to occur, the result of large temperature fluctuations. The room approaches the appearance of a semi-outdoor space, such as a conservatory

If the only windows in the room are roof lights, there tends to be less light falling on the walls of the room. The percentages above need to be approximately doubled to achieve the same sensation of room brightness.

$\overline{D}$ is the ratio of the daylight in a room to the light outdoors on open ground. More precisely, it is the mean illuminance on a room surface expressed as a percentage of the simultaneous illuminance on an unobstructed horizontal plane under an overcast sky. There is no direct sunlight: the sun is entirely hidden by clouds.

The average daylight factor is often used in standards as a measure of adequate daylight.

METHOD 1: THE BRE FORMULA

This is used when the skyline is approximately horizontal.

The formula gives the average daylight factor across the room at desktop height:

$$\overline{D} = \frac{\theta A_w \tau_w}{A_r (1 - \rho_r^2)}$$

If there are several windows in one room, the total daylight factor is the sum of the values calculated for individual windows. The only requirement is that the average room reflectance ρ_r must be calculated with all the windows present.

The main equation can be inverted to give the window area needed for a given daylight factor:

$$A_w = \frac{\overline{D}\left(1 - \rho_r^2\right) A_r}{\theta \, \tau_w}$$

where the meanings of the symbols are shown in Figure W4.1. The sky angle is the same as in Worksheet 3; the room surface reflectance is the weighted average of the floor, walls including window, and ceiling reflectances.

EXAMPLE

What window area is needed to obtain a 2% average daylight factor in the room in Figure W4.1?

- Room dimensions: plan, 5.5 m × 4.5 m, height, 2.9 m
- Surface finishes: walls, light stone colour; ceiling, white; floor, timber
- Window: clear double-glazed
- Angle of visible sky: 48°

Step-by-step:

1 *Calculate areas:* floor, 24.75 m²; walls, 53.00 m²; total 107.5 m².
2 *Estimate room reflectances:* From Worksheet 14, for a wood floor, the reflectance is 0.2; for light stone walls, 0.4; and for white paint, 0.85. The wall area includes the windows, which normally have low reflectance (because

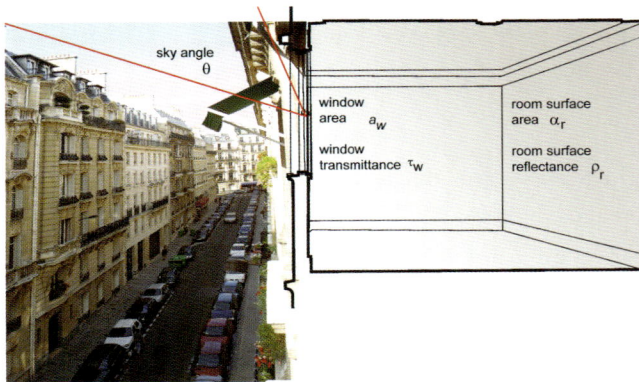

W4.1

the light mainly passes through them!): a typical overall reflectance for glazing, window bars and fittings is 0.1. The wall areas also include items such as doors, pictures and wall-mounted furniture, as well as the main wall finish. The effective reflectance can be calculated by making an estimate of the likely window area and of the other areas and reflectance, but for most purposes it is adequate to adopt an overall mean value. We assume an effective wall reflectance of 0.3.

The average reflectance of the room is thus

$$\rho_r = \frac{\rho_{floor}A_{floor} + \rho_{walls}A_{walls} + \rho_{ceiling}A_{ceiling}}{A_r}$$

$$= \frac{0.2 \times 24.75 + 0.3 \times 58.00 + 0.85 \times 24.75}{107.5} = 0.404$$

A result to three decimal places is nonsense considering the accuracy of the values entered. It should be presented as just 0.4, but we will leave rounding off until the end.

3   *Estimate window transmittance:* From Worksheets 15 and 16, the diffuse transmittance of clear double glazing is 0.65, with a reduction due to dirt of 8%. Then

$$\tau_w = 0.65 \times (1 - 0.08) = 0.6$$

4   *Calculate the required area of glazing:* Putting into the equation the 2% daylight factor, the sky angle and window transmittance, and the room area and mean reflectance, we have

$$A_w = \frac{2 \times \left(1 - 0.404^2\right) \times 107.5}{48 \times 0.6} = 6.25 \text{ m}^2$$

which should be interpreted as 'the area of glazing required is between 6 and 6.5 m²'.

METHOD 2: USE THE VERTICAL DAYLIGHT FACTOR

When the skyline is complicated, the room daylight factor can be calculated from D_v, the vertical daylight on the face of the window. This can be found with a dot diagram and the sky component to daylight factor conversion table, as in the previous worksheet, or by any other method.

The equation is then

$$\overline{D} = \frac{2D_v A_w \tau_w}{A_r\left(1 - \rho_r^2\right)}$$

Example

If the vertical sky component on the window exterior is 20%, then, from Table W3.2 in the previous worksheet, the vertical daylight factor would be 20% × 1.20 = 24.0.

With a window area of 6 m² and the other parameters the same as above,

$$\overline{D} = \frac{2 \times 24.0 \times 6 \times 0.6}{107.5 \times \left(1 - 0.404^2\right)} = 1.92\%$$

And for presentation this should be rounded to 2%.

5 *How to* calculate the daylight factor at a point in a room

For two or three decades after World War II, this was a standard calculation. The daylight factor at a point was the principal measure of daylight adequacy: a value of 2% was a requirement for a school desk or an office workplace that was embodied in many regulations and codes of practice. As a consequence, many methods were produced for estimating the result of what is at heart a complex lighting process. These methods were mainly graphical. They used charts, tables of pre-calculated values, and tools such as the BRS protractors (produced by the then Building Research Station in the UK).

The 2% criterion (the point value on a desk) remains a useful guide. It became discredited because if the criterion is a *minimum* value of 2% at the back of a classroom for 30 children, the window area required is large. Thermal problems of excessive solar heat gain or convective draughts are inevitable unless high-technology glazing is used. Fifty years ago, windows in the UK had only single glazing, so many post-war classrooms were uncomfortable.

In a side-lit room, a minimum daylight factor of 2% is broadly equivalent to an average daylight factor of 5% over a horizontal working plane at desk height.

Point daylight factors are tedious to calculate. It is much better to let the computer do it: there are several programs, or procedures within architectural software, that are available. Be careful, though. Often answers are given with several decimal points of implied precision where this is quite unjustified by either the precision of the input values or the assumptions implicit in the software.

METHOD 1: A RULE OF THUMB FOR FINDING WHERE 2% OCCURS

This is another form of Rule 5 in Worksheet 1 – the limit of strong daylight:

- In a side-lit room, 2% daylight factor on desk-tops occurs a distance from the window equal to twice the height of the window head above the working plane.

The rule applies when external obstructions are not more than about 25° and the windows have normal glazing and normal proportions.

METHOD 2: USING FISH-EYE PROJECTIONS AND DOT DIAGRAMS

The daylight factor is calculated by splitting it into three components.

The sky component

1 Either take a fish-eye picture looking upwards from the reference point (the place for which the daylight factor is needed) or plot the outline of the windows on a sky diagram (Worksheet 8 explains how this is done).

2 Select one of the dot diagrams in the data sheets labelled Horizontal Sky Component. Scan this and superimpose it on the fish-eye figure, enlarged so that its outer circle lies over the perimeter of the sky diagram. Count the dots that lie over open sky seen through the windows. In Figure W5.1, each dot is worth 0.1% sky component; 30 dots lie on the sky, a sky component of 3.0%.

3 Now rotate the dot diagram by 30°, keeping the outer circle on the horizon, and count the dots again. If the number is significantly different, repeat the process a few times, then find the average number of dots.

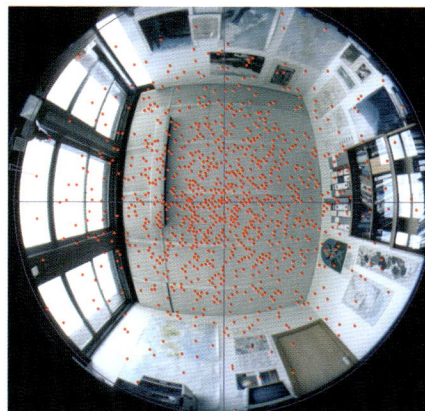

W5.1

The smaller the area of sky, the greater the variability and the more repeats needed. In the example above, five counts gave 30, 36, 29, 31 and 30 dots, an average of 31.2.

4   Find the glazing transmittance. From Worksheet 15, a panel with two sheets of 6 mm glass has a diffuse transmittance of 0.69 and a regular transmittance of 0.76. The diffuse transmittance is used for the average daylight factor and the regular transmittance for the sky component. Neither is exact, but both are satisfactory approximations.

5   Adopt a light loss value to account for dirt. From Worksheet 16, we choose a value of 0.9. Multiply this by the glazing transmittance to get an overall transmittance of $0.9 \times 0.76 = 0.68$.

6   The sky component is

average number of dots × dot weighting × transmittance

$$31.2 \times 0.1 \times 0.68 = 2.12\%$$

Externally reflected component

This is the light received directly after reflection from external surfaces such as buildings opposite. It includes light reflected from window reveals and solar shading.

Count the dots lying on external surfaces seen through the window. Multiply the number by the dot weighting divided by five. This takes the external surfaces to be one-fifth of the luminance of the sky they obscure. Obstructions that are very large or dark-coloured may be one-tenth or less of the obscured sky luminance, and appropriate weightings should be used.

In the example, an average of four dots lay on the window reveal; there are no obscuring buildings.

The externally reflected component is

$$4 \times 0.1 \times 0.2 = 0.08\%$$

Internally reflected component

1   *Calculate the average daylight factor for the room:* The average daylight factor can be found using any of the methods in Worksheet 4. The skyline in the present example is close to a horizontal roofline 20° above the horizon, so the BRE method is appropriate. To calculate the average daylight factor, we need the other parameters of the room:

- sky angle 60° (window head obstruction 10°)
- average room reflectance 0.5
- total room area 69 m^2
- total window area 7 m^2
- window transmittance $0.9 \times 0.69 = 0.62$

Then, entering these into the BRE formula,

$$\overline{D} = \frac{\theta A_w \tau_w}{A_r (1 - \rho_r^2)}$$
$$= \frac{60 \times 7 \times 0.62}{69 \times (1 - 0.5^2)} = 5.03\%$$

2   *Multiply this by the reflectance term in the daylight factor equation:* In the BRE equation, this is ρ_r^2, giving an internally reflected component of $5.03 \times 0.5^2 = 1.26\%$

Add the components

The total daylight factor at the point is

D = sky component + externally reflected component + internally reflected component

$$= 2.12 + 0.08 + 1.26 = 3.46\%$$

which should be rounded off to the nearest whole number, 3%, or rounded to the nearest 0.5% and the confidence range indicated: $3.5 \pm 0.5\%$. Presentation of daylight factor values is discussed in Chapter 8.

The calculated reflected component is the average value across the room. The lowest amount of reflected light occurs at the back of a sidelit room, where the sky component is also lowest. If the calculation is a test of the minimum daylight factor in the room, a smaller reflected component should be adopted. Typically, this might be half of the average value. In Algorithms and Equations, there are alternative formulae for the average and minimum internally reflected component, and other methods for daylight factors generally.

6 *How to* calculate the number of luminaires needed

This is the 'lumen method', used when there is a regular array of ceiling-mounted or pendant luminaires intended to provide uniform lighting at desk level over the whole room.

1 DECIDE THE ILLUMINANCE NEEDED

Multiply this by the floor area of the room to obtain the number of lumens required.

Example

The room shown in Figure W6.1 measures 8 m × 4 m in plan and the ceiling height is 3 m. It is a general office. The ceiling is to be white; the walls are to be painted, with a reflectance about 0.3; the floor will have a reflectance of about 0.2.

Worksheet 19 lists typical values of required task illuminances. We adopt 500 lx.

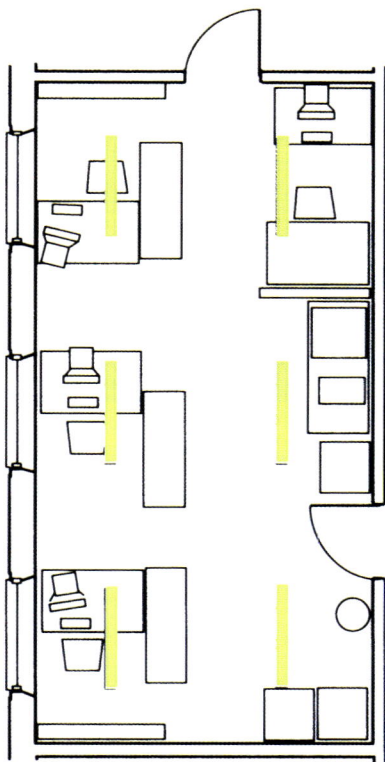

W6.1

The total flux required is 500 lx × 32 m² = 16,000 lm.

2 CHOOSE THE TYPE OF LAMP AND THE TYPES OF LUMINAIRE REQUIRED

In the example, we will use linear fluorescent fittings with two 1.2 m 28 W T5 lamps.

3 LOOK UP THE LUMEN OUTPUT OF THE LAMP AND THE UTILISATION FACTOR OF THE LUMINAIRE.

This information comes from manufacturers' web sites.

The lamp has an output of 2900 lm. It is higher when new; the figure given is a 'design output' to represent its long-term performance.

A utilisation factor (UF) is the fraction of the light emitted from lamps that falls on the working plane. It depends on the proportions of the room, because, with ceiling-mounted luminaires, more light reaches the working plane directly when the room is broad and the ceiling low than in a tall narrow room. It depends, too, on the reflectances of the room surfaces, because interreflection is taken into account.

To find the UF, it is necessary to calculate the room index, which is the ratio of the horizontal to vertical area in the room surfaces:

$$k = \frac{LW}{(L+W)H_m}$$
$$= \frac{8 \times 4}{(8+4) \times (3-0.8)} = 1.2$$

H_m is the height from the working plane to the luminaire.

Table W6.1 is a UF table for the chosen luminaire and is typical of manufacturer's photometric data. The values needed for this calculation are shown in bold type. Following the row for ceiling 0.8 and walls 0.3, we find UF = 0.56 for a room index of 1.0 and UF = 0.68 for a room index of 2.0. Interpolating, UF = 0.58.

Table W6.1 Example utilisation factors

Reflectances			Room index, k				
C	W	F	*1.0*	*2.0*	*3.0*	*4.0*	*5.0*
0.8	0.6	0.2	0.63	0.73	0.77	0.79	0.81
	0.5		0.60	0.71	0.76	0.78	0.80
	0.3		**0.56**	**0.68**	0.73	0.76	0.78
0.7	0.6	0.2	0.60	0.70	0.73	0.75	0.76
	0.5		0.58	0.68	0.72	0.74	0.75
	0.3		0.54	0.65	0.69	0.72	0.73
0.5	0.6	0.2	0.55	0.62	0.65	0.66	0.67
	0.5		0.53	0.61	0.64	0.66	0.67
	0.3		0.51	0.59	0.63	0.64	0.66

4 ESTIMATE THE EFFECTS OF DIRT AND AGEING

In large buildings with hundreds of luminaires, a detailed estimate of the performance of the lighting during its lifetime is worthwhile. With a small installation, only an approximate estimate is necessary. A typical maintenance factor is 0.8.

5 CALCULATE THE NUMBER OF LUMINAIRES NEEDED

$$N = \frac{\text{number of lumens required on the working plane}}{\text{number of lumens that reach the working plane from each luminaire}}$$

$$= \frac{\text{illuminance} \times \text{area}}{\text{lumens per lamp} \times \text{lamps per luminaire} \times \text{utilisation factor} \times \text{maintenance factor}}$$

$$= \frac{EA}{Fn\,\text{UF}\,\text{MF}}$$

$$= \frac{500 \times (8 \times 4)}{2900 \times 2 \times 0.58 \times 0.8} = 5.9$$

6 PLAN THE LAYOUT OF THE LUMINAIRES

Six luminaires are needed, and the obvious arrangement is a uniform spacing, shown in yellow on the plan in Figure W6.2. The first check to be made is on the uniformity of the illuminance that they give. Among the photometric data for a luminaire there is given a maximum spacing-to-height ratio. A value of 1.5 applies to this luminaire: it is the maximum

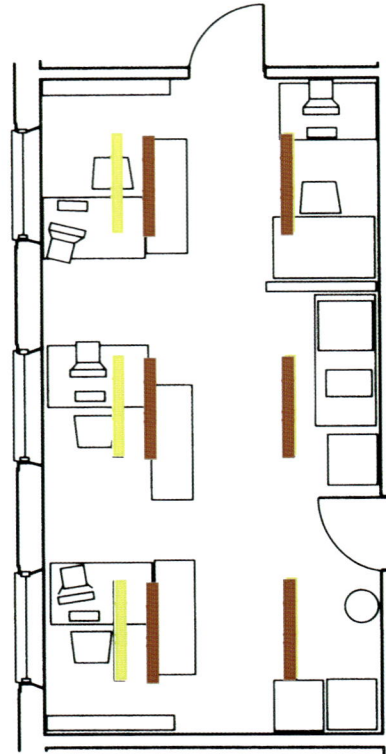

W6.2

distance apart of the centres of the luminaires in plan to the height of the luminaires above the working plane. The distance apart is 8/3 m on the longer axis and 4/2 m transversely, giving spacing-to-height ratios of (8/3)/2.2 = 1.21 and (4/2)/2.2 = 0.91. These are less than the maximum given, so the uniformity criterion is satisfied.

The second check is whether the luminaires will be visible as bright reflections on VDU screens or desktops.

Two problems emerge here with the proposed layout. Reflections of the luminaires next to the window will be visible in the desk surfaces beneath them. This is reduced by moving the row to the positions shown in brown. The second problem is that the inner row of luminaires could be visible in the screen of the workplace on the corner. To avoid that glare, the luminaires should have a sharp angular cut-off in the linear direction. Otherwise, the partition that separates the workplaces could be increased to ceiling height.

7 *How to* calculate the energy used when daylight and electric lighting are used together

The following method is a resume of the procedure adopted in the British and European Standard BS EN15193:2007. This worksheet covers side-lit rooms; the Standard, in addition, deals with roof-lit spaces.

The calculation is time-consuming and the Standard is not set out in a way that makes the procedure easy to follow. It is, however, important because it provides a common approach to energy assessment. The method is similar in principle to the use of daylight factors described in Chapter 8.

The electrical energy used by lighting is the power consumption of the system multiplied by the hours of use. The worst case of energy use is when all the lighting is switched on during the total period that the building is in use. The procedure adopted in the Standard is to take this value and calculate several factors that might reduce it: the penetration of daylight, the hours of strong daylight outside and the control system. Finally, a value termed the LENI (lighting energy numeric indicator) is calculated, and this is compared with the benchmark value.

The power consumption of the lighting is taken to be the power used directly plus the background power used by emergency lighting systems, the control system. This is termed the parasitic power consumption.

1 CALCULATE DAYLIT AND NON-DAYLIT AREAS

$h_g = h_{Li} - h_{Ta}$, where h_{Li} is the window head height and h_{Ta} is the working plane height

$a_{Dmax} = 2.5h_g$

$a_D = a_{Dmax}$ unless the depth of the room is less than $1.25a_{Dmax}$, in which case a_D = room depth

b_D = width of window + $a_D/2$, or the width of the room, whichever is smaller

And so the daylit area, $A_D = a_D b_D$

Note that the daylit area is taken to be slightly larger than the 'area of strong daylight' rule of thumb described in Chapter 4 and in Worksheet 1, where the penetration distance is $2.0h_g$.

2 CALCULATE THE TRANSPARENCY INDEX

I_T = area of glazing divided by daylit area of the working plane.

3 CALCULATE THE DEPTH INDEX

$$I_{De} = \frac{a_D}{h_g}$$

4 CALCULATE THE OBSTRUCTION INDEX

If the obstruction gives a horizontal roofline γ degrees above the horizon,

$$I_o = \cos(1.5\gamma) \text{ if } \gamma < 60°; \ I_o = 0 \text{ otherwise}$$

The Standard gives rules for calculating I_c when there are vertical fins, overhangs and courtyards.

5 CALCULATE THE DAYLIGHT FACTOR FOR AN UNGLAZED OPENING

$$D_c = (4.13 + 20I_T - 1.36I_{De})I_o$$

6 CALCULATE THE DAYLIGHT FACTOR FROM THE GLAZED OPENING

This requires the transmittance of the window system, which is

overall transmittance = normal transmittance of glazing (from data sheet)
× frame factor (typically 0.7)
× factor accounting for dirt (typically 0.8)
× factor to account for diffuse light on façade (typically 0.85)

It is worth noting that BS 8206-2 suggests a factor of 0.91 to convert direct glazing transmittance to diffuse transmittance.

7   LOOK UP THE DAYLIGHT PENETRATION CLASSIFICATION

This uses Table W7.1.

Table W7.1 Daylight penetration example

D_C	D	Daylight penetration
$D_C \geq 6\%$	$D \geq 3\%$	Strong
$6\% > D_C \geq 4\%$	$3\% > D \geq 2\%$	Medium
$4\% > D_C \geq 2\%$	$2\% > D \geq 1\%$	Weak
$D_C < 2\%$	$D < 1\%$	None

8   FIND THE DAYLIGHT SUPPLY FACTOR

The Standard gives three ways of doing this: an equation involving the latitude of the site, a graph and a table of examples (Table W7.2).

The example room requires 500 lx and has strong penetration, and the values in the table for Watford can be used: F_{os} = 0.75.

9   CALCULATE THE DAYLIGHT-DEPENDENT ARTIFICIAL LIGHTING CONTROL

This value, F_{DC}, is given by Table W7.3. This table gives the annual value. The Standard includes a table for determining monthly values.

Table W7.3 Daylight-dependent electric lighting

Control of artificial lighting system	F_{DC} as a function of daylight penetration		
	Weak	Medium	Strong
Manual	0.20	0.30	0.40
Automatic daylight-dependent	0.75	0.77	0.85

10   CALCULATE THE DAYLIGHT DEPENDENCY FACTOR

Here we bring together all that has been calculated so far:

$$F_D = 1 - F_{DS}F_{DC}$$

11   CALCULATE THE OCCUPANCY DEPENDENCY FACTOR

If the lighting is switched centrally or in blocks covering 30 m^2 or more, F_O = 1. It is taken that there is no effective control. Otherwise, F_O depends on two things: the lighting control system, F_{OC} (Table W7.4); and the proportion of time that the space is unoccupied.

Table W7.4 Lighting control factor, F_{OC}

Systems without automatic presence or absence detection	F_{OC}
Manual on/off switch	1.00
Manual on/off switch plus automatic switch-off when all users have left	0.95
Systems with automatic presence or absence detection	
Auto on/dimmed	0.95
Auto on/auto off	0.90
Manual on/dimmed	0.90
Manual on/auto off	0.80

Table W7.2 Daylight supply factor, $F_{D,S}$

Site	Latitude, °N	Maintained illuminance								
		300 lx			500 lx			750 lx		
		Weak	Medium	Strong	Weak	Medium	Strong	Weak	Medium	Strong
Athens	38	0.80	0.91	0.96	0.59	0.80	0.90	0.41	0.63	0.82
Lyon	46	0.70	0.82	0.89	0.51	0.70	0.82	0.36	0.55	0.72
Bratislava	48	0.68	0.80	0.87	0.49	0.68	0.79	0.35	0.54	0.70
Frankfurt	50	0.66	0.78	0.85	0.47	0.66	0.77	0.33	0.52	0.68
Watford	52	0.63	0.76	0.83	0.45	0.63	0.75	0.32	0.50	0.65
Gävle	60	0.54	0.67	0.78	0.38	0.54	0.66	0.27	0.42	0.56

The Standard includes a table of typical absentee factors, F_A. Table W7.5 is a selection from it.

Table W7.5 Absentee factor, F_A

Building type	Room type	F_A
Offices	Overall	0.2
	Cellular office, 1 person	0.4
	Cellular office, 2–6 persons	0.3
	Open plan office, >6 persons sensing/30 m²	0
	Plan office, 6 persons sensing/10 m²	0.2
	Conference room	0.5
Educational buildings	Overall	0.2
	Classroom	0.25
	Lecture hall	0.4
	Staff room	0.4
	Library	0.4
	Sports hall	0.3

The occupancy dependency factor is then given as follows:

when $0 \leq F_A < 0.2$,	$F_O = 1 - [(1 - F_{OC})F_A/2]$
$0.2 \leq F_A < 0.9$,	$F_O = F_{OC} + 0.2 - F_A$
$0.9 \leq F_A \leq 1.0$,	$F_O = [7 - (10F_{OC})](F_A - 1)$

12 FIND THE CONSTANT-ILLUMINANCE FACTOR

In a dimmer-controlled system where a constant illuminance is to be maintained, more energy is required to achieve the required illuminance when luminaires collect dirt or become discoloured. Lamps are initially run below their maximum power, and as time progresses the power is increased. Under such a regime, F_c may be taken as 0.9 in a clean environment under such a regime. Or, assuming a maintenance factor, MF,

$$F_c = (1 + MF)/2$$

In all other cases, $F_c = 1$.

13 ESTIMATE THE TOTAL ENERGY

The total energy use for lighting is given by

$$W = W_L + W_P$$

where the energy consumed for illumination is

$$W_L = \Sigma \, P_n F_c (t_D F_O F_D + t_N F_O)/1000 \text{ kWh}$$

The summation symbol, Σ, means that to find the total building energy, the equation is calculated for all the separate zones of the building and the results added up.

W_P is the parasitic consumption, including charging energy for emergency lighting. The Standard suggests a default value of 5 kWh/(m²·year) for daylight and occupancy control combined in the absence of manufacturer's data. In addition, the Standard suggests 1 kWh/(m²·year) for emergency lighting.

P_n is total installed power, W (= power/m² × floor area).
t_D is the daylight time usage, hours/year.
t_N is the non-daylight time usage, hours/year.

LENI for the building is defined as the total energy consumption per year for lighting per m² of floor area.

EXAMPLE

The building is in London. This calculation is of the lighting energy expenditure in a room used as an office. The space is 8 m long × 5 m deep × 2.9 m high. There is a window located centrally in the long wall with a sill height of 0.7 m and a head height of 2.7 m and length 6 m. There are no external obstructions, and double glazing is used with a normal transmittance of 0.75. On a working plane at height 0.7m, 500 lx is required.

There are 2250 hours of daytime usage and 250 hours of night-time usage per year. The installed lighting power is 15 W/m². We will compare the energy use with electric lighting used continuously during working hours, with simple manual switching and with auto switching plus an occupancy detector that switches off the lights serving a zone 15 minutes after the occupant departs.

1 Calculate daylit and non-daylit areas

In the example: $a_D = 2.5 \times 2 = 5$ m. This is the depth of the room, so there is no non-daylit area.

2 Calculate the transparency index

$$I_T = (6 \times 2)/40.0 = 0.3$$

3 Calculate the depth index

$$l_{De} = 5/2 = 2.5$$

4 Calculate the obstruction index

In the example, there is no obstruction, so $l_o = 1$.

5 Calculate the daylight factor for an unglazed opening

$$D_c = (4.13 + 20 \times 0.30 - 1.36 \times 2.5) \times 1 = 6.73\%$$

6 Calculate the daylight factor from the glazed opening

We adopt a frame factor of 0.76, normal transmittance of 0.75, a 10% reduction for dirt (referring to Worksheet 16 data), and a 0.91 diffuse correction factor. The corrected daylight factor is

$$D = D_c \times 0.76 \times 0.75 \times 0.9 \times 0.91 = 6.73 \times 0.47 = 3.14\%$$

7 Look up the daylight penetration classification

Using Table W7.1, the daylight penetration in the example room would be classified as 'strong'.

8 Find the daylight supply factor

Referring to Table W7.2, with 500 lx required and 'strong' penetration, for London at 51 °N latitude, we interpolate between Watford (52°) and Frankfurt (50°) to get $F_{DS} = 0.76$.

9 Calculate the daylight-dependent artificial lighting control

Using the table W7.3, for manual control and 'strong' penetration, $F_{DC} = 0.4$. With continuous lighting use, $F_{DC} = 0$.

10 Calculate the daylight dependency factor

$$F_D = 1 - F_{DS}F_{DC}$$

With continuous use, $F_D = 1$. For manual controls, $F_D = 1 - 0.4 \times 0.76 = 0.70$; for automatic controls, it is $F_D = 1 - 0.85 \times 0.76 = 0.35$.

11 Calculate the occupancy dependency factor

With no control, $F_O = 1$. In the other cases, we first look up F_{OC}, finding that for simple manual control, $F_{OC} = 1$, and with occupancy sensing and automatic dimming, $F_{OC} = 0.95$. Then

we look up the type of building and room occupancy, finding that for a cellular office with 2–6 occupants, $F_A = 0.3$. From these, $F_O = 1 + 0.2 - 0.3 = 0.9$ for manual switching and $F_O = 0.95 + 0.2 - 0.3 = 0.85$ with automatic control and occupancy detection.

12 Find the constant-illuminance factor

This does not apply, so $F_c = 1$.

13 Estimate the total energy

P_n is the lighting power (15 W/m^2 × 40 m^2). With continuous electric lighting, there is no parasitic load, so the annual energy use for the single zone is

$$W_L = P_nF_c(t_DF_OF_D + t_NF_O)/1000 \text{ kWh}$$
$$= (600 \times 1) \times [(2250 \times 1 \times 1) + (250 \times 1)]/1000$$
$$= 1500 \text{ kWh}$$

With simple manual switching,

$$W_L = (600 \times 1) \times [(2250 \times 0.9 \times 0.7)$$
$$+ (250 \times 0.9)]/1000 = 986 \text{ kWh}$$

With occupancy detection and automatic dimming control,

$$W_L = (600 \times 1) \times [(2250 \times 0.85 \times 0.35)$$
$$+ (250 \times 0.85)\}]/1000 = 529 \text{ kWh}$$

To these, however, must be added emergency lighting, and in the third case the parasitic load from the occupancy detection system and the emergency lighting. We assumed values of 1 kWh/(m^2·year) and 5 kWh/(m^2·year).

In the uncontrolled case, the total is 1540 kWh, giving a LENI value of 38.5 kWh/m^2.

With manual switching, the total is 1026 kWh, with a LENI value of 25.6 kWh/m^2.

The fully automatic case has a total of 769 kWh, with a LENI value of 19.2 kWh/m^2.

If the site were in Athens, the value of F_{DS} would be 0.9, $F_D = 0.235$, and the annual energy cost with automatic control and occupancy sensing would be 397 kWh plus 240 kWh emergency and parasitic, giving 637 kWh total, a LENI value of 15.9 kWh/m^2.

8 *How to* use sky diagrams and fish-eye images

Fish-eye camera lenses have a very short focal length and capture almost a hemisphere of view. If the camera is pointed vertically upwards, the image produced is a disc showing the horizon around the perimeter and the zenith of the sky at the centre.

Sunpath diagrams are normally plotted on a stereographic projection of the sky. This is a map projection that represents the surface of a hemisphere as a circle. The stereographic projection has useful properties: it preserves angles – angles on the hemisphere are reproduced in the diagram; therefore circles on the hemisphere become either circles or straight lines when plotted, and sunpaths plot as arcs of circles.

Some, but not all, fish-eye lenses produce a stereographic image. Others give an image that is close to the equal solid angle projection. The difference can be seen in the two grids in Figure W8.2: concentric circles, which correspond to view angles of 10°, 20°, … vary in their spacing.

The sky diagrams printed in the data sheets are intended to be used as overlays on site photographs. They can be photocopied and enlarged, then superimposed on prints; this is easiest if they are printed on acetate. Nowadays, more conveniently, they can be scanned and laid over digital images. They can be stored as a set of layers in Photoshop or another graphics program, easily available for use.

The azimuth scale on the diagrams, the numbers around the perimeter, goes clockwise from zero to 360°, as if looking downwards on to a sky dome. Fish-eye photographs of the sky look upwards, so either the image or the diagram must be laterally inverted, flipped left–right. In this book, the images are inverted.

The diagrams are given in two projections: stereographic and equal solid angle. The latter is nearer to the projection produced by most fish-eye lenses, and should be used as a default. Figure W8.2 shows the two projections side by side, the equal solid angle on the left.

The accuracy of estimates from dot diagrams depends on the number of dots in a zone. The confidence range of a measurement is inversely proportional to the square root of the number of dots on which it is based. As a working rule, the number of dots in a sky patch should be 30 or more. If only a small zone of sky is visible on an image, the process should be repeated with different dot patterns. The vertical sky component diagram is printed in two versions, differing in the number of dots. Each can be flipped about the centre line to give a second sample. The horizontal sky component and the configuration factor diagrams do not have any orientation, so they can be rotated about the centre to produce different dot patterns under a sky patch.

It is possible to generate scaled random dot patterns in daylighting analysis software and count automatically the number lying in a patch of visible sky on an image. The number of sample points is then limited only by the number of pixels in the image.

W8.1

A photograph taken through a fish-eye lens. The camera is on the ground, pointing upwards.

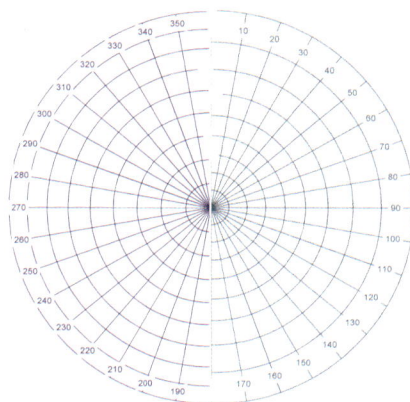

W8.2

Comparison of equal solid angle (left) and stereographic (right) projections.

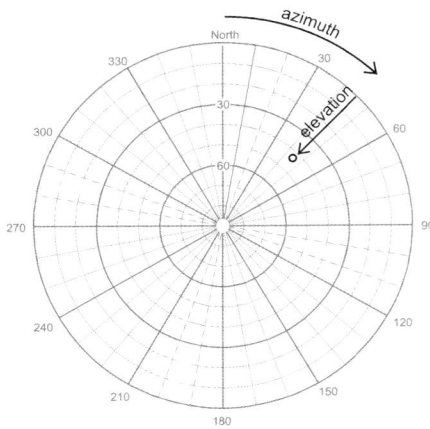

W8.3

The hemisphere of sky is represented by a circular map. The compass direction of a sky point (the azimuth) is plotted directly by an angle from north; the height above the horizon is measured along the radial lines. This example is an equal solid angle projection.

Plotting buildings on a sky diagram

Figure W8.3 represents the world that is visible from a specific viewpoint; each point on it corresponds with a direction of view, defined by its azimuth (the bearing from north) and its elevation (the angle above the horizon). All that is necessary is to select the location of the viewpoint on a site plan and to find from there the angles in plan and section to the corners of the building to be plotted. These angles can be measured from scale drawings or calculated. Working manually, it is usually easiest to measure the azimuth and calculate the elevation.

Example

Figure W8.4 shows two blocks. The viewpoint is at **a**. To find the point on the sky diagram that represents **c**, the corner of an adjacent block:

1 Measure the angle between north and the line in plan from **a** to **c**. This is 61°, the azimuth, α.
2 Measure the distance in plan, d (28 m); then get the height difference between **a** and **c**, and calculate the angle of elevation. The plan distance is 28 m. The height difference is (25.0 m − 2.5 m) = 22.5 m. Then

$$\gamma = \arctan\frac{h}{d} = \arctan\frac{22.5}{28} = 39°$$

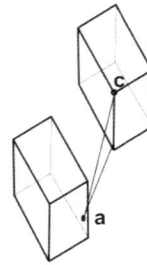

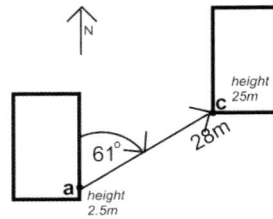

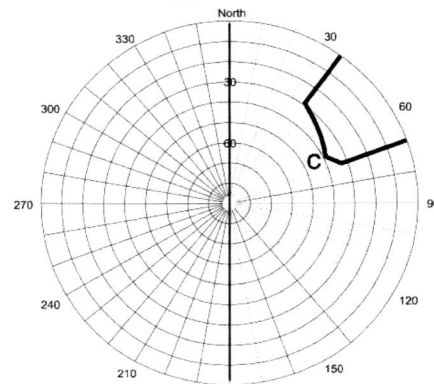

W8.4

Sky plot example 1.

3 Find the point on the diagram and mark it. Repeat with the other corners of the building and join them to get the outline of the building.

Two points should be noted. Firstly, straight horizontal lines, such as the roofline in this example, become curves on the diagram. To plot the curve accurately, it is helpful to calculate one or two intermediate points along the line. Secondly, the vertical line though the centre of the diagram represents the plane of the window. No sky is visible to the west of this line.

Figure W8.5 shows the two buildings plotted from a point **b** on the ground between the blocks.

If an obstruction has a simple shape and the study is limited to only a few positions, this method of plotting the diagram is feasible. If the building forms are complex or their impact needs to be evaluated at many viewpoints, then calculating and plotting the outlines is tedious and time-consuming.

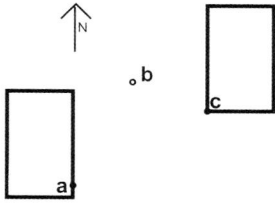

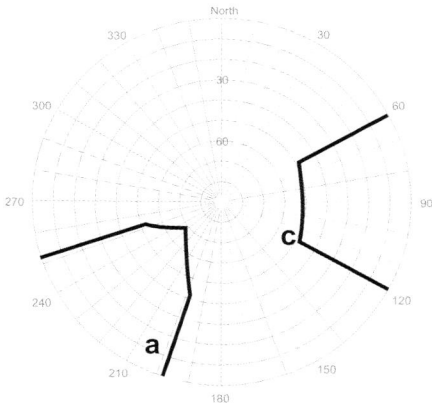

W8.5
Sky plot example 2.

The easiest way of automating the process is to set up a spreadsheet. Putting a grid on the site plan can give x and y coordinates for the corners and other key points on the buildings. Then these can be entered on the spreadsheet together with the height values, z. Multiple values of x_p, y_p, z_p for the viewpoint can be entered. Then, for each, the horizontal distance from viewpoint to building point is

$$d = \sqrt{(x - x_p)^2 + (y - y_p)^2}$$

and the vertical angle, γ, is given by the equation in the example above.

If the site plan grid has north at the top (i.e. north–south lines are parallel with the y axis) the azimuth angle, α, is given by

$$\alpha = \arccos\left(\frac{y - y_p}{d}\right), \quad (x - x_p) \geq 0$$

$$= 360° - \arccos\left(\frac{y - y_p}{d}\right), \quad \text{otherwise.}$$

Algorithms and Equations Section 1.11 describes how stereographic and other sky diagrams can be constructed.

9 *How to* use sunpath diagrams

Chapter 4 describes how sunpath diagrams are used in conjunction with site photographs to estimate periods of sunlight when the sky is partly obstructed. This worksheet gives an example.

A house in London has large windows opening onto a terrace. It faces approximately south-west and enjoys sunlight throughout the day from about 8 am. The morning sunshine in particular is much valued by the users. A neighbour plans to extend the adjacent house so that it projects further into the garden. How much sunlight would be blocked?

Figure W9.1, a fish-eye image taken on the terrace, shows the site at present. Figure W9.2 has the proposed building superimposed.

A sunpath diagram overlaid on the image and rotated (Figure W9.3) shows that sunlight would be blocked from the viewpoint until about 11.30 in June and about 11.15 in December. The probable sunlight hours dot diagram (Figure W9.4) indicates the hours of sunshine loss, taking into account cloudiness. Counting the dots gives red (summer semester) 225 and blue (winter semester) 114, of which 66 were in the period 1 November to 28 February.

In Figure W9.4, each dot is equivalent to 0.1% of probable sunlight; therefore, the total loss of sunlight caused by the proposed building would be (225 + 114) × 0.1 = 33.9% of the hours of sunlight in London. At present, the terrace receives 88.5% of probable sunlight, so more than one-third of this would be lost.

Note that only the dots above the existing skyline are counted in assessing the effect of the new building.

W9.1

The site as existing.

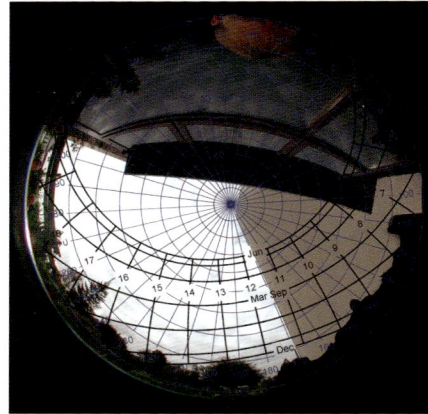

W9.3

Sunpath diagram superimposed.

W9.2

With proposed building.

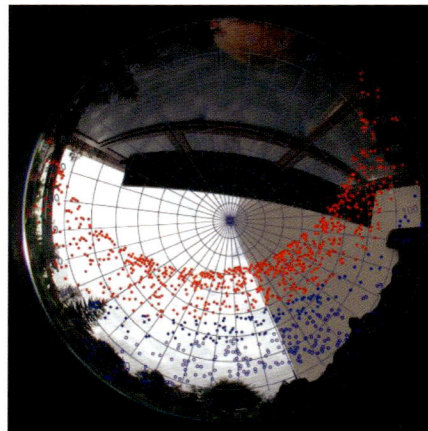

W9.4

Dot diagram for percentage of probable sunlight hours.

10 *How to* calculate sunlight and skylight in the urban canyon

Chapter 8 describes how the direct and interreflected light in an urban street can be calculated. This worksheet gives a step-by-step example. It is a tedious calculation with several stages, but once it has been set up in a spreadsheet it is convenient and quick to use. The formulae are explained in Chapter 8.

The example is a narrow street with continuous facades on either side (Figure W10.1). The room being studied is at first-floor level and its windows face north-west, $\alpha_b = 315°$. The ground has a reflectance 0.2 and the buildings are painted white, but, taking into account doors and windows, and that the façades have prominent moulding, the overall façade reflectance is 0.5. The site is at latitude 35° N and the time is 11 am on 15 May.

1 SET UP A TABLE OF THE BUILDING PARAMETERS

Throughout the calculation, angles are given in degrees, lengths in metres and illuminance in kilolux. Input numbers in bold type, calculated values in normal type.

Orientation of window façade	α_b	**315.00**
Width of street	w	**8.50**
Height of street above window centre	h_u	**2.75**
Height from ground to window centre	h_b	**4.75**
Reflectance of ground	ρ_g	**0.20**
Reflectance of building	ρ_b	**0.50**

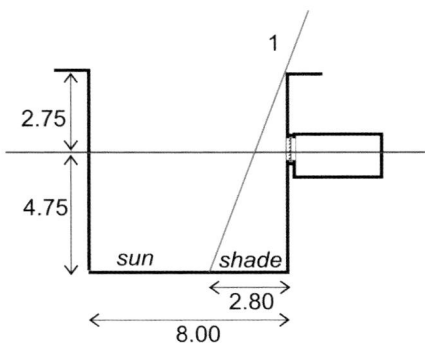

W10.1

2 GET SUN AND SKY PARAMETERS

These can be calculated from formulae given in Equations and Algorithms, taken from graphs given in Chapter 4, or measured data.

Solar azimuth	α_s	**139.01**
Solar elevation	γ_s	**69.46**
Solar normal illuminance	E_{sn}	**92.69**
Diffuse horizontal illuminance	E_{dh}	**45.38**

3 CALCULATE ANGLES USING DIRECTION COSINES

$$c_1 = \cos\alpha\cos\gamma, \quad c_2 = \sin\alpha\cos\gamma, \quad c_3 = \sin\gamma.$$

The cosine of the angle of incidence of a ray on a plane is

$$\cos\theta = c_1 n_1 + c_2 n_2 + c_3 n_3$$

where c gives the direction cosines of the ray and n those of the plane.

The length of the shadow cast by the window façade is the absolute value of

$$W_{sh} = \frac{(h_u + h_d)}{w}\frac{\cos|a_b - a_s|}{\tan\gamma'_s}$$

If this is greater than the street width, the lower part of the opposite façade is in shadow to a height of

$$h_{sh} = \frac{(h_u + h_d)(w_{sh} - w)}{w_{sh}}$$

	c_1	c_2	c_3
Sun	−0.26	0.23	0.94
Window façade	0.71	−0.71	0.00
Opposite facade	−0.71	0.71	0.00
Ground	0.00	0.00	1.00

Cos angle sun on façade	0.00
Cos sun on opposite façade	0.35
Cos sun on ground	0.94
Length shadow cast by facade	2.80

4 DIVIDE THE STREET SECTION INTO ZONES

The sunlight and shaded areas, and the surfaces above and below the level of the centre of the window are given separate zones (Figure W10.2).

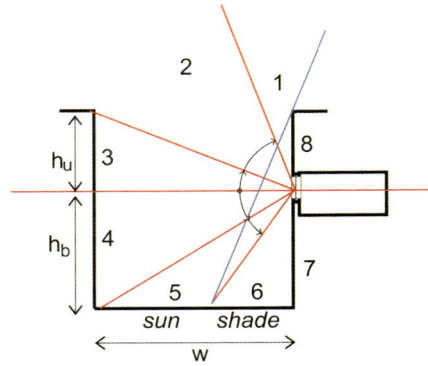

W10.2

5 CALCULATE THE ILLUMINANCE FROM SKY AND SUN IN EACH ZONE

If there is sunlight on the ground, the sky luminance distribution can be any of many patterns. Fortunately, however, its influence is a second-order effect compared with sunlight. The sky is therefore taken to be of uniform luminance, which greatly simplifies the calculation. On the upper part of the façade facing the window, zone 3, the illuminance from the sky is

$$\bar{E}_{sky3} = E_{hd} \frac{1 + H_3 - \sqrt{1 + H_3^2}}{2}, \quad \text{where } H_3 = \frac{w}{h_u}$$

The mean skylight illuminance over all the opposite façade is

$$\bar{E}_{sky3\&4} = E_{hd} \left(\frac{1 + H_4 - \sqrt{1 + H_4^2}}{2} \right), \quad \text{where } H_4 = \frac{w}{h_u + h_d}$$

The mean illuminance on the lower façade (zone 4) is

$$\bar{E}_{sky4} = \frac{\bar{E}_{sky3\&4}(h_u + h_b) - \bar{E}_3 h_u}{h_b}$$

The mean sky illuminance on the ground is

$$\bar{E}_{skyg} = E_{hd} \left(\sqrt{1 + H_g^2} - H_g \right), \quad \text{where } H_g = \frac{w}{h_u + h_b}$$

and on the window façade it is the same as on the zones opposite.

The solar illuminance on the sunlit surfaces is the solar normal illuminance multiplied by the cosine of the angle of incidence, which was found earlier.

Zone	Illuminance from sky	Illuminance from sun	Total
3	19.11	32.44	51.55
4	11.22	32.44	43.66
5	17.16	86.80	103.96
6	17.16	86.80	103.96
7	11.22	0.00	11.22
8	19.11	0.00	19.11

6 CALCULATE THE INTERREFLECTED LIGHT ON THE ZONES

There are two parts to this. First find the mean reflectance of the canyon,

$$\bar{\rho} = \frac{2(h_u + h_b)\rho_b + w\rho_g}{2(h_u + h_b) + 2w}$$

then the mean interreflected illuminance, which is done by adding up the flux reflected from each zone (illuminance × area × reflectance), then dividing by the total area and the term (1 − mean reflectance):

$$\bar{E}_r = \frac{E_{zone3}\, h_u\rho_b + E_{zone4}\, h_b\rho_b + E_{zone5}\,(w - w_{sh})\rho_g + E_{zone6}\, w_{sh}\rho_g + E_{zone7}\, h_b\rho_b + E_{zone8}\, h_u\rho_b}{[2(h_u + h_b) + 2w](1 - \bar{\rho})}$$

7 CALCULATE THE DIRECT LIGHT FROM THE SKY PLUS THE REFLECTED LIGHT FROM THE GROUND AND THE OPPOSITE FAÇADE ONTO THE WINDOW

The general equation is

$$E_{wz} = E_z \rho_z \frac{\sin \omega_{z1} - \sin \omega_{z0}}{2}$$

where E_z is the illuminance in a zone, ρ_z is the reflectance, and ω_{z1} and ω_{z0} are the angles defining the zone seen from the window.

Adding these to the table gives the following:

Zone	Illuminance from sky	Illuminance from sun	Inter-reflected	Total	Upper angle	Lower angle	Reflectance	Illuminance on window From above	From below
1	0.00	0.00	8.32	8.32	90.00	80.00	0.50	0.03	
2					80.00	17.93			
3	19.11	32.44	8.32	59.87	17.93	0.00	0.50	4.61	
4	11.22	32.44	8.32	51.98	29.20	0.00	0.50		6.34
5	17.16	86.80	8.32	112.28	59.48	29.19	0.20		4.20
6	17.16	0.00	8.32	25.48	90.00	59.48	0.20		0.35
7	11.22	0.00	8.32	19.53	90.00	90.00	0.50		
8	19.11	0.00	8.32	27.43	90.00	90.00	0.50		
Window					Direct illuminance from sky			15.36	
					Interreflected light on window			4.16	4.16
							Totals	24.16	15.05

8 THE FINAL STAGE IS TO USE THE SPLIT-FLUX FORMULA TO CALCULATE DAYLIGHT WITHIN THE ROOM

The room measures 8 m × 4 m in plan, with a ceiling height of 3 m. There are three windows, each 2.1 m high and 1.67 m wide. They are identical in construction and face the same obstruction; therefore, they can be treated as a single opening. They have louvres integral with the glazing, and these cut out the majority of downward light on the window.

From Chapter 8, the equations are

$$F_{il} = a_w \left(E_{ws} \tau_{sl} + E_{wg} \tau_{gl} \right) \text{ downward light}$$

$$F_{iu} = a_w \left(E_{ws} \tau_{su} + E_{wg} \tau_{gu} \right) \text{ upward light}$$

then

$$E_{lower} = \frac{2(F_{il} + F_{iu}\rho_u)}{a_r (1 - \rho_u \rho_l)}$$

$$E_{upper} = \frac{2(F_u + F_{il}\rho_l)}{a_r (1 - \rho_u \rho_l)}$$

Length of window wall	L	**8**
Depth of room from window	W	**4**
Height of ceiling	h_u	**3**
Height of window	h_w	**2.1**
Total width of windows	w_w	**5**
Window transmittance:	Up to up, τ_{gu}	**0.4**
	Up to down, τ_{gl}	**0.1**
	Down to up, τ_{su}	**0**
	Down to down, τ_{sl}	**0.1**
Reflectance of upper half of room	ρ_u	**0.6**
Reflectance of lower half of room	ρ_l	**0.2**

The results show the large effect of high-reflectance finishes to the façades of buildings in a narrow street. The mean illuminance on the lower half of the room is 1.32 klx, which, rounded, should be expressed as 1300 lx. A major component of this is diffusely reflected sunlight.

The calculation also shows the potential problem of glare from sunlight on white-painted façades. The total illuminance

Window area, a_w	Room area, a_r	Initial downward flux, F_{il}	Initial upward flux, F_{ul}	Illuminance on lower room surfaces, E_{lower}	Illuminance on upper room surfaces, E_{upper}
10.50	136.00	41.17	63.20	1.32	1.19

on the upper sunlit façade opposite to the window is about 60 klx, a luminance of $60 \times 0.5/\pi$ kcd/m², about 9550 cd/m². This is the same order of magnitude as the diffuse sky. In this situation there is a delicate balance to be made between view out, room illuminance and glare, and the best solution depends of the use and layout of the room and on the needs and wishes of users. It is essential that users can control the blinds and other devices that limit the transmittance of the window.

To create a general-purpose spreadsheet in an application such as Excel, different configurations of sunlight must be taken into account. As the solar angles change, different façades become illuminated and the shadows on the floor and walls of the canyon take different forms. This can be programmed with the use of conditional statements, 'if' functions. Chapter 8 gives the formulae for dealing with different geometries.

11 *How to* measure light

This worksheet is a guide to measuring daylight on site and in scale models.

MEASURING ILLUMINANCE

An illuminance meter measures the light falling onto a surface, in units of lux or, in the USA, lumens per square foot or 'footcandles'. Its photographic equivalent is an incident-light meter. The sensor in the instrument is usually recognisable by a white plastic disk, which covers a photocell. This disk and the shape of the mount holding it ensure that the instrument responds correctly to incident light at different angles. This is known as cosine correction, which is essential. The instrument should also be colour-corrected, which ensures that it compensates correctly for spectral differences in the light. This is sometimes referred to as V_λ (vee-lambda) correction.

When taking readings with a portable illuminance meter, it is essential to check two things:

- *Is the meter level?* Make sure that the sensor is parallel with the surface being studied – for example, that it is truly horizontal if you are measuring desk or floor illuminance. A small tilt can cause a large error if the light shines obliquely on the surface.
- *Are you obstructing light that would fall on the sensor?* Many light meters have the sensor on a cable about a

metre long so that the reading can be taken without overshadowing the sensor. If your lightmeter has the sensor built in, be careful!

When assessing the lighting in a room, record the following, because they are often necessary when the measured illuminances are analysed.

- electric lighting switched on or off
- positions of window blinds, curtains, solar shading
- date and time
- sky conditions, whether the sun is shining
- people and objects that might be affecting the light at measuring points.

If you are measuring daylight, take a series of readings over a few minutes to check how much it is fluctuating. If you need to know the relative contributions of daylight and electric lighting, take readings with and without the electric lighting, during a period when the sky is not changing rapidly. Subtracting the daylight-only reading from the combined reading yields the electric lighting illuminance. Similarly, if moving clouds give intermittent sunlight on the building and its surroundings, subtracting readings with the sun obscured from those taken when it is visible give approximately the illuminance due to sunlight, direct and reflected.

When presenting the results of a lighting survey, make sure that figures given do not imply an incorrectly high precision. See 'The accuracy of lighting measurements and calculations' in Chapter 8.

MEASURING THE DAYLIGHT FACTOR IN A ROOM

Strictly, this is not possible. A daylight factor is a number calculated on the basis of several assumptions that never exactly match reality. It is better to put it as follows:

MEASURING THE RATIO OF INTERNAL TO EXTERNAL ILLUMINANCE AND USING THIS AS AN ESTIMATE OF DAYLIGHT FACTOR

This is possible but notoriously prone to error. The requirements are as follows.

The internal and external measurements should be simultaneous. Two illuminance meters are needed, and these must be matched in calibration – it is normal practice to compare these side by side under the high illuminances outside and under low interior illuminances. The importance of this matching is made obvious by a quick calculation: suppose the exterior illuminance is 50 klx and the illuminance at an indoor point is 1000 lx, which is 2% of the external value. If meter A reads 10% low and is used for the exterior measurement, and meter B reads 10% high and is used inside, the measured indoor outdoor percentage would be $900/55{,}000 \times 100 = 1.6\%$. If the two meters were used the other way round, the result would be $1100/45{,}000 \times 100 = 2.4\%$, one-and-a-half times the previous amount. An alternative is to repeat all readings with the meters interchanged, as described below under 'Using paired cells to eliminate calibration differences'.

The other requirement is a static, heavily overcast sky. Outside, where there is as little obstruction as possible, measure the horizontal illuminance (the sensor facing directly upwards), then take readings with the sensor facing north, south, east and west. Assuming a normal ground reflectance of about 0.2, the vertical readings should be similar to each other and about half the horizontal value. If they differ significantly from this, measure the vertical illuminance in the direction that the windows face; then scale the interior

measurements as follows to compensate for the sky irregularity:

$$\text{compensated reading} = 0.5 \times [(\text{external horizontal illuminance})/(\text{exterior vertical illuminance})] \times \text{actual reading.}$$

If the purpose of the measurements is to check calculated daylight factors, measure the dimensions of the room, the actual window sizes (taking into account such things as curtains and objects on the window sill), the actual reflectance of surfaces, and the transmittance of glazing, including weathering and dirt. Record what external obstructions there are, and whether, like trees, they could change significantly with time. Then insert these values into the formulae and re-calculate the daylight factors.

MEASURING LIGHT IN MODEL ROOMS UNDER AN ARTIFICIAL SKY

An artificial sky provides a steady approximation to the CIE Overcast Sky. The most common type is the mirror-lined box with a luminous ceiling and walls. In this, the distribution of light over the ceiling and the effect of multiple interreflections between walls create a luminous distribution increasing in brightness towards the zenith. Sometimes, patterns on the mirror surface are used to fine-tune the distribution In another type of artificial sky, a dome is illuminated by luminaires around the circumference at the base. A further type uses a translucent dome with lamps above.

The model must be significantly smaller in plan area than the sky. The maximum recommended size varies with sky type, but for rectangular mirror skies the upper limit tends to be a model width of about one-third the sky width in each direction. A maximum model area of about one-tenth of an artificial sky plan area is a convenient rule of thumb.

The model must be accurately scaled, and its surface materials must match the colours and reflectances as closely as possible. A model room made in white card can look stunning, but the interreflected light is grossly exaggerated.

Illuminances within the model are measured by small photocells linked by cables to a meter or a laptop outside the sky. These sensors, because of their relative size, measure the mean illuminance over a finite area, not the value at a point. For example, a cell diameter of 10 mm corresponds to a circle of 1 m at scale 1 : 100.

It is difficult to reproduce window transmittance in a small model, not only because the necessary miniaturisation demands much skill, but also because there are scale effects. A pane of body-tinted glass 8 mm thick differs in transmittance from the same material in a sheet 0.8 mm thick in a 1 : 10 model. It is normal practice to leave windows in a model as blank openings in the wall, and to apply corrections to the measured illuminances. The correction factors must include every reduction of transmittance: window frames, glazing bars, the glazing materials, dirt, blinds. The overall transmittance is typically 0.5, and can be much less.

MODELS FOR VISUAL APPRAISAL OF DAYLIGHT

A physical model can be as quick to build as a virtual model, and can be useful when exploring alternative solutions when designing. It is especially helpful for students when learning to design, because it directly links the physical qualities of a space with their perceptual effect. An artificial sky is not needed: it is better to take models outside under the real sun and sky or, if the scheme has only side windows, simply to view it indoors with the model windows next to the glass of a real window.

The following points are important:

1   The model must be large enough to look inside comfortably, preferably with both eyes; the view through a small peephole can be misleading. Miniature models are hard to appraise: apart from the physical limitations of close focus and monocular vision, a small well-made model has a cuteness that can affect critical observation. It is satisfactory to have a miniature TV camera on a probe, and to view the scene on a VDU. Screen-based images are so familiar that we are able to perceive them as real spaces.
2   The reflectances of surfaces must be realistic. Patterned materials such as carpets can be a problem: full-size samples in a model look grossly large. It is not necessary to produce a scaled reproduction for use in the model; a sheet of plain colour with a reflectance equal to the average of the actual material can be used. If assessment of colour is one of the purposes of the study, the hue and colour saturation of surfaces must also be realistic.

Sunlighting appraisal can be done by taking a model outdoors, then tilting and rotating it so that the pattern of shadows on the model is what would occur at the times and dates being evaluated. This is most easily done by fixing a sundial to the model, oriented correctly to model north; this indicates the rotations needed.

If a lamp is used indoors as a substitute sun, the angle of light on the model varies significantly if the source is too close. As a rule of thumb, the lamp should be a distance away at least five times the model's largest dimension.

MEASURING REFLECTANCE

For lighting calculations, what is usually required is not the laboratory-measured reflectance of a small sample of a material, but the average reflectance of the material in its context on site, affected by weathering and dirt.

Method 1: incident and reflected illuminance

This works only with large matt surfaces. Use an illuminance meter to measure the light falling on the surface, then, at a distance of about a metre from the surface, take a reading with the sensor facing the surface. The disadvantage is that the backward- or downward-facing reading covers a hemisphere of view angle, and this is greater than the angle subtended by the surface being measured. Approaching the surface to take closer readings tends often to obstruct the light falling on the area to be measured.

Method 2: visual comparison

A set of about eight cards in various shades of grey of known reflectance is useful for quickly estimating reflectance of materials on site. Cards of A5 size are the most convenient to work with, and the colour should run to the edge of the card, with no white border; the small chips on paint sample cards are too small.

The procedure is to lay the cards against the material and select the two cards that are just brighter and just darker than the sample, and estimate from these the sample reflectance. In the viewing, it is sometimes helpful to half-close the eyes; and if the sample has a strong hue, an effort of will is necessary to visualise this on a black–white scale.

Shiny surfaces can be assessed if the surface of the cards is similarly shiny. The usefulness of a set of cards in matt grey can be increased by pressing a transparent film across half of each card.

Method 3: measuring luminance

With most types of luminance meter, the user looks into an eyepiece that superimposes a target circle on the view, and that also shows a digital display of the luminance of the target. The units used are candelas per square metre or, in the USA, foot-Lamberts. The photographic equivalent is a reflected-light spot meter.

Luminance readings are taken of the surface being studied and of a reference surface such as a card of known reflectance under the same illuminance. Usually, this can be laid on the surface and side-by-side readings made. If the reference has reflectance ρ_r, and the luminances of the test material and the sample are L_x and L_r, the reflectance of the test material is

$$\rho_x = \rho_r \, L_x / L_r.$$

This gives the diffuse reflectance of the material. If the material is glossy, its specular reflectance at a given angle of incidence is found by measuring the luminance of the card and the luminance of the reflection of the card seen at that angle. The reflected luminance divided by the directly viewed luminance gives the specular reflectance.

Using paired cells to eliminate calibration differences

There are two major sources of error in field measurement: calibration differences and changeability of daylight. When measuring ratios, such as indoor-to-outdoor illuminance or the transmittance of glazing, these errors can be eliminated by duplicating measurements with paired cells. These cells need not be cross-calibrated.

Example: measuring transmittance loss due to dirt on glazing. A patch of glazing is cleaned; one illuminance cell, *a*, is placed against this, facing the sky. A second cell, *b*, is placed by a nearby uncleaned area of glazing, also facing the sky. Simultaneous readings are taken: E_{1a} and E_{1b}. The cells are then swapped about and another pair of simultaneous readings recorded: E_{2a} and E_{2b}. It does not matter if the sky illuminance has changed. The transmittance of the film of dirt on the glazing (the dirty glass illuminance divided by the clean glass illuminance) is then given by

$$\tau_{dirt} = \sqrt{\frac{E_{1b}E_{2a}}{E_{1a}E_{2b}}}$$

HIGH-DYNAMIC-RANGE (HDR) PHOTOGRAPHS

Digital cameras have a relatively small brightness sensitivity range on any individual exposure, but a series of images at different exposures or sensitivities enables a scene of wide luminance range to be recorded, and the numerical value of the pixels then makes it possible to derive luminance and chromatic data. The technique is, at the time of writing, largely confined to research units and specialist departments, but the potential is so great that the methodology will become widespread.

Figure W11.1 shows an image of a tree together with a false-colour map that emphasises luminance differences.

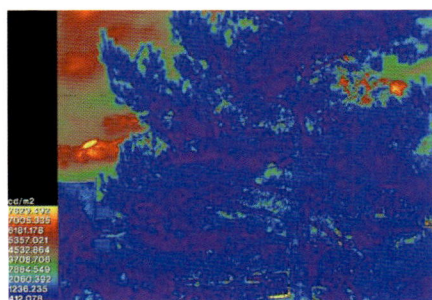

W11.1

A false-colour and a conventional image. The false-colour image quantifies brightness and maps luminance to hue. Pixel values from the original digital photograph were converted to luminance measures after calibration of the camera. Usually, two or more photographs at different exposures are used to compensate for the restricted brightness sensitivity range of the camera sensors.

12 *How to* identify faults in workplace lighting

This worksheet focuses on desk-based tasks such as in offices, classrooms and areas in the home where computers are used. The principles apply, though, to work places generally – in the kitchen, for example, or an industrial workshop – and also to situations not normally considered as 'work' but where there is a significant visual task, such as walking along an unfamiliar route or looking at museum exhibits.

Users often identify the problem incorrectly when the lighting is faulty. It is, for example, normal to complain of 'too much light' when the cause is not exceptionally high illuminance but shiny reflections. Sometimes, complaints about poor lighting reflect dissatisfaction with other factors, such as a general dislike of the job, or discomfort due to other environmental conditions.

Where side windows provide daylighting, problems are most likely to occur in vertical or near-vertical surfaces, especially when VDUs are used – either because the bright view outside is close within the field of view to the screen, or when the user is facing away from the window but view outside is reflected in glossy surfaces. With ceiling-mounted luminaires and roof lights, problems occur on near-horizontal surfaces – keyboards, glossy printed paper, pencil writing. Figure W12.1 shows the three main causes of troublesome reflections in office-like workplaces.

Almost all of the faults arise from the geometry of the layout – the relative positions of light source, task object and user, and the consequent angles between them. Successful workplace lighting design begins by determining what the user needs to see, then planning the layout so that the light falling on the task enhances the critical features, and finally ensuring that the user's view of the task is clear and comfortable.

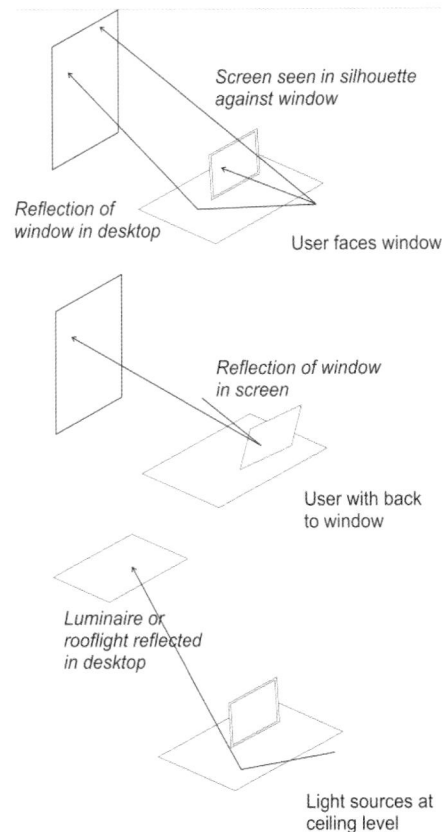

Screen seen in silhouette against window

Reflection of window in desktop

User faces window

Reflection of window in screen

User with back to window

Luminaire or rooflight reflected in desktop

Light sources at ceiling level

W12.1

Different ways in which troublesome reflections can occur.

PROCEDURE

1 Talk to users and observe them working. Ask them to demonstrate the circumstances that cause difficulty or discomfort.

2 Sit or stand in users' working positions and follow the check list. The procedure works by systematically blocking the light in different ways and then, in each case, judging whether visibility or comfort are altered. A piece of card (usually an A4 sheet) is used as a blocking screen.

	Problem	Cause	Test
1	**Discomfort from direct glare**	The sky or another bright object is close to the task in the user's field of view and causes discomfort, which usually increases with time.	**From the viewpoint of the user, screen the bright source from the eye.** Does this increase comfort?
2	**Disability from direct glare**	Task visibility is inhibited by a light source within the field of view or a bright background to the task. This can occur with no discomfort. The eye adapts to the overall brightness and not to the task area, which is 'under-exposed'.	**Screen the source from the eye and look at the task.** Does it become easier to see fine detail and low contrast?
3	**Discomfort from bright shiny reflections outside the task**	Glossy surfaces close to the task area give a mirror-like reflection of the sky or other sources. These are uncomfortable.	**Screen the surfaces around the task from each source in turn.** Does this increase comfort? Which light sources cause shiny reflections?
4	**Disability from bright shiny reflections outside the task**	Task visibility is inhibited by bright reflections.	**Repeat 3: screen the surfaces around the task from each source in turn.** This time, does it become easier to see fine detail and low contrast in the task?
5	**Disability from reflections in the task itself**	Partially glossy surfaces in the actual task area give bright reflections that are superimposed on the task detail. This is often called a 'veiling reflection'. It makes the task visually more difficult. It is a very common problem with VDUs, with pictures in art galleries and with white boards in classrooms.	**Screen the task from the light source.** Is visibility of detail improved? Alternatively, move the source or the task, or look at the task from different angles. Does task visibility change as positions change?
6	**Distraction**	Moving objects or rapidly changing patterns of light distract the eye from the task area. The movement does not need to be in the immediate field of view: the peripheral visual field is especially sensitive to movement. Flicker from old and poor-quality fluorescent lamps can be a serious nuisance.	**Screen the eye from the movement.** Does this make it easier to concentrate on the task?
7	**Dazzle**	The task brightness is greater than the eye can tolerate. The level at which this occurs depends on the state of the eye's adaptation. A dark-adapted eye experiences dazzle for a few seconds when normal lighting is switched on. When the eye is adapted to strong daylight, the brightness of sunlight on white paper is dazzling, and this does not improve: it remains above the range to which the eye can adapt.	**Screen the sun or other powerful source from the task. Wait several minutes for the eye to adapt.** Are comfort and visibility improved?
8	**Shadows reduce task illuminance**	The position of the light source is such that direct light on the task is blocked by the user's body, furniture or other objects.	**Experiment by changing the relative positions of source, task and user.** Is task visibility improved?
9	**The wrong features of the task object are enhanced**	Typical faults: lighting at a shallow angle exaggerates the texture of a surface, masking colour and pattern; shiny reflections over-emphasise 3D shape; silhouette is enhanced at the expense of detail.	**Experiment with different directions of incident light and by replacing small bright sources with large sources of lower brightness, and vice versa.** Is the visibility of particular features of the task improved?
10	**Insufficient illuminance**	None of the above faults occur, but the user has difficulty in discerning small detail or minor contrast differences. This may occur especially with older users.	**Check maintenance.** Are blinds closed unnecessarily? Are luminaires clean and lamps in good condition? **Check whether vision can be aided.** Can visibility be enhanced with magnification, selective colour coding, a different background, or other means? **Measure illuminance and compare with code values.** Take user age and disabilities into account.
11	**Insufficient control**	The user is not able to control his or her immediate environment or is prevented from adapting to changes when they occur.	**Imagine conditions different from those at the time of testing.** For example: direct sunshine on the window; decreasing daylight during the afternoon; activities of nearby users. Can the user respond by controlling blinds, external shading or electric lighting? Can the user change his or her working position?

13 *How to* use the right word

Lighting has its own vocabulary of specialist words. Some of these are ordinary words in everyday use, but are used in lighting with a precise technical meaning; some are unfamiliar terms that are found only in technical writing.

UNITS

Many units of measurement are familiar from everyday use. For some, we have a good sense of their magnitude: we know that 1000 volts is likely to be dangerous and that a suitcase weighing 40 kg would feel heavy and be expensive to take on an aircraft. Other units become familiar when studying science and engineering and are used throughout the physical world to describe phenomena such as velocity, force, power and mass: watts, joules and newtons are examples. The units of light are in neither category. At first

sight, the words used seem strange and, because the units are not used in any other context, we lack the experience that gives a sense of their magnitude.

These units are unique to lighting, because 'light' is not an independent physical quantity. It is merely a part of the spectrum of electromagnetic radiation, as are infrared radiation, ultraviolet, x-rays, radio waves, and several other phenomena. It has meaning only in terms of human vision, and is defined arbitrarily by a standardised graph of the sensitivity of the human eye to radiation at different wavelengths.

These units are parts of the international metric system. In a system widely used in North America, the linear unit is the foot instead of the metre; the corresponding unit of illuminance is the lumen per square foot. Luminance is measured in foot-Lamberts instead of candelas per square metre.

The technical word	What it means in the context of lighting
Light	Electromagnetic radiation that can be sensed by the human eye.
Sunlight	The light of the direct beam of the sun.
Skylight	Light from the sun that has been scattered in the atmosphere. It forms the sky, an apparent hemisphere of light. It is often called 'diffuse daylight' and, in older publications, just 'daylight', which conflicts with the present-day use of that word. 'Skylight' is sometimes used to describe a window in a roof.
Daylight	Sunlight and skylight together.
Direct light	Light falling on a surface that has not been reflected by another surface but comes directly from the source. Some publications use the expression 'initial light'.
Illumination	A general word used to mean the light falling on a place, the process of lighting. It is distinct from 'illuminance', one of the units of light, which is described below.
Daylight factor	The daylight illuminance on a surface expressed as a percentage of the illuminance on a horizontal surface with an unobstructed view of the sky (such as open ground). It excludes direct sunlight and is normally based on the assumption of a densely overcast sky. It does include light reflected from other buildings and the ground; and, indoors, it includes the effects of interreflection within the room.
Sky component	The part of the daylight factor due to light received directly from the sky. It is often used to describe the skylight falling on the outside face of a window, and referred to as the 'vertical sky component'. Other parts of the daylight factor are the 'externally reflected component' and the 'internally reflected component'.
Sky factor	A precursor of daylight factor, which has remained fossilised in legal proceedings, particularly Rights of Light cases. Technically, it is the sky component calculated on the basis of a uniformly bright sky and unglazed windows.
Luminaire	A light fitting. The enclosure that protects a lamp and controls the directional distribution of light.
Lamp	The actual source of light within a luminaire.

Unit, *abbreviation*	*What it describes*	*Symbol*	*Typical values*
lumen, lm	Luminous flux The flow of light, the total output from a source	F	100 W incandescent lamp: 1,360 lm
lux, lx	Illuminance The light falling on a surface: lumens per square metre, lm/m²	E	From a candle 1 m away: 1 lx Typical value in a general office: 500 lx From sun and bright sky in summer: 100,000 lx
candela, cd	Intensity The quantity of light flowing in a particular direction from a lamp or a small patch of sky: lumens per steradian, lm/sr	I	From a small display spotlight: 10,000 cd
candelas per square metre, cd/m²	Luminance The measurable brightness of a surface or of the sky: lumens per steradian per square metre, lm/(sr·m²)	L	Typical overcast sky: 3,000 cd/m² white paper in strong sunlight: 30,000 cd/m²

If the illuminance on a surface measured 100 lx on a lightmeter in SI units, the reading in US customary units would be 100/10.764 = 9.290 lumens per square foot.

If a bright surface had a luminance of 100 candelas per square metre, its luminance in US customary units would be $100\pi/10.764 = 29.186$ foot-Lamberts.

14 Data sheet *Typical reflectance of materials under diffuse daylight*

Exterior			*Interior*	
Snow (new)	0.8		White paper	0.8
Sand	0.3		Stainless steel	0.4
Paving	0.2		Cement screed	0.4
Earth (dry)	0.2		Carpet (cream)	0.4
Earth (moist)	0.1		Wood (light veneers)	0.4
Green vegetation	0.1		Wood (medium colours)	0.2
White glazed tile	0.7		Wood (dark)	0.1
Portland stone	0.6		Quarry tiles	0.1
Medium limestone	0.4		Window glass	0.1
Concrete	0.4		Carpet (deep colours)	0.1
Brickwork (buff)	0.3			
Brickwork (red)	0.2			
Granite	0.2			
Window glass	0.1 (see Algorithms and Equations, Section 5.5–5.8)			
Tree foliage	0.1 (see Chapter 8)			

Paint colours, with Munsell reference				
White N9.5	0.85		Strong red 7.5R4.5/16	0.18
Pale cream 5Y9/2	0.81		Strong blue 10B4/10	0.15
Light grey N8.5	0.68		Dark grey 5Y4/0.5	0.14
Strong yellow 6.25Y8.5/13	0.64		Dark brown 10Y3/6	0.10
Mid-grey N7	0.45		Deep red-purple 7.5RP3/6	0.10
Strong green 5G5/10	0.22		Black N 1.5	0.05

15 Data sheet *Light transmittance of glazing*

For calculating the diffuse light entering a window, the value of the glazing transmittance should take into account the directional distribution of the incident light. The mean value of this is lower than the regular transmittance, which is the most commonly published value. An approximate conversion rule is that diffuse transmittance is 0.9 × regular transmittance. Algorithms and Equations, Section 5.5 gives a formula for calculating the mean transmittance over a rectangular opening.

The figures given below for glass products are typical values and may be used in preliminary calculations, but specific values for particular products should be obtained from the manufacturer. The transmittance of louvres such as Venetian blinds depends on the material (specular and diffuse reflectances), the blade angle and the incident direction of the light.

Material	Transmittance of diffuse light	Transmittance of light beam at normal incidence
Clear glass 6mm	0.80	0.87
Body-tinted glass 6 mm: bronze	0.46	0.50
Double glazing: sealed unit, clear + clear	0.69	0.76
Sealed unit, clear + low-emissivity coated	0.66	0.73
Sealed unit, clear + clear with silver reflective coating	0.27	0.30
Translucent fabric blinds	0.1–0.4	
Venetian blinds: louvres fully open in direction of incident beam		0.6
Venetian blinds: louvres fully closed		<0.1
Venetian blinds: horizontal louvres, diffuse incident light	0.3	

16 Data sheet *Reduction of glazing transmittance due to dirt*

The tables give typical numbers based on the medians of measured values in Sheffield, UK. Very high and very low transmittances can occur.

Typical percentage reduction in glazing transmittance due to dirt deposition

Room function	Location	
	Rural/suburban	Urban
Residential Private rooms and communal areas, few occupants, good maintenance, no smoking	4	8
Commercial, educational Rooms used by groups of people, areas with office equipment or with some smoking	4	10
Polluted and heavily used interiors Swimming pools, gymnasia, areas with industrial machinery or heavy smoking	16	20

Corrections to be applied for various exposure conditions

Exposure	Slope of glazing		
	Vertical	Inclined	Horizontal
Exposed to heavy rain	×0.5	×1.5	×3
Normal exposure for location	×1	×2	×3
Exposed to snow	×1	×3	×4
Glazing sheltered from rain by overhang. Weathered glazing or leaded windows	×3	—	—

Blank values indicate that general data are not available.

Maintenance factors to be used in daylighting calculations

Room function	Exposure	Slope of glazing					
		Vertical		Inclined		Horizontal	
		Rural/suburban	Urban	Rural/suburban	Urban	Rural/suburban	Urban
Residential Private rooms and communal areas, few occupants, good maintenance, no smoking	Driving rain exposure	0.98	0.95	0.94	0.88	0.88	0.76
	Normal exposure	0.96	0.92	0.92	0.84	0.88	0.76
	Heavy snow exposure	0.96	0.92	0.88	0.76	0.84	0.68
	Sheltered by overhang	0.88	0.76	—	—	—	—
Commercial, educational Rooms used by groups of people, areas with office equipment or with some smoking	Driving rain exposure	0.98	0.95	0.94	0.85	0.88	0.70
	Normal exposure	0.96	0.90	0.92	0.80	0.88	0.70
	Heavy snow exposure	0.96	0.90	0.88	0.70	0.84	0.60
	Sheltered by overhang	0.88	0.70	—	—	—	—
Polluted and heavily used interiors Swimming pools, gymnasia, areas with industrial machinery or heavy smoking	Driving rain exposure	0.92	0.90	0.76	0.70	0.52	0.40
	Normal exposure	0.84	0.80	0.68	0.60	0.52	0.40
	Heavy snow exposure	0.84	0.80	0.53	0.40	0.36	0.20
	Sheltered by overhang	0.52	0.40	—	—	—	—

Blank values indicate that general data are not available.

17 Data sheet *Current daylight criteria in the UK*

The publication of BS 8206 Pt 2 in 1992 and BRE 209 'Site layout planning for daylight and sunlight: a guide to good practice' in 1991 introduced new guidelines, in particular for dwellings. They used as criteria the average daylight factor linked to rules covering room depth, and sunshine availability measured in probable sunlight hours. They assessed the impact of a development on existing buildings in terms of the reduction in the vertical sky component and available sunlight.

BS 8206–2:2008 'LIGHTING FOR BUILDINGS. CODE OF PRACTICE FOR DAYLIGHTING'

The British Standard was revised in 2008. The current edition acts as the ultimate reference for daylighting criteria in the UK. It is a guidance document, not a mandatory standard, and it is one of a series of Standards on environmental conditions in buildings. It is intended to complement BS EN 12464, which covers electric lighting design.

In revising the Standard, a greatly increased emphasis was placed on daylight and health.

On health generally:

'... it is important that occupants of buildings, particularly those of limited mobility in, for example, hospitals and nursing homes, and people who might be unable to go outside much, are given access to high levels of daylight, particularly in the mornings, to assist the entrainment of circadian rhythms ... buildings used by such people should have spaces with high levels of daylight, such as conservatories, which are readily accessible.'

On view:

'Unless an activity requires the exclusion of daylight, a view out-of-doors should be provided irrespective of quality. All occupants of a building should have the opportunity for the refreshment and relaxation afforded by a change of scene and focus. Even a limited view outside can be valuable. If an external view outside cannot be provided, occupants should have an internal view possessing some of the qualities of a view-out-doors, for example, into an atrium.'

The Standard states that all occupants of a building should have the opportunity for the refreshment and relaxation afforded by a change of scene and focus. Any outside view is better than none. The need to supervise a particular outside area might be required and the need for privacy must be considered. A table (reproduced as Table 6.2 in this book) gives minimum recommended window areas when windows are restricted to one wall.

Daylight and room brightness

The function of daylighting extends beyond task illumination. There are two general requirements – to give an attractive character to a room and to convey information about the outside – and both sunlight and skylight must be considered. The Standard states that controlled entry of sunlight into buildings is rarely unwelcome in the UK, provided it can be controlled by users; but uncontrolled entry of sunlight is intolerable. In rooms where the occupants have a reasonable expectation of sunlight, it should be present for at least 25% of probable sunlight hours, including at least 5% during winter months (September to March).

Skylight is measured by the average daylight factor. The provision of electric lighting in a room is associated with this. If the daylight factor is 5% or more, daytime electric lighting will rarely be necessary, but the large area of windows might cause thermal problems. A value of 2–5% gives an attractive daylit appearance, but supplementary electric lighting is usually necessary. Below this, electric light becomes the principal source of illumination.

In dwellings, there should be at least 1% in bedrooms, 1.5% in living rooms and 2% in kitchens, with a best practice minimum of 2% throughout.

Task lighting

Illuminance should be as specified in BS EN 12464; it is assumed that daylight illuminances for tasks should be the same as for electric lighting. Glare and bright specular reflections in the field of view must be avoided.

BRE 209 'SITE LAYOUT PLANNING FOR DAYLIGHT AND SUNLIGHT: A GUIDE TO GOOD PRACTICE, 1991'

This publication of the Building Research Establishment is the document most used by planning authorities in development control. It covers daylight within new developments, gardens and open spaces, existing buildings, and adjoining development land. In the introduction, it states that it is advisory and not mandatory, that it should not be seen as an instrument of planning policy and that numerical guidelines other than those given may be adopted. But, by the nature of development control, it is useful to have a rigid and authoritative reference, and 'Site layout planning' tends to be adopted to fulfil this need.

For the purpose of ensuring adequate daylight in a development, the vertical sky component on the exterior face of the building is used. Taking reference points at a height of 2 m above the ground at window positions in plan or, if window positions are not fixed, at a series of points not more than 8 m apart, a vertical sky component of 27% is stated to indicate the potential for good daylighting. This corresponds to the light received when there is a continuous obstruction 25° above the horizon.

Where the daylight of an existing building may be reduced by the construction of a new building, the general aim should be to make the impact as small as possible. Any reduction to below 27% vertical sky component should be minimised, especially if the value is reduced to less than 0.8 of its previous value. The effect of a new obstruction on an existing building can be assessed also by plotting the no-sky line with and without the obstruction. If, with the obstruction, the room area that receives direct daylight (the area in front of the no-sky line) is reduced to less that 0.8 of its value without the obstruction, the occupants will notice a significant reduction in daylight.

The value of a site and its potential for development can be reduced if the development of a neighbouring site reduces the available daylight. The recommendation in 'Site layout planning' is that reference points 2 m above ground on the boundary line should have a minimum vertical sky component of 17% or more, a value equivalent to a horizontal obstruction of 43°. The reference points should be spaced so that every part of the boundary lies within a horizontal distance of 4 m from one of them.

Sunlight in dwellings and in non-residential buildings with a particular requirement for sunlight is considered. The criterion used is that in a building that has one or more walls facing within 90° of south, on at least one of these walls there should be sunlight for at least one-quarter of probable sunlight hours, including 5% or more during the period 21 September to 21 March. This is measured, as with the vertical sky component, at 8 m centres along a line 2 m above ground. When sunlight on existing buildings is affected, a reduction to 0.8 of its former value of either the annual or the winter sunlight hours is considered to be an adverse effect.

Sunlight in gardens or other external amenity spaces is desirable for comfort and for vegetation growth. The presence of possible sunlight on 21 March is used as a criterion. It is suggested that no more than two-fifths and preferably less than a quarter of the ground area in such a space should not receive some sunlight on that day.

'Site layout planning' also considers access to sunlight for passive solar heating, and discusses other aspects of a site's physical environment, including solar dazzle by reflection in glazed façades.

CALCULATIONS

Both BS 8206 and 'Site layout planning' contain methods of calculation. The Standard gives the BRE average daylight factor formula and a maximum room depth procedure. It also provides diagrams for sunpaths and probable sunlight hours. 'Site layout planning' gives graphical tools – indicators using overlays and dot diagrams for sunlight availability, sunpaths and solar gain, and for skylight.

In practice, there is often uncertainty in daylight calculations submitted with planning applications and in disputes about adjacent sites. Several software packages are available for daylight factor calculation. Some compute point daylight factors and derive average daylight factors from these; it is not uncommon to obtain results that differ significantly from those calculated with average daylight factor formulae. Errors arise from lack of consistency in the use of factors such as for dirt on windows, the use of direct instead of diffuse glass transmittance, and the treatment of balconies and secondary spaces. A particular source of error occurs when a window area below working plane level is included in the overall window area; its contribution to working plane illuminance is only about 15% of the same area of higher windows. Sometimes in estimating the impact of a new development on an existing building, the decrease in average daylight factor is used instead of the vertical sky component; although the relationship is linear except at very low levels, the proportionality is not 1 : 1. A reduction of 20% in the average daylight factor is equivalent to a reduction of more than 24% in the vertical sky component. A misinterpretation of the guidelines leads to a larger reduction than allowed.

RIGHTS OF LIGHT

English law provides a remedy when a long-established access to daylight is blocked. If a window has had an uninterrupted view of the sky for more than 20 years, a Right of Light over neighbouring property is acquired. If the construction of a building on the neighbouring property blocks the light, the owner or tenant of the affected property can sue.

The criterion of infringement is a very low illuminance. For a case to succeed, the level of daylight must be dramatically reduced: a room is taken to be adequately lit if, on a plane across the room at a height of 0.85 m, more than about half of the area has a sky factor of 0.2%. The precise proportion of area is the subject of debate.

The figure of 0.2% sky factor was established in the 1930s. It is based on an assumption that for office work the threshold of adequate lighting is 1 lumen per square foot (or 1 foot-candle, approximately 10 lx) and that the light from cloudy sky is equivalent to 500 lumens per square foot.

In terms of present-day lighting practice, this is nonsense, for several reasons: a sky factor itself is a poor predictor of daylight quantity; current standards typically require 500 lx for general office lighting, an illuminance 50 times greater than the supposed threshold; electric lighting and daylight are used in conjunction; energy costs must be taken into account; and so on.

But this is not necessarily relevant. There are good grounds for protecting the access of existing buildings to daylight and for giving recourse to legal action when this is threatened by development. The criterion has been in place for 80 years, and there is little evidence to suggest that it is either too high or too low when all the attributes of daylighting are considered. This condition of 0.2% sky factor over half the room area cannot be justified by the requirements of office lighting, but it may be an acceptable indicator of whether compensation is appropriate.

The acquisition to a Right of Light can be blocked by serving a notice of a 'notional obstruction', which has the same effect in law as the construction of a blocking screen on the site. Rights cannot be acquired over Crown land or by an unbuilt site; it applies only to specific windows.

The law applies only to skylight: there is no right to sunlight or to a view.

There is further discussion on calculations and accuracy in Chapters 6 and 8; the sky factor and daylight factor methods are developed in Chapter 7.

18 Data sheet *Sky diagrams*

LIST OF DIAGRAMS

Each sky diagram is given in stereographic projection, 's', and equal solid angle projection 'e':

1 Projection grid
2 Sunpath diagram for London
3 Probable sunlight hours for London
4 Vertical sky component 0.1% per dot
5 Vertical sky component 0.2% per dot
6 Horizontal sky component 0.1% per dot
7 Horizontal sky component 0.2% per dot
8 Sunpath diagram 35° N
9 Sunpath diagram 45° N
10 Sunpath diagram 55° N
11 Configuration factor
12 Horizon factor (horizon index)

Stereographic projection

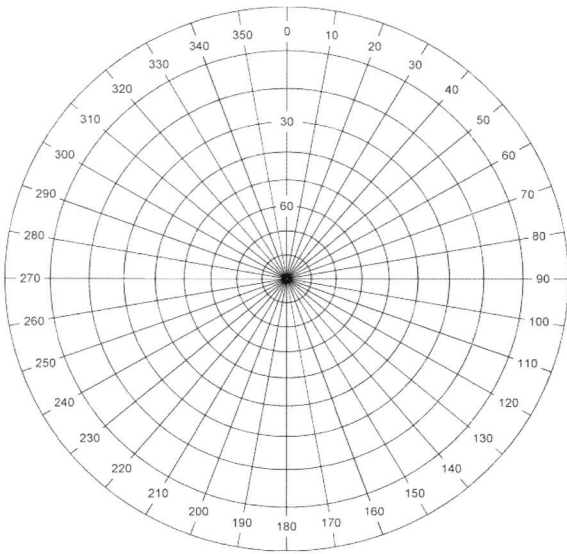

1s

Equal solid angle projection

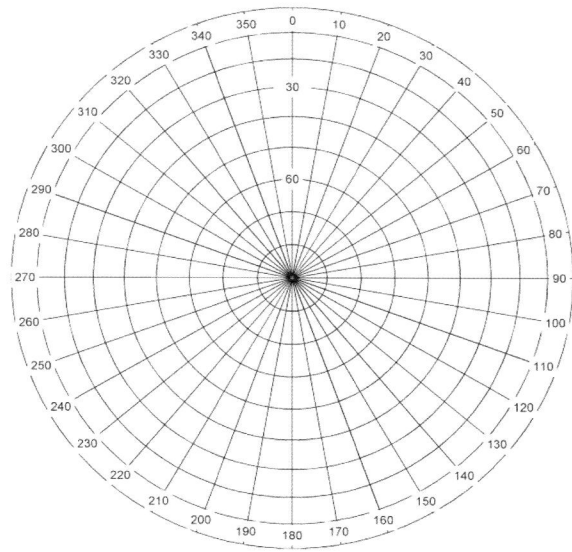

1e

Sunpath diagram
Latitude 51° N
Stereographic projection

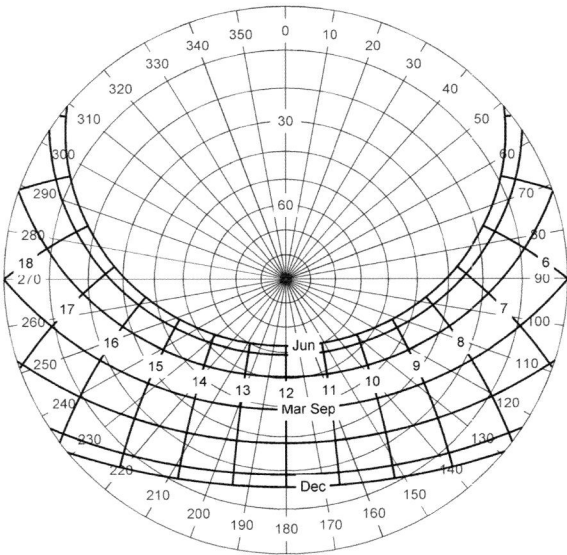

2s

Sunpath diagram
Latitude 51° N
Equal solid angle projection

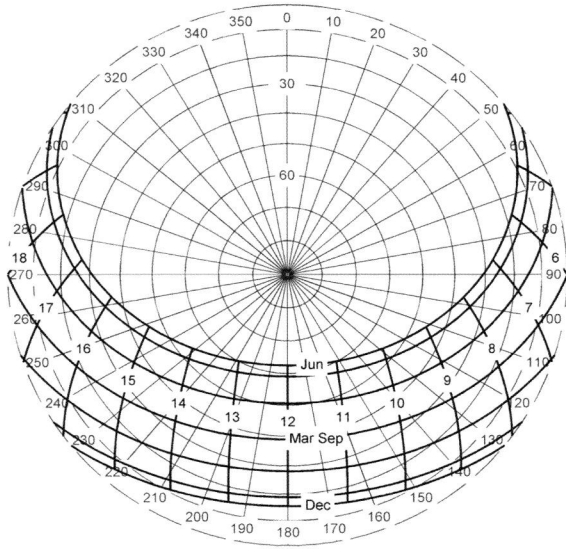

2e

Probable sunlight hours
Stereographic projection
Each dot represents 0.2%
summer half-year red
winter half-year blue
1 Nov — 28 Feb o
51° N

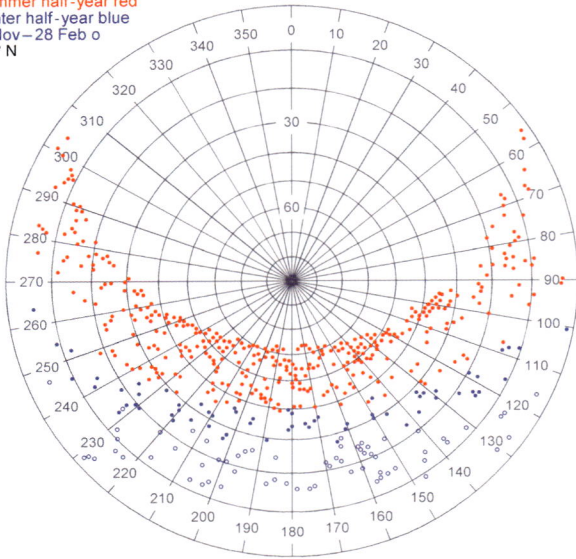

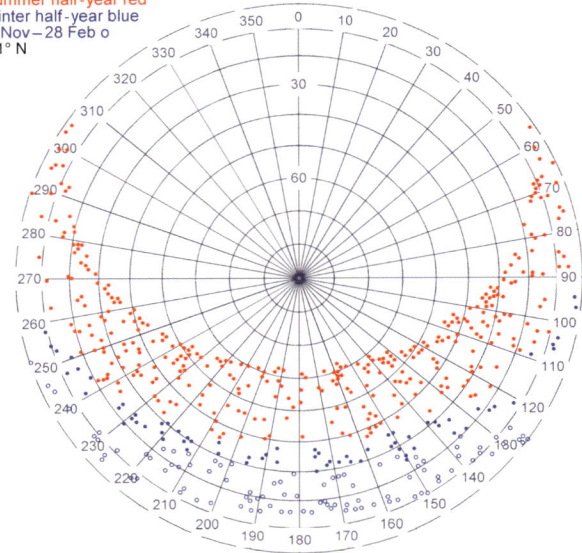

3s

Probable sunlight hours
Equal solid angle projection
Each dot represents 0.2%
summer half-year red
winter half-year blue
1 Nov — 28 Feb o
51° N

3e

Vertical sky component
Stereographic projection
Each dot represents 0.1%

direction of view

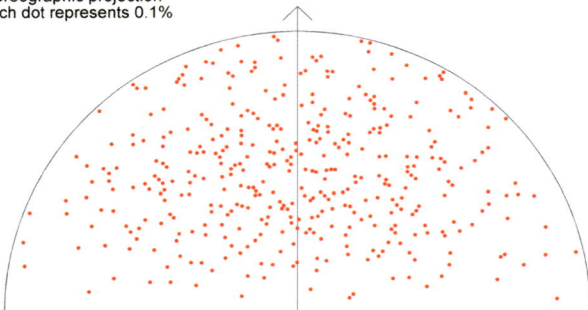

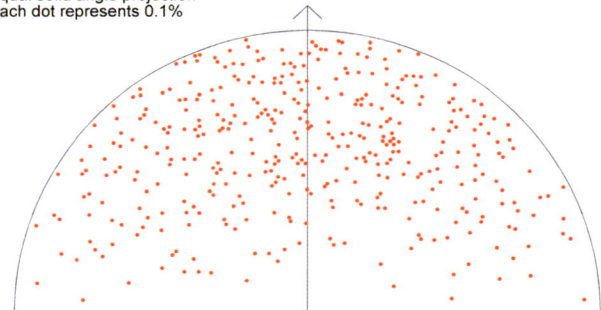

4s

Vertical sky component
Equal solid angle projection
Each dot represents 0.1%

direction of view

4e

Vertical sky component
Stereographic projection
Each dot represents 0.2%

direction of view

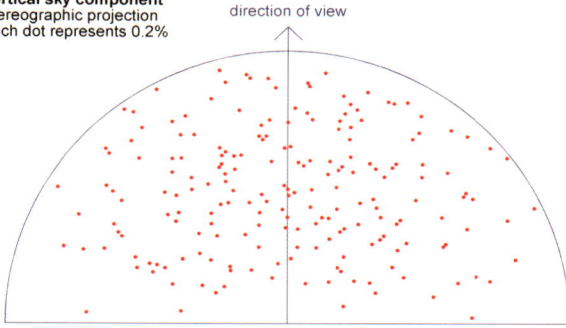

5s

Vertical sky component
Equal solid angle projection
Each dot represents 0.2%

direction of view

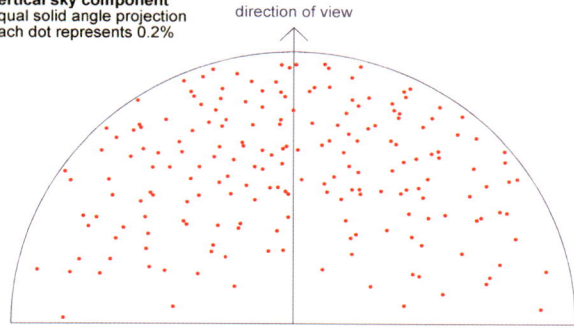

5e

Horizontal sky component
Stereographic projection
Each dot represents 0.1%

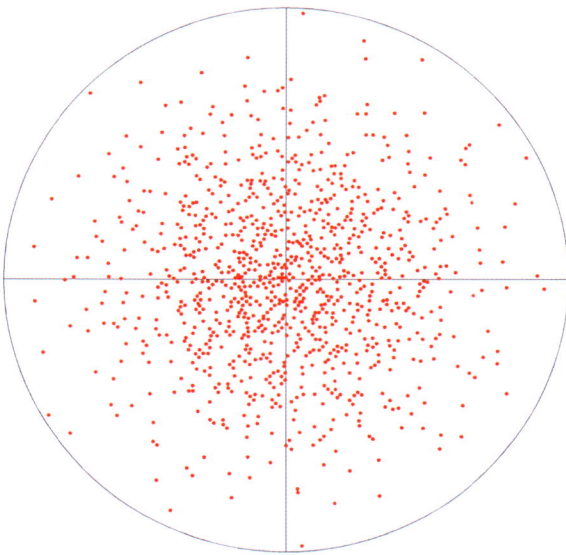

6s

Horizontal sky component
Equal solid angle projection
Each dot represents 0.1%

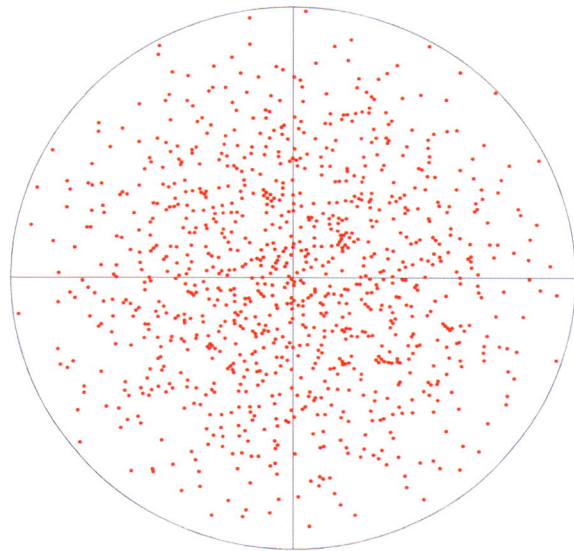

6e

Horizontal sky component
Stereographic projection
Each dot represents 0.2%

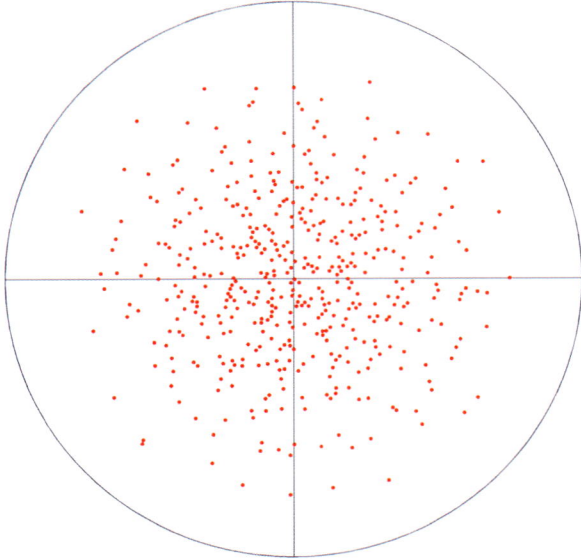

Horizontal sky component
Equal solid angle projection
Each dot represents 0.2%

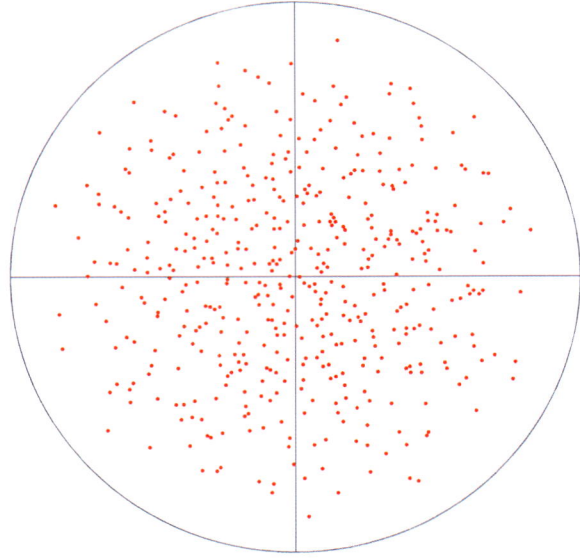

7s

7e

Sunpath diagram
Latitude 35° N
Stereographic projection

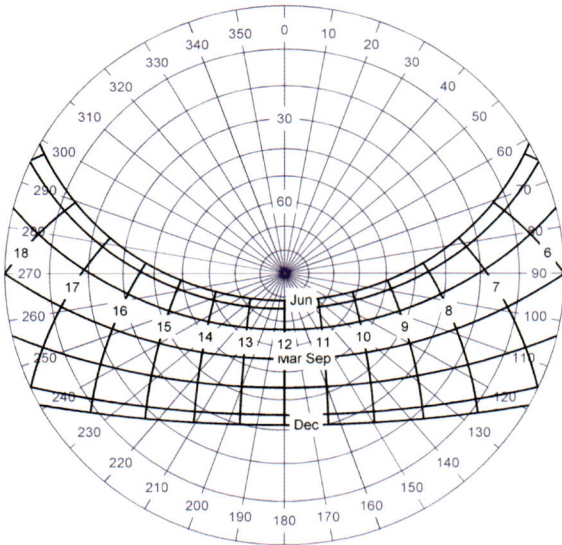

Sunpath diagram
Latitude 35° N
Equal solid angle projection

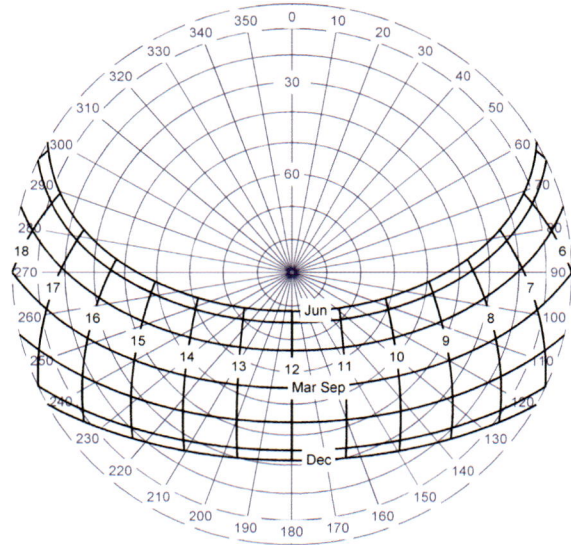

8s

8e

Sunpath diagram
Latitude 45° N
Stereographic projection

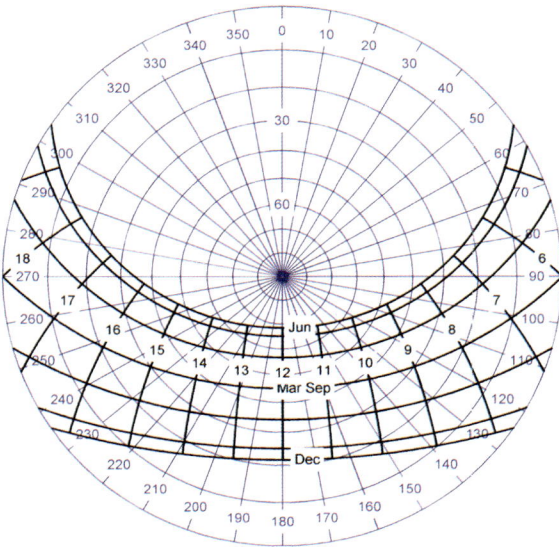

9s

Sunpath diagram
Latitude 45° N
Equal solid angle projection

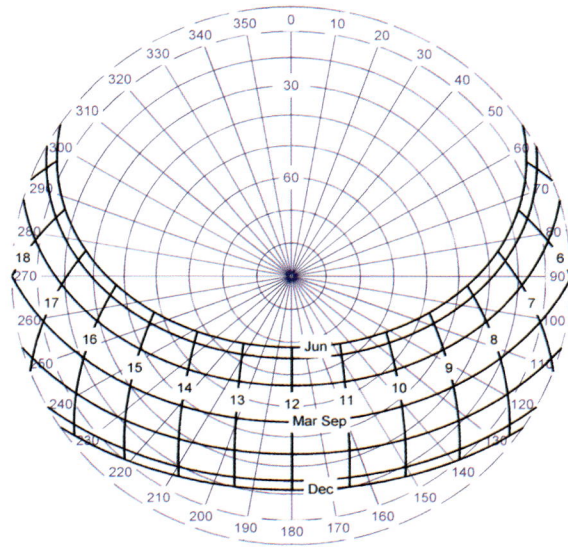

9e

Sunpath diagram
Latitude 55° N
Stereographic projection

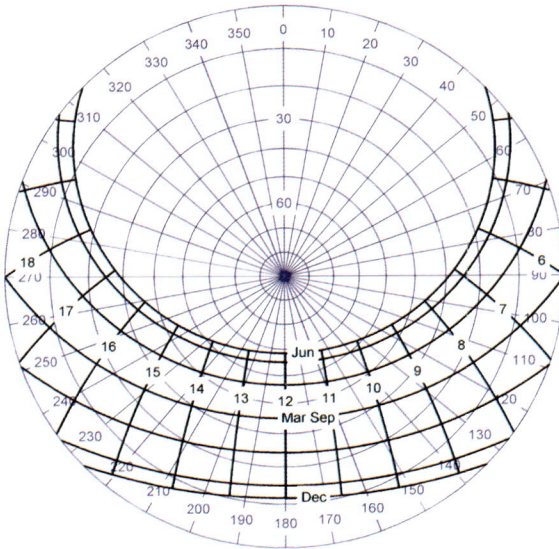

10s

Sunpath diagram
Latitude 55° N
Equal solid angle projection

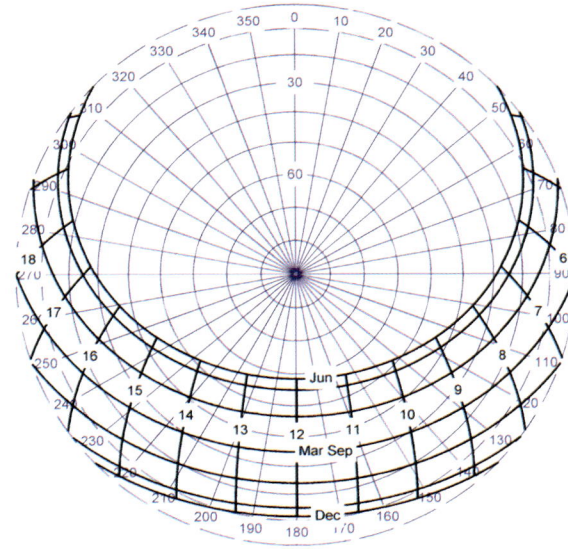

10e

Configuration factor
Stereographic projection
Each dot represents 0.001

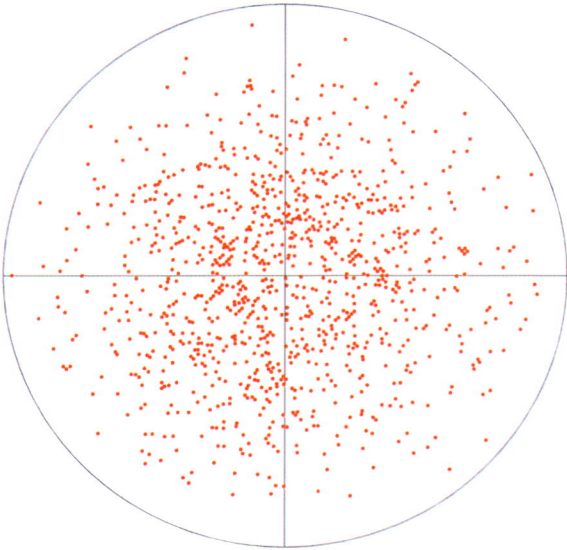

11s

Configuration factor
Equal solid angle projection
Each dot represents 0.001

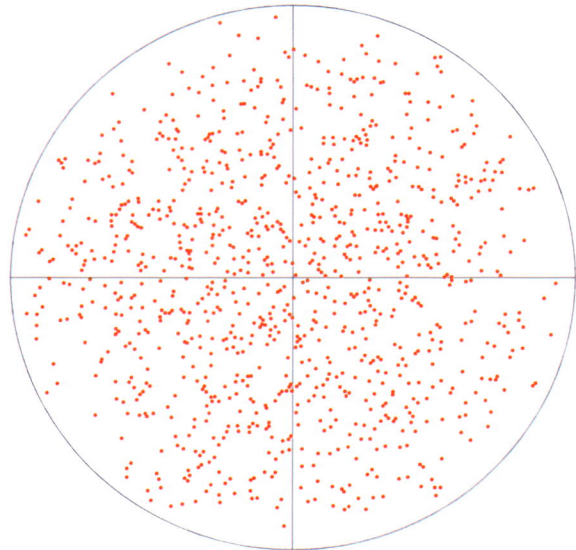

11e

Horizon factor (horizon index)
Enlarge or reduce this diagram to plan scale
33 lines: for percentage, multiply zone counts by 3.03 and round to nearest whole number

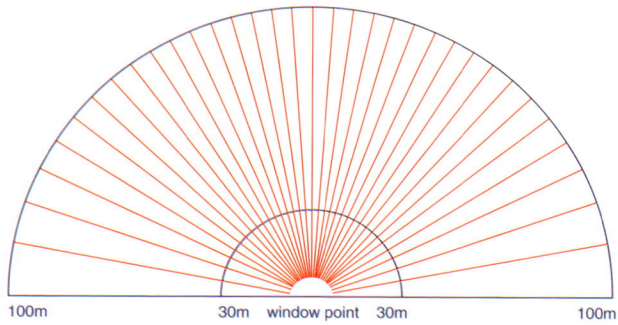

100m   30m   window point   30m   100m

12

19 Data sheet *Typical recommended task illuminances*

National and international standards and codes of practice specify working plane illuminances for various activities. They are intended primarily for electric lighting installations. This table gives typical values.

Task requirements	lux	Examples
General awareness of space; perception of detail is unimportant	50	Access routes to service areas
Movement of people; recognition of detail for short periods; background lighting	100	Corridors, storerooms for large items, auditoria, bedrooms
Recognition of detail for short periods in areas where errors may be serious	150	Plant rooms, domestic bathrooms
Areas without difficult visual tasks but occupied for long periods; short-period tasks with moderate contrast or size of detail	200	General lighting in control booths, foyers, factory areas with automated processes
Tasks such as reading normal print (moderate contrast and size of detail) over long periods	300	Workshops for large items, general library areas, school classrooms, domestic kitchens
Tasks with some details of low contrast and moderate size	500	General offices, laboratories
Tasks with low contrast and small size	700	Traditional drawing offices
Very small visual and low-contrast tasks	1000	Electronic assembly, tool rooms
Tasks with extremely small detail and low contrast	1500	Fine work and inspection
Tasks with exceptionally small detail and very low contrast	2000	Assembly of minute mechanisms

Algorithms and Equations

This list brings together all the procedures and formulae in the book. Items numbered on the left (e.g. 1.1) are set out in the pages that follow. The references down the right-hand column are to the main text.

ALGORITHM IN THIS SECTION			EQUATION, TABLE OR FIGURE IN MAIN TEXT, OR WORKSHEET
		SYMBOLS	
1		GEOMETRICAL RELATIONSHIPS	
	1.1	General coordinates	
	1.2	Local surface coordinates	
	1.3	Conversion between coordinate systems	
		Direction cosines generally	Equations (8.6)–(8.10)
	1.4	Direction cosines of the normal to a plane	
	1.5	Angle between two vectors	
	1.6	Distance and direction between two points	
	1.7	Interception of a ray and a plane	
	1.8	Test whether a point lies on a plane	
	1.9	Sides, internal angles and area of a spherical triangle	
	1.10	Subdivision of a spherical triangle	
	1.11	Stereographic and other projections of the sky	Figures 3.9–3.12; Worksheet 8 generally
2		SOLAR GEOMETRY	
	2.1	Solar declination	
	2.2	The equation of time	
	2.3	True solar time and hour angle	
	2.4	Solar elevation and azimuth	Figures 3.7 and 3.8
	2.5	Astronomical daylength	
	2.6	Shadow length	Figures 4.6–4.8
	2.7	Ground shadow area of a rectilinear building	Figure 4.9
3		LIGHT FROM THE SKY	
	3.1	Relative optical air mass	
	3.2	Illuminance turbidity	
	3.3	Extraterrestrial illuminance	
	3.4	Illuminance from direct sunlight	Figures 3.14–3.16
	3.5	Global and diffuse illuminance	Figures 3.18–3.25
	3.6	Clear sky luminance and illuminance	Figure 3.17
	3.7	Overcast sky luminance and illuminance	
4		STANDARD SKIES	
	4.1	CIE Standard General Sky	Figure 3.30
	4.2	CIE Standard Overcast Sky	Figure 3.27
	4.3	Dot diagrams based on the CIE Standard Overcast Sky	Figure 3.12; Worksheets 5 and 18

ALGORITHM IN THIS SECTION			EQUATION, TABLE OR FIGURE IN MAIN TEXT, OR WORKSHEET
5		DAYLIGHT AND OBJECTS	
	5.1	Light reflected from the ground	Figures 4.20 and 4.21
	5.2	Luminance of nearby external obstructions	Worksheet 5
	5.3	Luminance of distant objects under an overcast sky	Figure 8.20; Tables 8.3 and 8.4
	5.4	Specular reflection in external surfaces	Figures 8.22–8.24
		Sumpner's equation (integrating sphere)	Equation (2.12), Figures 2.27 and 2.28
		Cavity reflectance	Equation (2.14)
	5.5	Directional transmittance of clear glass	
	5.6	Directional transmittance of non-clear glass	
	5.7	Diffuse reflectance and transmittance of non-clear glass	
		Illuminance from reflected sunlight	Equations (8.11) and (8.12)
		Illuminances within an urban canyon	Equations (8.14)–(8.29); Worksheet 10
		Lumen method	Worksheet 6
		Energy use by lighting	Worksheet 7
	5.8	Combined overall transmittance and reflectance of non-clear glass	
6		DAYLIGHT FACTORS	
		Sky component and daylight factor on a vertical surface	Equations (7.1)–(7.9); Worksheet 3
		Average daylight factor	Equations (7.10)–(7.14); Worksheet 4
		Point daylight factor	Figures 7.18 and 7.19; Worksheet 5
	6.1	Sky factor for an unglazed vertical rectangular opening	
	6.2	Sky component for an unglazed vertical rectangular opening	
	6.3	Sky component for an unglazed horizontal rectangular opening	
	6.4	Average internally reflected component for vertical windows	
	6.5	Minimum internally reflected component for vertical windows	
7		DAYLIGHT COEFFICIENTS	
		The fundamental equation	Equations (10.1)–(10.8)
		Subdivision of the sky	Figure 10.4; Table 10.1
8		NUMERICAL METHODS	
	8.1	Configuration factor and form factor definitions	Equations (8.3)–(8.5)
	8.2	Form factors for parallel rectangles	
	8.3	Configuration factors for rectangular sources	
	8.4	Configuration factor and form factor with triangular subdivision	
	8.5	Solution of interreflection equations	Equations (10.12)–(10.16)
	8.6	Random emission from point source and diffusing surface	Equation (10.21)
		List of sources	

Symbols

Each symbol consists of a letter and one or more subscripts. For example E_{hd} refers to illuminance (E) on a horizontal surface (h) from diffuse light (d).

GENERAL SUBSCRIPTS	
e	Radiant quantities (omitted when there is no ambiguity)
v	Luminous quantities (omitted when there is no ambiguity)
s	Direct sun
o	Extraterrestrial
g	Global
d	Diffuse
cl	Clear sky
oc	Overcast sky
av	Average sky
pc	Partly cloudy sky
h	A horizontal surface
v	A vertical surface
z	Zenith

Symbol	Quantity
$\bar{a}$	Mean extinction coefficient
α	Azimuth angle
$cf_{a\text{-}b}$	Configuration factor between infinitesimal area a and finite area b
γ	Angle of elevation above the horizon
δ_s	Angle of the solar declination
D	Daylight factor
D_s	Sky component of the daylight factor
D_e	Externally reflected component of the daylight factor
D_i	Internally reflected component of the daylight factor
d_k	Daylight coefficient for sky zone k
d_{sk}	Direct component of daylight coefficient for sky zone k
E	Irradiance or illuminance
E_v	Illuminance (lux). The subscript is omitted if there is no ambiguity
E_e	Irradiance (W/m^2). The subscript is omitted if there is no ambiguity
ET	Equation of time (h)
ε	Angular distance from the zenith
$F_{a\text{-}b}$	Form factor between finite areas a and b
Hi_w	Horizon factor from a window
Hi_s	Spatial horizon factor

Symbol	Quantity
ϕ	Geographical latitude of a station (positive north of the equator, negative south of the equator)
λ	Geographical longitude of a station (negative east of Greenwich, positive west of Greenwich)
GMT	Greenwich mean time (h)
LT	Local time (h)
K	Luminous efficacy (lm/W)
L	Radiance or luminance
L_e	Radiance (W/(sr·m^2)). The subscript is omitted if there is no ambiguity
L_v	Luminance (cd/m^2). The subscript is omitted if there is no ambiguity
$L_{(\gamma,\alpha)}$	Luminance of a sky element altitude γ and azimuth α
L_z	Luminance of the sky at the zenith (cd/m^2)
m	Relative optical air mass
ρ	Diffuse reflectance
ρ^g	Reflectance of the ground
σ	Attenuation coefficient
T_c	Correlated colour temperature (K)
T_L	Linke turbidity factor
T_{il}	Illuminance turbidity factor
t_{sr}	Time of sunrise (h)
t_{ss}	Time of sunset (h)
τ	Transmittance
θ	Angle between a sky element and the sun

	PARAMETERS AND NOTES

1 Geometrical relationships

This section defines three axis systems that are commonly used in daylight modelling, then lists some useful formulae from analytic geometry.

1.1 GENERAL COORDINATES

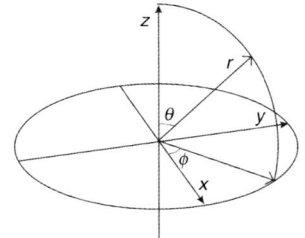

A point may be given in either Cartesian form (x, y, z) or with spherical coordinates $\{r, \phi, \theta\}$, where

$$x = r \cos\phi \, \sin\theta, \quad 0 \le \phi \le 2\pi, 0 \le \theta \le \pi$$
$$y = r \sin\phi \, \sin\theta$$
$$z = r \cos\theta$$

The path of a ray or the direction of a straight line in space is described by its direction cosines:

$$c_1 = r \cos\phi \, \sin\theta$$
$$c_2 = \sin\phi \, \sin\theta$$
$$c_3 = \cos\theta$$

Homogeneous coordinates are used in matrix operations on points and vectors. A point (x_a, y_a, z_a) is written

$$[x_a \ y_a \ z_a \ 1] \text{ or } \mathbf{a}$$

1.2 LOCAL SURFACE COORDINATES

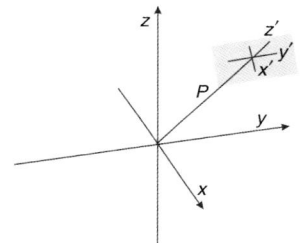

A plane surface may be defined by the direction coordinates of its normal, n_1, n_2, n_3, and its perpendicular distance, P, from the general origin. P is positive when the normal faces away from the origin. Local coordinates, (x', y', z'), have their origin at the point on the surface where the z' axis would pass through the general origin. The y' axis is always parallel with the general x–y plane; furthermore, when the x'–y' plane is parallel with the x–y plane, the y' and y axes are parallel.

It follows from these conventions that when the general origin is situated at a lower corner of a rectangular room, the local surfaces axes are oriented as shown. Direction cosines of the surface normals take the values given in the following table:

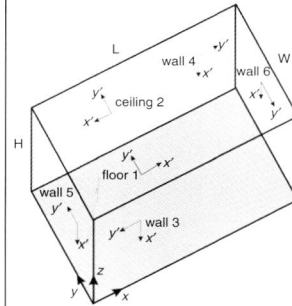

	Surface		Direction cosines		
		n_1	n_2	n_3	P
1	floor, $z = 0$	0	0	1	0
2	ceiling, $z = H$	0	0	−1	−H
3	wall, $y = 0$	0	1	0	0
4	wall, $y = W$	0	−1	0	−W
5	wall, $x = 0$	1	0	0	0
6	wall, $x = L$	−1	0	0	−L

1.3 CONVERSION BETWEEN COORDINATE SYSTEMS

The coordinates of a point with respect to one axis system may be converted to the corresponding coordinates of another axis system by matrix multiplication. The equation for the transformation takes the form **b** = **aT**, or

$$
\begin{bmatrix} x_b & y_b & z_b & 1 \end{bmatrix} = \begin{bmatrix} x_a & y_a & z_a & 1 \end{bmatrix} \begin{bmatrix} a_{11} & a_{12} & a_{13} & 0 \\ a_{21} & a_{22} & a_{23} & 0 \\ a_{31} & a_{32} & a_{33} & 0 \\ t_x & t_y & t_z & 1 \end{bmatrix}
$$

where the 3×3 submatrix determines scaling and rotation while t_x, t_y and t_z are translations along the corresponding axes. Direction cosines may be converted in the same way as the coordinates of a point.

Where an algorithm uses quantities in more than one system, a single prime indicates the use of local surface coordinates – for example (x', y', z') or c_1', c_2', c_3'; a double prime indicates sky coordinates; otherwise, general coordinates are assumed.

	PARAMETERS AND NOTES
Local surface to general 1 $$[x \quad y \quad z \quad 1] = [x' \quad y' \quad z' \quad 1] \begin{bmatrix} \cos\phi_n \cos\theta_n & \sin\phi_n \cos\theta_n & -\sin\theta_n & 0 \\ -\sin\phi_n & \cos\phi_n & 0 & 0 \\ \cos\phi_n \sin\theta_n & \sin\phi_n \sin\theta_n & \cos\theta_n & 0 \\ P\cos\phi_n \sin\theta_n & P\sin\phi_n \sin\theta_n & P\cos\theta_n & 1 \end{bmatrix}$$	$\{P, \phi_n, \theta_n\}$ is the origin of the local surface axes (x', y', z') are the coordinates of a point with respect to local surface axes
Local surface to general 2 If $n_3 = 1$, $$[x \quad y \quad z \quad 1] = [x' \quad y' \quad z' \quad 1] \begin{bmatrix} 1 & 0 & 0 & 0 \\ 0 & 1 & 0 & 0 \\ 0 & 0 & 1 & 0 \\ 0 & 0 & P & 1 \end{bmatrix}$$ if $n_3 = -1$, $$[x \quad y \quad z \quad 1] = [x' \quad y' \quad z' \quad 1] \begin{bmatrix} -1 & 0 & 0 & 0 \\ 0 & 1 & 0 & 0 \\ 0 & 0 & -1 & 0 \\ 0 & 0 & -P & 1 \end{bmatrix}$$ otherwise, $$[x \quad y \quad z \quad 1] = [x' \quad y' \quad z' \quad 1] \begin{bmatrix} \frac{n_1 n_3}{w} & \frac{n_2 n_3}{w} & -w & 0 \\ -\frac{n_2}{w} & \frac{n_1}{w} & 0 & 0 \\ n_1 & n_2 & n_3 & 0 \\ Pn_1 & Pn_2 & Pn_3 & 1 \end{bmatrix}$$ where $w = \sqrt{1 - n_3^2}$	n_1, n_2, n_3 are the direction cosines of the surface normal P is the perpendicular distance of the surface from the general origin

1.4 DIRECTION COSINES OF THE NORMAL TO A PLANE n_1, n_2, n_3, P

The plane is defined by three non-collinear points on its surface, $\mathbf{a}_1$, $\mathbf{a}_2$, $\mathbf{a}_3$, in anticlockwise order when viewed facing the surface. The points are specified by their Cartesian coordinates with respect to the general axes:

$\mathbf{a}_1 = [x_1, y_1, z_1]$, etc.

$n_1 = \dfrac{w_1}{r}, n_2 = \dfrac{w_2}{r}, n_3 = \dfrac{w_3}{r}$, provided $r \neq 0$

$P = x_1 n_1 + y_1 n_2 + z_1 n_3$

where

$w_1 = (y_2 - y_1)(z_3 - z_1) - (y_3 - y_1)(z_2 - z_1)$

$w_2 = (x_3 - x_1)(z_2 - z_1) - (x_2 - x_1)(z_3 - z_1)$

$w_3 = (x_2 - x_1)(y_3 - y_1) - (x_3 - x_1)(y_2 - y_1)$

and

$r = \sqrt{w_1^2 + w_2^2 + w_3^2}$

If $r = 0$ then the points are collinear

	PARAMETERS AND NOTES

1.5 ANGLE BETWEEN TWO VECTORS, ω

$$\cos \omega = c_1 d_1 + c_2 d_2 + c_3 d_3$$

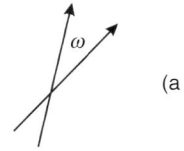
(a

This gives directly the angle between two vectors and the angular distance between two sky points (a). It also gives the angle between the normals of two planes (d), and hence the angle of intersection of the planes.

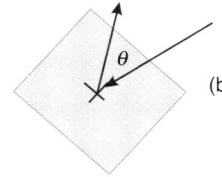
(b

Where one set of cosines refers to a sky point (e.g. the position of the sun) and the other set represents a plane, the angle ω is the angle of incidence of light from that sky point onto the plane (b),

Where one set of cosines describes the direction of a ray and the other set a plane, the ray will intercept the plane only if travelling towards the surface (c). Hence, the angle of incidence θ is

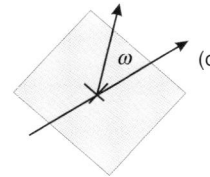
(c

$$\theta = \pi - \omega$$
that is
$$\cos \theta = -\cos \omega$$

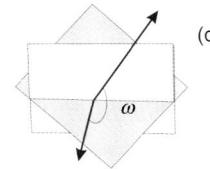
(d

c_1, c_2, c_3 and d_1, d_2, d_3 are direction cosines

1.6 DISTANCE r AND DIRECTION c_1, c_2, c_3 BETWEEN TWO POINTS

This gives the length r and the direction cosines c_1, c_2, c_3 of the line from (x_1, y_1, z_1) to (x_2, y_2, z_2):

$$r = \sqrt{(x_2 - x_1)^2 + (y_2 - y_1)^2 + (z_2 - z_1)^2}$$
and
$$c_1 = \frac{(x_2 - x_1)}{r}, c_2 = \frac{(y_2 - y_1)}{r}, c_3 = \frac{(z_2 - z_1)}{r}$$
provided $r > 0$

	PARAMETERS AND NOTES
1.7 INTERCEPTION OF A RAY AND A PLANE (x, y, z), r If a ray starts from point (x_1, y_1, z_1) and strikes a plane surface, the point of interception is (x_2, y_2, z_2) and the distance travelled is r: $$r = \frac{n_1 x_1 + n_2 y_1 + n_3 z_1 - P}{c_1 n_1 + c_2 n_2 + c_3 n_3} \quad \text{provided } c_1 n_1 + c_2 n_2 + c_3 n_3 < 0$$ $$x_2 = x_1 + r c_1$$ $$y_2 = y_1 + r c_2$$ $$z_2 = z_1 + r c_3$$ The expression $-(c_1 n_1 + c_2 n_2 + c_3 n_3)$ gives the cosine of the angle of incidence. If this is zero, the ray is parallel with the surface; if negative, the ray is travelling away from the surface.	n_1, n_2, n_3, P are the direction cosines of the normal to the plane c_1, c_2, c_3 are the direction cosines of the ray (x_1, y_1, z_1) is the start point of the ray
1.8 TEST WHETHER A POINT LIES ON A PLANE The cross-product of a vector normal to a plane and a vector lying on the plane is zero. The point lies on the plane provided $$n_1(x - x_p) + n_2(y - y_p) + n_3(z - z_p) = 0$$	(x, y, z) are the coordinates of the point to be tested (x_p, y_p, z_p) are the coordinates of any other point lying on the plane n_1, n_2, n_3 are the direction cosines of the normal to the plane
1.9 SIDES, INTERNAL ANGLES AND AREA OF A SPHERICAL TRIANGLE *Sides* $$\cos A = c_{b1} c_{c1} + c_{b2} c_{c2} + c_{b3} c_{c3}$$ $$\cos B = c_{c1} c_{a1} + c_{c2} c_{a2} + c_{c3} c_{a3}$$ $$\cos C = c_{a1} c_{b1} + c_{a2} c_{b2} + c_{a3} c_{b3}$$ $$\sin A = \sqrt{1 - (\cos A)^2}$$ $$\sin B = \sqrt{1 - (\cos B)^2}$$ $$\sin C = \sqrt{1 - (\cos C)^2}$$ *Interior angles* $$\alpha = \arccos\left(\frac{\cos A - \cos B \cos C}{\sin B \sin C}\right) \quad \text{rad}$$ $$\beta = \arccos\left(\frac{\cos B - \cos C \cos A}{\sin C \sin A}\right) \quad \text{rad}$$ $$\gamma = \arccos\left(\frac{\cos C - \cos A \cos B}{\sin A \sin B}\right) \quad \text{rad}$$ *Area* $$S = \alpha + \beta + \gamma - \pi \quad \text{srad}$$	c_{a1}, c_{a2}, c_{a3} c_{b1}, c_{b2}, c_{b3} c_{c1}, c_{c2}, c_{c3} are the direction cosines of the vertex points

PARAMETERS AND NOTES

c_{a1}, c_{a2}, c_{a3}

c_{b1}, c_{b2}, c_{b3}

c_{c1}, c_{c2}, c_{c3}

1.10 SUBDIVISION OF A SPHERICAL TRIANGLE

This algorithm gives the direction cosines of the point d found by subdividing side C. It gives also the lengths of the new sides C' and B'.

are the direction cosines of the vertex points

A, B, C are the sides of the triangle

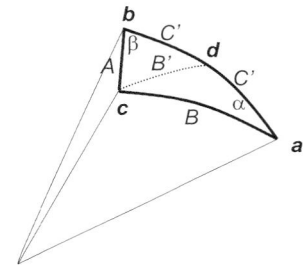

$$\cos C' = \sqrt{\frac{1+\cos C}{2}}, \quad \sin C' = \sqrt{\frac{1-\cos C}{2}}$$

If point a is on the zenith, i.e. $c_{a3} = 1$, the direction cosines of d are

$$c_{d3} = \cos C'$$

$$c_{d2} = c_{b2}\frac{\sin C'}{\sqrt{1-c_{b3}^2}}, \quad c_{d1} = c_{b1}\frac{\sin C'}{\sqrt{1-c_{b3}^2}}$$

if point b is on the zenith, i.e. $c_{b3} = 1$, the direction cosines are

$$c_{d3} = \cos C'$$

$$c_{d2} = c_{a2}\frac{\sin C'}{\sqrt{1-c_{a3}^2}}, \quad c_{d1} = c_{a1}\frac{\sin C'}{\sqrt{1-c_{a3}^2}}$$

otherwise the direction cosines are found as follows:

$$c_{d3} = \frac{\sin C'}{\sin C}\left(c_{b3} + c_{a3}\right)$$

if $c_{d3} = 1$ or $c_{d3} = -1$ then $cd_2 = 0, \quad cd_1 = 0$

else

if $\frac{c_{a2}}{s_{a3}} = \frac{c_{b2}}{s_{b3}}$ then $c_{d2} = \frac{c_{b2}}{s_{b3}}s_{d3}, \quad c_{d1} = \frac{c_{b1}}{s_{b3}}s_{d3}$

if $\frac{c_{a2}}{s_{a3}} < \frac{c_{b2}}{s_{b3}}$ then $c_{d2} = \frac{s_{d3}}{s_{b3}}\left(c_{b2}c_q - c_{b1}s_q\right), \quad c_{d1} = \frac{s_{d3}}{s_{b3}}\left(c_{b1}c_q + c_{b2}s_q\right)$

if $\frac{c_{a2}}{s_{a3}} > \frac{c_{b2}}{s_{b3}}$ then $c_{d2} = \frac{s_{d3}}{s_{b3}}\left(c_{b2}c_q + c_{b1}s_q\right), c_{d1} = \frac{s_{d3}}{s_{b3}}\left(c_{b1}c_q - c_{b2}s_q\right)$

where $s_{d3} = \sqrt{1-c_{d3}^2}, \quad s_{b3} = \sqrt{1-c_{b3}^2}$

and $c_q = \frac{\cos C' - c_{b3}c_{d3}}{s_{b3}s_{d3}}, \quad s_q = \sqrt{1-c_q^2}$

The length of side B' is given by

$$\cos B' = c_{d1}c_{c1} + c_{d2}c_{c2} + c_{d3}c_{c3}$$

$$\sin B' = \sqrt{1-(\cos B')^2}$$

1.11 STEREOGRAPHIC AND OTHER PROJECTIONS OF THE SKY

Sunpath diagrams and other charts of the sky are often plotted in stereographic projection, mapping a hemisphere onto a plane.

If a sky point has azimuth α and elevation γ degrees, it is represented on the diagram by the point (r, α) in polar coordinates, where

$$r = R \tan\left(\frac{90° - \gamma°}{2}\right)$$

R is the radius of the horizon circle line.

Alternatives are the equiangular projection

$$r = R\left(\frac{90° - \gamma°}{90°}\right)$$

and the equal solid angle, equal area or ellipsoid projection

$$r = R\sqrt{2} \sin\left(\frac{90° - \gamma°}{2}\right)$$

Algorithm 4.3 describes how to construct dot diagrams for the sky component.

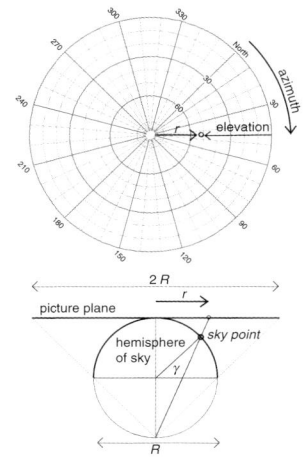

	PARAMETERS AND NOTES
# 2 Solar geometry	*J* is the day number: *J* = 1 on 1 January, *J* = 365 on 31 December. February is taken to have 28 days.

2.1 SOLAR DECLINATION, δ_s

δ_s is the angle between the sun's rays and the earth's equatorial plane, the latitude at which the sun is directly overhead at midday. Declination values are positive when the sun is north of the equator (March 21 to September 23) and negative when the sun is south of the equator. Maximum and minimum values of δ_s are +0.409 rad (+23.45°) and −0.409 rad (−23.45°).

Day angle:

$$\tau_d = \frac{2\pi(J-1)}{365} \quad \text{rad}$$

Solar declination:

$$\delta_s = 0.006918 - 0.399912\cos\tau_d + 0.070257\sin\tau_d$$
$$-0.006758\cos 2\tau_d + 0.000907\sin 2\tau_d$$
$$-0.002697\cos 3\tau_d + 0.001480\sin 3\tau_d \quad \text{rad}$$

2.2 THE EQUATION OF TIME, ET

ET describes variation between clock time and solar time due to eccentricity in the earth's orbit. It is positive when sun time is before clock time.

$$ET = 0.170 \sin[4\pi(J-80)/373] - 0.129 \sin[2\pi(J-8)/355] \quad \text{hours}$$

(The argument of the sine function is in radians)

2.3 TRUE SOLAR TIME, TST, AND HOUR ANGLE, ξ

Solar time differs from clock time. The difference is due to (a) differences between the site longitude and the standard meridian (for example: 0°, Greenwich meridian), (b) the equation of time, and (c) summer time or daylight-saving conventions.

$$TST = LT + \frac{\lambda_s° - \lambda°}{15} + ET - TD \quad \text{hours}$$

$$\xi = \frac{\pi}{12} TST \quad \text{rad}$$

LT is the local clock time, *hours* from midnight
$\lambda°$ is the longitude of the site, *degrees* (positive west of Greenwich)
$\lambda_s°$ is the longitude of the standard meridian, the longitude used as the basis of local clock time (e.g. 0° for GMT), *degrees*
ET is the equation of time, *hours*
TD is summer time or daylight saving, *degrees* (positive when clock time is later than standard time)

	PARAMETERS AND NOTES
## 2.4 SOLAR ELEVATION, γ_s, AND AZIMUTH, α_s	δ_s is the solar declination, *radians*
	ξ is the solar hour angle, *radians*
Solar elevation (or solar altitude) is defined as $\pi/2$ – *solar zenith angle*, the angle between the centre of the sun and the zenith. The elevation angle is only approximately the angle of the centre of the sun above the horizon, because near the horizon the apparent position of the sun is affected by refraction in the atmosphere.	ϕ is the latitude of the site, *radians* (positive north of the Equator)

Solar azimuth is sometimes given as an angle from north, from 0 to 2π radians.

$$\sin\gamma_s = \sin\varphi\,\sin\delta_s - \cos\varphi\,\cos\delta_s\,\cos\xi$$
$$\cos\gamma_s = \sqrt{1-(\sin\gamma_s)^2}$$

therefore

$$\gamma_s = \arcsin(\sin\varphi\,\sin\delta_s - \cos\varphi\,\cos\delta_s\,\cos\xi)$$

$$\cos a_s = \frac{-\sin\varphi\,\sin\gamma_s + \sin\delta_s}{\cos\varphi\,\cos\gamma_s}$$
$$\sin a_s = \sqrt{1-(\cos a_s)^2}, \quad 0 < \xi \le \pi$$
$$\quad\quad = -\sqrt{1-(\cos a_s)^2}, \quad \pi < \xi \le 2\pi$$

Therefore,

$$a_s = \arccos\left(\frac{-\sin\varphi\,\sin\gamma_s + \sin\delta_s}{\cos\varphi\,\cos\gamma_s}\right), \quad 0 < \xi \le \pi$$
$$\quad\quad = 2\pi - \arccos\left(\frac{-\sin\varphi\,\sin\gamma_s + \sin\delta_s}{\cos\varphi\,\cos\gamma_s}\right), \quad \pi < \xi \le 2\pi$$

Direction cosines

$$c_{s1} = \cos a_s\,\cos\gamma_s$$
$$c_{s2} = \sin a_s\,\cos\gamma_s$$
$$c_{s3} = \sin\gamma_s$$

	PARAMETERS AND NOTES
2.5 ASTRONOMICAL DAYLENGTH, S_o Astronomical daylength or astronomical sunshine duration, is defined as the period during which the solar elevation is greater than zero. The sun is actually hidden only when the solar elevation is below about $-0.84°$ $(-0.0147$ rad), owing to the apparent radius of the sun $(0.27°)$ and atmospheric refraction. $$S_o = \frac{24}{\pi} \arccos(-\tan\varphi \tan\delta_s), \text{ hours, } -1 \le -\tan\varphi \tan\delta_s \le 1$$ where arccos gives a result in radians Within the Arctic and Antarctic Circles, $$S_o = 0, \quad \text{if } (-\tan\varphi \tan\delta_s) > 1$$ $$S_o = 24, \quad \text{if } (-\tan\varphi \tan\delta_s) < -1$$ Times of sunrise and sunset in solar time are given by $$t_{sr} = 12 - \frac{S_o}{2}, \text{ hours}$$ $$t_{ss} = 12 + \frac{S_o}{2}, \text{ hours}$$	δ_s is the solar declination, *radians* ϕ is the latitude of the site, *radians* (positive north of the Equator)
2.6 SHADOW LENGTH This equation gives the length L of the shadow cast by a point H metres high above an inclined surface: $$\cos\theta = c_{s1}n_1 + c_{s2}n_2 + c_{s3}n_3$$ $$L = H\frac{\sqrt{1-(\cos\theta)^2}}{\cos\theta} \quad \text{metres, provided } \cos\theta > 0$$	n_1, n_2, n_3 are the direction cosines of the normal to the plane c_{s1}, c_{s2}, c_{s3} are the direction cosines of the solar azimuth and altitude H is the perpendicular height of the point above the plane, *metres*

	PARAMETERS AND NOTES
2.7 GROUND SHADOW AREA OF A RECTILINEAR BUILDING This gives the area, a_g, of the shadow cast on level ground by a building that is rectilinear in plan and section: $$a_g = \frac{H \cos \gamma_s}{\sin \gamma_s} [L \cos(\omega) + W \sin(\omega)] \text{ square metres}$$ *where* $$\omega = |a_s - a_b|$$	*L, W* are the plan dimensions of the building, *metres* *H* is the height of the building above ground level, *metres* a_b is the orientation of the building (the azimuth of the normal to the façade of length *L*), γ_s and α_s are the solar altitude and azimuth

	PARAMETERS AND NOTES
# 3 Light from the sky	h is the height of site above sea level, *metres* γ_s is the solar elevation, *radians*

3.1 RELATIVE OPTICAL AIR MASS, m

Air mass, m, is the length of an oblique path through the atmosphere divided by the path length when the sun is directly overhead. The third formula gives the relative air mass.

The ratio of mean atmospheric pressure at the station height to that at sea level is

$$\frac{p}{p_0} = 1.0 - \frac{h}{10000}, \text{ where } h < 4000$$

$$\frac{p}{p_0} = \exp\left[\frac{h}{1000}\left(-0.1174 - 0.0017\frac{h}{1000}\right)\right], \text{ where } 4000 \leq h < 10000$$

The air mass is then

$$m = \frac{p}{p_0}\frac{1}{\left[\sin\gamma'_s + 0.50572\left(\frac{180\gamma'_s}{\pi} + 6.07995\right)^{-1.6364}\right]}$$

When the sun is higher than 10° above the horizon and the site is near sea level, a good approximation is

$$m \approx \frac{1}{\sin\gamma'_s}$$

3.2 ILLUMINANCE TURBIDITY, T_{il}

T_L is the Linke turbidity

The illuminance at the earth's surface from the solar beam depends on attenuation in the atmosphere; an index of this attenuation is the illuminance turbidity. The corresponding index of attenuation for total radiation is the Linke turbidity. More extensive data are available for Linke turbidity than illuminance turbidity, and the following equation is an empirical relationship between the two for European clear skies:

$$T_{il} = 0.7868 + 0.12652T_L + 0.08666T_L^2, \text{ provided } T_L > 1.06$$

	PARAMETERS AND NOTES

Typical values of T_{il} under cloudless skies are given in the following table:

Region	T_{il}
Perfectly dry clean air	1.0
Dry mountain areas	1.5
Rural areas	2.5
Urban areas	3.0
Industrial areas	5.0

3.3 EXTRATERRESTRIAL ILLUMINANCE

The solar radiation incident on the upper atmosphere varies during the year owing to the ellipticity of the earth's orbit.

$$E_{vo} = \overline{E_{vo}}\left[1 + 0.034\cos\left(\frac{2\pi(J-2)}{365}\right)\right] \ \text{klx}$$

J is the day number, $\overline{E_{v0}}$ is the luminous solar constant: extraterrestrial illuminance at mean distance between earth and sun, *kilolux*.

The luminous solar constant is derived by mathematically integrating the solar spectrum outside the atmosphere with the photopic luminous efficacy function, $V(\lambda)$, of the human eye. Both have been revised in recent years, and thus published illuminances vary.

Current recommendations are
133.3 klx with standard $V(\lambda)$
134.1 klx with $V_m(\lambda)$
133.8 klx for calibration of International Daylight Measurement Project instruments.

For normal lighting calculations, the difference between these is unimportant.

3.4 ILLUMINANCE FROM DIRECT SUNLIGHT, E_{vs}

Solar illuminance on a surface is derived from the extraterrestrial illuminance by calculating attenuation in the atmosphere and the angle of incidence.

The first expression gives the mean extinction coefficient of light in clean dry air; the second gives solar normal illuminance (the illuminance on a surface at ground level perpendicular to the sun's beam).

$$\overline{a_{vR}} = \frac{0.1}{1 + 0.0045\,m}$$
$$E_{vsn} = E_{vo}\exp(-\overline{a_{vR}}\,mT_{il}) \ \text{klx}$$

Solar illuminance on an inclined plane can then be found:

$$E_{vs}(a_k, \gamma_k) = E_{vsn}(n_1 c_{s1} + n_2 c_{s2} + n_3 c_{s3}) \ \text{klx}$$
For a horizontal surface,
$$E_{vsh} = E_{vsn}c_3 = E_{vsn}\sin\gamma'_s \ \text{klx}$$

T_{il} is the illuminance turbidity
m is the relative optical air mass
E_{vo} is the extraterrestrial illuminance, *kilolux*
n_1, n_2, n_3 are the direction cosines of the normal to the plane
c_{s1}, c_{s2}, c_{s3} are the direction cosines of the solar azimuth and altitude
γ_s is the solar elevation

	PARAMETERS AND NOTES
3.5 GLOBAL ILLUMINANCE, E_{vgh}, AND DIFFUSE ILLUMINANCE, E_{vdh}	γ_s is the solar elevation, *radians* $\gamma_s°$ is the solar elevation, *degrees*

These empirical equations give the frequency distributions of global illuminance (illuminance on unobstructed ground from both sunlight and skylight) and of diffuse illuminance (skylight alone). By computing first the solar elevation at regular intervals during the day and regular intervals of days throughout the year, the cumulative frequency distributions through the year (or any arbitrary period) can be found.

The first set of equations are based on measurements made in Nottingham, UK, during 1984–85 and may be applied to other sites in north-west Europe with similar climate. The second set is based on measurements made in Hong Kong between 2003 and 2005.

Mean global illuminance. Nottingham:

$$\gamma'_s{}° = \frac{180\gamma'_s}{\pi}$$

$$\bar{E}_{vgh} = 0.0105(\gamma'_s{}° + 5)^{2.5} \text{ klx}, \quad -5 \leq \gamma'_s{}° \leq 2.5$$

$$= 73.7\sin^{1.22}\gamma'_s{}°, \quad 2.5 < \gamma'_s{}° \leq 60$$

Mean diffuse illuminance. Nottingham:

$$\gamma'_s{}° = \frac{180\gamma'_s}{\pi}$$

$$\bar{E}_{vdh} = 0.0105(\gamma'_s{}° + 5)^{2.5} \text{ klx}, \quad -5 \leq \gamma'_s{}° \leq 5$$

$$= 48.8\sin^{1.105}\gamma'_s{}°, \quad 5 < \gamma'_s{}° \leq 60$$

Mean diffuse illuminance. Hong Kong:

$$\gamma'_s{}° = \frac{180\gamma'_s}{\pi}$$

$$\bar{E}_{vdh} = 0.010(\gamma'_s{}°+5)^{2.61} \text{ klx}, \quad -5 \leq \gamma'_s{}° \leq 5$$

$$= 39.6\sin^{0.931}\gamma'_s{}°, \quad 5 < \gamma'_s{}° \leq 90$$

Centre value of band as a fraction of mean illuminance (bands mean/4 wide)

	0.125	0.375	0.625	0.875	1.125	1.375	1.625	1.875	2.125
Nottingham									
Global, %	9.1	15.8	16.2	14.6	11.4	9.1	10.6	8.7	3.9
Diffuse, %	5.9	12.6	16.1	17.7	17.3	16.5	8.7	3.9	1.6
Hong Kong									
Diffuse, %	2.2	9.0	16.4	23.4	24.9	15.5	4.3	3.4	0.9

	PARAMETERS AND NOTES
## 3.6 CLEAR SKY LUMINANCE AND ILLUMINANCE	γ_s is the solar altitude, *radians*

3.6 CLEAR SKY LUMINANCE AND ILLUMINANCE

The CIE clear sky was superseded by the Standard General Sky (Algorithm 4.1). This version gives the luminance of a sky point as a fraction of the zenith luminance. The original CIE formulation gives two separate equations that correspond to $T_{il} = 2.45$ and $T_{il} = 5.5$, for clean and industrial atmospheres, respectively. Illuminance turbidity is used as a factor here.

The relative luminance of a sky point at altitude γ and angular distance θ from the sun is

$$\frac{L_{vcl}(\gamma,\theta)}{L_{vclz}} = \frac{f(\theta)}{f(\pi/2 - \gamma_s)} \frac{\phi(\gamma)}{\phi(\pi/2)}, \quad 0 \le \gamma_s \le \frac{\pi}{2}, 0 < \gamma \le \frac{\pi}{2}$$

where the functions f and ϕ are

$$f(\theta) = 1 + N[\exp(-3\theta) - 0.009] + M\cos^2\theta$$

using

$$N = 4.3 T_{il}^{1.9} \exp(-0.35 T_{il})$$

$$M = \frac{0.71}{\sqrt{T_{il}}}$$

and

$$\phi(\gamma) = 1 - \exp\left(\frac{-0.32}{\sin\gamma}\right)$$

hence

$$\phi(\pi/2) \approx 0.27385$$

An alternative luminance distribution formula was developed from luminance measurements made in Japan. This formula gives absolute luminance values with a distribution similar to the CIE equation. It may be used to predict zenith luminance with atmospheres of given turbidity.

$$L_{vclz} = E_{vo}\, g(\tau_v, m)\, f(\pi/2 - \gamma_s) \quad kcd/m^2, \quad 0 \le \gamma_s < \pi/2$$

where the function g is

$$g(\tau_v, m) = \frac{(2.5 - 1.4\tau_v)(\tau_v^{\,m} - \tau_v)}{19.6(1 - m)}, \quad \tau_v \ge 0.75$$

$$= \frac{[1.6 - 0.4\tau_v + (0.75 - \tau_v)m](\tau_v^{\,m} - \tau_v)}{22.07(1 - m)}, \quad \tau_v < 0.75$$

and $f(\pi/2 - \gamma_s)$ is given in the algorithm above.

τ_v, the atmospheric transmittance, is found from

$$\tau_v = \exp(-\bar{a}_{vR} T_{il}) \approx \exp(-0.1 T_{il})$$

PARAMETERS AND NOTES

γ_s is the solar altitude, *radians*

γ is the altitude of the sky point, *radians*

θ is the angular distance of the sky point from the sun, *radians*: Algorithm 1.5 or using

$\cos\theta = \sin\gamma\sin\gamma_s + \cos\gamma\cos\gamma_s\cos(\alpha - \alpha_s)$

T_{il} is the illuminance turbidity factor (algorithm 3.2)

m is the relative optical air mass (algorithm 3.1)

E_{vo} is the extraterrestrial solar illuminance, klx $\bar{a}_{vR}$ is the mean extinction coefficient

	PARAMETERS AND NOTES
With moderate turbidity (approximately $T_{il} = 3$), the illuminance on the ground from the clear sky may be estimated from the following empirical equation (illuminance from direct sun is, of course, excluded): $$E_{vclh} = 0.8 + 15.5\sqrt{\sin\gamma_s} \quad \text{klx}, \quad 0 < \gamma_s \le \pi/2$$	
### 3.7 OVERCAST SKY LUMINANCE AND ILLUMINANCE The light received from a fully cloudy sky depends on the solar elevation even if the solar disc is completely obscured. The following formulae are empirical and are based on different sets of measurements, so that they match only approximately. They may be taken to represent mean values under skies that resemble the brightness pattern of the CIE standard, but actual values may range from half to twice the mean. The luminance in cd/m² of a sky point k, at an angle γ_k above the horizon is $$L_{vock} = E_{vo}(1 + 1.5\sin\gamma_s)\left(\frac{1 + 2(1 - \rho_g{}^3)\sin\gamma_k}{4 + 90(1 - \rho_g)}\right)\sin\gamma_s$$ The horizontal illuminance is $$E_{voch} = 0.3 + 21\sin\gamma_s, \text{ klx}$$	γ_s is the solar elevation, *radians* γ_k is the elevation of the direction of view, *radians* ρ_g is the reflectance of the ground E_{vo} is the extraterrestrial illuminance, *lux*

4 Standard skies

4.1 CIE STANDARD GENERAL SKY

The standard parameters are shown in the following table

		a	b	c	d	e
1	**CIE Standard Overcast Sky, alternative form.**	4.0	−0.70	0	−1.0	0
	Steep luminance gradation towards zenith, azimuthal uniformity					
2	Overcast, with steep luminance gradation and slight brightening towards sun	4.0	−0.70	2	−1.5	0.15
3	Overcast, moderately graded with azimuthal uniformity	1.1	−0.8	0	−1.0	0
4	Overcast, moderately graded and slight brightening towards sun	1.1	−0.8	2	−1.5	0.15
5	**Sky of uniform luminance**	0	−1.0	0	−1.0	0
6	Partly cloudy sky, no gradation towards zenith, slight brightening towards sun	0	−1.0	2	−1.5	0.15
7	Partly cloudy sky, no gradation towards zenith, brighter circumsolar region	0	−1.0	5	−2.5	0.30
8	Partly cloudy sky, no gradation towards zenith, distinct solar corona	0	−1.0	10	−3.0	0.45
9	Partly cloudy, with obscured sun	−1.0	−0.55	2	−1.5	0.15
10	Partly cloudy, with brighter circumsolar region	−1.0	−0.55	5	−2.5	0.30
11	White–blue sky, with distinct solar corona	−1.0	−0.55	10	−3.0	0.45
12	**CIE Standard Clear Sky, low illuminance turbidity**	−1.0	−0.32	10	−3.0	0.45
13	**CIE Standard Clear Sky, polluted atmosphere**	−1.0	−0.32	16	−3.0	0.30
14	Cloudless turbid sky, with broad solar corona	−1.0	−0.15	16	−3.0	0.30
15	White–blue turbid sky, with broad solar corona	−1.0	−0.15	24	−2.8	0.15

The General Sky specification includes as type 16 the original Standard Overcast Sky. This is given in Algorithm 4.2.

	PARAMETERS AND NOTES
	zenith

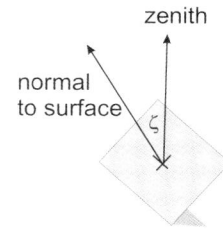

4.2 CIE STANDARD OVERCAST SKY

Luminance distribution

   The luminance of a sky point at elevation γ is given as a fraction of the zenith luminance:

$$L_{voc} = \frac{1+2\sin\gamma}{3}L_{vocz}$$

γ is the elevation of a point in the sky
ζ is the tilt of the surface normal from vertical (zenith angle), *radians*
γ_s is the solar elevation

Horizontal illuminance ($\zeta = 0$):

$$E_{voch} = \frac{7\pi}{9}L_{voc} \approx 2.4435L_{voc}$$

Vertical illuminance ($\zeta = \pi/2$):

$$E_{vocv} = \frac{3\pi+8}{18}L_{voc} \approx 0.9680L_{voc} \approx 0.3962E_{voch}$$

Illuminance on an inclined plane:

$$E_{voc}(\zeta) = \left[\frac{\pi(1+C)}{6} + \frac{4S^3}{9} + \frac{4C(\pi-\zeta+SC)}{9}\right]L_{vocz}, \ 0 \leq \zeta \leq \pi$$
where $C = \cos\zeta$, $S = \sin\zeta$

Horizontal illuminance from a patch of sky bounded by azimuth angles α_1 and α_2, and from γ_L above the horizon to γ_H above the horizon (angles in radians):

$$E_{voc}(\alpha_1,\alpha_2,\gamma_L,\gamma_H) = L_{vocz}\left(\frac{\sin^2\gamma_H - \sin^2\gamma_L}{6} + \frac{2\sin^3\gamma_H - 2\sin^3\gamma_L}{9}\right)(\alpha_2 - \alpha_1)$$

Vertical illuminance from a patch of sky bounded by α_L and α_R to the left and right of the normal to the surface and from γ_L above the horizon to γ_H above the horizon (angles in radians):

$$E_{voc}(\alpha_L,\alpha_R,\gamma_L,\gamma_H) = \frac{L_{vocz}(\sin\alpha_L + \sin\alpha_R)}{3}\left(\frac{\gamma_H - \gamma_L}{2} + \frac{\sin2\gamma_H - \sin2\gamma_L}{4} + \frac{\cos^3\gamma_H - \cos^3\gamma_L}{3}\right),$$
$$0 \leq \alpha \leq \frac{\pi}{2}, 0 \leq \gamma \leq \frac{\pi}{2}$$

	PARAMETERS AND NOTES

4.3 DOT DIAGRAMS BASED ON THE CIE STANDARD OVERCAST SKY

Production of a dot diagram for the sky component on a horizontal or vertical surface
N dots are required.

Subdivide the sky, preferably into zones of approximately equal size. The subdivision described in Chapter 10, Table 10.1, is suitable.

Assume a zenith luminance of unity. Use Algorithm 4.2 to find the total illuminance (horizontal or vertical surface). Denote this by E_T.

Then, taking each sky zone in turn:

1. Use Algorithm 4.2 to determine the illuminance due to this sky zone (vertical or horizontal). Denote this by E_z.
2. Let N_z be the number of dots in the zone; then $\dfrac{N_z}{N} = \dfrac{E_z}{E_T}$

   Since an integer is desirable, we take $N_z = \text{Round}\left(\dfrac{E_z N_T}{E_T}\right)$

3. Randomly select N_z points in the range $\{[a_1 \le a < a_2],[\gamma_L \le \gamma < \gamma_H]\}$, where α_1 and α_2, γ_L and γ_H, are the azimuth and elevation limits of the sky zone.
4. Use Algorithm 1.11 to find the coordinates of these points on the final diagram.

The procedure will normally include a check on the total number of dots on the diagram after rounding. It may also include a method for dealing with overlapping dots.

	PARAMETERS AND NOTES
# 5 Daylight and objects	E_{vg} is the Illuminance on the ground. ρ_g is the ground reflectance ζ is the tilt of the surface normal from vertical (as in Algorithm 4.2)

5.1 LIGHT REFLECTED FROM THE GROUND

These equations deal with the ground as a diffuse reflector. Specular reflection is covered by Algorithm 5.4.

Ground luminance, L_g:

$$L_g = E_{vg}\frac{\rho_g}{\pi}$$

Illuminance on an inclined plane from ground-reflected light, E_{gk}:

$$E_{gk} = L_g\frac{\pi(1-\cos\zeta)}{2}$$
$$= E_{vg}\frac{\rho_g(1-\cos\zeta)}{2}$$

5.2 LUMINANCE OF NEARBY EXTERNAL OBSTRUCTIONS, L_k

The surface is assumed to be diffusing.

$$L_k = \frac{E_{vk}\rho_k}{\pi}$$

E_{vk} is the illuminance on the surface, *lux* (sky illuminance + total reflected illuminance) ρ_k is the reflectance of the surface

---

5.3 LUMINANCE OF DISTANT OBJECTS UNDER AN OVERCAST SKY, L_x

The luminance of a distant object depends on the viewing distance and on the effects of atmospheric scattering. For the majority of daylight calculations, external obstructions may be assumed to be diffuse reflectors and sufficiently close for atmospheric effects to be negligible.

The following expression gives the luminance of a distant surface as a proportion of the luminance of the overcast sky at the horizon:

$$L_x = L_s\left[1-(1-\rho\,k_\zeta)\exp(-\sigma x)\right] \text{ cd/m}^2$$
where
$$k_\zeta = \frac{7}{3}\left[\frac{3(1+C)}{14} + \frac{4S^3}{7\pi} + \frac{4C(\pi-\zeta+S\,C)}{7\pi} + \rho_g\frac{1-C}{2}\right], \quad 0\leq\zeta\leq\pi$$
where $C=\cos\zeta$, $S=\sin\zeta$

L_s is the luminance of the horizon sky, cd/m^2 ζ is the tilt of the surface normal from vertical (as in Algorithm 4.2), *radians* ρ is the reflectance of the surface ρ_g is the reflectance of the ground x is the distance, *kilometres* σ is the mean atmospheric attenuation coefficient, km^{-1} (For normal calculations under an overcast sky, it is recommended that the value of σ be taken as 0.3)

	PARAMETERS AND NOTES
5.4 SPECULAR REFLECTION IN EXTERNAL SURFACES A specular reflection of the sky can occur in glossy external surfaces, such as a glazed curtain wall. If the reflected sky zone includes the sun, glare or overheating can be caused. The same equations may be used to trace the reflection of rays in an interior. *Direction of a reflected ray* The direction cosines of the reflected ray are $c_1' = (-n_1^2 + n_2^2 + n_3^2)c_1 + (-2n_1n_2)c_2 + (-2n_1n_3)c_3$ $c_2' = (-2n_1n_2)c_1 + (n_1^2 - n_2^2 + n_3^2)c_2 + (-2n_2n_3)c_3$ $c_3' = (-2n_1n_3)c_1 + (-2n_2n_3)c_2 + (1 - 2n_3^2)c_3$ provided $-(c_1n_1 + c_2n_2 + c_3n_3) > 0$ For matrix multiplication, the transformation matrix is $$\begin{bmatrix} -n_1^2 + n_2^2 + n_3^2 & -2n_1n_2 & -2n_1n_3 & 0 \\ -2n_1n_2 & n_1^2 - n_2^2 + n_3^2 & -2n_2n_3 & 0 \\ -2n_1n_3 & -2n_2n_3 & 1 - 2n_3^2 & 0 \\ 0 & 0 & 0 & 1 \end{bmatrix}$$ It follows that, when the surface is horizontal, (water, for instance) the cosines of the reflected ray are $c_1' = c_1$ $c_2' = c_2$ $c_3' = -c_3$	c_1, c_2, c_3 are the direction cosines of the original ray or line of sight n_1, n_2, n_3 are the direction cosines of the surface normal
Luminance of reflected sky, L_v' The angle of incidence is $\theta = \arccos(-c_1n_1 - c_2n_2 - c_3n_3)$ Then the reflected luminance is $L_v' = L_v\,\rho'(\theta)$	L_v is the luminance of the sky zone $\rho'(\theta)$ is the specular reflectance of the surface at angle of incidence θ

	PARAMETERS AND NOTES

### 5.5 DIRECTIONAL TRANSMITTANCE OF CLEAR GLASS, T_i 	
 	
Transmittance of a beam at angle of incidence i
  The angle of incidence is the angle between the direction of the beam and the normal to the glass:
 	
$$\tau_i = -0.028378 + 3.156075\cos i - 3.058376\cos^2 i - 1.428919\cos^3 i$$
$$+ 4.014235\cos^4 i - 1.775827\cos^5 i$$
 	
Mean transmittance of a rectangular opening
  This enables the sky component of the daylight factor to be derived from the value calculated with an unglazed opening. For 6 mm clear glass, a polynomial function was derived that gives an effective glass transmission correction factor T:
 	
$$T = 0.623 + 0.3\cos b - 0.137\cos^2 b + 0.5^{\cdot}\cos a - 0.66\cos a \cos b$$
$$+ 0.346\cos a\cos^2 b - 0.285\cos^2 a + 0.427\cos^2 a\cos b - 0.246\cos^2 a\cos^2 b$$
	Altitude and azimuth angles a and b are as in Algorithm 6.1

### 5.6 DIRECTIONAL TRANSMITTANCE OF NON-CLEAR GLASS, T_i This gives the directional daylight transmittance of non-clear, heat-absorbing solar control glasses: $$\tau_{ix} = \frac{(1-r_x)^2 g}{1 - r_x^2 g^2}$$ The x subscript signifies that each component must be evaluated separately for radiation polarised with its planes of vibration parallel (r_{pl}) and perpendicular (r_{pd}) to the plane of the glass, where $$r_{pl} = \frac{\sin^2(i - i_r)}{\sin^2(i + i_r)} \text{ and } r_{pd} = \frac{\tan^2(i - i_r)}{\tan^2(i + i_r)}$$ The angle of refraction, i_r, is found from Snell's law : $\sin i = n \sin i_r$. For non-polarised radiation, the value of τ_i is based on the average of the parallel and perpendicular reflectances.	r_x is the specular monochromatic reflectance i is the angle of incidence n is the refractive index of the glass KL is the normal-incidence KL value for daylight If the normal-incidence KL value for daylight is not known, it can be derived from the normal-incidence daylight transmittance τo via the equation $KL = \log e$ X, where $$X = \frac{(1-r)^2 + \sqrt{(1-r)^4 + 4\tau_0 r^2}}{2\tau_0} \text{ and } r = \left(\frac{n-1}{n+1}\right)^2$$

	PARAMETERS AND NOTES

The parameter g represents the fraction of the incident energy remaining after transmission through the glass, and is found from

$$g = \exp\left[\frac{-KL}{\sqrt{1-\left(\dfrac{\sin i}{n}\right)^2}}\right]$$

For completeness, the directional absorptance α_{ix} and the directional reflectance ρ_{ix} are given here:

$$\alpha_{ix} = 1 - r_x - \frac{(1-r_x)^2 g}{1-r_x g} \quad \text{and} \quad \rho_{ix} = r_x + \frac{r_x g^2 (1-r_x)^2}{1-r_x^2 g^2}$$

5.7 DIFFUSE REFLECTANCE AND TRANSMITTANCE OF NON-CLEAR GLASS, S_d AND T_d

KL is the normal-incidence value (see Algorithm 5.6)

Reflectance:

$$\rho_d = 0.0123(KL)^4 - 0.0676(KL)^3 + 0.140(KL)^2 - 0.138(KL) + 0.154$$

Transmittance:

$$\tau_d = 0.845 \exp(-1.15\ KL)$$

5.8 COMBINED OVERALL TRANSMITTANCE AND REFLECTANCE OF MULTIPLE LAYERS

ρ_2 and τ_2 are the reflectance and transmittance of the upper layer
ρ_1 and τ_1 are the reflectance and transmittance of the lower layer

If there are multiple layers of stratus cloud or glazing consists of several partly transparent materials, interreflection occurs between layers.
For two layers,

$$\tau_{\text{combined}} = \frac{\tau_1 \tau_2}{1 - \rho_1 \rho_2}$$

$$\rho_{\text{combined}} = \rho_2 + \frac{\tau_2^2}{\rho_1 \left(1 - \rho_1 \rho_2\right)}$$

For more than two layers, find the combined reflectance and combined transmittance of the lowest two layers, then of the lowest three (using the combined values of the lowest two), continuing until all layers are included.

	PARAMETERS AND NOTES

6 Daylight factors

Angles *a*, *b* and *c*, *radians*

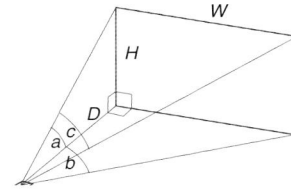

6.1 SKY FACTOR FOR AN UNGLAZED VERTICAL RECTANGULAR OPENING, *SF*

The sky factor is used as a measure of daylight obstruction in legal cases, such as those concerned with Rights of Light. The formula is an alternative form of the equation for the configuration factor for a rectangle to a perpendicular element:

$$SF = \frac{b - c\cos a}{2\pi} \times 100\%$$

When the opening is *H* high, *W* wide and a perpendicular distance *D* away

$$b = \arctan\frac{W}{D}$$

$$a = \arctan\frac{H}{D}$$

$$c = \arctan\frac{W}{\sqrt{H^2 + D^2}}$$

6.2 SKY COMPONENT FOR AN UNGLAZED VERTICAL RECTANGULAR OPENING, D_s

Angles *a*, *b* and *c*, *radians*, as in Algorithm 6.1

This algorithm gives the sky component (from a CIE Overcast Sky) on a horizontal plane due to an unglazed vertical rectangular opening that has its lower edge in the reference plane and one vertical edge in a plane perpendicular to the opening and containing the reference point:

$$D_s = \frac{1.5(b - c\cos a) + 2\arcsin(\sin b \sin a) - \sin 2a \sin c}{7\pi} \times 100\%$$

To obtain the sky component for a glazed opening, the value D_s obtained from this algorithm may be multiplied by the transmittance *T* obtained from Algorithm 5.5.

6.3 SKY COMPONENT FOR AN UNGLAZED HORIZONTAL RECTANGULAR OPENING, D_{sh}

Angles *a*, *b*, *c* and *d*, *radians*

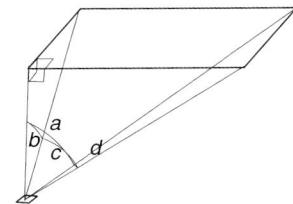

This algorithm gives the sky component (from a CIE Overcast Sky) on a horizontal plane at a point directly below one corner of the opening:

$$D_{sh} = \begin{Bmatrix} 1.5z(d\sin a + c\sin b) + z\pi + z(\sin 2b \sin c + \sin 2a \sin d) \\ -2z[\arcsin(\cos\alpha\cos a) + \arcsin(\sin a \cos b] \end{Bmatrix} \times 100\%$$

where

$$z = \frac{1}{7\pi}$$

$$\alpha = \arctan\frac{\tan a}{\tan b}$$

	PARAMETERS AND NOTES

6.4 AVERAGE INTERNALLY REFLECTED COMPONENT FOR VERTICAL WINDOWS

The average internally reflected component of the daylight factor represents the daylight reaching a reference point after reflections and inter-reflections from the surfaces inside a room. The value of the interreflected light will vary throughout the room, but for most purposes it is sufficient to calculate an average value to assign to most of the room and a minimum for points distant from the window. This algorithm is based on the split-flux method.

$$\bar{D}_i = \tau \, \frac{A_w}{A} \, \frac{C\rho_{fw} + 25\rho_{cw}\rho_g}{1-\bar{\rho}} \quad \%$$

The value of C is given by

$$C = \frac{9}{7\pi} k_1 \left(1 + \frac{\rho_b}{\pi(1-\rho_o)} k_2 \right)$$

where

$$k_1 = \frac{\sin\phi_L + \sin\phi_R}{3} \left(\frac{\gamma_H - \gamma_L}{2} + \frac{\sin 2\gamma_H - \sin 2\gamma_L}{4} - \frac{2\cos^3\gamma_H - 2\cos^3\gamma_L}{3} \right)$$

$$k_2 = \frac{\pi}{2} - \left(\sin\phi_L + \sin\phi_R \right)\left(\frac{\gamma_H - \gamma_L}{2} + \frac{\sin 2\gamma_H - \sin 2\gamma_L}{4} \right)$$

$$\rho_o = \frac{\rho_g + \rho_b}{4}$$

Alternatively, when there is a simple obstruction $\omega°$ degrees above the horizon, and any shading by the window head and to the sides is insignificant,

$$C = b_o + b_1\omega° + b_2\omega^{°2} + b_3\omega^{°3}$$

where

$b_0 = +3.89698 \times 10$

$b_1 = -2.97065 \times 10^{-1}$

$b_2 = -7.67589 \times 10^{-3}$

$b_3 = +7.56675 \times 10^{-5}$

When $\omega° \le 60°$, $\quad C \approx 40 - \dfrac{\omega°}{2}$

If obstructions form an irregular skyline, the overall value of C can be calculated by dividing the external scene into several zones in plan angle f, finding the value of C for each, and adding these together.

C is the daylight factor on the vertical external face of the window. The sky component on a vertical external surface is

$$C_{sv} = \frac{9}{7\pi} k_1$$

Parameters and notes column:

τ is the diffuse light transmittance of glazing, including effects of dirt,

A_w is the glazed area of the window (after subtracting the area of window bars and other obstructions), *square metres*

A is the total area of ceiling, floor and walls, including windows, *square metres*

$\bar{\rho}$ is the area-weighted average reflectance of ceiling, floor and walls, including windows

ρ_{cw} is the area-weighted average reflectance of ceiling and wall surfaces above the centre height of the windows, excluding window wall surfaces

r_{fw} is the area-weighted average reflectance of floor and wall surfaces below the centre height of the windows, excluding window wall surfaces

ρ_g is the reflectance of the ground

ρ_b is the reflectance of external obstructions

φ_L, φ_R, γ_H and γ_L are angles of obstruction, as in the diagram, *radians*

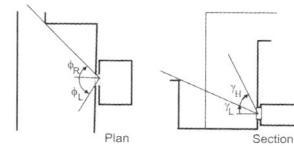

	PARAMETERS AND NOTES
6.5 MINIMUM INTERNALLY REFLECTED COMPONENT FOR VERTICAL WINDOWS	$\bar{D}_i$ is the average IRC $\bar{\rho}$ is the area-weighted average reflectance of ceiling, floor and walls, including windows, ρ_f is the area-weighted average reflectance of the floor

$$\frac{D_{im}}{D_i} = \left[(4.7676 \times 10^{-3})r_f - 0.214579\right] + \left[(-7.5428 \times 10^{-8})r_f + 0.029467\right]\bar{r}$$
$$+ \left[(8.3808 \times 10^{-7})r_f - 0.000208\right](\bar{r})^2$$

where

$$\bar{r} = 100\bar{\rho} \quad \text{and} \quad r_f = 100\rho_f$$

This equation is based on the assumption that the ceiling has a reflectance of 0.7, with a range of $\bar{\rho}$ from 0.3 to 0.6 and a range of ρ_f from 0.15 to 0.4. The following table provides conversion factors to apply to D_i for other values of ceiling reflectance.

Ceiling reflectance	Conversion factor
0.4	0.7
0.5	0.8
0.6	0.9
0.7	1.0
0.8	1.1

7 Daylight coefficients

THE FUNDAMENTAL EQUATION

See Equations (10.1)–(10.8).

SUBDIVISION OF THE SKY

See Figure 10.4 and Table 10.1.

	PARAMETERS AND NOTES
# 8 Numerical methods	

8.1 CONFIGURATION FACTOR AND FORM FACTOR DEFINITIONS

Flux density and emittance

The flux density is defined as

$$\frac{\text{flux incident on an infinitesimal element of surface}}{\text{area of that element}}$$

For luminous quantities, the units are lux.

The emittance is defined as

$$\frac{\text{flux emitted by an infinitesimal element of surface}}{\text{area of that element}}$$

For luminous quantities, the units are apostilbs (a value of emittance or luminance in apostilbs is the figure in candelas per square metre multiplied by π). It is assumed that the emitting surface is a uniform diffuser.

Configuration factor

The configuration factor describes flux transfer between an infinitesimal surface element δs_1 and a finite area s_2 on another surface:

$$cf_{\delta s_1 - s_2} = \frac{\text{flux density on } \delta s_1}{\text{emittance of } s_2}$$

$$= \frac{\text{illuminance on } \delta s_1 \text{ in lux}}{\text{luminance of } s_2 \text{ in apostilbs}}$$

Form factor

The form factor is the fraction of radiation leaving one finite surface element s_1 that reaches another finite element s_2:

$$F_{s_1 - s_2} = \frac{\text{mean flux density on } s_1}{\text{emittance of } s_2}$$

$$= \frac{\text{mean illuminance on } s_1 \text{ in lux}}{\text{luminance of } s_2 \text{ in apostilbs}}$$

When the surface elements are of different areas, A_1 and A_2, then by reciprocity, $Fs_1\text{-}s_2 A_1 = Fs_2\text{-}s_1 A_2$.

	PARAMETERS AND NOTES
### 8.2 FORM FACTORS FOR PARALLEL RECTANGLES	Parameters H and W, where $H = \dfrac{a}{c}$ and $W = \dfrac{b}{c}$ as in the diagram

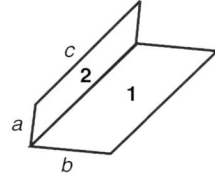

Form factor for two perpendicular rectangles of the same length, having one common edge, and at right angles to each other

$$F_{1-2} = \frac{1}{\pi W}\left[W\arctan\frac{1}{W} + H\arctan\frac{1}{H} - A\arctan\frac{1}{A} + \frac{\log_e(BC^{W^2}D^{H^2})}{4} \right]$$

where

$$A = \sqrt{H^2 + W^2}$$

$$B = \frac{(1+W^2)(1+H^2)}{1+W^2+H^2}$$

$$C = \frac{W^2(1+W^2+H^2)}{(1+W^2)(W^2+H^2)}$$

$$D = \frac{H^2(1+H^2+W^2)}{(1+H^2)(H^2+W^2)}$$

Form factor for identical, parallel, opposite rectangles

$$F_{1-2} = \frac{2\left(\log_e A + B + C\right)}{\pi XY}$$

where

$$A = \sqrt{\frac{(1+X^2)(1+Y^2)}{1+X^2+Y^2}}$$

$$B = X\sqrt{1+Y^2}\arctan\left(\frac{X}{\sqrt{1+Y^2}}\right)$$

$$C = Y\sqrt{1+X^2}\arctan\left(\frac{Y}{\sqrt{1+X^2}}\right) - X\arctan X - Y\arctan Y$$

Parameters X and Y, where $X = \dfrac{a}{c}$ and $Y = \dfrac{b}{c}$ as in the diagram

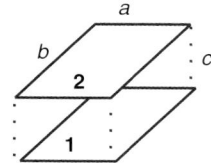

	PARAMETERS AND NOTES

8.3 CONFIGURATION FACTORS FOR RECTANGULAR SOURCES

Configuration factor for an element perpendicular to a rectangle

The small element δs_1 is perpendicular to rectangle 2, with its centre line passing through the corner.

$$cf_{\delta_1 \cdot \delta_2} = \frac{\arctan A - B \arctan C}{2\pi}$$

where

$$A = \frac{1}{Y}$$

$$B = \frac{Y}{\sqrt{X^2 + Y^2}}$$

$$C = \frac{1}{\sqrt{X^2 + Y^2}}$$

Angles are expressed in radians.

The algorithm is another form of the equation for the sky factor, Algorithm 6.1.

Configuration factor for an element parallel to a rectangle

The small element δs_1 is parallel to rectangle 2 and lies on a line perpendicular to one corner of the rectangle. The configuration factor can be used to compute the illuminance at a point on a surface facing a rectangular source or the mean illuminance from a small-area source onto a rectangle.

$$cf_{\delta s_1 \cdot \delta s_2} = \frac{A \arctan B + C \arctan D}{2\pi}$$

where

$$A = \frac{X}{\sqrt{1 + X^2}}$$

$$B = \frac{Y}{\sqrt{1 + X^2}}$$

$$C = \frac{Y}{\sqrt{1 + Y^2}}$$

$$D = \frac{X}{\sqrt{1 + Y^2}}$$

Parameters X and Y, where $X = \dfrac{a}{b}$ and $Y = \dfrac{c}{b}$ as in the diagram

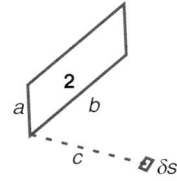

Parameters X and Y, where $X = \dfrac{a}{c}$ and $Y = \dfrac{b}{c}$ as in the diagram

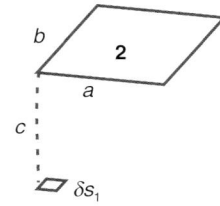

8.4 CONFIGURATION FACTOR AND FORM FACTOR WITH TRIANGULAR SUBDIVISION

Triangle 1 subtends a spherical triangle from a vertex of triangle 2. If the spherical triangle is sufficiently small to be treated as a point source, the configuration factor is a simple function of the angular size and the angle of incidence at the vertex.

Test for size of subtended triangle for configuration factor calculation

   In lighting calculations, an area source may be treated as a point if the ratio of its maximum dimension to its distance to the illuminated surface is less than an arbitrary value ε, often taken to be 1/5:

$a_\varepsilon = \arctan \varepsilon$
if $\sin A \leq \sin a_\varepsilon$ and $\sin B \leq \sin a_\varepsilon$ and $\sin C \leq \sin a_\varepsilon$
then the spherical triangle is sufficiently small

Note: $\sin[\arctan(1/5)] \approx 0.2$.

Configuration factor

   The configuration factor of triangle 1 at vertex 1 of triangle 2 is

$$cf_{21-1} = \frac{S(\cos\theta_a + \cos\theta_b + \cos\theta_c)}{3\pi}$$

Form factor

   The form factor that relates the illuminance of triangle 2 to the emittance of triangle 1 is found by determining the mean configuration factors over regular points on the receiving triangle. If the receiving triangle is small, the form factor can be found from the vertex values, as follows:

$$F_{2-1} = \frac{cf_{21-1} + cf_{22-1} + cf_{23-1}}{3}$$

$\sin A$, $\sin B$, $\sin C$ are the sides of a spherical triangle (Algorithms 1.9 and 1.10)
ε is the maximum ratio of source dimension to distance (1/5)

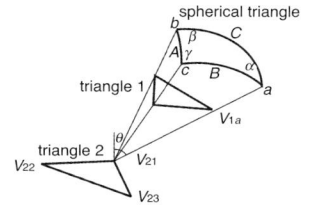

θa, θb, θc are the angles between the surface normal of triangle 2 and the directions of the vertices, *radians*
S is the area of the spherical triangle, *steradians*

	PARAMETERS AND NOTES
### 8.5 SOLUTION OF INTERREFLECTION EQUATIONS This algorithm is the Gauss–Seidel iterative method, with initial estimates based on Sumpner's formula for interreflected light. For every element i, the final illuminance E_i is given by $$E_i = E_{di} + F_{i\text{-}1}\rho_1 E_1 + F_{i\text{-}2}\rho_2 E_2 + \ldots + F_{i\text{-}n}\rho_n E_n$$ To form an iterative method, the previously calculated value of each E_I is used on the right-hand side of the equation. Hence the estimate of illuminance after m iterations is $$E_i^{(m)} = E_{di} + F_{i\text{-}1}\rho_1 E_1{}^* + F_{i\text{-}2}\rho_2 E_2{}^* + \ldots + F_{i\text{-}n}\rho_n E_n{}^*$$ where $E_k{}^*$ is the most recent value, which is $E_k{}^* = E_k^{(m)}$ for $k = 1, \ldots, i-1$, and $E_k{}^* = E_k^{(m-1)}$ for $k = i, \ldots, n$. The iterations are repeated until $|E_i^{(m)} - E_i^{(m-1)}| < \varepsilon$ for all finite areas. The initial estimates of illuminance are given by the direct illuminances plus an estimate of interreflected light: $$E_i^{(0)} = E_{di} + \frac{E_{d1}\rho_1 A_1 + E_{d2}\rho_2 A_2 + \ldots + E_{dn}\rho_n A_n}{A(1-\overline{\rho})}$$	A is the total surface area $\overline{\rho}$ is the area-weighted mean surface reflectance ε is the tolerance in the numerical solution, For every finite area patch i, where $i = 1, \ldots, n$: A_i is the area E_{di} is the direct illuminance ρ_i is the reflectance, $F_{i\text{-}j}$ is the form factor between patch i and patch j

	PARAMETERS AND NOTES

8.6 RANDOM EMISSION FROM POINT SOURCE AND DIFFUSING SURFACE

These formulae are obtained by using random numbers in the inverse of the equations that describe the distribution of luminous intensity. The symbol **R** represents a function that gives a different random number on the interval [0, 1] each time it is called.

Isotropic point source
   This gives a scaled random distribution of the angles θ and ϕ in general coordinates:

$$\cos\theta = 1 - 2\mathbf{R}_1$$
$$\phi = 2\pi\mathbf{R}_2$$

Diffusing surface source
   This gives a scaled random distribution of the angles θ' and ϕ' in the local coordinates of the surface:

$$\sin\theta' = \sqrt{\mathbf{R}_1}$$
hence
$$\cos\theta' = \sqrt{1 - \mathbf{R}_1}$$
$$\phi' = 2\pi\mathbf{R}_2$$

Alternative modes of reflection and transmission ('top-hat' method)
   Consider a ray that may be split with m different modes of reflection or transmission at a surface. Let p_1, p_2, ..., p_m be the fraction of the ray in each of the modes ($p_1 + p_2 + ... + p_m = 1$). Let array P be a cumulative distribution, (p_1, $p_1 + p_2$, $p_1 + p_2 + p_3$, , 1).
   If P can be represented by an analytical function with an inverse P^{-1}, the mode k ($1 \le k \le m$) is given by
   $k = \text{floor}(P^{-1}(R)) + 1$
   where floor(x) is the largest integer less than or equal to x.
   If P^{-1} cannot be obtained, an empirical equation can be fitted.
   The basic 'top-hat' method is the following procedure:
   rand = **R**
   k=1
   while rand $\le P^{-1}(k)$
        k=k+1
   end while
   The final value of k is the mode selected.

Sources of algorithms

Most of these formulae were included in a 1993 report 'Daylighting algorithms', by Peter Tregenza and Steve Sharples. We acknowledge with gratitude the contribution made by Professor Sharples to this collection. We are indebted also to J. A. Lynes for his review and advice on the original submission. The report was the outcome of a project sponsored by the Energy Technology Support Unit on behalf of the Department of Trade and Industry to collect and evaluate methods of lighting calculation, especially those suited to computer use.

During the International Energy Authority's Task 21 project on daylight in buildings, which ran from 1995 until 1999, most of the algorithms were made available on the Internet by the US Laurence Berkeley Laboratory; they remained available for several years. Unfortunately, they are not easily accessible now and the report is out of print.

The original collection has been revised. A few formulae have been corrected or brought up to date and some new methods have been added.

The following list gives the original published sources. Where none is given, the algorithm, equation or list of data is either published widely or is derived from general theory.

2.1   H.M. Nautical Almanac Office *The nautical almanac* (London: HMSO) (published annually).
       Roy, G.G., M. Rodrigo and W.K King, *A note on solar declination and the equation of time.* Architectural Science Review, 1989. **32**(2): p. 43–51
       Spencer, J.W., *Fourier series representation of the position of the sun.* Search 1971. **2**(5): p. 172.

2.2, 2.3 IES Calculation Procedures Committee, *Recommended practice for the calculation of daylight availability.* Journal of the Illuminating Engineering Society of North America, 1984. **13**(4): p. 381–392.

2.4   CIE, *Guide to daylighting of building interiors, draft 1990*, N.C. Ruck, ed. 1990, Paris: Commission Internationale de l'Eclairage.

2.5   Page, J.K. and S. Sharples, *The SERC meteorological data base. Volume II: Algorithm manual,* 2nd ed. 1988, Department of Building Science, University of Sheffield.

2.7   Tregenza, P.R., *The proportions of a rectangular building for minimum ground shading.* Building and Environment, 1977. **12**: p. 221–222.

3.1   Page, J.K. and S. Sharples, *The SERC meteorological data base. Volume II: Algorithm manual,* 2nd ed. 1988, Department of Building Science, University of Sheffield.
       Page, J.K. and J.L. Thompson, *Modelling daylight availability,* in *National Lighting Conference, Chartered Institution of Building Services.* 1982, Warwick.

3.2   Kasten, F. and A.T. Young, *Revised optical air mass tables and approximation formula.* Applied Optics 1989. **28**(22): p. 4735–4738.
       Rogers, G.G., C.G. Souster and J.K. Page, *The development of an interactive computer program SUN1 for calculation of solar irradiances and daily irradiations.* 1978, Department of Building Science, University of Sheffield.

3.3   Darula, S., R. Kittler and C.A. Gueymard, *Reference luminous solar constant and solar luminance for illuminance calculations.* Solar Energy 2005. **79**(5): p. 559–565.

3.4   Navvab, M., *Analysis of atmospheric turbidity for daylight calculations.* Energy and Buildings, 1984. **6**: p. 293–303.

3.5   Tregenza, P.R., *Measured and calculated frequency distributions of daylight illuminance.* Lighting Research and Technology, 1986. **18**(2): p. 71–74.

3.6   CIE, *Standardisation of luminance distribution on clear skies.* 1973, Paris: Commission Internationale de l'Eclairage.
       Kittler, R., *Luminance distribution characteristics of homogeneous skies: a measurement and prediction strategy.* Lighting Research and Technology, 1985. **17**(4): p. 183–188.
       Nagata, T., *Luminance distribution of clear skies, part 1: measurements of the luminance distribution.* Transactions of the Architectural Institute of Japan, 1971. (185): p. 65–70.
       Nagata, T., *Luminance distribution of clear skies, part 2: theoretical considerations.* Transactions of the Architectural Institute of Japan, 1971. (186) p. 41–48.
       Nagata, T., *Luminance distribution of clear sky and the resulting horizontal illuminance.* Journal of Light and Visual Environment, 1983. **7**(1): p. 23–27.
       IES Calculation Procedures Committee, *Recommended practice for the calculation of daylight availability.* Journal of the Illuminating Engineering Society of North America, 1984. **13**(4): p. 381–392.

3.7   Krochmann, J. and M. Seidl, *Quantitative data on daylight for illuminating engineering.* Lighting Research and Technology, 1974. **6**(3): p. 165–171.
       The luminance equation is by Kittler in an unpublished paper quoted in the reference above.

4.1   CIE, *Spatial distribution of daylight: CIE Standard General Sky.* 2003, Paris: Commission Internationale de l'Eclairage, CIE S 011/E:2003.

4.2   CIE, *Natural daylight: official recommendations 13th Session.* 1955, Paris: Commission Internationale de l'Eclairage.

         Wilkinson, M.A., *Natural lighting under translucent domes.* Lighting Research and Technology, 1992. **24**(3): p. 117–126.

5.3   Tregenza, P.R., *Luminance of distant objects under overcast skies.* Lighting Research and Technology, 1992: **24**(3), p. 155–159.

5.6   Mitalas, G.P and J.G. Arseneault, *Division of Building Research Computer Program No. 28: Fortran IV program to calculate absorption and transmission of thermal radiation by single and double glazed windows.* 1968, Ottawa: National Research Council.

         Littlefair, P.J., *Effective glass transmittance under a CIE sky.* Lighting Research and Technology, 1982. **14**(4): p. 232–235.

5.7   Petherbridge, P., *Transmission characteristics of window glasses and sun controls*, in *Sunlight and buildings, CIE Conference.* 1967, Rotterdam: Bouwcentrum.

         Sharples, S., J.K. Page, and C.G. Souster, *Incorporating body-tinted glazing into daylight computer models.* Lighting Research and Technology, 1984. **16**(3): p. 143–145.

6.1, 6.2   Walsh, J.W.T., *The science of daylight.* 1961, London: Macdonald.

6.3   Seshadri, T.N., *Equations of sky component with a CIE standard overcast sky.* Proceedings of the Indian Academy of Sciences, 1960. Paper 57A: p. 233–242.

6.4   Tregenza, P.R., *Modification of the split-flux formulae for mean daylight factor and internal reflected component with large external obstructions.* Lighting Research and Technology, 1989. **21**(3): p. 125–128.

         Sharples, S., J.K. Page and C.G. Souster, *Modelling the daylight levels produced in rectangular, side-lit rooms by vertical windows containing clear or body-tinted glazing.* 1981, Department of Building Science, University of Sheffield.

6.5   Hopkinson, R.G., P. Petherbridge and J. Longmore, *Daylighting.* 1966, London: Heinemann.

         Building Research Establishment, *Estimating daylight in buildings: Part 2. BRE Digest 310.* 1986, Garston, Watford, UK: Building Research Establishment.

         Sharples, S., J.K. Page and C.G. Souster, *Modelling the daylight levels produced in rectangular, side-lit rooms by vertical windows containing clear or body-tinted glazing.* 1981, Department of Building Science, University of Sheffield.

6.6   Building Research Establishment, *Estimating daylight in buildings: Part 2. BRE Digest 310.* 1986, Garston, Watford, UK: Building Research Establishment.

8.1   Bellchambers, H.E., P. Petherbridge and R.O. Phillips, *Nomenclature and symbols associated with radiation transfer calculations.* Transactions of the Illuminating Society (London), 1961. **26**(3): p. 136–142.

8.2, 8.3   Seigel, R. and J.R. Howell, *Thermal radiation heat transfer,* 3rd ed. 1992, New York: McGraw-Hill.

8.4   Tregenza, P.R., *Daylighting calculations: radiosity method using triangular patches.* Lighting Research and Technology, 1994. 26(1): p. 1–7.

8.5   Sumpner, W.E., *The diffusion of light.* The London, Edinburgh, and Dublin Philosphical Magazine and Journal of Science, 5th Series, 1893. **35**(213): p. 81–97.

         Littlefair, P.J., *Interreflection calculations: Improving convergence.* Lighting Research and Technology, 1991. **23**(4): p. 175–177.

8.6   Tregenza, P.R., *The Monte Carlo method in lighting calculations.* Lighting Research and Technology, 1983. **15**(4): p. 163–170.

         Tocher, K.D., *The art of simulation.* 1963, London: English Universities Press.

Index